STATISTICAL PROCESS CONTROL

Second Edition

STATISTICAL PROCESS CONTROL

Second Edition

Leonard A. Doty

Industrial Press Inc.

Library of Congress Cataloging-in-Publication Data

Doty, Leonard A.
Statistical process control / by Leonard A. Doty. — 2nd ed.
392p., 15.6 x 23.5 cm.
Includes bibliographical references and index.
ISBN 0-8311-3069-5
1. Process control—Statistical methods. 2. Quality control—Statistical methods. I. Title.
TS156.8.D67 1996
658.5′62′015195—dc20 95-44408
CIP

INDUSTRIAL PRESS INC.
200 Madison Avenue
New York, New York 10016-4078

Second Edition, 1996

STATISTICAL PROCESS CONTROL

10 9 8 7 6 5 4 3 2

CONTENTS

TABLES

PREFACE TO THE SECOND EDITION

SPC/TQM (statistical process control/total quality management) is a quality management system, as opposed to a production or accounting system which many firms, especially American firms, have had for many years (many, if not most, still do). There are two parts to this system—technical and humanistic. This book, the first of a series (hopefully), concentrates on the technical portion of the SPC/TQM quality system, called SPC (thus the name of the book). The next book of the series, now being written, will be entitled *TQM*, and it will concentrate on the humanistic aspect of the system.

It is very important for both the teacher and the practitioner to understand the nature of the quality system explained here. SPC/TQM is a system that essentially depends on the cooperation of people (hence the use of many people skills in the complete system). The people skills are what I call humanistic, and are explained mostly in the second book of the series (although many are necessary to SPC and are, therefore, woven into many SPC subjects). The system has essentially four objectives: 1) quality (make a "good" product or service), 2) productivity (get the product "out the door"), 3) accounting (make the product or service at the least cost), and 4) help people to work together harmoniously. The fourth objective is, of course, also the nature of the system itself.

A good SPC program, especially if it also includes TQM principles, should have a quality manual and quality procedures (the rules for the use of the quality management program). Since this book is basically technical in nature, it does not cover these topics. The best type of manual and procedures are those that meet ISO standards. An example ISO manual and ISO procedures will be given in the next book of this series (also see Kanholm, 1993 and Fawcett, 1993).

This second edition has been changed in several ways. First, more and better explanations have been added in several places (notably in Chapters 1, 2, and 4). Next, Chapters 2 and 3 have been combined, and a new Chapter 2, entitled the "Tools of Quality," has replaced the old. Chapter 2 now has a list of the tools of quality, and a fairly complete explanation of the seven basic tools (these seven tools are also called the tools of SPC, and sometimes of TQM). Then, a better explanation of the nature of SPC (Chapter 1) and the nature of control charts (Sections 4.1–4.10) has been added. Also, Chapters 4 and 5 have been changed somewhat to better facilitate what is actually going on with SPC. Finally, the important SPC concepts that were in Chapter 11 have now been put into Chapter 1, and Chapter 11 has been eliminated.

As far as the system is concerned, Chapters 2–6 explain SPC, Chapters 8 and 9 explain acceptance sampling, Chapter 7 explains the probability rules and distributions needed for acceptance sampling (except for the normal curve in Chapter 3), and Chapter 1 gives some important SPC humanistic concepts. Chapter 10 presents a summary of DOE (Design of Experiments). A more complete explanation of many of the humanistic concepts will be presented in my next book, entitled *TQM*. Acceptance sampling and DOE are often assumed to be part of SPC (which is my contention).

This book can easily be organized in two different ways. If the curriculum follows a regular semester format, the text should be taught in about the way it is organized. Chapter 5 is just a chapter of many different types of control charts, and could easily be dismissed (or only part of it could be taught). Just help the students understand the nature of the different types of charts and what they can do. This chapter is quite good at explaining the charts if, and when, needed.

If the curriculum follows a quarter system, the course could be divided into two parts, for two quarters. First, teach Chapters 1, 2, 3, 4, and some 6. Then, on the second quarter, review Chapters 1, 4, and 6 and then teach Chapters 7–10.

I am indebted to many colleagues for their encouragement and assistance, especially the Tucson chapter of the ASQC (American Society for Quality Control), Mr. Luis Soto, and Dr. Michael N. Leeming. I am especially indebted to my wife, Lucy, without whose help and encouragement this book could not have been written.

STATISTICAL PROCESS CONTROL

Second Edition

CHAPTER 1

THE NATURE OF STATISTICAL PROCESS CONTROL (SPC)

Statistical process control (SPC) is mostly technical in nature—it is actually just the technical arm of the author's SPC/TQM quality management system. It concentrates on finding process variations; correcting these variations depends on the creativity and ingenuity of the people involved. This chapter, unlike the remaining chapters of this book, emphasizes the humanistic aspects of the system—those that are most important to SPC. Although humanistic concepts are normally thought of as TQM (total quality management), they are needed in most, if not all, of the SPC technical subjects in the remainder of this book, and so are woven into these subjects as needed. These humanistic concepts, especially when they involve quality, are absolutely essential to the full understanding and use of SPC.

Objectives

1. Describe the SPC/TQM quality management system.
2. Give a brief history of quality control and statistical process control.
3. Define quality control and quality responsibilities, and explain how much quality is needed.
4. Define variation and how it affects SPC.
5. List and explain the various types of quality costs, and describe the types of quality cost controls.
6. Define the nature of the two modern quality standards—ISO and the Malcolm Baldrige award.
7. Explain the philosophy of the basic SPC/TQM system.
8. Understand how SPC relates to nonmanufacturing.
9. Understand how SPC is implemented.

1.1 The SPC/TQM Quality System

SPC (statistical process control) began as a means of controlling production in a manufacturing plant. It soon became obvious that SPC principles could be extended into other areas, such as nonmanufacturing (areas other than production in a manufacturing firm, and all areas of a service-type industry), management, health care, education, politics, the family, and even life itself. When used in these areas, these concepts are usually called something other than SPC, such as TQ (total quality), WCQ (world class quality), CWQC (company wide quality control), QI (quality improvement), TI (total improvement), TQI (total quality improvement), TCQ (total company quality), TQM (total quality management), and others. TQM is the favorite of most (including this author). Although this book stresses the manufacturing function, the concepts are equally useful to all other areas.

People have often explained, or at least inferred, that each new term is some kind of new system. This is not true, and can be extremely confusing to those who are trying to understand these concepts. The only real difference, then, between a quality management system (such as SPC/TQM) and the old productivity/accounting system (where people were thought of as only another production factor) is quality's emphasis on people. Any of the concepts involved (the "tools" of Chapter 2), may or may not be useful to any quality management system. It takes knowledgeable people—people who understand just which concepts can be used and just how they can be used. This book will define and explain many (at least the most important) of these concepts.

One reason for the change of terms (from SPC to TQM) was the meaning of the words. The word "statistical" had an unfortunate mathematical connotation to most people (too many people think that anything mathematical is bad), and the word "control" suggested something other than cooperation (the concept of cooperation was becoming too important to the new system). Also, everything is a process whether or not it is in production (although most people think of a process as being only a production system).

The system that has evolved from SPC is in two parts—technical and humanistic. Some firms call everything in a quality management system TQM, with SPC being the technical arm of TQM. A part of SPC, which is highly mathematical and experimental, is often called DOE (Design of Experiments, see Chapter 10). However, some firms think of DOE as separate from SPC. Some firms also think of acceptance sampling (Chapters 7–9) as something separate from SPC, mostly because many SPC practitioners are advocating the abolition of acceptance sampling (they say that acceptance sampling is no longer needed for suppliers who practice SPC). Sometimes the humanistic aspect is called TQM, while the technical part is called SPC—although just which technical parts constitute SPC and which parts are TQM is often very hard to determine.

That is why I call this system the SPC/TQM quality management system, and refer to SPC as the technical part and TQM as the humanistic. I include acceptance sampling in with SPC because I believe it will never really be abolished; and I also include DOE in with SPC because of its technical nature. Chapters 2–6 cover SPC, Chapters 8 and 9 cover acceptance sampling, and Chapter 10 gives a short summary of DOE. Chapter 7 explains the statistical rules and probability distributions necessary to acceptance sampling (except for the normal curve of Chapter 3). This first chapter covers some critical humanistic concepts that are important for all of these things—for SPC, TQM, acceptance sampling, and/or DOE. Unfortunately, it is difficult (frequently impossible) to completely separate the humanistic principles from the technical side. This is why humanistic aspects are often woven into the SPC technical subjects in this book.

SPC/TQM is a system of management: one that concentrates on quality rather than on productivity or accounting (as used to be the case in the past, and still is in many firms). A quality management system concentrates on the customer while the old productivity/accounting management system appears to concentrate on things (how many and/or how much). An emphasis on things, rather than people, seems to cause an autocratic management system to develop. A quality system, however, insists on customer satisfaction and seems to result in supportive type management systems (see Section 1.7). In fact, a good quality management system (such as TQM) cannot really continue over time under autocratic type management.

Actually, quality is included in a production and/or an accounting management system, and production and accounting are included in a quality management system. The problem is in the way we think about it and the way we approach it. In production or accounting systems, quality tends to become only an appended function; it tends to be somewhat forgotten. The problems associated with getting a product out the door tend to become more important than the problems associated with getting a "good" product out (making "quality" products).

An excellent description of quality problems (a list of these problems will be given in the next paragraph of this first section), and the problems that beset the American production culture, was formulated by Bhote in his book *World Class Quality*. He compared American firms to a man who had lost a gold coin and who was looking for it in an area where he had not lost it. When asked why, the man replied, "The light is better here."

"This tale suggests," Bhote writes, "American industry's frantic search for ways of reducing costs. It looks in the wrong places—because it is easier. Mindless layoffs, arbitrary cuts in headcounts, the flight offshore to reduce the costs of direct labor (which account for a tiny 5% of sales), and musical-chair reorganizations—all of which are easily mandated, but their effectiveness remains a mirage."

Bhote continues, "Although there are many dimensions to the quality problems caused by management, its sins of omission and commission with respect to variation include: the lack of knowledge about the impact of variation on overall costs, no coherent policy on variation reduction, no allocation of resources, no leadership, no stated goals, no action on goals even if stated, and little or no training." I heartily concur.

In summary, the SPC/TQM quality management system is a system where people work together to accomplish certain goals. The goals are: 1) quality (making a "good" product), 2) productivity (getting the product "out the door"), 3) accounting (making the product at the least cost), and 4) people working together harmoniously. This last objective is, of course, the same as the system itself. There are many concepts, and subsystems, used to accomplish these purposes. They are, in general, divided into two aspects—technical (called SPC) and humanistic (called TQM). Since this book is mostly technical in nature, it is entitled SPC.

Quality Problems

Some of the problems that helped SPC/TQM come into existence are listed below. These problems—problems that resulted from using the wrong management system, more than anything else—have probably caused the quality system known as SPC/TQM to be developed. (If the reader desires more information on these problems, he or she can read Johnson's *Keeping Score,* Deming's *Out of the Crisis,* and Peters' two books, especially the first chapter of his book *Thriving on Chaos.* There are others, but these are probably the most important.)

1. Increased costs (especially of scrap, rework, inefficiency, waste, repairs, recalls, etc.).
2. Customer complaints, especially about poor quality and poor service. It was noted (by *Fortune* magazine, 1985) that the Koreans preferred Japanese products 2 to 1 over American products. It has also been noted that American quality is a joke overseas. Those of us who are older can remember when this joke was true of the Japanese (it certainly is not true now).
3. Competition that threatens the vitality of our business. A friendly spirit of striving and winning is good; competition is important. But when it becomes all compelling, it can be deadly. In the long run, cooperation

is more important than competition. This is the reason that SPC stresses the importance of working together (team problem solving, single suppliers, suppliers and customers involved in designing products and in solving problems, a caring culture, etc.).

4. A total misunderstanding of the nature of quality; a concentration on "product" quality (100% inspections) versus "process" quality (SPC). Even after quality became more important, most American firms seemed to emphasize the difficulty of quality rather than its ease and naturalness. If quality is so difficult—we tend to think—how can we trust that letdowns, unconscious or otherwise, will not occur, perhaps frequently. However, the Japanese seem to concentrate on the ease and naturalness of quality, as when they compared their products to ancient Japanese combs, which had always been handcrafted with careful and loving attention (implying that quality is an attitude inherent in, and pervading, their work and culture and, therefore, is just a natural result of their way of life). If quality is that precious to them—we tend to ask ourselves—maybe we can trust them to do it always in all things. This is the type of quality attitude that SPC/TQM would like to foster in all firms.
5. A preoccupation with short-term profits, corporate mergers, many top management changes, etc., as opposed to long-term stability.
6. Using sales gimmicks as a substitute for solid quality products; not focusing on customer satisfaction.
7. A preoccupation with limiting customer complaints rather than focusing on producing quality products.
8. A lack of effective planning for long-term stability.
9. Quality treated as an added burden instead of the key to profitability and increased market share.
10. Failure to utilize the inherent abilities of workers to contribute to process improvement, with the tendency to treat workers as units of production with no individuality, creativity, or imagination of their own. This results in apathy, lassitude, paranoia, withdrawal, resentment, indifference, and loss of self-esteem and pride of workmanship—which then leads to absenteeism and poor quality. These results are then used as proof of the "decline of the American worker." SPC practitioners have basically proven that over 85% (probably over 95%) of quality problems are "systems" problems that are management, not operator, controllable.
11. A culture permeated by negative attitudes and an atmosphere of distrust, which leads to labor/management/government schisms (internal strife, strikes, government interference, etc.) instead of cooperation to solve problems.
12. Massive bureaucracy with intricate checks and balances for controlling every action (no one trusts anyone).
13. A focus on failures, with elaborate procedures for assessing punishment instead of solving problems. A "shoot the messenger syndrome" develops which leads to "hiding" problems rather than "solving" them

("shoot the messenger" means to punish the bearer of bad news). Remember that most (probably over 95%) quality problems are "systems" problems, so that most problems can only be solved with the cooperation of top management. If top management just gets angry and punishes (instead of trying to fix the problem), we can see how a "hiding" syndrome can develop.

14. Management's inconsistency toward quality, which leads to cynical/negative attitudes. Cynical/negative attitudes eventually become cynical/negative actions.
15. "Elitism" as a tool for management control. (Ishikawa said, in *Quality Progress* (1989), "Top and middle management must put an end to elitism and promote industrial democracy and respect for humanity and creativity.") Elitism is an attitude that only certain people with certain characteristics are capable of effective planning and decision making—or even effective thinking. Also, the hoarding and blocking of information is one tool that elitists use to maintain control.
16. The tendency to control quality to the customer by inspecting defects out (massive inspections) instead of building quality in (SPC).
17. The tendency to build rigid systems that fight change, and thus actually discourage and impede any progress toward improvement. Creativity is actively discouraged and the status quo and obedience are emphasized. (In many cases, change has seemed to take place but the attitudes have not. Under these conditions, how long can we expect the change to continue?)
18. The use of massive advertisements to counteract a poor quality image.
19. Putting increased pressure on productivity without first correcting the underlying systems problems (which just creates more bad products faster).
20. Cutting expenses arbitrarily (even if doing so hurts quality).
21. A dependence upon authoritarian management and single-track single-minded structures for control.
22. Antagonistic relationships with suppliers; relationships based only on price and competition instead of cooperation. A large supplier base, it was claimed, tends to lower prices through competition. In actuality, this only leads to decreased quality as suppliers cut quality to lower costs.
23. Internal function oriented, rather than customer oriented, goals (people and systems evaluated on partial department goals rather than on overall company goals). This leads to uncertainty as to the relationships between process steps and customer requirements, and then to a rigid conformance to rules designed to satisfy internal function goals rather than customer satisfaction. This insistence on conformance to "the rules" then became an alibi for poor quality, and for a poor quality image.
24. A passion for "bigness for bigness sake" (see Peters' *Thriving on Chaos,* Chapter 1). This tends to reduce the flexibility needed for quick responses to market changes; which then increases the dependence on long-term, rigid, nonchanging systems and massive production runs;

which then requires long-term, rigid, nonchanging markets and large sales orders; which then increases the reluctance to accept small sales orders (increasingly important in today's market). As someone once said, "Blessed are the flexible, for they shall not be bent out of shape."

1.2 History of Quality

Quality control as a separate function of manufacturing basically began with the "division of labor" of the industrial revolution (1819) and the "Scientific Management" system of Fredrick W. Taylor (1876). At this time (1819 to 1924), workers were separated from the results of their labor, i.e., from the final product; they were given only small portions of the work to do on each product.

In addition, the very motions they were to use were proscribed by management (this was Taylor's "time study" portion of his "Scientific Management" system). Before this, when a worker or a small team of workers built the whole product, the responsibility for quality could also be included in their duties. Now, however, all responsibility was removed from the worker (except for the responsibility to produce) and given solely to management. Under these conditions, something had to be done to guarantee quality. The method used, for the most part, was 100% inspection, done by a separate inspector or inspection function.

Statistical process control (called statistical quality control until after World War II) was introduced in 1924 by W. A. Shewhart of Bell Laboratories. Shewhart developed a statistical chart (now called a control chart) for control of product variables, along with the procedures and mathematical proof that make the use of these charts scientifically viable. Basically, his procedure was to analyze and chart averages of small sample sizes (4 or more—the charts actually show 2 or more) rather than individual values. The resultant distribution of the averages of these small subsamples is normal, or close enough to it (even though, in all cases, the larger the subsample size, the closer to normality it becomes).

For example, the data from Table 3.1 are not normal, i.e., do not form a normal curve when graphed. However, when divided into subsamples of 4, the subsample averages (Figure 4.1) do provide a normal curve when charted. With this system, quality could be controlled with a sampling procedure rather than with the 100% inspection then being used. (Please note that this was not fully accepted until long after World War II—or until the Japanese proved it to be true.)

In developing the mathematical proof for his procedure, Shewhart utilized the Central Limit Theorem, which states that the distribution of sample averages will be normal (or nearly so—usually close enough for all practical purposes), even though the individual values are drawn from a nonnormal distribution. The reason for this is the mathematical relationship between the standard deviations, as follows:

$$s_x = \sigma/\sqrt{n}$$

where

s_x = the standard deviation of the sample means

σ = the standard deviation of the individual values (also called the standard deviation of the universe or distribution from which the sample was taken)

n = the sample size (should be 4 or greater).

The experience of quality practitioners over the intervening 70 years has shown conclusively the validity of Shewhart's theories. In fact, in the experience of these practitioners, a sampling procedure is superior to 100% inspection in most cases; due mostly to the mind-numbing boredom of 100% inspection which all too often results in a totally unacceptable level of inspection errors—much more than would normally result from sampling. (Of course, some 100% inspections will always be necessary, especially of small amounts of very high-cost items.)

Shortly after Shewhart invented the control chart, two of his fellow workers at Bell Laboratories, H. F. Dodge and H. G. Romig, developed acceptance sampling as a substitute for 100% inspection (see Section 9.2). The concept of acceptance sampling is based upon the statistical concept that an unbiased sample (random and homogeneous) of the proper size will resemble the population from which it was drawn (see Chapter 3 for a definition of "unbiased," and Chapters 8 and 9 for an explanation and discussion of "acceptance sampling"). Therefore, information about the population can be inferred from measurements taken from the sample.

In general, these statistical concepts were not completely accepted until World War II, when the need for, and viability of, these procedures became apparent (Dr. W. Edwards Deming was very instrumental in this effort). At that time, the United States government basically forced American manufacturers to adopt SPC principles in order to reduce the enormous amount of defective material being produced during the early days of the war. The success of this endeavor is a matter of record—quality was enormously improved. Although some of the SPC principles were adopted by American business at this time (and called SQC), much of it was not. It was the Japanese, after World War II, who successfully implemented the entire gamut of the SPC principles and practices, and even expanded them by adding some ideas of their own. It was also at this time that the various motivational theories showed the need for a more humanistic approach to quality (see the last of this section).

It was after World War II, when Japan was rebuilding its productive base, that W. Edwards Deming and Joseph M. Juran introduced Japan to the concepts of SPC. (Dr. W. Edwards Deming became affectionately known in Japan as "Papa San Deming," and an award, the "Deming award," was named after him.) SPC was the next logical progression beyond the SQC procedures that proved so effective during the war. However, American manufacturers almost totally rejected it, leaving the Japanese to organize and perfect it into the powerful tool for increasing quality and decreasing costs that it is today. Not only has the original SPC theory been successfully implemented by the Japanese, but they have expanded and refined the procedures for increased effectiveness.

The contributions of two Japanese theorists are especially noteworthy. The Taguchi Design of Experiments (DOE) models have added understandability and simplicity to an otherwise complex subject. And the Ishikawa Cause and Effect diagram (see Chapter 2) has become widely accepted as an excellent tool for analyzing incoming data and identifying critical design criteria.

Some Motivational Theories of the 1950s and 1960s

The concept of the "team approach to problem solving" (a central theme of SPC) has been a natural outgrowth of a host of motivational theories of the 1950s and 1960s (see Doty, 1989). The most notable of these are the following.

1. Maslow's hierarchy of needs, which proposed that people satisfy needs from a lower level (physiological) to higher level (ego and self-actualization), in that order, and that they cannot operate on higher level needs until lower level needs are reasonably satisfied (see Maslow, 1970).
2. McGregor's Theory X and Theory Y, which were essentially sets of assumptions about people that cause or contribute to certain management styles. Theory X managers believe that people are inherently lazy and uncreative and must be tricked or coerced into doing a good job. These managers will be authoritarian in their styles. Theory Y managers believe that people have inner needs to achieve worthwhile goals and be creative and self-directed. These managers will be supportive in their styles. Supportive styles are supposed to be much more preferable (see McGregor, 1960).
3. Herzberg's two factor theory, which divided Maslow's hierarchy of needs into two categories, called satisfiers and motivators. According to this theory, lower level (physiological) needs can only satisfy; it takes the higher level needs (ego and self-actualization) to truly motivate. If this theory is true (and there is much evidence that it is), then it follows that workers must operate within the higher level needs in order to be

truly happy and to be truly quality oriented. It also follows that workers can be both productive and happy at the same time, a theory not well received by managers at the time (see Herzberg, 1959).

4. Glasser's group identity theory, which proposed that people are happiest and most content when working in groups. This was in sharp contrast to the methods of the day where workers were deliberately separated and encouraged to work alone and in competition with all other workers—an attitude inherent in the "division of labor" concept of the scientific management theories of Fredrich W. Taylor (see Glasser, 1975).
5. Livingston's "Pygmalion" effect, which stated that workers (everyone actually) tend to respond to high expectation with high performance and to low expectation with low performance. We tend to do what is expected of us, especially if that expectation comes from recognized and accepted authority figures (see Livingston, 1969).
6. Rensis Likert's system 1, 2, 3, and 4, which basically described, in some detail, a desired evolution from authoritarian, Theory X orientation, lowered performance, unhappy workers (system 1) to supportive, Theory Y orientation, increased performance, happy workers (system 4) (see Likert, 1961).
7. Job enrichment, whose main characteristics are: variety of skill usage, greater responsibility and autonomy, increased closure (doing the whole job), timely feedback, more recognition, and group membership and team effort. Job enrichment was highly touted in the 1950s and 1960s, and still is, to some extent.

1.3 Define Quality

Scientific researchers have long known that the definition of a problem is critical to its efficient solution. This is the critical first step of the so-called "scientific process." This step is no less important to the concept of "quality" and to SPC application. The way we define our subject is crucial to the way we think about it—which, in turn, is fundamental to how we apply it. A good definition will also include measurable standards of comparison so that applications can be consistently directed toward the goals described in the definition. Only when we can clearly explain and define our subject, and its goals and objectives, do we really know what it is. And if we do not have a clear understanding of our subject, how can we possibly apply it correctly?

This need for clear and understandable definition can be illustrated by the following diagram of the "traditional" versus the SPC (statistical process control) definition of "good" quality.

The traditional definition of "good" quality has been "conformance to specifications," which is anywhere between the upper and lower specification limits (between USL and LSL). The newer SPC definition is "as close to the target value as possible." According to Taguchi, there is a "loss to society" that increases exponentially the further the character-

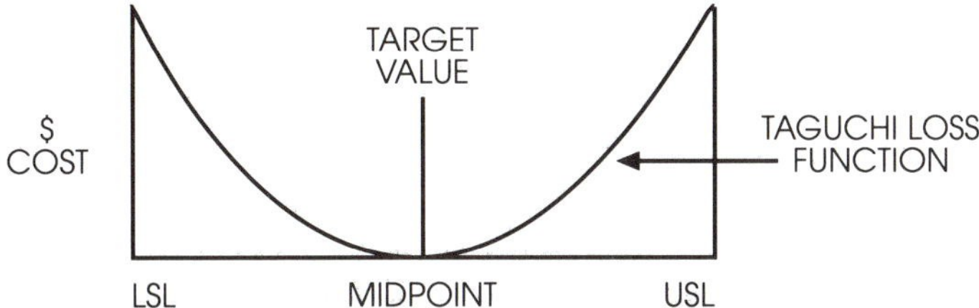

istic is from the central, or target, value—even if it is still within the specification limits (due to many factors, not the least of which is excessive wear on mating parts).

Workers who are taught the "traditional" definition will think that products produced within the limits will be "good quality" even if very close to the limit. They will not realize that they may be actually producing fairly poor quality because their definition is flawed. The fact that the Japanese, who do work to the SPC definition, forged ahead so dramatically on quality is a clear indication of the viability of the SPC, or Taguchi, approach.

Unfortunately, quality means different things to different people. It even often means different things to the same people at different times, and under different circumstances. Therefore, quality is often difficult, at best, to precisely define. This is certainly one of the reasons that the control of quality has seldom, if ever, attained the same level of precision and attention as has productivity, or any other aspect of the control of production. However, through the years, several types of definitions have evolved from this confusion surrounding the concept of quality. By themselves, none of these is usually adequate to provide the definition of quality needed at any one time or any one circumstance; some combination of two or more is usually required.

1. **Statistical.** A statistical definition of quality is almost always a part of one of the other definitions, although it can be stated separately. There are several forms. First, a simple statement of percent defectives (or, as it is often called, process quality) can constitute a statistical definition. Charts and graphs (especially the control charts to be explained in later chapters) can be added for clarification. Finally, a special inspection plan, such as MIL-STD-105E (which takes an entire book to completely explain) can be used. (An inspection plan, such as MIL-STD-105E, is actually an acceptance sampling plan, as explained in Chapter 9.) Many different derivations and combinations of these three basic statistical formats are used at various times and in various circumstances.
2. **Fitness for use.** Basically, "fitness for use" is determined by the customer and transmitted to the producer through the customer's buying patterns. It is what the customer is willing to pay. In our modern complex world, this is not always easy for the producer to determine. Vari-

ous types of marketing surveys are often needed, along with sophisticated statistical analyses, to determine just what the customer actually wants and is willing to pay. "Fitness for use" is also measured by comparing the various quality cost categories. In actual practice, then, fitness for use is measured as a combination of quality cost factors with some measure of customer satisfaction added. Customer satisfaction can be inferred from the amount of external failures, which can be measured to a great extent by the amount of customer returns and complaints. It should be noted that Dr. W. Edwards Deming, one of the greatest quality "gurus" of this generation and an expert on statistics, did not believe that "fitness for use" can be measured.

3. **Quality of design.** It is the duty of Design Engineering to translate the customer desires, the information that defines "fitness for use," into the various functional requirements (called specifications) needed by Production to manufacture the product. However, "quality of design" is normally thought of as the "intentional variation in grades and/or levels." Customer desires (as determined by marketing) can define a single level of quality or several levels. The customer may desire one level or grade at one time, and another, perhaps higher, grade under different circumstances. Designing to these levels, in order to reach specific markets, is what is known as "design quality." For instance, a small simple automobile might be designed to a level of quality that allows the car to be sold at a relatively low cost, while another might be specially designed for long-term luxurious use that would cost much more. The decision as to quality level is a complex Management/Marketing/Design/Production problem. It involves marketing surveys to determine available levels, types of markets, possible number of customers and probable profit; design engineering analysis of standards and specifications at each possible level; and production analyses of processes, people, skills, and costs. Although this problem clearly involves quality and SPC input, it is a high-level management decision that should not occur very often. This book will not address this problem specifically, although the concepts and techniques explained herein will usually all apply.
4. **Process quality.** Once the design quality is determined, the product must be produced to the specifications set by the design function. How well this is done is known as "process quality" or "quality of conformance." This is the duty of Production: to build to the standards set by Design. Process quality is the true measure of the firm's ability to produce a quality product. The measurement and determination of this concept is the proper function of Quality Control and/or SPC. This is the type of quality that is most addressed in this book, although it necessarily includes the other types at various times—especially statistical quality. In fact, process quality is almost always presented as a simple statistic—percent defective—which is frequently expressed as the symbol p (a p of 0.05, for instance, means a process quality, or percent defective, of 5%).
5. **Relative usefulness.** Because of the different expectations of different customers, and even of the same customers at different times and in

different circumstances, some think that quality can never be precisely measured. Instead, they feel, quality can only be measured in relation to the expectations of the moment, and in relation to different markets and customer types. Needless to say, this makes it very difficult to translate quality into useful manufacturing specifications.

6. **Most effectively meets its functional needs.** One way to overcome the problem of relative usefulness is to concentrate solely on the functions of the product—what it was made to do. In this viewpoint, the customer is expected to limit his/her expectations to the product functions as defined by the manufacturer. Unfortunately, this is something the customer, especially the general buying public, is seldom willing to do. The simple hairdryer is an excellent example of this problem. Although originally designed for the single function of drying hair, it was continually used for many other purposes; many of which compromised the safety of the original design. Manufacturers were finally obliged to change the design to fit all possible uses (mostly in order to protect themselves from possible product liability lawsuits).
7. **Meets its functional objectives with the least time, effort, and cost.** Unfortunately, people tend to consider some nonfunctional aspects of the product to be almost as important as the product itself. Sometimes it seems that not only do users want the product to do what it is supposed to do, but they want it immediately (as soon as they perceive the need), they want it to work instantly (without needing to wait for results), and they want it to be cheaper (for nothing, if possible). These and other nonfunctional needs must also be considered in the overall quality requirements.
8. **Customer expectations.** Some think that quality can only be measured in terms of customer expectations. However, as has already been discussed, the differences in these expectations makes this measurement extremely difficult—and even, at times, all but impossible.

In general, then, a product is considered to be a quality product when it most effectively discharges the requirements of its function; when it meets its objectives with the least expenditure of time, effort, and money; and when it does what the customer wants it to do with no perceived problems. Defining and measuring these requirements, however, can be frustratingly difficult.

Quality, in the manufacturing setting at least, is the ability of the product and/or process to meet the various standards—the engineering specifications. Quality control is the engineering and management activity by which the quality characteristics of the process, and thus the product, are measured, compared to a standard, and corrected as needed. The setting of the standards is the duty of Design Engineering. Measuring, comparing, and analyzing the quality characteristic, and its process, should be the duty of Production, with assistance (especially in the use of statistics) from quality control and/or statistical process control. It is the duty, then, of production personnel to properly manufacture the product to the standards set by design and, when informed by quality analysis (their own or SPC's), apply corrective action to quality deviations.

It should be noted that quality also includes the little things that add to comfort (ease of operation, ease of maintenance, etc.)—maybe *especially* these "little" things. They include such things as: bucket and reclining seats, trip meters, trouble/diagnostic lights, interlocks to prevent inadvertent activation or inactivation (such as inability to shut off engine until gear is in park), computer discs in permanent jackets for safety, etc. Quality includes the identification, and implementation, of these things even when not specifically perceived by the customer (if not done, someone else soon will and take your customers away!).

Responsibility for Quality

To some extent, quality impinges upon the objectives and duties of all the functions of the firm. Thus, it has been truly stated that quality is the responsibility of everyone in the firm, from the highest ranking officer (who sets quality policies) to the actual operator (who must build quality into the product). It is the objective of Quality Control and/or SPC, as it is in all other functions of the firm, to assist in building the best product possible at minimum cost.

It is not enough, however, just to state that quality is the responsibility of everyone. Quality responsibilities must be carefully defined and then clearly assigned so that everyone is thoroughly aware of his or her specific duties regarding quality; otherwise, the responsibility for quality tends to become diffuse and everyone tends to expect everyone else to control the quality. In this way, a policy of "everyone is responsible for quality" tends to become, informally, "everyone else but me is responsible for quality," which usually means that no one but Quality Control is responsible for quality.

It is this deterioration of quality responsibilities, in the past, that the new SPC philosophy is designed to eliminate (one of the things, at least). In general, SPC attempts to move the quality decision-making responsibility, as much as possible, down to the operator, to the person actually making the item. Thus, the operator assumes a level of responsibility, control, and authority, which was seldom, if ever, known in the old quality philosophy. Production supervisors, instead of being "arbiters" of quality, now become just another resource for the operator to use in order to improve quality.

It is interesting to note that this tends to lead to cost conservation, as well as quality improvement, due to the elimination of duplication of effort. The inspection function under most old quality systems was performed by both operator and quality inspector. Under the new SPC philosophy, this function is given solely to the operator (after suitable training, of course).

Another interesting effect of SPC is the change in attitude among the workers (an equally profound change must also be generated in management for SPC to be completely effective). In fact, most SPC practitioners would maintain that this is a fundamental requirement of SPC—as it most certainly is. However, this attitudinal change is also brought into being, to a great extent, by the operational and decision-making needs of the system. With more decision-making power comes more control which, in the opinion of most behavioral experts, leads to increased worker satisfaction and decreased job stress. Workers who are more satisfied with their jobs, and who are happier and calmer (less stressed), SPC contends, will almost always produce increased product quality (and decreased costs).

How Much Quality?

We live in an imperfect world, where nothing lasts forever and, sooner or later, something is going to go wrong. We even make jokes about it. It has been called Murphy's law: "The perversity of the universe tends to a maximum," and, "If anything can go wrong it will, and at the worst possible moment." We have learned by experience and instinct not to expect perfection; yet the dream, and hope, persists. So we learn to expect imperfection and, therefore, tend to design that expectation into our measurement methods. Most of the past quality measurement systems, for instance, started with the assumption of a certain degree of error. We are apparently willing to accept that error will exist even before the measurement begins. Yet, in many areas of our environment, we instinctively reject this attitude.

If we were to define "good quality," for instance, as a 99.9% error-free environment (most of our past production measurement systems, for instance, have assumed only a 99% error-free environment), this would seem almost perfect and certainly would appear to be sufficient. But what does this really mean in certain key areas? It means:

- 20,000 wrong drug prescriptions each year
- 4 wrong numbers on each page of the telephone book
- 730 short or long landings per year at each major airport in the country
- 140,000,000 lost pieces of mail per year
- 26,000 wrong surgical operations per year
- 19,000 babies dropped at birth each year
- 193,000,000 checks deducted from wrong accounts per year
- heart fails to beat 32,000 times per year (it only takes one failure to kill, although the heart can usually be restarted each time if a physician happens to be at hand with the proper equipment).

Obviously, even 99.9% quality is not acceptable in many cases. Unfortunately, modern complex high technology demands this kind of quality even in many (or most?) manufacturing systems. To illustrate the problem further, suppose that control chart limits were to be set at the specification limits. Control charts assume a 3 sigma (3σ), or 99.73%, good quality (see Chapter 3 and Section 4.1). For a product with 1000 parts, each controlled to this level of quality, there will only be 1 good unit for every 15 produced ($1/0.9973^{1000} = 14.9$). This problem, and its solution, is discussed in more detail in Chapter 6, especially in the section on process capability ratios.

Phil Crosby, one of the three "gurus" of modern quality control in the United States, has suggested that we act as if only 100% quality (zero defects) is acceptable. Most quality professionals tend to reject this idea as unattainable because of the facts of existence; errors will certainly occur eventually. It is obviously impossible to live an error-free life and to produce totally error-free products, over time.

Yet perhaps Crosby's theory can have some merit if applied as an attitude rather than as a demand on nature. His philosophy seems to imply that with this attitude mistakes will be kept to a minimum. Without this attitude errors tend to become institutionalized and to gradually increase over time. This institutionalization of errors appears to be exactly what has happened in the United States over the past 80 years, and to have contributed to the decline in quality in American-made products in that time. What is more, the Japanese, in their insistence on higher and higher quality, appear to have substantiated Crosby's theory. This, and other sources of SPC activity, have pretty well substantiated that a "defect-free" attitude can lead to long-term increases in both quality and productivity at the same time.

1.4 Variation

The basic objective of SPC is the reduction of variation. No two objects are ever exactly the same. Variation in measurements is a fact of life and must be properly dealt with. In a manufacturing setting, these variations are caused by the following (most of these things, with the proper change of names, can also be seen in nonmanufacturing and service processes).

1. **The process.** This includes such things as poor workholding and positioning, machine vibration, machine looseness, hydraulic and electrical fluctuation, machine breakdown, machine wear, machine speeds and feeds, poor preventive maintenance, poor repairs, dirty machinery, wrong process used, poor setup, change in setup, poor fixture design, too much play in part positioning, incorrect use of fixture, etc.
2. **The material.** These types of variations are caused by differences in

material characteristics, such as hardness, moisture content, tensile strength, ductility, hard/soft spots, too hard or too soft, high or low concentration, mixing of different lots, change in supplier and/or change in material, more than one supplier, etc.

3. **The operator.** This is perhaps the greatest source of variation. The personal, emotional, and mental problems of the operator, along with inattentiveness and lack of understanding, lead to misalignment, frequent machine adjustments, errors, improper handling, etc. Other operator problems are: new and/or untrained operator, operator fatigue (the most common cause of cycles in the R chart), change in shift, operator morale, etc. Probably 80% or more of quality problems are, or can be, solved by simply observing, or by asking the operator (getting the operator personally involved on a quality improvement team is by far the best way).
4. **Tooling.** Tooling problems can be caused by such things as: using the wrong tool, tool made incorrectly, tool used incorrectly, tool wear, etc.
5. **Quality control.** If quality control inspectors do not fully understand the implications and proper uses of statistical control techniques, they can cause excessive variations by requiring too-frequent adjustments to the process. This, along with faulty measuring equipment and incorrect measurements, can be a large source of variation in the product.
6. **Measurement.** These types of problems are caused by such things as: errors in measurement, using the wrong gauge, using an inaccurate gauge, misreading the measurement instrument, incorrect calculations, new and/or untrained inspector, etc.
7. **Methods (procedures).** Some common errors in this area are: incomplete operation, missing operation, wrong methods used, wrong methods specified, etc. A good production work order system can do a lot to reduce errors in this area.
8. **Engineering.** Engineering can cause variation through: incorrect or incomplete process designs, specifying engineering specifications outside the range of process capability, incorrect product specifications, unsafe product and/or methods design causing fear and hesitation on the part of the operator, and product design specifications unnecessarily critical (not "robustly" designed). (Robust means to design so that systems are not so dependent on changes in production; so that changes in production do not cause very many errors.)
9. **Management (systems or organizational errors).** Most of the preceding causes of quality problems are systems or organizational errors and thus management causes. Most quality professionals estimate that as much as 95% of quality problems (the estimate used to be 85% but it was revised in 1993) are systems or management controllable, not operator controllable.
10. **Environment.** This includes temperature, moisture, sun, etc.
11. **Miscellaneous.** Many very small variations in the product are caused by changes in temperature, humidity, light, air pressure, dust, etc. Sometimes, with certain products, these variations can be quite significant and require special procedures to control (such as steam vents for

humidity to control static in knitting mills, as well as the closing of certain windows during certain hours of the day so that the sun does not make the presses too hot).

For quality control purposes, these causes are classified either as chance causes or as assignable (special) causes. Chance causes are those that are small in magnitude and present a stable picture of variation where no long-term patterns are discernible. Assignable causes, on the other hand, are more readily recognized through one or more of a group of different types of long-term trends (see Chapter 6). They are assumed to be correctable, and their identification is one of the most important objectives of SPC (and quality control).

In essence, variation is reduced by two different approaches: by identifying assignable causes and *correcting* the process, and by using information about causes, both assignable and chance, to *improve* the process (see Chapter 6 for a fuller discussion of these two important concepts). Correcting the process—changing those things in the process that are out of control—is usually accomplished by the operator and his/her immediate supervisor. Improving the process is usually done by top management after the process has settled into its steady-state condition, after no more out-of-control situations remain to be corrected. Control charts give this important information to management.

1.5 Quality Costs

(*Note:* Much of this section has been derived from Crosby, *Quality is Free* and Juran and Gryna, *Quality Planning and Analysis.*)

One of the great lessons learned from the Japanese experience is that quality produces profits. But just how much quality is needed to optimize profits is, and should be, a matter of utmost concern for management. Quality costs must be identified and controlled, and their relationship to profits analyzed, just like any other cost. And, like any other cost, quality costs can be budgeted, measured, and analyzed to achieve the goal of higher quality at lower cost.

One of the biggest problems in the past has been management's attitude toward quality. Quality costs have, for the most part, been looked upon as a necessary evil. They have been considered as necessary costs of doing business and, as such, should be minimized and reduced as much as possible. The trouble with this attitude is that it does not consider the impact that quality has on profits.

The fact that quality costs frequently affect profits even more than do other costs, even production costs, has been largely ignored in American business. When quality costs are analyzed and evaluated, it must be from the attitude of quality costs' long-range effect on company profits and stability. If this effect is a desirable one, if it contributes to profits, it should not be reduced, necessarily, but perhaps even increased until its effects on profits are maximized (for instance, costs associated with reducing scrap). For best analysis, quality costs must be divided into their various categories, and the factors that affect these costs must be examined.

There are three types of quality cost: prevention, appraisal, and failure. Failure costs are further subdivided into internal failures and external failures (failures in the field after the customer uses the product). Failure costs are the most undesirable of all, especially external failure costs (because of their direct effect on customer satisfaction). In general, both prevention and appraisal costs have a direct, and opposite, effect on failure cost. As prevention and appraisal costs increase, failure costs tend to decrease, and vice versa.

The goal is to increase prevention and appraisal costs until they exactly offset the failure costs. In this respect, then, prevention and appraisal costs are considered to be controllable but failure costs are not (direct control, that is). Of course, the watchword must be "effective" control. Prevention and appraisal costs must be increased in such a way that this increase maximizes the reduction of failure costs. Since this kind of maximum effect seldom occurs, there is almost always room for improvement in all cost categories.

One of the problems with controlling quality costs is the difficulty in identifying them in most firms (at least, American firms). Costs must be measured in order to be properly managed. If you can't measure it, you don't really know what it is, and you most certainly won't be able to effectively control it. In the past, most charts of accounts (Accounting's way of summarizing and controlling costs) did not separate most quality costs. Instead, they were added in with other cost categories. Thus the separation and identification of these costs become a major problem to the quality analyst. Of course, if Accounting can be prevailed upon to separate these costs in the chart of accounts (change the chart of accounts), this problem would disappear. But this, then, would present Accounting with a major difficulty, as it will usually require extensive changes in their cost collecting procedures (also, many quality costs are quite difficult to measure). The solution to this problem is seldom easy.

Prevention Costs

These are the costs of designing, implementing, and maintaining a quality system—the costs of all activities associated with creating a product or service and the error prevention activities that are applied during the business cycle. It is important to clearly distinguish between prevention and appraisal costs. Prevention costs are associated with the creation and design of cost control systems, while appraisal costs are the costs of using those systems to detect errors. Some of the more important cost categories involved are the following.

1. The development of the quality, inspection, and reliability plans, and the data gathering and analysis system associated with these plans. Only the development of, and any subsequent refinements or alterations to, the system are prevention costs. The costs of running the system are appraisal costs.
2. Design and development of quality control equipment (including any subsequent upgrading, redesigning, and/or improvement). The cost of maintaining and using the equipment would be appraisal costs.
3. Time, effort, and cost on the part of others in the organization who are not directly part of the quality control function. The cost of ongoing quality activities of these others, of course, would be appraisal and/or failure costs.
4. Training of quality personnel and quality training for other department personnel.
5. Miscellaneous is mostly a general office management category.
6. Design review.
7. Product qualification.
8. Zero defects and other error prevention programs.
9. Quality orientation for new employees.
10. Supplier evaluations—initial qualification appraisal.
11. Process capability studies (see Chapter 6).
12. Tool control.
13. Quality system audits.
14. Preventive maintenance.
15. Acceptance planning.
16. Specification reviews.
17. Checking of drawings.
18. Supplier quality seminars.

Appraisal Costs

This category includes the cost of assessing and analyzing the condition of the product and measuring and evaluating conformance to quality standards. Cost categories are as follows.

1. Inspection and test of incoming material and periodic audits of the supplier's quality control system.
2. Inspection and testing.
3. Product quality audits.
4. Equipment calibration and maintenance.
5. Data gathering and analysis.
6. Supplier audits.
7. Specification conformance analysis.
8. Product acceptance.
9. Process control acceptance.
10. Status measuring and reporting.

Failure Costs

These are the costs associated with the failure of a product to meet quality standards. These costs cannot occur if there are no defects in the product (100% quality). Failure costs are subdivided into internal and external failure costs.

Internal Failure Costs These costs occur when product defects are identified prior to transfer of ownership (prior to the customer receiving the product). The categories are as follows.

1. Scrap.
2. Rework.
3. Failure analysis.
4. Reinspection.
5. Supplier fault analysis.
6. Downgrading. (The product is sold at a discount due to defects or failure.)
7. Redesign due to internal failures.
   a. Engineering change orders.
   b. Purchasing change orders.
   c. Corrective action costs.

External Failure Costs These costs occur after the customer receives the product, after transfer of ownership. These types of failures have a direct effect on customer satisfaction, and therefore on sales. Because of this, any failure or defect reduction system must first concentrate on the reduction, and control, of these most critical defect types before extending the control to other areas. The categories are as follows.

1. Adjustment for complaints.
2. Handling and replacement of returned product.
3. Product repairs.
4. Warranty expenses.
5. Liability cost and litigation expense.
6. Consumer affairs.
7. Redesign due to external failures.
   a. Engineering change orders.
   b. Purchasing change orders.
   c. Corrective action costs.

Controlling Quality Costs

Management's job is to keep all costs as low as possible while maximizing profits. In this respect, quality costs are no different than other costs. The only difference is in the measurement, analysis, and evaluation of these costs. Quality costs, for the most part, are difficult to relate directly to profits. Just how much a particular quality cost affects the profit picture is usually difficult to determine. Several techniques have evolved that attempt to solve this problem, but none of them alone can make these necessary comparisons effectively.

1. Compare to other companies. This type of analysis must be made at the lowest level; individual categories must be compared rather than total costs. Thus a total breakdown of costs must be available in order for proper comparisons to be made. Unfortunately, other companies' costs are frequently unavailable, especially if they are competitors. And, of course, it is imperative that the products be, at least, similar (better if they are identical). This concept has been expanded into a system of total comparison called "benchmarking" (it is one of the requirements for the Malcolm Baldrige award).
2. Analyze the interrelationships among cost categories. The ideal is to have the prevention and appraisal costs together equal the failure costs.
3. Optimize the individual costs. In general, this is accomplished when no profitable projects for reducing these costs (and maintaining long-range profits at the same time) can be readily identified; and when quality costs are controlled by sound budgeting.
4. Compare to previous periods. If quality costs are steadily declining from cost period to cost period (while sales and profits are increasing, and with customer complaints decreasing), then it can probably be assumed that quality costs are being properly optimized.

None of these schemes is completely effective in and of itself, but if they are all used carefully, along with judicious management judgment, quality costs can be reasonably controlled while, at the same time, keeping profits effectively maximized.

1.6 General Quality Standards

In the United States, there are two sets of generally accepted quality standards: ISO 9000 and Malcolm Baldrige. These two quality systems are presented here as a matter of information only; they are clearly part of the quality concepts that every SPC practitioner should know.

The ISO 9000 Series

ISO 9000, also called Q90 by the American Society for Quality Control (ASQC, 611 East Wisconsin Ave., Milwaukee, WI 53201; also see Kanholm, 1993 and Fawcett, 1993) is a French acronym that, translated, means something like international organization for standards. It provides a minimum standard for all quality systems and a general quality system model for all types of businesses and for all types of products and services. ISO 9000 is mandated by the EEC (European Economic Community) and enjoys an almost unanimous worldwide acceptance. Eventually most companies of the world will probably demand an ISO 9000 "third party" registration for product certification.

(In ISO, "third party" audits are conducted each six months, after the initial "third party" audit and certification. "Third party" means someone other than the company or its customers.)

Actually, ISO 9000 (and Q90) only explains the others; it is a guideline for selection and use. This is also true of ISO 9004 (and Q94). ISO 9004 also provides standards for internal use—for evaluating a firm's internal quality system. Certification is handled through ISO 9001, ISO 9002, and ISO 9003 (called Q91, Q92, and Q93 by ASQC). ISO 9001 (Q91) provides certification for every function of the firm, ISO 9002 (Q92) omits Design Control and Servicing, and ISO 9003 (Q93) is designed to cover inspection and testing only. ISO 9001 includes all 20 functions within a firm, ISO 9002 only 18, and ISO 9003 only 10. Since ISO 9001 (Q91) has all 20 functions, only it needs to be explained (ISO 9001 necessarily includes ISO 9002 and 3).

There are several important things about ISO to remember. One is that a general system for managing through quality is mandated. The firm is left completely free to organize within the broad ISO guidelines. These guidelines are so broad and so general that no coercion is intended or included. Second, the system is constantly audited so that changes must always be for the better. Auditing continues every six months, by an outside auditor, and the auditor must be convinced that any changes fall within the ISO guidelines. Finally, ISO demands not only that the proper documents be included in the system, but that people use these documents properly. In other words, everything must be properly documented (in accordance with ISO standards) and everyone must be properly working; properly using these documents. This is probably the greatest message of ISO: have a system and work that system. For ISO we must have both.

The ISO 9001 standards are divided into 20 sections. Each of these sections has requirements (documents, procedures, and records) that must be included in the company's quality system. Documents are descriptions of what must be done, and are included in the actual ISO procedures. Records are descriptions of what has been done in specific instances. Records can be shown, in general, in the procedures, but all actual records are separate from the ISO procedures. All records, when completed, must be stored and controlled. Procedures are written descriptions (usually documents) that explain just how the firm will proceed to accomplish the ISO requirements in each area.

All of these things (documents, procedures, records, and their ISO requirements) must be installed in order to pass an ISO audit. They should also be included in a good quality system. And they should be memorized and constantly applied. If an SPC (and/or TQM) system is added, it can become part of Section 20 on Statistical Procedures (such as PC 20.2 and/or PC 20.3).

The following summary is listed in the order of the 20 ISO 9001 requirements (for instance, 1 means 4.1 of the standards, 2 is 4.2, etc.). Only ISO 9001 gives all 20 sections, and therefore only it will be used. All others are only portions of the full 9001.

1. Management Responsibility (4.1).
   a. Assign, document, understand, implement, and maintain quality policy and objectives.
   b. Assign quality responsibilities and authorities.
   c. Make resources and personnel available.
   d. Assign a Management Representative.
   e. Make, and record, periodic management reviews.
2. Quality System (4.2).
   a. Establish, document, implement, and maintain an effective quality system (the quality system is contained in the rest of the standards).
   b. Prepare a quality manual and quality procedures.
   c. Prepare a quality plan (this can be referenced in other parts of the quality system).
   d. Keeps records.
3. Contract Review (4.3).
   a. Establish and maintain procedures for contract review.
   b. Review contracts (orders) for customer requirements.
   c. Review company capacity (know-how, material, equipment, personnel, time, etc.).
   d. Resolve differences.
   e. Keep records.
4. Design Control (4.4).
   a. Plan the design process.
   b. Assign responsibilities, personnel, and resources.
   c. Assign design activities.
   d. Identify, document, and review the organizational and technical interfaces.
   e. Control communication between the various groups.
   f. Identify and document design input.
   g. Document design output—make sure that it matches the input requirements.
   h. Verify the design.
   i. Control design changes.
5. Document Control (4.5).
   a. Review and approve all documents prior to issue.
   b. Establish a control system that assures that documents are properly identified.
   c. Establish a control system that assures that documents are where they belong.
   d. Remove old documents.
   e. Maintain a master list, with current revision.
   f. Review and approve document changes.

6. Purchasing (4.6).
   a. Assess quality capabilities of suppliers and subcontractors.
   b. Keep records of contractors.
   c. Use only approved suppliers and subcontractors.
   d. Clearly and completely define the products.
   e. Review and approve purchasing documents.
   f. Verify purchased product.
   g. If applicable, allow customers to verify purchased products.
7. Purchaser Supplied Product (4.7).
   a. Verify, store, and protect customer products.
   b. Notify customers in the event of loss or damage.
8. Product Identification and Traceability (4.8).
   a. Label, tag, or otherwise mark products to identify them.
   b. Be sure that product labels are correlated with their documentation (drawings, specifications, etc.).
   c. If required, identify individual products or batches to ensure traceability.
9. Process Control (4.9).
   a. Identify, plan, document, and control each production process.
   b. Comply with proper references and procedures.
   c. Have documented work instructions for personnel.
   d. Use suitable processes and equipment.
   e. Approve, and maintain, processes and equipment.
   f. Provide workmanship criteria.
   g. Monitor those processes that cannot be verified by subsequent inspection (welding, painting, etc.).
   h. Maintain records.
10. Inspection and Testing (4.10).
    a. Inspect all received products.
    b. Where received products are used prior to production, identify and record for possible recall.
    c. Restrict access to products before acceptance.
    d. Before dispatching a product, verify that all production activities, processes, and inspections are completed satisfactorily.
    e. Establish and maintain inspection records.
11. Inspection, Measuring, and Test Equipment (4.11).
    a. Calibrate, maintain, and safeguard inspection equipment.
    b. Establish and maintain calibration and/or control records.
    c. Identify and mark calibration status—even on equipment that is not calibrated.
    d. Select, plan, and use the proper measuring and test equipment.
12. Inspection and Test Status (4.12).
    a. Mark products that have been inspected.
    b. Record inspection authorities.
13. Control of Nonconforming Product (4.13).
    a. Segregate and control nonconforming products.
    b. Review and consign (rework, accept, regrade, or reject) nonconforming product.

   c. If required by contract, get permission from customer to use or repair a nonconforming product.
   d. Reinspect repaired or reworked products.
14. Corrective and Preventive Action (4.14).
   a. Investigate causes for nonconformances.
   b. Analyze trends.
   c. Carry out preventive actions, as needed.
   d. Follow up on corrective actions.
15. Handling, Storage, Packaging, and Delivery (4.15).
   a. Provide appropriate product handling methods.
   b. Provide secure and adequate storage.
   c. Control the movement of products to and from storage.
   d. Periodically assess condition of stocks.
   e. Control packing of product.
   f. Protect quality and delivery of product after final inspection.
16. Quality Records (4.16).
   a. Organize and store quality records.
   b. Maintain quality records in proper condition.
   c. Assign retention periods for quality records.
17. Internal Quality Audits (4.17).
   a. Plan, conduct, and document internal quality audits.
   b. Implement corrective actions as needed.
18. Training (4.18).
   a. Determine personnel training needs.
   b. Provide the required training.
   c. Keep proper records.
19. Servicing (4.19).
   Apply the proper quality system elements to servicing.
20. Statistical Methods (4.20).
   Use adequate statistical techniques.

The Malcolm Baldrige Annual Quality Award

(Contact: U.S. Department of Commerce, National Institute of Standards and Technology, Gaithersburg, MD 20899.) This award has proven in the past to be quite difficult to obtain. It takes a lot of time, energy, and money, and is clearly much more complex and involved than is the simple ISO model. A firm that receives the Baldrige award has clearly shown an excellent quality system that works. Although the ISO system appears to be overshadowing it by quite a bit (at least in 1995), this award does provide another excellent model for building a good quality system.

There are seven categories.

1. **Leadership.** This category examines: 1) how senior executives create and sustain a clear and visible quality value system; 2) the supporting management system; 3) the company's and senior executives' quality leadership in the external community; and 4) integration of the company's public responsibilities with its quality values and practices.

2. **Information and analysis.** This category examines: 1) the company's total quality management data including the scope, validity, use, and management of the system; and 2) the adequacy of the data to support a responsive prevention approach.
3. **Strategic quality planning.** This category examines: 1) the company's planning process for achieving or retaining quality leadership; 2) how the company integrates quality improvement planning into the overall business planning; and 3) short- and long-term priorities to achieve and/or attain quality leadership.
4. **Human resource utilization.** This category examines: 1) the company's effectiveness in developing the full potential of the workforce; and 2) the company's effectiveness in maintaining an environment conducive to full participation, quality leadership, and personal and organizational growth.
5. **Quality assurance of products and services.** This category examines: 1) methods for achieving total quality control; 2) process design and control; 3) control of procurement; and 4) integration of quality control with continuous quality improvement.
6. **Quality results.** This category examines: 1) objective measures of quality levels and quality improvement derived from analysis of customer requirements and of business expectations; and 2) current quality levels in comparison to the competition.
7. **Customer satisfaction.** This category examines: 1) knowledge of the customer; 2) overall customer service systems; 3) responsiveness; 4) ability to meet requirements and expectations; and 5) current levels and trends in customer satisfaction.

1.7 SPC Philosophy

SPC (statistical process control) is defined as a system that uses statistics to identify special (assignable) causes of variation in a process. Once the variations are identified by SPC, it is up to the various people involved to use their creativity and ingenuity to correct these variations. This is SPC's way of controlling the processes.

If the processes are in control, it is assumed that the products produced from these processes will also be in control (this does *not* assume that the products will meet the specifications, see Chapter 6). Thus, instead of controlling the products with mostly 100% inspections, the processes are controlled with sampling procedures (a much cheaper, and potentially surer and longer lasting, control system).

In this book, SPC is considered to be the technical arm of the quality management system called SPC/TQM by the author. In order to properly explain SPC, it is best to describe the philosophy surrounding the entire concept of the quality management system called SPC/TQM.

If a company really is serious about quality, and really wants to have a quality product over time, it will need a long-term SPC/TQM quality management program, one that cannot be destroyed by a single person—even a new top manager. This is where ISO comes in. If an SPC/TQM quality management system is described in ISO (mostly ISO, Section 20), it is likely to survive changes in management (which has not been the case so often in the past, especially the American past).

The SPC/TQM quality management system is a natural extension of SPC into all aspects and functions of the firm, not just the production function. It is a totally integrated effort toward improving performance at every level and in every activity in the firm. As in SPC, this system stresses continuous improvement of quality: a continuous commitment to manage the firm around the concept of quality. This is a systems-oriented approach involving all functions of the firm. Quality is organized, assignments are made, schedules are constructed, an overseer function (either a person or a committee) is organized, reports are made, files are kept, and results are compared to keep the system on course.

The main goal of SPC/TQM is customer satisfaction. The focus is to increase this satisfaction with a disciplined approach to continuous improvement involving any and all functions of the firm and any and all available tools.

It is impossible to say which of the following elements are likely to be present in any SPC/TQM firm. Most of them overlap with many of the others, some considerably so. Nevertheless, they are all listed here so that the different philosophical concepts can be properly presented. Therefore, the extent and amount of these elements are left to the analyst, and the management, of the firm using them. The following are the quality system elements that are likely to be present in any firm that has a well-run SPC/TQM quality management system. (Read the author's new book, now being written, on TQM; and Covey, 1989; Senge, 1990; Deming, 1986; Johnson, 1989; Peters, 1982; Schatz, 1986; Scholtes, 1988, and Scott, 1991.)

1. A top management team acts as the steering group (or is, at least, in obvious control of the quality function). Ideal top management TQM teams will include some workers.
2. The firm will have a top-level SPC/TQM coordinator (usually called SPC coordinator, TQM coordinator, improvement coordinator, or something else) plus enough coordinators and facilitators to assist the improvements teams as needed. A good rule of thumb is: one coordinator for every 250 employees.
3. An SPC/TQM policy is in place (this can be included in the ISO Quality Manual).
4. Department, team, and company mission statements are available. Team mission statements will change as the team activities change, and as the process being analyzed changes (see Covey, 1989).
5. Established procedures, rules, and criteria for team formation, team activity, and people empowerment (the authority to act) are available.

The worker has the responsibility for quality rather than QC, including the right to make critical decisions about quality and what to do to maintain it.

6. Management is supportive and committed, rather than autocratic. In SPC/TQM, operators and management both are expected to be involved in all aspects of the quality function, including all the details of quality management, control, and improvement.
7. Department and team performance improvement goals are available—in conformance to, and within the guidelines of, the overall company improvement goals (see Covey, 1989).
8. The firm has an effective evaluation and review procedure, and is using it effectively (see Section 1.8 on the Deming evaluation procedure and red bead experiment).
9. A program of continuous lifelong education and training for all is in place and working.
10. A free-flowing network of information, including informational feedback on performance, goal attainment, and activity interrelationships (the glue that holds the system together) is operating. This network gives the worker the critical informational inputs necessary to make rational and effective decisions.
11. The firm is using an integrated system for identifying and controlling quality costs.
12. There is a long-term focus and commitment.
13. There is a company-wide customer orientation.
14. There is an internal customer/supplier orientation. (The last person working on the part becomes your supplier, while the next person to work on the part becomes your customer.)
15. An organization for customer/supplier involvement in quality improvement is in place and operating.
16. All systems are organized for flexibility and for necessary change. The firm has a means of learning, adapting, and managing dynamic change. Change is not considered something to be feared, but something to control for the benefit of the firm.
17. A system is in place for monitoring competition (benchmarking) and organizing for product/process leadership. The firm is committed to process/product leadership.
18. Provision has been made for periodic meetings and award ceremonies (quality day, quality award, etc.).
19. The necessary resources (time, materials, money, etc.) are provided.
20. A system of self-directed, interrelated, cross-functional, empowered teams is operating (empowered means authority to act).
21. Workers and processes are "certified" and "process owners" are appointed. When people are properly trained, they are "certified" to do their jobs (by the supervisor, mostly). "Process owners" refers to those process experts who have been assigned to be responsible for the processes for which they work (one "process owner" to a process).
22. Periodic audits of people and processes are conducted to maintain certification (an ISO standard).

23. People are treated with trust, dignity, and respect. Employees are empowered and involved, and a humanistic cultural environment is obvious (employees are self-actualized, feel good about themselves and their work, and are happy—and absenteeism and lateness are reduced).
24. A statistical control of processes (SPC) is operating (the reduction of variation, a concentration on prevention rather than on correction, an orientation toward continuous quality improvement, etc.).
25. A systems approach to quality is in place (everyone assigned rather than slipshod or no or little organization), including a company-wide, all-inclusive, quality attitude and commitment. A proper assignment of quality duties has been made to all (quality duties are not just assumed, with the resultant constant harangue on quality duties at every meeting).
26. Everyone in the firm has a total commitment to profit improvement.
27. A cultural environment of caring, cooperation, mutual respect and concern, continuous process improvement, goal achievement, etc., by all is operating in the firm, at all levels.
28. Quality control, as a separate function, is used as technical support to assist the worker in making quality products. The quality system is left free to provide technical support to the worker, plan and install the quality systems, train the worker as needed to operate the system (including a thorough understanding of the theory as well as the operational dynamics), audit the system periodically to see that it still functions effectively, provide statistical analysis of control charts, conduct experiments (usually called DOE or Design of Experiments), provide critical information to management for the control of process variables, and provide critical information to design for proper determination of engineering specifications.
29. The system (actually the process) rather than the product is audited for control of quality. Under SPC, the prime directive is to reduce the dispersion (the standard deviation) of the process—to get closer and closer to the central value of the product (see Chapters 3 and 6). This activity is continuous, even when the product is produced within the specifications (see Chapter 6 and the discussion on the Taguchi loss function in Section 1.3). With SPC, the control of quality centers on the control of the process. It is felt that if the process is controlled and improved, product quality will automatically be maximized. After the process has been perfected, product specifications are compared to process control limits to determine if the process is capable of producing the product to these specifications (see Chapter 6).

An individual SPC philosophy can be assembled from almost any combination of the above elements. In modern SPC, there are three philosophies that have become universally accepted—each philosophy has its own recognized expert. These experts (called "the three gurus of quality control" in some circles) are: Philip B. Crosby *(Quality is Free, Quality Without Tears)*, Joseph M. Juran *(Quality Control Handbook,*

Quality Planning and Analysis), and W. Edwards Deming *(Quality, Productivity, and Competitive Position, Out of the Crisis).*

They all agree, for the most part, on all important elements. Therefore, the philosophy of Dr. W. Edwards Deming, probably the most notable of all the quality experts, will be used to explain and define what a quality philosophy should be.

Deming's Philosophy

Dr. Deming, who died in 1994, agreed that an effective SPC/TQM program must be structured and planned. However, he did not provide the detail for this that the other two do. He provided a general outline for a good quality program with his 14 points (Figure 1.1). He also agreed that management commitment and involvement is critical, using his 14th point to define a structure in top management that will control and direct the other 13 points.

Deming's philosophy supports a participative management style, as his Quality Circles approach in Japan clearly demonstrates. His Quality Circles are a series of committees, mostly at the worker level and mostly permanent, designed to effect quality improvements. Each circle (committee) is trained in SPC/TQM and then allowed to exercise full control in all three areas of quality improvement: identification, analysis, and implementation. Under this approach, management is viewed as just another resource the circle can use to accomplish its goals (clearly a participative management approach).

Deming's philosophy places much more emphasis on statistical analysis as a measure of quality than do the other experts'. He opposed the

1. Create constancy of purpose for improvement of product and service.
2. Adopt the new philosophy of refusing to allow defects.
3. Cease dependence on mass inspection and rely only on statistical control.
4. Require suppliers to provide statistical evidence of quality.
5. Constantly and forever improve production and services.
6. Train all employees.
7. Give all employees the proper tools to do the job right.
8. Encourage communication and productivity.
9. Encourage different departments to work together on problem solving.
10. Eliminate posters and slogans that do not teach specific improvement methods.
11. Use statistical methods to continuously improve quality and productivity.
12. Eliminate all barriers to pride in workmanship.
13. Provide ongoing retraining to keep apace with changing products, methods, etc.
14. Clearly define top management's permanent commitment to quality.

Figure 1.1. W. Edwards Deming's 14 points.

use of cost of quality as a measurement tool because it does not include customer satisfaction (an almost impossible cost to quantify, according to Deming). He, along with Dr. Juran, believed that 85% of all quality problems are management controllable and that it is the duty of the committees to point this out, and the duty of management to correct the problems and to improve the process (in 1993, he changed the 85% to 95%). He believed in more statistical training for the committees and placed less emphasis on organizational and strategic training.

Back in the 1920's, W. Edwards Deming was a student of W. A. Shewhart (the man who invented control charts). During that time, he was indoctrinated into Shewhart's "Plan, Do, Check and Act" philosophy. That indoctrination stuck for a lifetime. The term "plan" (or, as Deming has said, "organizing") refers to planning a project, or planning an improvement project before it begins (so that everyone knows what is going to happen, as far as is possible). Next, a project is tried, or executed (Do a pilot project?), to see if the plan will work. Then all relevant characteristics are checked (inspected). If any problems are found, the original plan is revised and the cycle is started again. If no problems are found, the entire production run can be started (act or produce), although the cycle (Plan, Do, Check, and Act) can always be run over and over again as needed. Shewhart, and then Deming, showed the cycle as follows.

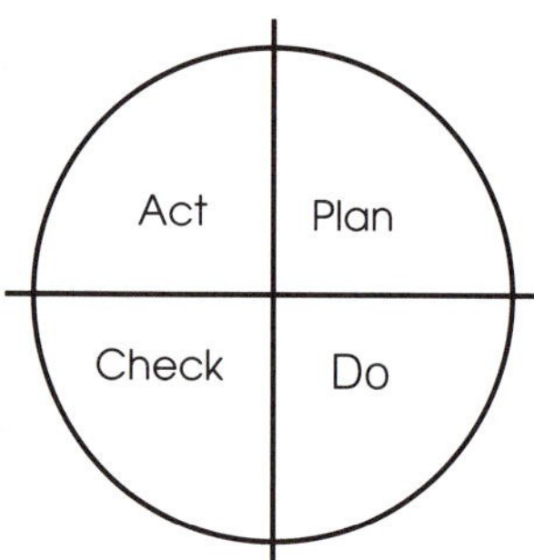

1.8 Nonmanufacturing SPC

It is usual for new practitioners to be uncertain as to how to apply SPC control charts. A complete understanding of chart theory and construction, a knowledge of the types of processes used, and some actual use of the charts (some actual experience) is about the only way for a new practitioner to gain insight into how to apply the charts. This is even more true of nonmanufacturing activities (i.e., the nonmanufacturing sections of a manufacturing firm, and a totally service firm with no manufacturing at all). Although this section refers to nonmanufacturing (thus, some form of manufacturing tends to be stressed), all other areas are also included (such as education, health care, politics, family life, and self-improvement).

Any of the charts explained in Chapters 4 and 5 can be used in nonmanufacturing in exactly the same way as they are used in manufacturing. About the only real difference between the two areas is the type of process, which emphasizes the need for the SPC practitioner to become very familiar with the charts as well as with his or her processes (in other words, study hard). The charts are explained in this book (especially in Chapters 4 and 5).

Types of nonmanufacturing data include actual, or 100%, times and sampling times (nonmanufacturing is often 100%). Types of nonmanufacturing charts are, usually: a moving average chart if the charting is of individual data items; a weighted *u* chart if charting all categories together and weighting (weighted *p* or *c* charts can also be used); a regular attributes chart if all categories are charted and not weighted; and/or a zero base chart if short runs are being charted.

Weighted attribute charts are used to some extent in nonmanufacturing and hardly at all in manufacturing (they should probably be used more often). The reason average charts are usually used so much is that most nonmanufacturing activities are of such a nature that variable sample sizes are necessary. And the reason for using the *u* rather than the *p*, for most nonmanufacturing applications, is that the *p* requires that each type of weighting be less than 100% and that the *p* weightings total to 100%. If constant sample sizes can be used, of course, weighted charts instead of weighted average charts should be employed. Also, the basic charts, instead of weighted charts, should always be used if at all possible (see Chapters 4 and 5).

Another difference for nonmanufacturing is the closer ties with the customer. Even though SPC (actually the entire SPC/TQM quality management system) emphasizes closer customer considerations (for all), it is still true that most manufacturing activities can proceed to a great extent without even thinking of the customer. This is not true of most nonmanufacturing processes. Most of these have a direct interaction with the customer. Customer needs and expectations must be more clearly identified and then translated into product and service goals. The customer must be able to see that the processes are being made simpler, that quality control and improvement methods are being implemented, and that many things (such as customer waiting time, for instance) are being reduced to their absolute limit.

Following are some examples of types of nonmanufacturing processes (a checklist of possibilities). Find characteristics that affect quality and productivity; then edit. Then use customers and internal surveys. The use of teams and brainstorming can, and should, be done at any time.

1. Paperwork processing—volume, CRT.
2. Dollar savings.
3. Cost of quality.
4. Quality ratings.
5. Productivity.
6. Sales.
7. Receivables—dollars paid in 30, 60, 90 days, dollars paid over a certain dollar amount, etc.
8. Payables.
9. Man hours per man hour.
10. Line items per man hour.
11. Documents per man hour.
12. Boxes, etc., per man hour.
13. Receptionist (call her randomly and rate her response). Number of rings after 5, courtesy, no answer, on hold more than 2 minutes, disconnect, transfer to wrong party, etc.
14. Volume of activity.
15. Cycle time; timeliness.
16. Percent don't pay; percent don't deliver.
17. Percent contaminants; percent moisture.
18. Customer goals—quality improvement program, waiting time, quality of products, courtesy, timeliness, etc.
19. Perceptions of quality (internal and external).
20. Programmers, writers, and managers can use peer review and self-assessment.
21. Correspondence—substantive errors, errors of content, typos, misspellings, timeliness, lost work, etc.
22. Issuing or storing to inventory—errors (accuracy), different charts for different aisles(?), weighted as to aisles(?).
23. Quality instead of quantity?
24. Lawyers—missing the crux of the argument, failure to counter, perception (appearance, lofty, lengthy, wordy, sentence structure, etc.).
25. Purchasing—quality of supply of product or service (chart rating of suppliers), weighted Pareto, quality in job performance reviews, cost reduction (quantity and dollar amount—composite weighted index), dollar amount of purchase orders processed, reduction of supply base (reduction of suppliers), improvement results by teams, individuals, and/or departments (weighted scale, usually).

SPC and Employee Rating—A Deming Example

Dr. Deming provided an excellent example of how a control chart can be used very effectively in the management of a firm (see Deming, 1986, pp. 109–114). This example is then extended to other control charts by the author in this book. (Please note that these are examples of the use of control charts in both manufacturing and nonmanufacturing situations.)

One of the most important nonmanufacturing areas constantly used by managers is employee rating. According to Dr. Deming, employee rating is constantly done incorrectly by supervisors, mostly because they do not understand the implications and effects of statistical procedures. Dr. Deming's red bead experiment (Example 1.1 below) shows clearly that the award of most merit increases is extremely unjust if statistics is not used properly (which is the situation in almost every such case, especially in the United States). Listen to what Dr. Deming had to say about his red bead experiment.

> The performance of anybody is the result of a combination of many forces . . .
>
> It would be difficult to construct physical circumstances so nearly equal for six people, yet to the eye, the people vary greatly in performance.
>
> . . . apparent differences between people arise almost entirely from action of the system that they work in, not from the people themselves.
>
> . . . What is worse, anybody that would seek a cause would come up with an answer, action on which could only make things worse henceforth.
>
> If the work of a group forms a statistical system [none are outside the limits and there are no patterns], then the prize [special recognition for a job well done] would be merely a lottery . . . To call it an award of merit when the selection is merely a lottery, however, is to demoralize the whole force, prize winners included. Everybody will suppose that there are good reasons for the selection and will be trying to explain and reduce differences between [people]. This would be a futile exercise when the only differences are random deviations . . .

Example 1.1 Six people draw 50 beads each, with replacement, from a box containing white and red beads (20% red). The aim is to produce white beads. The results were (use the *np* chart):

Name	**Red Beads (np)**
Paul	9
Stephen	5
Karen	15
Brian	4
Debora	10
Keith	8
Total	51

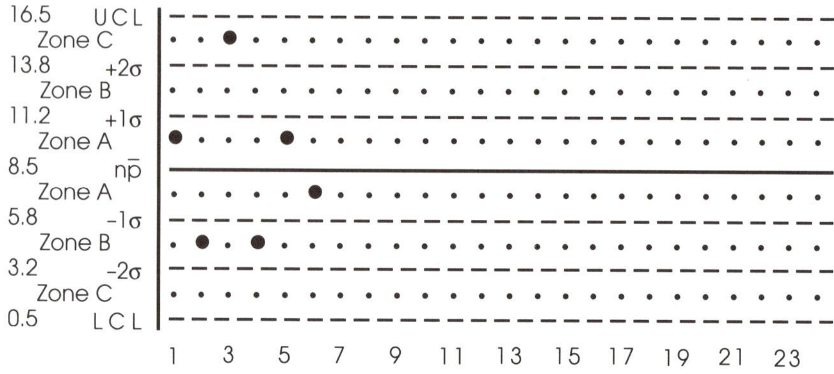

Figure 1.2. Control chart for Example 1.1.

Solution:

$$\bar{p} = \Sigma n\bar{p}/\Sigma n = 51/(6 \times 50) = 0.17$$

$$n\bar{p} = 50(0.17) = 8.5$$

$$\text{CL}p = n\bar{p} \pm 3\sqrt{n\bar{p}(1-\bar{p})} = 8.5 \pm 3\sqrt{8.5(1-0.17)} = 16.5 \;\&\; 0.5$$

Please note that the charted values (Figure 1.2) are just the number of undesirable events (number of red beads).

Since none of the people is above the upper limit of 16.5 nor below the lower limit of 0.5, the distribution is a chance one (occurring by chance alone)—which it *better* be considering the nature of the experiment. Any deviation from chance causes in the above experiment would have had to result from some kind of cheating; such as removing the red beads and replacing them with white ones. All too often, such is also the case in production—cheating is used to offset the unfairness of most of management's evaluative procedures. Any reward or punishment based on ranking (a favorite management evaluation tool) would be completely spurious and cause only resentment and, eventually, decreased performance (the opposite of the evaluation purpose).

Example 1.2 You are a manager with nine employees reporting directly to you. They have essentially the same responsibilities. In the past year, they have recorded the following number of mistakes. Each employee had about the same chance as another to make a mistake. This equal probability is very important. If these probabilities are not equal, the following analysis will not work—a weighted model will be needed instead (see Example 1.4).

Name	**Mistakes**
Paul	10
Stephen	15
Karen	11
Brian	4
Debora	17
Charlie	23
Keith	11
David	12
Joanne	10
Total	51

Whom to reward? Whom to penalize? *Why?*

Solution (use the c chart):

$$\bar{c} = 113/9 = 12.55$$

$$\text{Control Limits} = 12.55 \pm 3\sqrt{12.55} = 23.2 \text{ and } 1.9$$

The results are recorded on Figure 1.3. The recorded values are the number of mistakes for each person.

Because no one made more than the upper nor less than the lower limit, the apparent differences between the nine people could all be attributed to the action of the system (however, watch Charlie—his errors are extremely close to the limit). They should all be rewarded the same. However, if ranking (management's favorite evaluation system) were to be used, we would reward Brian and penalize Charlie. Brian's

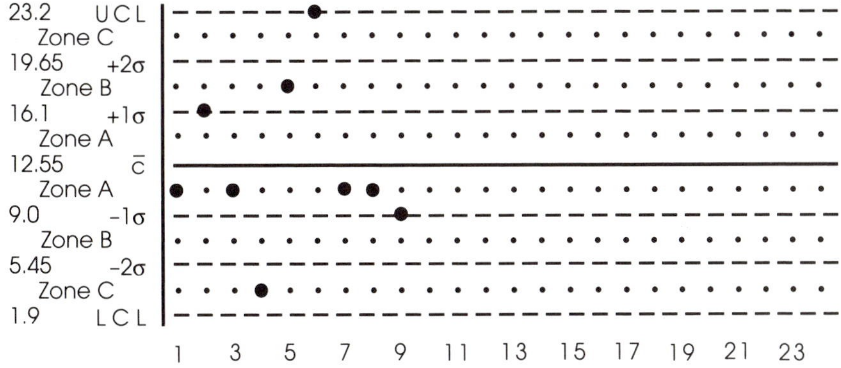

Figure 1.3. Control chart for Example 1.2.

reward would probably happen just because of luck—this period. Luck (chance or probability) alone probably made the difference, not ability.

Example 1.3 How many times in a row does Charlie have to be above average to be *justly* (statistically) penalized? (This expands Example 1.2 to many periods.)

Answer

Actually, there are several situations, and several patterns, that would justify some kind of action (see Chapter 6). All of these patterns have the same decision criteria—they can only occur by chance alone less than 1% of the time (in statistical parlance, $\alpha < 0.01$). The most important, in this case, is the first, i.e., above the upper limit or below the lower limit (1–0.9973). When there are many more people, the rest of the rules from Chapter 6 will also apply. For instance: seven times in a row above, or below, the average; seven in a row going up or down; seven in a row going up and down; 2 in zone C, between 2 and 3 sigmas (σ) above or below the mean; or any other regular pattern that calculates to a probability of less than 1%.

The normal curve and area under the curve procedures are used for the above calculations, since control charts are based on the normal curve (see Chapter 3). The binomial is also used to calculate probabilities of more than one occurrence (see Chapter 7). Multiple appearances (two in a row, for instance) means appearances in the same chart area in multiple charts (the same person appearing in zone C for two charts in a row, for instance). Of course, separate charts could also be constructed for each employee, and then two in a row would refer to two in a row in the same zone on the same chart (for the same person).

Example 1.4 Weighting of Example 1.2. The entries, in Figure 1.4, are the composite scores of the table below.

Name	Errors	Critical (20)	Major (5)	Minor (1)	Composite
Paul	10	1	0	9	29
Stephen	15	1	3	11	46
Karen	11	0	2	9	19
Brian	4	2	0	2	42
Debora	17	0	1	16	21
Charlie	23	0	2	21	31
Keith	11	1	6	4	54
David	12	5	1	6	111
Joanne	10	0	5	5	30
Total	113	10	20	83	

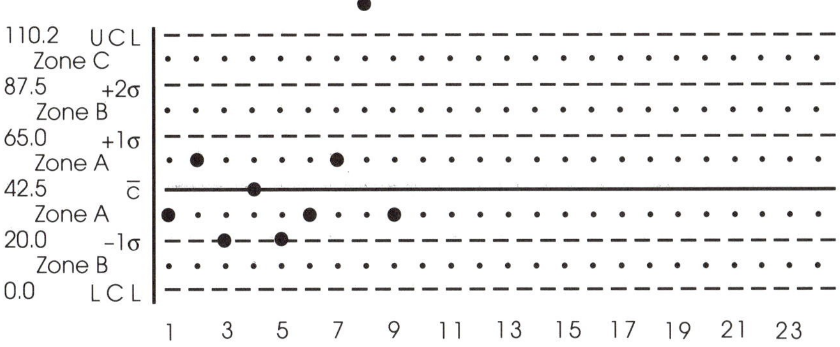

Figure 1.4. Control chart for Example 1.4.

Problem

Now whom to reward and whom to penalize?

Answer

Reward none, penalize David (or reward 8 and penalize David). Why? None below the lower limit of 0.0 and David above the upper limit of 110.2. Statistical calculations (using the c chart) are:

$$c = 20(10/9) + 5(20/9) + 1(83/9) = 42.55$$

$$\text{Control Limits} = 42.55 \pm 3\sqrt{20^2(10/9) + 5^2(20/9) + 1^2(83/9)}$$
$$= 110.2 \text{ and } 0.$$

1.9 An SPC/TQM Implementation Model

The following implementation steps are not static (that is, each always following in the same order) but are dynamic, systematic procedures that require constant attention as well as the flexibility to adapt to any and all special problems that may be found. At any one step, information found there can suggest improvements and refinements to the system so that backtracking, repeating, and/or resequencing of steps may often be commonplace.

SPC/TQM implementation procedures should be kept as simple as possible, although complex interacting process variables may sometimes require more complex implementation procedures. For example, complex mathematical models (such as control charts, DOE, or regression techniques) may be needed at any of the steps for identification and/or analysis of the important factors. The following list is a simple summary of the important quality implementation steps, and is given to present an overall picture to the quality analysts involved. Everything that will be presented in succeeding chapters in this book may apply at the appropriate steps in the list.

Remember that SPC makes no claim of miraculous cures to problems. The techniques presented in this book can only assist the only miracle available to the analyst—the human brain. The creative imagination, ingenuity, and flexibility available in any normal human mind must be applied properly to make effective quality decisions. It only follows, of course, that the proper use of this brain must be allowed; the proper system (an SPC/TQM quality management system) must be established by management.

The SPC implementation steps are as follows.

1. Develop a flowchart (Section 2.2) of each major product (a simple list of operations in the order in which they occur can often do). Make sure that all quality measurement spots are shown (see Chapter 4). Each measurement spot becomes a candidate for a control chart.
2. Identify critical operations. Ask operators, engineers, etc. Do Pareto analyses, cause and effect analyses, etc. (see Chapter 2). Analyze defect rates, costs, etc.
3. List these operations in order of criticality and by cost, defect rate, percent defective, product, operation importance, etc.
4. Install a chart at the most critical operation as a pilot project. Choose one, at first, that will be easy to improve. In this way, the rest of the firm can be shown that SPC really works; that it actually produces cost cutting procedures.
5. Collect the data and plot the charts.
6. Analyze the charts as enough data become available.
7. Correct assignable causes and make process improvements as suggested by chart data and chart interpretation.
8. After this first process has been changed, and after improvement using SPC has been proved, gradually install SPC in all other areas, following the steps listed above.
9. Finally, extend the SPC/TQM system into all areas (such as non-manufacturing, service activities, management, etc.).

Although single analysts can be used occassionally, especially at the beginning, team approach problem solving and supportive management styles are a must in the long run. Organize committees at each chart installation, make appropriate assignments, and train as needed. Include operators, workers, engineers, coordinators, supervisors, and any others deemed necessary. New teams can be formed until all employees are on teams and all processes are being controlled using SPC. Remember that team brainstorming can, and almost always should, be used at every step along the way. Also, any (and sometimes all) of the seven basic tools can be used (Chapter 2).

SPC can be installed using this book only. A total quality system (TQM), however, usually requires much more study, understanding and commitment on the part of everyone, especially management. Besides this book, read: the one now being written by the author, entitled *TQM;* Atkinson, 1990; Brassard, 1989; Covey, 1989; Deming, 1986; Ishikawa, 1990; Jones, 1990; Peters, 1997 (especially his Chapter 1); Pyzdek, 1989; Schatz, 1986; Scholtes, 1988; Scott, 1991; and *The Total Quality Management Guide* from the DoD.

It is probably best to install the SPC/TQM system by using ISO 9001 principles (the principles explained in the Baldrige award can also be quite helpful). In this regard the ISO guides from ASQC (Q90 to Q94) should also be studied, as well as Fawcett and Kanholm (see the Bibliography). If an ISO certification is pursued (as it certainly should), the SPC/TQM quality system can be included into its Section 20 (for instance, Section 20.2, 20.3, etc.). In this way, a more certain quality system continuity can be guaranteed.

It has been all too prevalent in the past, in American firms anyway, for changes in management to bring about changes in the quality system as well. (In fact, a good SPC/TQM quality system was often disbanded as a result of management changes.) But if the quality system is included in ISO, new management will have a much more difficult time changing it, as they must explain to the certifier that any change would be the same or better (certification is renewed every six months, by an outside party).

A good SPC/TQM system requires a lot of creativity and ingenuity on the part of the analyst (as well as management), a new type of management, and an entirely different culture, i.e., a quality culture (as opposed to a productivity or accounting culture, as has been all too prevalent in the past).

It must be stressed that many problems can be solved by simple observation (for example, a simple observation on how environmental aspects can impinge the process can be a powerful problem solver, especially if the analyst is resourceful and ingenious). Many other problems can be solved by a simple defect analysis (flow, Pareto, etc., see Chapter 2). This is why the "seven basic tools" in Chapter 2 are usually considered an integral part of SPC.

Another very effective tool is a simple summary listing of the defect types, along with any time, operator, process, or material effects. An examination of these defect types (starting, of course, with the one that occurs most often)—in relation to the time they occurred, the reactions and activities of the operator at that time, the actions and levels of the applicable process variables at that time, and/or the material characteristics that may affect the product in the way noted—is usually enough to isolate the causes of defects and suggest the proper cure (a good control chart system may or may not be included). If not, a more complex mathematical model (DOE, correlation analysis, etc.) is then usually indicated.

One last thing! A good SPC program, especially if it also includes TQM principles, should have a quality manual and quality procedures (the rules for the use of the quality management program). The best type of manual and procedures are those that meet ISO standards. An example ISO manual and ISO procedures will be given in the next book of this series, called *TQM* (also see Kanholm, 1993 and Fawcett, 1993).

CHAPTER 2 THE TOOLS OF QUALITY

SPC is about quality. Therefore, many of the following "quality tools," especially those of a statistical nature, can also be considered SPC "tools." All of them are also TQM tools since TQM is the complete system of which SPC is only a part. Actually, TQM is only a term applied to SPC when it began to be applied to all aspects of the firm. All of them, however, must be adapted to the particular environment in which they are used. This requires a complete knowledge of the underlying theory, as well as their practical application, in order to make the adaptation effective.

These tools can be used at any point in the SPC system, at any one of the steps. However, they are probably even more useful when used prior to control charts. Control charts can be complex, and can take some time to implement, in order to find the problem solution. A thorough knowledge of these tools can be extremely helpful in finding quick solutions to problems. Most of these tools can be used almost instantly, at one time or the other, to find solutions to quality problems. In fact, quality problem solutions can often be found just by observation, if the analyst is reasonably alert and intelligent.

This chapter will start with a simple listing of the many "tools," and then continue with explanations and examples of the seven basic tools (except for control charts, which are so extensive that they are explained separately in Chapters 4 and 5). For the most part, only the essential, or basic, tools will be detailed here. The others will be defined briefly, and references will be supplied (for the reader's own research). Some of the tools covered in this book are not strictly statistical but are nevertheless included here because of their usefulness to the SPC system.

However, SPC tools are not SPC! In essence, SPC is a philosophy that embodies total knowledge and total control of the process. These tools are simply the best means found so far to accomplish that purpose. This knowledge answers the questions: What? Who? Why? Where? When? and How? It includes information (where appropriate) about the firm, other processes, internal and external customers, the environment, etc. Motivational theory has shown that when people are supplied with this information, they feel more relaxed and comfortable with the process and tend to do better work with less errors (a good summary of motivational theory can be found in Doty, *Work Methods and Measurement for Management,* Delmar Press, 1989, Chapter 8).

One last note. The mere existence of these tools is not enough—people must be trained and then empowered (given the authority) to use them. This takes commitment and action by top management.

Objectives

1. List and briefly describe the various tools of quality.
2. Describe flowcharts and explain how they are used for improving quality.
3. Describe how checksheets are used in the quality system. Also describe the use and function of the location (measles) chart.
4. Explain the function and use of histograms and bar charts.
5. Define Pareto analysis and explain how it can be used in the quality improvement process.
6. Explain the cause and effect diagram and how it is used in the quality system.
7. Define scatter diagrams and explain how they are used.

2.1 The Quality "Tools" List

Every attempt has been made to make this list exhaustive, but this is, of course, impossible. New tools are constantly being added and the old ones are constantly being changed (improved). This is why the analyst (everyone, actually) must keep current with any new development; and this is why the SPC/TQM quality management system emphasizes the concept of lifelong education.

All of these tools are humanistic in nature, or a mixture of humanistic and technical. The seven basic tools, explained in this chapter, are actually tools of quality (tools of the SPC/TQM quality management system). However, they are often called "tools of SPC," and sometimes "tools of TQM." In fact, all of these "tools" are called many things: tools of quality, tools of SPC, tools of TQM, and tools of anything else the firm may be calling the management system at that time. However, they are actually "tools of quality," i.e., tools of the quality management system called SPC, TQM, etc. In this book, the system will be called the "SPC/TQM quality management system," or just the SPC system.

The use of any one (or more) of these "tools" can often lead to solutions without using a full-fledged SPC system (one of the reasons they are given such prominence). Also, any one (or more) of these tools can be used to supply and/or analyze information at any of the SPC steps. In fact, a simple observation (creative observation) can often show solutions without even using any of these "tools" (another reason that the concept of "creative imagination" is stressed).

The Seven Basic Tools of Quality

These are on the "must" list for all SPC programs (also for all TQM systems). Anyone installing and using an SPC program will use most (probably all) of these seven tools. Some of the most excellent books on these and other quality tools is Brassard, 1989 and Ishikawa, 1990.

1. **Flowcharts** (see Section 2.2 of this chapter). A pictorial (graphical) representation of the process flow—showing the process inputs, activities, and outputs in the order in which they occur.
2. **Checksheets** (see Section 2.3 of this chapter). A list of items inspected (checked). The list is usually organized in a standardized format designed to facilitate information gathering and, later, quantitative analysis. It also assures that different people will collect required information in the same way.
3. **Histograms** (see Section 2.4 of this chapter). A graphical summary of variation in a set of data. A pictorial means of organizing, summarizing, analyzing, and displaying data.
4. **Pareto analysis** (see Section 2.5 of this chapter). Uses a specially organized histogram (the Pareto chart) to provide a picture that instantly identifies those problems of the greatest concern—those problems that should be addressed first.
5. **Cause and effect diagram** (see Section 2.6 of this chapter). As the name implies, this tool is just a group of causes and effects diagrammed to show the interrelationships. The diagram is a form of tree diagram on its side so that it looks like a fishbone (which is why it is also called the fishbone diagram). It is also called the Ishikawa diagram, after the man who invented it.
6. **Scatter diagram** (see Section 2.7 of this chapter). Cartesian coordinate-type graphs (X,Y graphs) that illustrate cause and effect relationships between two types of data.
7. **Control charts** (see Chapters 4 and 5). Graphs of one or more important characteristics of a product. They use statistical techniques to analyze the process, and to provide information for correction and improvement of the process, and thus the products produced on that process.

The Seven Basic Organizational Tools

These analysis and management tools are called the "new seven" quality tools in Japan. All of these use a form of matrix and/or tree diagram to reach their goals (see Brassard, 1989).

1. **Relations diagram** (also called the interrelationship diagraph). Analyzes the interrelationships of complex systems, i.e., which portions of the system relate to which other portions, and how and to what extent.
2. **Affinity diagram.** A brainstorming technique whereby ideas are grouped and arranged by subject. Interrelationships can also be diagnosed (see Brassard, 1989).
3. **Tree diagram.** Analyzes the interrelationships among goals and measurements. Can also organize plans and contingencies.
4. **Matrix diagram.** Analyzes relations between two different factors. Also used in deploying customer requirements into design requirements, then into vendor or purchasing requirements, and then into production requirements (in this form, it is known as the Quality Function Deployment—QFD—Diagram).
5. **Matrix data-analysis diagram.** Applies quantitative analysis to the matrix diagram.
6. **PDPC (Process Decision Program Chart).** Used to guide the implementation process. It organizes each possible chain of events in a complex plan so that all possible events are identified and planned. For instance, anything that can possibly go wrong will be identified, and a plan, and resources, already formulated in case any of these problems occur.
7. **PERT/CPM** (also see Doty, 1989, Chapter 5). An arrow method of quantitatively analyzing complex relationships among work tasks in a complex job, with the purpose of organizing efficient work schedules, determining the critical task sequence (called the "critical path") within the arrow diagram upon which the schedule depends, reducing overall schedule time, and determining the most efficient allocation of critical resources among the many interrelating tasks.

Other Quality Tools and Analysis Techniques

Please note that there are many more managerial and engineering techniques than the ones presented here. These are just the more important ones for quality control.

1. **Process capability and C_{pk} analysis** (see Chapter 6). A technique for analyzing and improving processes.
2. **The normal curve** (see Chapter 3). One of the most fundamental, and most used, statistical analysis techniques.
3. **Normal curve economic analysis** (see Chapters 3 and 6). A means of using the normal curve to determine the most cost effective process settings.
4. **Location (measles) chart** (explained in Section 2.3 of this chapter). A method of determining nonconformance causes by locating them on a picture of the part.
5. **Quality cost analyses** (see Chapter 1). Provides information to management for the control of quality costs.
6. **Gantt charts.** A scheduling technique. (See Doty, 1989, Chapter 5.)
7. **FMECA (Failure Modes, Effects, and Criticality Analysis).** A means of

determining which problems are the most critical, i.e., which should be worked on first). (See Doty, 1989, Chapter 10.)

8. **Fault tree analysis.** Determines the probability of an event, or series of events, occurring. (See Doty, 1989, Chapter 10.)
9. **Procedures analysis.** Uses FMECA techniques to analyze the effects of human errors. (See Doty, 1989, Chapter 10.)
10. **Methods analyses/work analyses.** These are procedures that are used to assist in the design of efficient motion patterns. (See Doty, 1989, Chapter 2.)
11. **Work sampling.** The use of statistical sampling techniques to get information about the job in order to determine the most efficient job design. See Doty, 1989, Chapter 4.
12. **DOE (Design Of Experiments).** Uses experiments in which test runs have been deliberately designed to vary critical characteristics to see what occurs. The results of these experiments are then used to determine the process's ability to make the product according to the specifications, and to assist Design in determining process and product parameters. DOE includes the various factorial-type experiments, ANOVA (ANalysis Of VAriance), the Taguchi methods, and hypothesis testing. (See Barker, 1985; Montgomery, 1991; and Chapter 10 of this book.)
13. **Motivational theories-principles-procedures.** These are models of the interaction between humans and their work (what some analysts have called the innate human drive for production), which attempt to explain the past long-term trend toward worker dissatisfaction. Understanding these things can assist (hopefully) in designing work systems that lead to worker satisfaction (and thus to increased quality and productivity). (See Chapter 1, this book; Doty, 1989, Chapter 8; Fein, 1971; and Deming, 1982 and 1986.)
14. **QFD (Quality Function Deployment).** Used in deploying customer requirements into design requirements, then into vendor or purchasing requirements, and then into production requirements. (See ReVelle, 1989.)
15. **Benchmarking.** A method of comparison to other firms in the same business, for the purpose of setting realistic competitive goals and objectives. (See Watson, 1994.)
16. **A team approach to problem solving.** Teams are groups of individuals who work together for the common good. This is an important concept (a central value, actually) for the SPC/TQM quality management system. (See the new book now being written by the author, called *TQM;* Scholtes, 1988; Schatz and Schatz, 1986; Scott and Jaffe, 1981; and Deming, 1986.)
17. **Prioritization matrix.** Prioritizes all known tasks and issues. In general, the options are narrowed until only those that are most desirable or effective are left. (See Brassard, 1989.)
18. **Value engineering (value analysis).** Used to define production plans and materials, and engineering procedures, in order to find lower cost alternatives. (See Doty, 1989, p. 69.)

19. **The hypergeometric, the binomial, the Poisson, and the *t* distributions** (see Chapter 7 of this text). Other statistical distributions that are fairly important in SPC, especially in the use of sampling techniques. Any statistical tool, technique, procedure, or distribution is (or will probably soon become) of use to SPC (and to TQM, of course).
20. **Control chart analysis** (see Chapter 6 of this text). Analyzes control charts for corrections (correct problems that show up on the process) and for changes (change the process after it is corrected—in order to provide for even better products and services).
21. **TQM (total quality management).** An umbrella system for all other quality programs (all quality programs become a part of TQM). Thus, SPC becomes the statistical or technical arm of TQM (teams, managerial procedures, environmental attitudes, and customer attitudes are some of the more important others). TQM is ". . . a management philosophy that creates an environment of participation, empowerment, accomplishment, and a sense of self-esteem by using a totally integrated effort towards improving quality in products, services and work life" (Stanley Pessok, *ASQC Quality Newsletter,* Tucson, AZ, April 1992). Some (including this author) contend that this also implies the general improvement of the "quality of life" for everyone and in every facet of society. (See the new book, now being written by this author, called *TQM;* Covey, 1989; Senge, 1990; Deming, 1986; Johnson, 1989; Peters, 1982; Schatz, 1986; Scholtes, 1988; and Scott, 1991.)
22. **SPC (statistical process control).** SPC is the statistical, or technical, arm of TQM. It is essentially a means of controlling the processes through statistics. It is assumed that the products of the controlled processes will be in control if the processes are in control. This book discusses SPC procedures.
23. **ISO 9000.** A European Economic Market quality certification plan which most nations of the world have embraced (ISO refers to a French phrase which translates approximately to International Organization for Quality). The 20 sections (for ISO 9001, at least) of the plan are of special interest to those attempting to install or improve a quality plan. (See Section 1.6.)
24. **EVOP (EVolutionary OPeration).** In EVOP, a series of individual experiments are run in such a way that the result of each experiment suggests the variable level for the next trial. The number of variables involved is usually no more than two, and never more than three. (See Section 10.6.)
25. **Regression/correllation.** Mathematical relationships (usually cause and effect) between two or more variables are determined. The logical successor to scatter diagrams (see Section 2.7). When only two variables are compared, Cartesian coordinate-type graphs (X,Y graphs) are often used to illustrate the relationships.
26. **The Malcolm Baldrige award.** An award given to American firms, by the American government, for excellence in quality management. Although the award is quite difficult to achieve, the various standards

within the award are of special interest to those attempting to install or improve a quality plan. (See Section 1.6.)

27. **Multivari charts, components search, paired comparisons, variables search, *B* versus *C* analysis (Bhote's own terminology), and scatter diagrams.** All are methods of limiting the variables to a major, or several interacting, causes (as well as the interactions). They can be used before, with, or after a DOE experiment. Quite often, one or more can be used to pinpoint the major cause without the full expense of a complete factorial experiment. (See Bhote, 1988.)

2.2 Flowcharts

A flowchart is a pictorial (graphical) representation of the process flow showing the process inputs, activities, and outputs in the order in which they occur. As such, it assists in the collection and organization of knowledge of the process. (To some extent, all of the tools listed here do this; however, flowcharts are specifically designed for this purpose.)

The chart is constructed as follows.

1. Identify a flow for study—preferably one that has a lot of problems to solve. This can be a materials flow, a paperwork flow, an information flow, a people flow, a decision procedure flow, etc. The best way to do this is to use a team and to brainstorm, unless such a flow is already obvious.
2. Identify necessary information. This includes information about inputs into the flow, outputs from the flow, activities and processes within the flow, measurements, people, dates, frequencies, operation times, documents, location, and equipment used. Use a team, and brainstorm.
3. Identify and list the sequence of operations in the flow. Study the process, ask questions of everyone, use a team, and brainstorm.
4. Identify the decision points in the flow. When charted, these decision points will appear as yes or no questions only. Sometimes a decision point is charted as a diamond, but in this book only a box will be used to keep it simple. If the main question to be answered cannot be a simple yes or no question (such as "What color is it?"), ask a series of yes or no questions (as shown below).

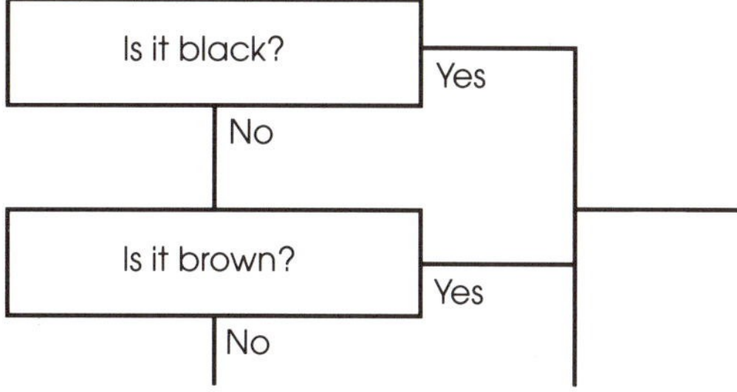

Continue until all possible colors have been covered.

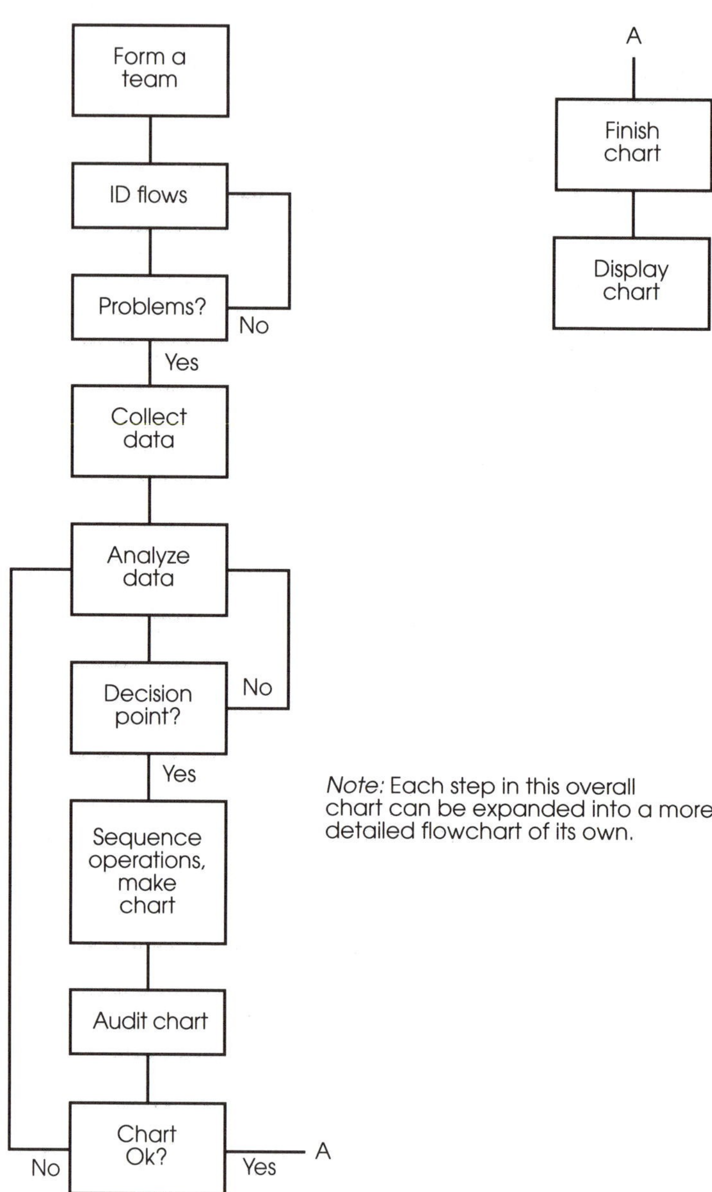

Figure 2.1. Flowchart of a typical flowchart project.

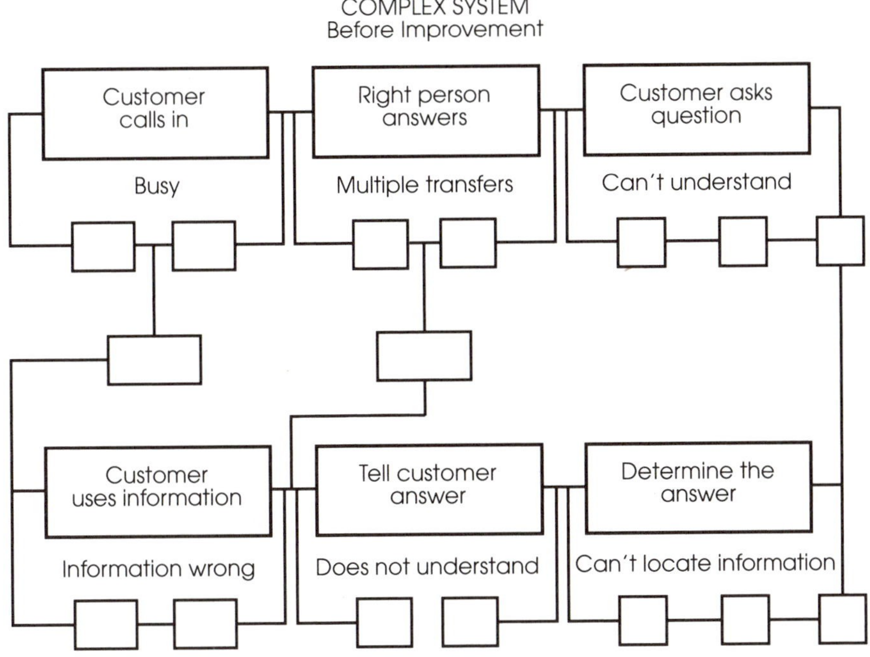

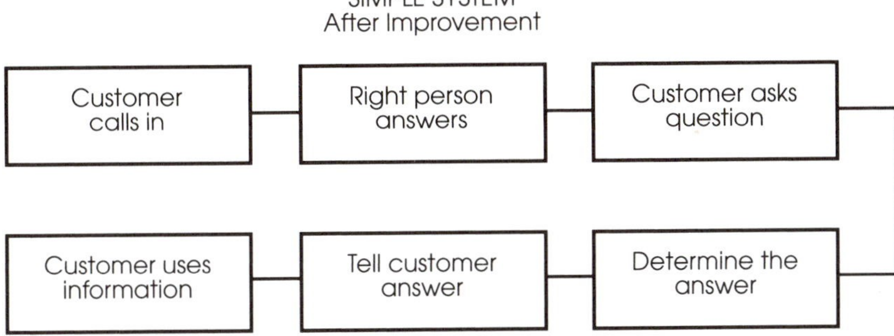

Figure 2.2. Reduction of organizational complexity.

5. Make the chart (see Figures 2.1 and 2.2; also note Pyzdek, 1986 & 1989). Keep it simple! Use a box for all activities, even for decision points. The more formal charts use a diamond shape for decision points, as well as other types of figures for different types of activities. The multiple lines (arrows) extending from the decision box will instantly and clearly identify it as a decision point. Use a capital letter as a connector (for example, A) to other parts of the chart on the same page, where a

line or arrow cannot be used (use a different letter for each connector). Use a page number (for example, p. 2) as a connector to another page.

6. After completion, make an audit of the flowchart. Check the inputs, outputs, activities, sequencing, etc., to see that nothing has been forgotten, and that the chart actually depicts what is being done at all times, with all people and at all places where the flow is being used.
7. Creativity and intelligence are needed, by everyone, at all of these steps. The best way is to form a team of those concerned with the area or process under study. Of course, an individual can do this, but a team is better.

Some Notes and Comments

1. Start the first analysis, and controls, early in the process. The earlier the operation, the greater the possibility of greater savings.
2. Flowcharts assist in identifying critical activities in the flow; those that are high cost, contribute many errors, form a bottleneck to the process, and/or affect customer needs the most.
3. Look for operations to improve that are operator controllable, measurable, and integral to the process, and where there is a high expectation of results (especially at the start so that a history of success can be established early in the improvement process).
4. Flowcharts collect and organize everyone's knowledge so that the entire group has the same level of understanding about the process. Therefore, keep the chart in a central, accessible, and visible location so that it can be used by everyone as needed.
5. Make sure the right people are involved in making the analysis and the chart. These should include: area workers and supervisors, suppliers and customers of the process (if possible), and an independent facilitator (if available).
6. Make sure that enough time is allotted. More than one session may be, and usually is, necessary.
7. Consider using an independent and trained facilitator to direct the team's efforts.
8. Make sure the flowchart looks good and is easy to read. Keep it simple, at least to start (for instance, a completely formal flowchart can contain more than a dozen different symbols, whereas a very simple chart will have but one—a box). If a flowchart is attractive, simple, and clear, it will be much more likely to be used; if unattractive, complex, and confusing, it will not. Line up arrows, use off-page and on-page connectors properly, and make it neat, orderly, and professional looking. "Professional" does *not* mean complex—as one famous scientist once said, "the true test of genius is simplicity."
9. Make sure that all members of the group participate. An independent facilitator can be invaluable here.
10. Questions are the key. Remember the five W's and an H—What, Where, When, Who, Why, and How (see Section 2.3). But be careful of the Why; some members of the group may get too defensive at too many Why's.

Advantages of a Good Flowchart Analysis

Most of these advantages also apply to most of the other quality tools.

1. The people involved begin to better understand the process in the same terms.
2. Helps to control the process, rather than the process controlling the people.
3. Improves communications. People can now visualize their suppliers and customers as a part of the overall process, of which they also are a part.
4. Better support of the entire quality effort, especially from those directly involved in the flowcharting activity.
5. Better training of new employees. The flowchart is an excellent training tool.
6. Happier employees. They now feel in better control of their own destinies; they feel more like an integral and important part of the team and not just a cog in the machinery; and they get a better feeling of approval for their efforts (their ideas count, and are accepted as worthy).
7. More economical processes.
8. Less waste in administrative functions (flowcharting is probably even more effective in analyzing and improving administrative processes).
9. Reduces confusion. The goal is to get workers so well versed in what is expected of them that the thought of deviating just doesn't occur.
10. Assists in reducing organizational slack (idle and waiting time).
11. Assists in reducing the chance for errors (by reducing the number of process steps).
12. Assists in reducing throughput time.

2.3 Checksheets

Checksheets are basically a list of items inspected (checked). The list is usually organized in a standardized format designed to facilitate information gathering and, later, quantitative analysis. It also assures that different people will collect required information in the same way. Figure 2.3 shows a simple tally sheet of errors, which is the simplest of all checksheets. Figures 2.4 and 2.5 show two other types of checksheets, where the errors (or defectives) are categorized as they are observed.

The data-gathering procedure is extremely simple. It is only necessary to note (observe) what is occurring, categorize it into one of the categories on the checksheet, and mark a tally in the proper column. The only really difficult part is knowing which categories to use on the checksheet. That comes with knowledge of the process, and some pre-

OPERATOR	MON	TUE	WED	THURS	FRI
1. Paul	11	1	1111	1	11
2. Stephen	1111	1	11	111111	111
3. Karen	1		111	1	1
4. Brian	1	1	11111	111111	1111111
5. Debora	1	1	11	1	11
6. Keith	11	11111	111	1	1
7. David	1	11	111	11	1

Figure 2.3. A rejects checksheet for a data entry file.

CHECKSHEET

Product: ______________________ Date: __/__/______

Name: ______________________

Total Examined: ______________

DEFECT TYPE	DEFECT COUNT	TOTAL
1. Bent	++++ ++++ ++++ ||	17
2. Chipped	++++ ++++ ++++ ++++ ||||	24
3. Burnt	++++ |	6
	Grand Total	37

Figure 2.4. A checksheet for counting rejects.

EQUIPMENT	WORKER	MONDAY AM	MONDAY PM	TUESDAY AM	TUESDAY PM	WEDNESDAY AM	WEDNESDAY PM
MACH 1	A	0x1x0	2	x0	00	000	xx10
	B						
MACH 2	C						

Data are coded (0, 1, x, etc.) to indicate type of defect.

Figure 2.5. A defective cause checksheet.

analysis (observing which categories occur through at least one complete operational cycle).

In the early stages of problem solving, we frequently don't know which data will end up being useful. Therefore, it is best to be as thorough as possible in the collection process, i.e., use as many categories as is reasonably possible. Also, the sources and times of the data should always be referenced, as this frequently gives valuable information for subsequent improvements.

Defect Location Checksheet (Measles Chart)

This type of chart shows the location of defects on a graphic representation (a sketch or drawing) of the object. The position on the object can provide clues as to the cause(s). Figure 2.6 shows the two ways this tool can be used: a simple tally of defects (chart A) and a categorization procedure (chart B).

This chart can also be combined with a Pareto and/or Cause and Effect Analysis to determine degree of urgency (Pareto) and cause(s) of defects (Cause and Effect).

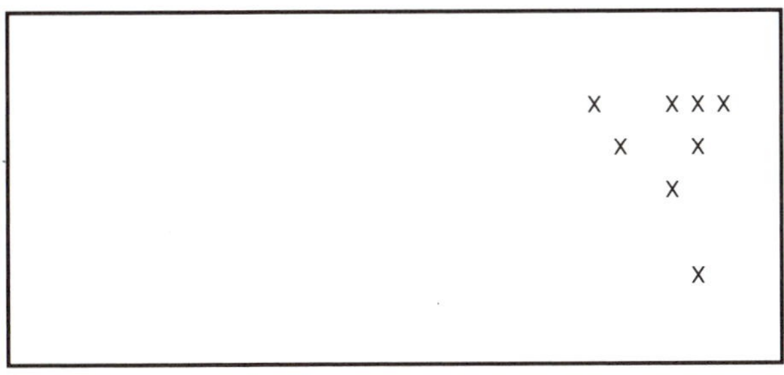

Chart A

1 1 1 1
2 2 2
1 1 2 2
1 3 1
3 3
1 1 1 1
1

Chart B

Figure 2.6. Examples of a measles chart—the chart should show, or be, the outline of the part.

Check-up/Confirmation Checksheet

This type of chart is comprised of a list of items to check for possible problems, and for information (data). Examples are a check-off list for aircraft start-up, or the two examples shown below—the 5-M checklist and the 5 W's and an H checklist. The 5-M checklist can be extended into a checklist for many things (for instance, see the list for variation in Section 1.4).

The 5-M Checklist (5 Manufacturing Factors)

1. Man (worker, operator).
   - Follow standards?
   - Efficiency?
   - Problem conscious?
   - Responsible (accountable)?
   - Qualified?
   - Experienced?
   - Assigned to the right job?
   - Willing to improve?
   - Maintain good human relations?
   - Healthy?
2. Machine (processes, tools).
   - Capability?
   - PM (Preventive Maintenance) adequate?
   - Good wording order?
   - Mechanical trouble?
   - Operation stopped often?
   - Any unusual noises?
   - Is the layout adequate?
   - Capacity?
3. Material.
   - Enough material?
   - Proper grade? Brand?
   - Impurities? Hard spots, soft spots?
   - Waste?
   - Handling?
   - Quality standards adequate?
4. Method (operation).
   - Work standards?
   - Safety?
   - Does the method ensure good product?
   - Efficient?
   - Resequence?
   - Simplify?
   - Combine steps?
   - Eliminate steps?
   - Layout?
   - Setup?

- Temperature and humidity?
- Lighting and ventilation?

5. Measurement.
   - Are measuring instruments adequate?
   - Calibration?
   - Are instruments used properly?
   - Dirt, grease, vibration, etc.?

The Five W's and an H Checklist

1. Who?
   - Who is doing it?
   - Who is supposed to be doing it?
   - Who else could do it?
   - Who else should do it?
2. What?
   - What is being done?
   - What should be done?
   - What else can be done?
   - What else should be done?
3. When?
   - When is it done?
   - When should it be done?
4. Where?
   - Where is it done?
   - Where else can it be done?
   - Where should it be done?
5. Why?
   - Why do it?
   - Why do it this way?
   - Why do it there?
6. How?
   - How is it done?
   - How can it be done?
   - How should it be done?

2.4 Histograms

A histogram is a graphical summary of variation in a set of data—a pictorial means of organizing, summarizing, analyzing, and displaying data. It contains the same information as the tally sheet, but in a picture form, i.e., a picture of the tally sheet. The pictorial nature of the graph displays patterns that are difficult (usually impossible) to see in a simple table of numbers, where anything of value is usually hidden in a morass of numbers. Even small amounts of raw data (data that have not yet been organized) can seem overwhelming, confusing, and/or intimidating unless organized in some way (see Chapter 3). The histogram is an excellent means of organizing large amounts of data so that important information becomes apparent (usually readily apparent).

A histogram is a bar chart, and the two terms are often used interchangeably. However, statisticians like to refer to bar charts of simple tallies as bar charts, while reserving the term histogram for a bar chart of data evenly divided into equal cells. Figure 2.7 is an example of the simple tally bar chart, while Table 3.2 (of Chapter 3) shows the more sophisticated histogram. Table 3.2 also illustrates a frequency distribution—the tallies from Table 3.1 are evenly spaced and boxed by a computer so as to form the distribution. Note how Table 3.2 provides almost instant information about the data (approximately where the central value is, how the data are distributed from the central value, etc.) that is completely unavailable from tables of measurements only (without extensive analysis, that is).

Using Histograms

The main purpose of histograms is to provide clues and information for the reduction of variation. This comes mainly from identification and interpretation of patterns of variation. There are two types of variation patterns: random (from chance or common causes) and nonrandom (from assignable or special causes).

Some of the random variation patterns, because they are repeated frequently in real life, have been found to be quite useful and have, therefore, been documented and quantified. They are called frequency, or probability, distributions in statistics and have been given special names (such as binomial, Poisson, etc.). Nonrandom patterns are patterns of error and are used in SPC, especially control charting, to assist in the reduction of variation (see Chapter 6).

Besides the patterns of variation, there are three important characteristics of histograms that also provide information about the nature of the variation. These are: the center (where on the number line), the width (how far it extends on both sides of the center), and the shape (peaked, flat, number of peaks, skewedness, etc.).

Some of the more important histogram patterns are provided in the following list. Note how the shape can provide clues to the cause(s) of variation.

1. **Bell-shaped** (normal, Gaussian). Figure 3.6 gives an example of this pattern. This is the normal, natural, pattern of data from most processes. Any deviation from this pattern is usually abnormal in some way (assignable or special causes) and can usually, therefore, provide clues about the variation. Even if the pattern is normal, however, the variation may still be able to be reduced by decreasing the width of the distribution, by decreasing the standard deviation (see Chapters 3 and 6).
2. **Bi-modal** (two peaks). Figure 3.3 gives an example of this pattern. This

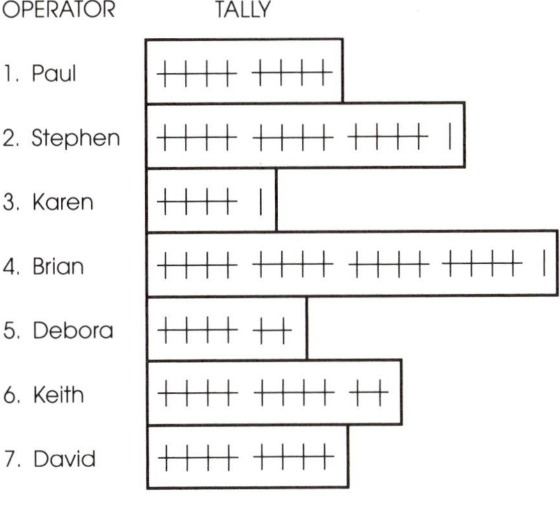

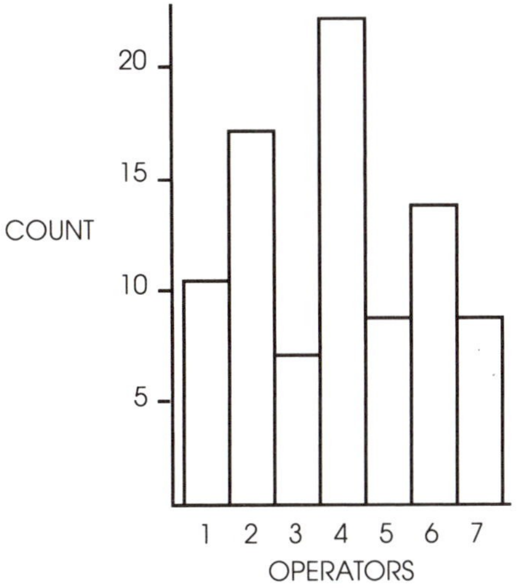

Figure 2.7. Tally and histogram of operator errors.

distribution is usually a mixture of two processes (a combination of two distributions) such as identical parts from two different machines.

3. **The plateau distribution** (flat on top, slight tails). This usually results from a mixture of many different processes, and can be analyzed by diagramming the flow and observing the processes.
4. **The comb distribution** (alternating high and low values). This usually indicates errors in measurement, errors in the organization of the data, and/or rounding errors.

5. **The skewed distribution** (a long tail on one side). Figure 3.3 gives an example of this pattern (as does Table 3.2, which is positively skewed). If the long tail is to the left, the distribution is negatively skewed; if it is to the right, it is positively skewed. This is not necessarily bad. Many skewed distributions occur naturally with certain types of data, and have been regularized with their own formulas (Poisson, log-normal, exponential, etc.). However, if the long tail can have a negative impact on quality, the process should be investigated and the cause determined and eliminated. Causes of skewed distributions include: short cycle tasks, one-sided specification limits, and practical limits on one side only.
6. **The truncated distribution** (a smooth curve with an abrupt ending on one side). This is often caused by external forces to the process, such as screening, 100% inspection, or a review process. Since truncating usually indicates added costs, it is a good candidate for improvement.
7. **The isolated peak distribution** (a small, separate, group of data to one side of the parent group). Look for poor inspection, measurement errors, or data entry errors.
8. **Edge-peaked distribution** (a peak right at the edge). This usually means that data from an otherwise long tail have been lumped together at one point (data from outside the limit have been recorded as being inside the limit).

Comments and Suggestions

1. Make sure the data are complete, unbiased, current, and typical of the process.
2. Make sure the sample is large enough. Statisticians usually consider that 30 or more measurements are needed to be statistically significant (100 or more is much better). If the data are being stratified, then each stratum needs a sample of 30 or more.
3. Try stratifying the data wherever possible (divide into separate groups and compare: compare operators, machines, material types, defect type, etc.).
4. Check all possible alternative conclusions before making a decision.
5. Confirm all theories before making changes.
6. Clarify and agree to what has been learned.
7. Make direct observations of the process.
8. Continue to collect data, analyze, diagnose, and improve.
9. Use a team, and brainstorm.
10. Consider using an independent and trained facilitator to direct the team's efforts.

2.5 Pareto Analysis

The Pareto law is named after an Italian economist who observed that about 20% of the people had about 80% of the money. Because of this, it is sometimes called the 80/20 rule. It illustrates the concept of the "vital few and the trivial many." The "vital few" refers to those things that affect us the most, those that have the greatest chance of the greatest return for our efforts, those that are larger in amount than the others (it is easier to reduce a larger amount or to reduce it by a larger reduction), etc. This rule, and its accompanying analysis, has an enormous number of applications in almost all facets of life and work. For instance, in work situations, it is usually true that about 20% of the products cause about 80% of the problems.

The Pareto chart gives us an instantaneous picture of these relationships—a picture that instantly identifies those problems we should address first (one look tells everyone what the major problem is). Since the objective of Pareto charts is improvement of the process, many Pareto analyses will use two charts showing the before and after conditions, before and after improvement (see Figure 2.9). As with almost all qual-

OPERATOR	TALLY	COUNT	RANK
1. Paul	1111111111	10	4
2. Stephen	1111111111111111	16	2
3. Karen	111111	6	7
4. Brian	111111111111111111111	21	1
5. Debora	1111111	7	6
6. Keith	111111111111	12	3
7. David	1111111111	10	5

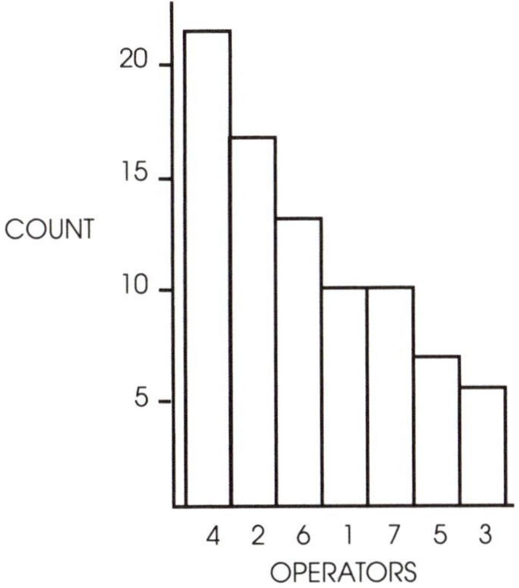

Figure 2.8. Basic Pareto chart—using counts only.

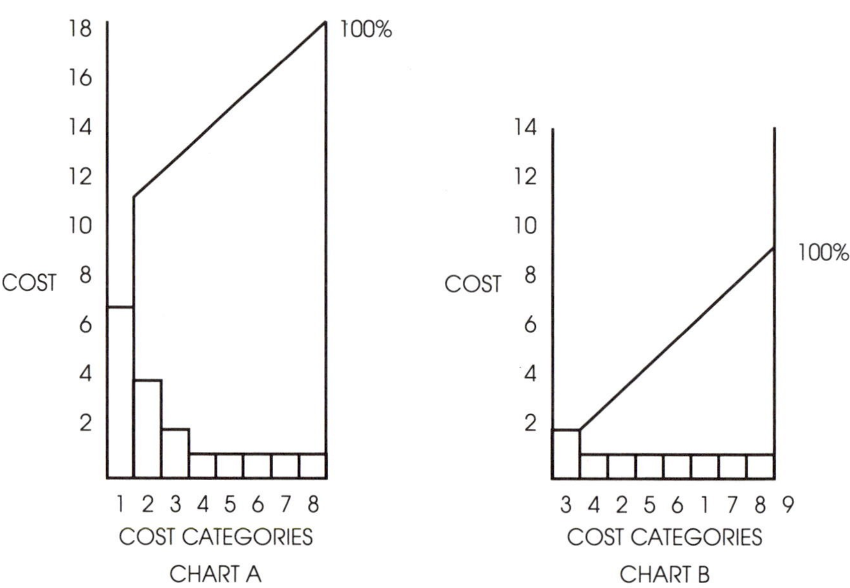

Figure 2.9. Pareto showing improvement from Chart A to Chart B.

ity tools, the construction and use of Pareto charts can be greatly enhanced by the use of teams and an independent facilitator.

A Pareto analysis can be illustrated in three ways: with a line chart showing the cumulative percent, with a bar chart arranged from high to low (a special kind of histogram, Fig. 2.8), and with a combination of these two (showing both the bars and the line on the same chart). The combination chart is the one most used (see Figure 2.10). Most Pareto charts also use two scales: one on one side for percent of total, and one on the other side for actual amount (see Figure 2.10).

Constructing the Pareto Chart

The vertical axis of the chart is used for the actual count, or measurement, and/or the percent of total count or measurement. The categories being counted or measured are then placed on the horizontal axis. Quality Pareto categories include operators, work groups, type of products, sizes, type of damage, type of defect or defective, type of injuries, cost, contribution to profit, etc. The count or measurement of the category can also be coded for severity, as follows.

1. Cost (multiply the cost by the ratio of total count).
2. Importance to customer (estimate on a scale of 1 to 10, 1 to 100, etc.).

OPERATOR	TALLY	COUNT	%	CUM %
4. Brian	111111111111111111111	21	26	26
2. Stephen	1111111111111111	16	20	46
6. Keith	111111111111	12	15	61
1. Paul	1111111111	10	12	73
7. David	1111111111	10	12	85
5. Debora	1111111	7	8	93
3. Karen	111111	6	7	100
		82	100	

Figure 2.8 table arranged from high to low, with percentages (%) and cumulatives (CUM) added. 21/82 = 26%, 16/82 + 20%, etc.; and 0 + 26 = 26, 26 + 20 = 46, etc.

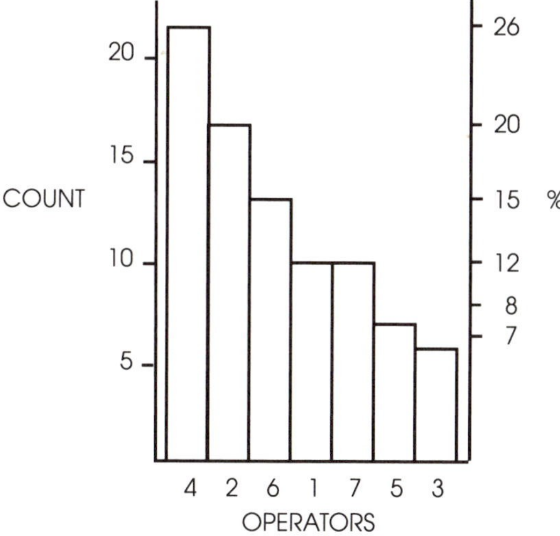

Figure 2.10. Basic Pareto chart—using counts and cumulative percent.

3. Importance to production (estimate on a scale of 1 to 10, 1 to 100, etc.).
4. Importance to safety (estimate on a scale of 1 to 10, 1 to 100, etc.).
5. Efficiency (multiply by the ratio of total count).
6. Conservation of materials (estimate on a scale of 1 to 10, 1 to 100, etc.).
7. Energy savings (multiply by ratio of total count).
8. Combinations of above, and others.

Example 2.1 Coded Pareto Using Incremental Costs. (See Figure 2.10.)

Defect Type	% Defects (1)	Cost/ Defect (2)	Incremental (1×2) (3)	% Incremental (4)
1	14	$ 4.00	$0.56	8
2	22	0.50	0.11	2
3	8	40.00	3.20	47
4	29	1.00	0.29	4
5	10	10.00	1.00	14
6	17	10.00	1.70	25
Totals	100		$6.86	100

Note: In % incremental column, 8 = 0.56/6.86 = 0.08 or 8%, etc.

Arrange from High to Low.

Defect Type	Incremental Cost	% Cost	% Defects	Cumulative % Costs	Cumulative % Defects
3	$3.20	47	8	47	8
6	1.70	25	17	72	25
5	1.00	14	10	86	35
1	0.56	8	17	94	52
4	0.29	4	29	98	81
2	0.50	2	22	100	100
Totals	$6.86	100	100		

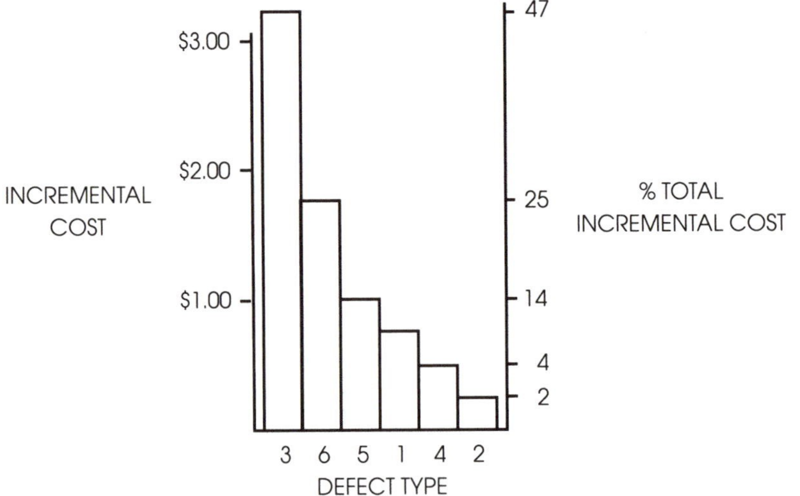

Figure 2.11. Pareto for Example 2.1.

Note that only 25% of the defects account for 72% of the costs. However, what about customer dissatisfaction on the remaining defects (assuming we start on the high-cost defects first)? Which items cause the most customer annoyance? What about safety, environment, etc.? Shouldn't these also be factored in for better decision rules? Obviously, the decisions are not simple, and require a great deal of knowledge and understanding, as well as creativity, ingenuity, and intelligence.

Example 2.2 Pareto Coded for Both. (See Figure 2.11.)

a. Importance to customer, rated on a scale of 1 to 1000.
b. Environment, rated on a scale of 1 to 10.

Defect Type	Importance to Customer (1)	Environment (2)	Composite (1 × 2) (3)	% Defect (5)	Rate (3 × 5) (6)
1	1000	2	2000	14	280
2	10	10	100	22	22
3	40	8	320	8	26
4	100	5	500	29	145
5	10	2	20	10	2
6	200	1	200	17	34
Totals				100	509

Arrange from High to Low.

Defect Type	Rate	% Rate	Cumulative % Rate
1	280	55	55
4	145	28	83
6	34	7	90
3	26	5	95
2	22	4	99
5	2	1	100
Totals	509	100	

Before the Pareto analysis of Figure 2.13, everyone just "knew" that the problem was the connectors (conn), and probably the dimensions (dim) as well, due to the type of information and the way it was being received. The Pareto analysis showed that the real problem was seals and boots. Problems in seals and boots are highly interrelated, and solving one tends to solve the other. Also, solutions to the boots and seals problems tend to solve dimension and connector problems as well. However, the opposite is not true; apparent solutions to connectors and dimension problems seldom help in solving boot and/or seal problems.

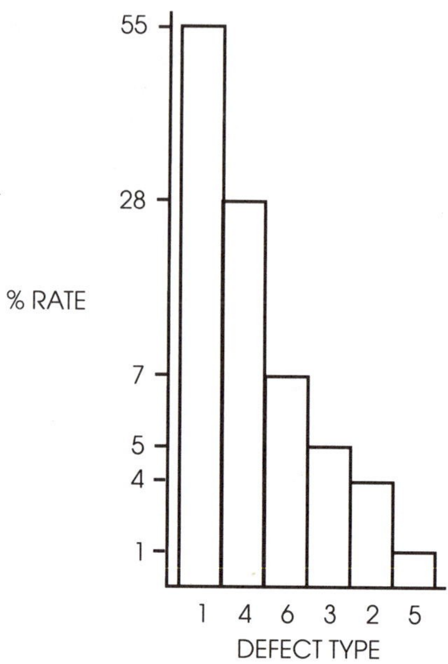

Figure 2.12. Pareto for Example 2.2.

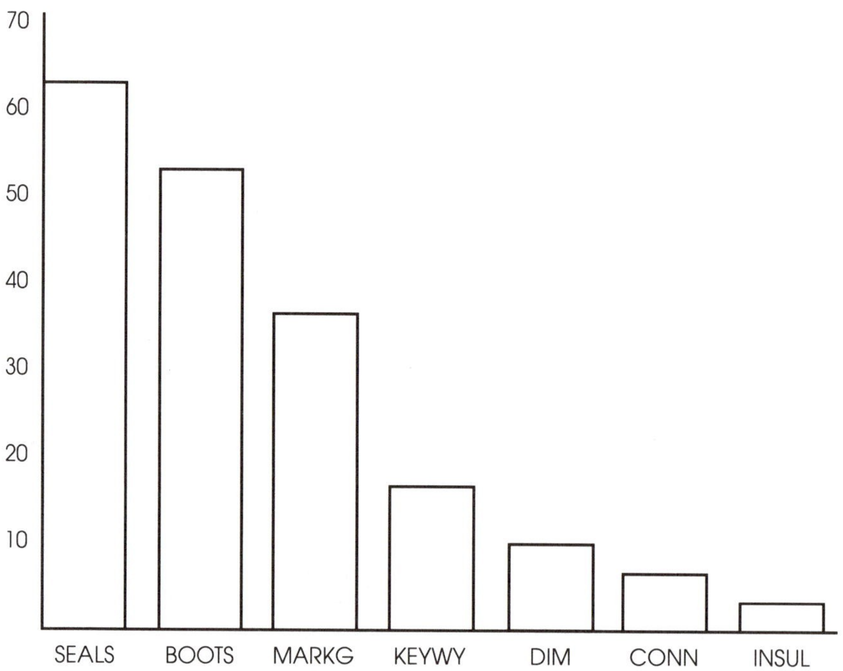

Figure 2.13. Pareto for wiring harness defects.

Once the real nature of the problem was uncovered, the incidence of defective units in this area dropped from 7% to less than 0.5%. This is an example of how properly diagnosed information can change the nature of "preconceived" ideas (change the bias). Much time and effort was lost in trying to solve the problem from the wrong direction. (Thanks to Lois Soto, Quality Assurance Manager, Charles E. Gilman Company, Nogales, AZ, for this example.)

2.6 Cause and Effect Diagram (Fishbone Chart or Ishikawa Diagram)

As the name implies, this tool is just a group of causes and effects diagrammed to show the interrelationships. The diagram is a form of tree diagram on its side so that it looks like a fishbone (see Figure 2.19). The name Ishikawa refers to the Japanese man who conceived the chart.

The diagram is formed by first stating the problem in the form of an effect. In Figure 2.14, the problem is to maximize hardness, within limits. Hardness, then, is the main effect. The main causes are then placed at the end of the lines extending up and down at an angle from the center line. These main causes are usually some form of the following manufacturing factors (note that they include the 5 M's checklist of Section 2.2): materials, equipment, work methods, operators/workers, processes, tooling, management (policies), measurement, environment, etc. The first three usually account for 80% of all problems.

Each of these main causes is now treated as effects and causes determined for each of them, then each of the secondary causes is treated as effects and causes found for each of them, and so on. The procedure is continued until all causes are identified.

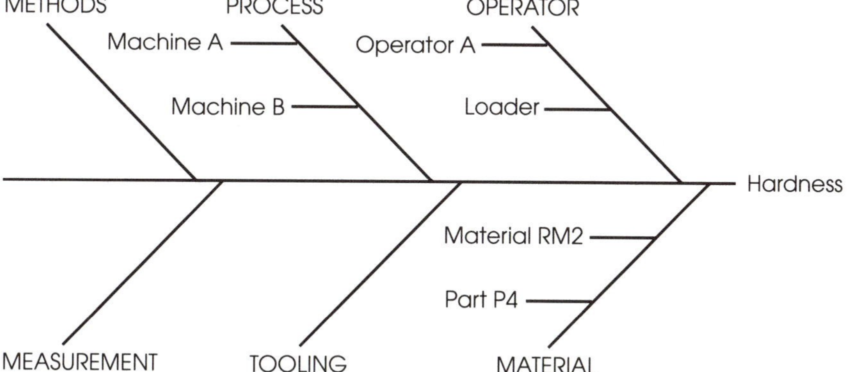

Figure 2.14. Basic cause and effect diagram.

Each cause, no matter where placed on the chart, must relate to the main effect (such as the effect hardness in Figure 2.14). If the chart is complex and extensive, secondary charts can be constructed from any of the causes. That cause then becomes the main effect of the secondary chart (always note on the main chart where a secondary chart is added).

The causes and effects are best determined by forming a team of those most concerned with the main problem, and then using the brainstorming procedure. Any quality characteristic (such as length, hardness, percent defectives, people, etc.) can become an effect around which a cause and effect chart is constructed. However, if the problem is people (how to change people, for instance), consider using a desired result (a goal) rather than a problem as the main effect. In other words, concentrate on the desired characteristics rather than on how to change people (which can degenerate into confrontation, resistance, decreased morale, etc.).

Cause and effect diagrams are especially effective in facilitating the brainstorming procedure, in examining and analyzing the processes (the root of all quality improvement lies in understanding the process), in planning procedures, and in determining the causes of dispersion. They are also used quite extensively by design engineering.

Notes and Comments

1. Use the diagram as an educational and training tool to learn about the process parameters and product characteristics and their interrelationships. Also use Paretos, histogram, and/or flowcharts. In fact, any of these seven tools can be effectively used in any good training program.
2. Use the diagram as a single picture of factor and characteristic relationships to replace, or accompany, more extensive checklists and explanations.
3. Use the diagram as a guide to focus discussion, to facilitate brainstorming sessions, to sort ideas into useful categories, to maintain focus on issues at hand.
4. Use the diagram as a summary of process/product data.
5. Continue to use and update the diagram. Review, correct, and embellish as necessary.
6. Indicate important relationships by boxing or circling the related causes/effects. If the exact quantitative relationships are known, enter them next to the proper cause/effect.
7. Consider the entire picture. Understand the impact of all factors, even those outside the team's control (such as government policies, local and national economy, employee issues, politics, environment, and other external factors).
8. Encourage a broad-based participation. Place a copy of the diagram on a wall in a conspicuous place, for all to see, and invite all to participate (remember, if suggestions are not acted upon, people will cease to participate).

9. To identify causes, ask the question, "Why does this effect occur and how does it add to dispersion?"
10. Consider using an independent and trained facilitator to direct the team's efforts.

2.7 Scatter Diagrams

These diagrams are Cartesian coordinate-type graphs (X,Y graphs) that illustrate cause and effect relationships between two types of data (see Figures 2.15–2.19). The two types of data relate in such a way that a change in one (called the independent variable) induces a change in the other (called the dependent variable). Pairs of points (X,Y) are plotted with the independent variable on the X-axis (horizontal axis or abscissa) and the dependent variable on the Y-axis (vertical axis or ordinate). Thus, a change in X causes (induces) a change in Y.

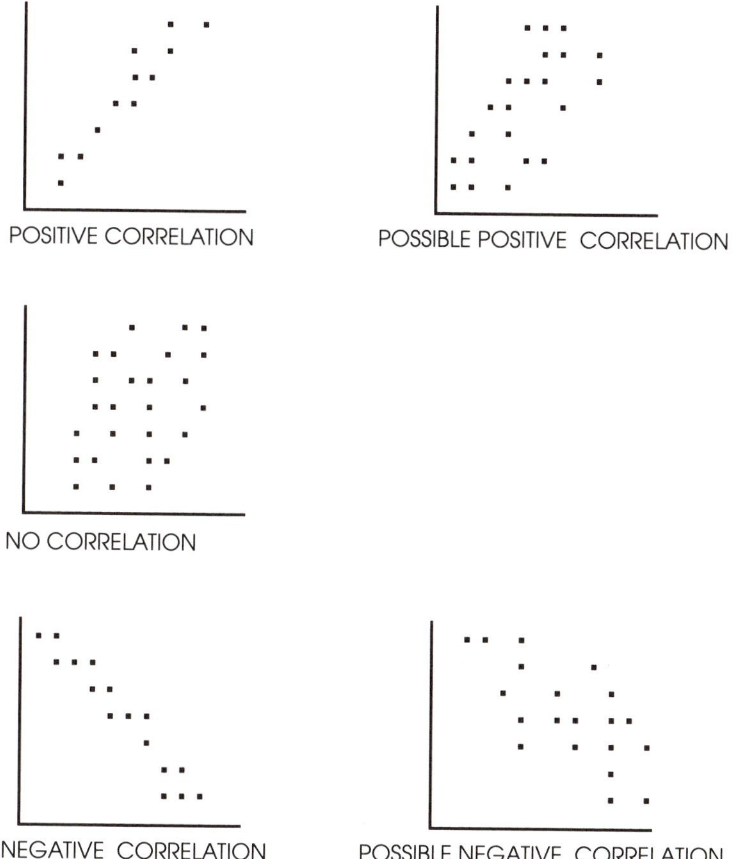

Figure 2.15. Scatter diagrams showing different types of relationships.

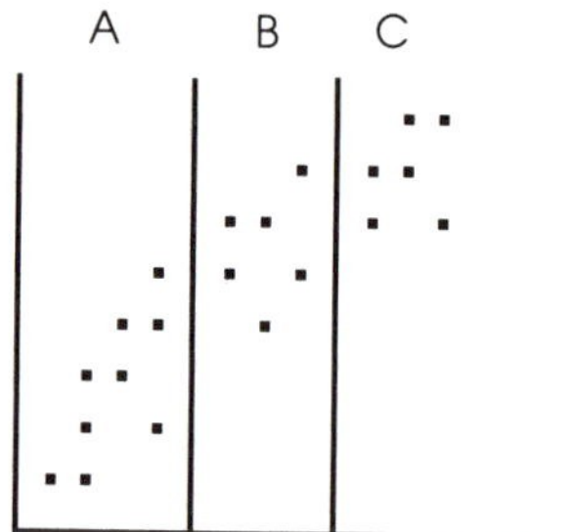

Figure 2.16. Scatter diagram.

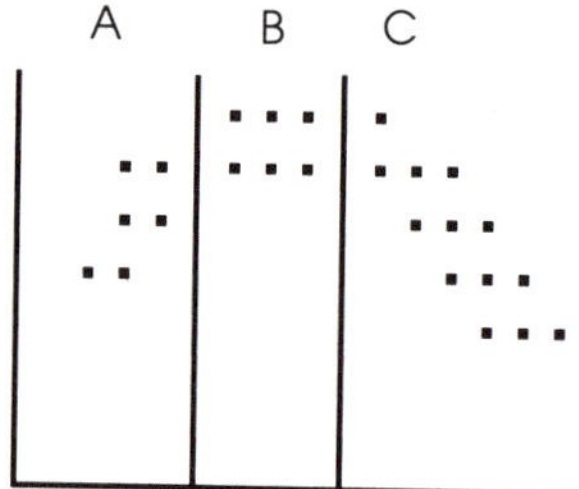

Figure 2.17. Scatter diagram.

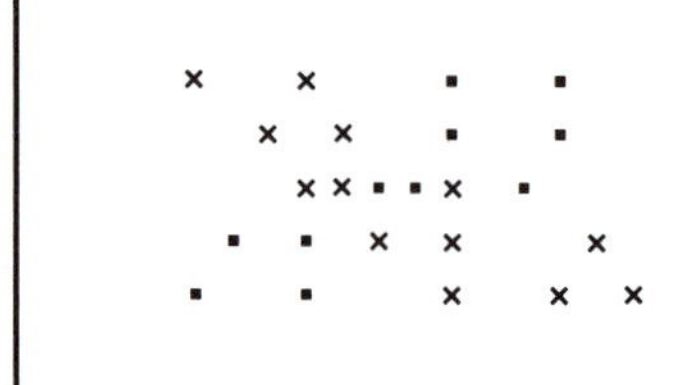

Figure 2.18. Scatter diagram.

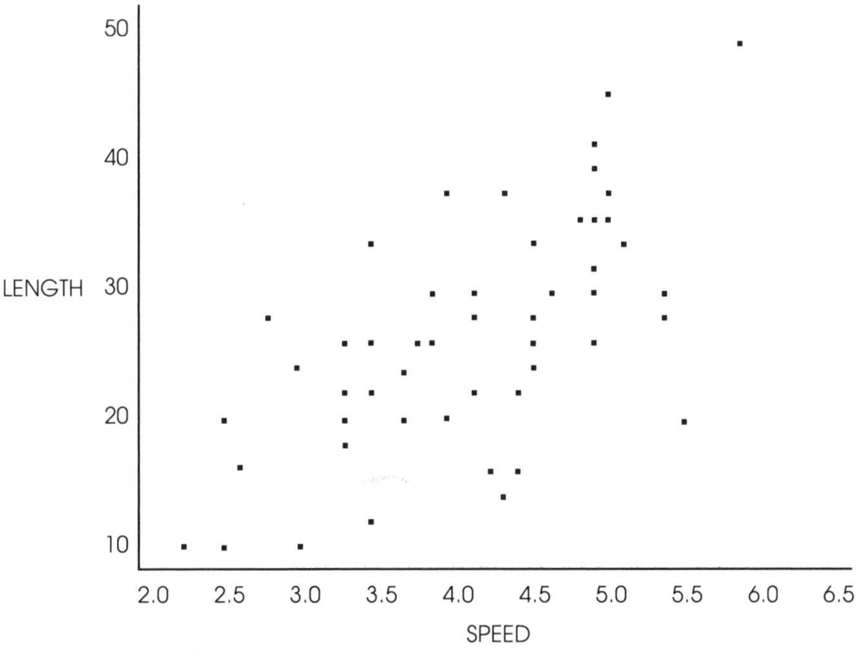

Figure 2.19. Scatter diagram for Table 2.3.

The different kinds of relationships between the two variables can provide clues and information to solve problems related to the process (see Figure 2.15).

Note that the relationships within the scatter diagrams are not quantized (the degree of change is not determined). This is left for a more advanced procedure called regression analysis. Scatter diagrams are not substitutes for regression analyses, and so must be used with care. For instance, an apparent relationship between two variables (as seen on the scatter diagram) can be negated, and even reversed, by the action of a third, interrelated, variable not on the chart. Also, scatter diagrams can be constructed for two variables only; more than two need a regression analysis.

Comments and Suggestions

1. The chart needs at least 30 pairs of data to be statistically significant (100 or more is much better, i.e., much safer statistically). Each pair of data refers to a measurement of an independent variable, such as temperature, and a resultant measurement of the dependent variable, such as hardness (the hardness that always results when that particular temperature is used).

2. Multiple relationships (more than two) must be analyzed using multiple regression/correlation analysis. Charts for multiple relationships are extremely difficult, and often impossible, to construct.
3. Be sure that the independent variable is measured over a sufficient range. The range of actual production conditions may not be sufficient to show the relationship (see Figures 2.16 and 2.17).
4. Consider extrapolation versus interpolation. Interpolation means to estimate a value between two measurements. This is a fairly safe procedure. However, extrapolation, which means to estimate a value outside the measurement range, is very risky. For instance, if only one or two of the three ranges (A, B, or C) on Figures 2.16 or 2.17 had been measured, an extrapolated value would have been very erroneous.
5. Stratify the data where possible. For instance, in Figure 2.18, the two variables show entirely different relationships for each vendor. But when combined together, the variables appear to have no relationship at all.
6. If a relationship exists, the variables are said to be correlated; if not, they are noncorrelated (not related). Be careful in assuming a relationship just because the graph seems to indicate it. There may be good reasons why the apparent relationship is completely spurious.
7. If the variables are directly related (a positive correlation), the dependent variable changes in the same direction as the change in the independent variable (when the independent variable increases, the dependent variable increases, and vice versa). The change does not have to be, but can be, one to one (that is, a one-inch change in the independent variable can, but does not have to, cause a one-inch change in the dependent variable—it can cause a two-inch, or other, change).
8. Indirect, or negative, correlation means that the dependent variable changes in the opposite direction as the change in the independent variable (an increase in the independent variable causes a decrease in the dependent variable).
9. A linear relationship means that as the change in the independent variable increases or decreases, the amount of resulting change in the dependent variable remains constant, for the same amount of change in the independent variable. A line of best fit would be a straight line. A one-to-one change (a one-inch change in the dependent variable) would be a 45 degree straight line.
10. For curvilinear relationships, the amount of change in the dependent variable increases or decreases at an increasing or decreasing rate. The line of best fit is a curved line.
11. Just because the two variables appear to be correlated on the chart does not necessarily mean that they are actually correlated in real life. The relationships (correlation) must be clearly established by logic and analysis (as well as by chart).

Table 2.1. Scatter Diagram Data for Figure 2.19

Number	Speed	Length	Number	Speed	Length
1	5.1	46	26	5.0	40
2	4.7	30	27	2.5	13
3	4.4	39	28	3.9	25
4	2.8	27	29	4.0	20
5	4.6	28	30	4.5	22
6	3.8	25	31	3.7	20
7	4.9	35	32	5.1	35
8	3.3	15	33	6.0	52
9	4.0	38	34	4.1	21
10	5.0	36	35	4.6	24
11	5.0	26	36	5.5	29
12	5.0	41	37	4.5	15
13	4.2	29	38	5.0	30
14	3.0	10	39	2.2	10
15	3.3	20	40	3.5	25
16	3.7	24	41	5.0	31
17	5.2	34	42	3.9	30
18	5.1	36	43	4.6	34
19	3.3	23	44	3.5	34
20	3.5	11	45	2.5	20
21	5.5	30	46	3.0	25
22	4.4	14	47	2.5	23
23	4.2	30	48	4.6	28
24	2.6	16	49	5.6	20
25	3.3	20	50	3.3	26

There appears to be some positive correlation between speed and length in Figure 2.19 (as the speed increases, the length increases), but it is not very strong. A line of best fit can be generated by observation to give a general idea of the degree of relationship, but a formal regression (and correlation) analysis is needed to determine the exact line and the exact quantitative relationship.

Practice Problems

2–1 Using the data reproduced below, determine the histogram.

Data (relative strengths of soldered joints)

1.5	1.2	3.1	1.3	0.7	1.3	0.1	2.9	1.0	1.3
2.6	1.7	0.7	2.4	1.5	2.1	3.5	1.1	0.7	0.5
1.4	1.7	3.2	3.0	1.7	2.8	2.2	1.8	2.3	3.3
3.1	3.3	2.9	2.2	3.1	2.1	3.5	1.4	2.8	2.8
1.9	2.0	3.0	0.9	3.1	1.9	1.7	1.5	3.0	2.6
1.0	2.9	1.8	1.4	1.4	3.3	2.4	1.8	2.1	1.6
0.9	2.1	1.5	0.9	2.9	2.5	1.6	1.2	2.4	3.4
1.3	1.0	1.5	2.2	3.0	2.0	1.8	2.9	2.5	2.0
1.0	1.3	1.3	3.8	1.1	2.0	2.1	2.4	1.6	1.4
2.2	2.3	2.4	1.8	1.8	2.8	1.4	1.8	2.1	3.0

2–2 Using the data reproduced below, determine the histogram.

Data

1.	40	45	37	37
2.	51	42	41	46
3.	39	45	39	41
4.	74	69	72	64
5.	43	39	49	45
6.	47	46	48	39
7.	49	46	46	51
8.	37	46	43	41
9.	53	57	54	56
10.	52	48	41	47
11.	43	46	44	43
12.	42	42	46	42
13.	45	43	52	40
14.	43	44	50	47
15.	55	47	48	50
16.	38	40	34	44
17.	46	45	34	39
18.	43	49	33	63
19.	38	36	42	43
20.	61	60	50	53
21.	43	45	50	42
22.	44	47	40	45
23.	47	44	44	41
24.	48	41	40	43
25.	44	43	48	49

2–3 Do a scatter diagram for the following data.

Temperature	Hardness
100	35
101	35
102	34
103	36
104	40
105	38
105	39
106	41
107	42
107	42
108	45
109	44
110	45
110	45
111	46
112	47
113	48
114	48
115	50
115	51

2–4 Do a simple Pareto analysis, using both counts and %, on the following error counts.

Operator	Errors
1	19
2	6
3	6
4	11
5	32
6	0

2–5 Do a Pareto analysis on the following data with the errors coded for environment on a scale of 1 to 100 and for safety on a scale of 1 to 10. The errors must be multiplied by the two codes.

Type of Errors	Number Errors	Environment Code	Safety Code
1	100	20	1
2	50	10	5
3	10	90	9
4	15	70	6
5	200	10	2

CHAPTER 3 THE NORMAL CURVE

In this chapter, a method of organizing raw data into cells for ease of analysis is presented. The more important analysis values that can be derived from this organization are also presented. These values form the basis for the normal curve, which is the most important and most used probability distribution in all of statistics. In SPC, it forms the theoretical foundation for all control charts. Although it can be used directly to determine various manufacturing values and to analyze the process, it is normally used in conjunction with control charts for this purpose. In this chapter, the normal curve is used directly to analyze production. Control charts are explained in Chapters 4 and 5. (Much of this chapter was derived from the author's book, *Reliability for the Technologies,* 2nd ed., 1991.)

Objectives

1. Know how to organize raw data into cells and frequency groupings that assist in the analysis of that data.
2. Know the differences between discrete and continuous data, and understand how these distinctions usually affect frequency groupings.
3. Understand the main differences between a universe and a sample, and between parameters and statistics. Also be able to distinguish between a biased and an unbiased sample, and understand why and when sampling is necessary.
4. Know the differences between measures of central tendency and measures of dispersion. Also, understand the various measures of central tendency, and be able to calculate their values from given data.

5. Understand the various measures of dispersion, and be able to calculate their values from given data.
6. Identify the normal curve and understand its characteristics.
7. Understand the area under the curve and how it relates to the mean and standard deviation.
8. Calculate the Z score, and determine probabilities from the table of Z scores.
9. Know the seven process applications of the normal curve and calculate each of these values.
10. Understand the relationship between the normal curve and quality control charts.

3.1 Organizing Into Cells

When large amounts of data are received, they must usually be organized in some manner in order for the pattern and structure of the data to be recognizable. One of the best ways to do this is to organize the data into frequency groupings (or cells). Table 3.2 shows an example of such a grouping derived from the raw data of Table 3.1.

The steps in organizing a frequency grouping are as follows.

1. Collect the raw data. Sometimes raw data are collected in no particular order, and listed as received or measured. However, in quality control and SPC, data are usually collected in a particular order, i.e., in a characteristic pattern easily recognizable by any quality control or SPC practitioner. Table 3.1 is an example of such a procedure. In this table, four items at a time are measured (for the desirable characteristic) as they are produced. The four measurements are then recorded on one line so that each line forms a subsample of the entire sample of 100 (thus there are 25 of these "subsamples" in the table). For grouping into cells, this order is unimportant. However, the order is critical later on when the data are used to determine control chart limits.
2. Determine the range of the data. The formula is

   $$R = X_h - X_l$$

   where

   $R =$ range

   $X_h =$ the highest data measurement

   $X_l =$ the lowest data measurement.

   In Table 3.1, the range is

   $$R = 1.091 - 1.050 = 0.041 \text{ inches.}$$

3. Choose the cell interval and determine the number of cells. The cell interval is the distance between cells, and is precisely defined as the difference between successive lower boundaries, successive upper

Table 3.1 Shaft Diameters (inches)

Sample	Measurements (observations)			
1	1.055	1.062	1.054	1.055
2	1.060	1.061	1.065	1.067
3	1.058	1.068	1.059	1.062
4	1.057	1.065	1.067	1.061
5	1.058	1.062	1.056	1.057
6	1.091	1.085	1.089	1.081
7	1.060	1.056	1.066	1.062
8	1.064	1.063	1.065	1.068
9	1.066	1.063	1.063	1.068
10	1.055	1.063	1.060	1.058
11	1.070	1.074	1.071	1.073
12	1.069	1.065	1.058	1.064
13	1.060	1.063	1.061	1.060
14	1.059	1.059	1.063	1.059
15	1.062	1.060	1.069	1.057
16	1.060	1.062	1.067	1.064
17	1.064	1.070	1.067	1.065
18	1.055	1.057	1.051	1.061
19	1.063	1.063	1.057	1.051
20	1.065	1.060	1.050	1.080
21	1.055	1.054	1.059	1.060
22	1.077	1.078	1.067	1.070
23	1.062	1.060	1.067	1.059
24	1.061	1.057	1.062	1.064
25	1.061	1.064	1.061	1.058

Table 3.2 Frequency Distribution of Shaft Diameters

Cell Boundaries	Midpoints	Frequency	Tally
1.048–1.052	1.050	3	III
1.053–1.057	1.055	15	~~IIII~~ ~~IIII~~ ~~IIII~~
1.058–1.062	1.060	36	~~IIII~~ ~~IIII~~ ~~IIII~~ ~~IIII~~ ~~IIII~~ ~~IIII~~ ~~IIII~~ I
1.063–1.067	1.065	28	~~IIII~~ ~~IIII~~ ~~IIII~~ ~~IIII~~ ~~IIII~~ III
1.068–1.072	1.070	9	~~IIII~~ IIII
1.073–1.077	1.075	3	III
1.078–1.082	1.080	3	III
1.083–1.087	1.085	1	I
1.088–1.093	1.090	2	II

boundaries, or successive midpoints. In Table 3.2, for instance, the interval is 0.005 inches (1.053–1.048 or 1.057–1.052 or 1.055–1.050, etc.). The cell interval must be an odd number and have the same number of decimal points as the original data. Thus, the cells can be organized in such a way that the midpoints also have the same number of decimal points as the original data. The cell interval and the number of cells are interrelated and must be determined together by trial and error. The procedure is as follows.

a. Divide the range (R) by successively larger odd numbers, starting with the digit 3 (that is, 3, 0.3, 0.03, 0.003, etc., depending on the number of decimal points in the original data). These divisors represent possible cell intervals, and the results represent possible (candidates for) number of cells.
b. Continue these divisions until a result exactly matches the square root of the sample size (not the subsample size), or is finally smaller than this square root. The result (number of cells) will decrease as the divisor (cell interval) is increased.
c. If the number of cells calculated is not a whole number, round up to a whole number—never round down. There cannot be a half a cell (or 1.5, or 2.3, etc.). If the number of cells is rounded down, the highest cell will not have enough room for all the data. If rounded up, some of the data points at the end of the highest cell will be empty—no measurements will be available for those particular numbers. In order to maintain normality (keep the curve normal), these empty data points must be evenly divided between the lowest and highest cells. The procedure for allocating these empty data points will be explained later.
d. Choose that cell interval which has the number of cells closest to the square root of the sample size. If two are equally close, choose the one that has the lowest number of cells.
e. The cell interval will be that number used in the divisor for determining the number of cells actually chosen for the grouping.

The calculations for Table 3.1 are

$$0.041/0.003 = 13.7 \text{ or } 14 \text{ cells}$$

$$0.041/0.005 = 8.2 \text{ or } 9 \text{ cells.}$$

Since 9 is less than the square root of the sample size of 100, the successive divisions can stop here. And since 9 is closer to 10 (the square root of 100) than is 14, choose 9 as the number of cells and 0.005 as the cell interval (note that if 14 had been chosen as the number of cells, the cell interval would have been 0.003).

4. Choose the lower boundary of the lowest cell. This is the step where the allocation of empty data points is made between the lowest and highest cells (if rounding had been necessary). The amount of allocation depends on the amount of rounding done. Note that 8 cells would have left only 40 data points ($8 \times 0.005 = 0.040$), which is one less than the 41 needed;

while 9 gives 45 ($9 \times 0.005 = 0.045$), which is 4 too many. The following procedure presents a good method of balancing the empty values at both ends of the distribution (dividing them as evenly as possible between the beginning of the first and the end of the last cell).

a. If the number of cells had been rounded up from 0.7 or above (8.7, 8.8, or 8.9, for instance), choose the lowest data value as the lower boundary of the lowest cell (for Table 3.1, this would have been 1.050).
b. If rounded up from 0.4, 0.5 or 0.6, choose one value below the lowest data value (for Table 3.1, this would have been 1.049).
c. If rounded up from below 0.4, choose two values below the lowest data value (for Table 3.1, this would have been 1.048).

Since the number of cells in Table 3.1 was actually rounded up from 8.2 to 9.0, the lower boundary of the lowest cell is two data points lower than the lowest data value, or 1.048 ($1.050 - 0.002 = 1.048$).

5. Determine the upper boundary of the lowest cell. This is done by adding the cell interval to the lower boundary and subtracting 1 from the last digit. This differentiates between the upper boundary of the previous cell and the lower boundary of the next cell (however, this digit must be added back later to the upper boundary of the highest cell). The upper boundary of the lowest cell for Table 3.1 is

$$1.048 + 0.005 - 0.001 = 1.052.$$

6. Determine the midpoint of the lowest cell. This is the assumed average of the cell (all measurements within the cell are assumed to have this value). In Table 3.2, for instance, three values are assumed to equal 1.050, 15 values are assumed to equal 1.055, etc. This may not always be true, of course; the real average may, and usually is, lower or higher than the midpoint. However, if the sample size is large enough (100 or more), errors in one cell will usually be offset enough by opposite errors in other cells so that the final result is close enough for all practical purposes (the statistical concept of compensating variations). The midpoint is calculated by adding the upper and lower boundaries and dividing by two. The midpoint of the lowest cell of Table 3.1 is then

$$(1.048 + 1.052)/2 = 1.050.$$

7. Determine the remaining boundaries and midpoints. This is accomplished by adding the cell intervals successively until the highest data value is included in the final cell. In Table 3.1, the boundaries and midpoint of cell 2 are

$$1.048 + 0.005 = 1.053 \text{ (lower boundary)}$$

$$1.052 + 0.005 = 1.057 \text{ (upper boundary)}$$

$$1.050 + 0.005 = 1.055 \text{ (midpoint).}$$

The boundaries and midpoint for cell 3 are

$$1.053 + 0.005 = 1.058 \text{ (lower boundary)}$$

$$1.057 + 0.005 = 1.062 \text{ (upper boundary)}$$

$$1.055 + 0.005 = 1.060 \text{ (midpoint).}$$

These calculations then continue until the ninth cell is complete. The upper boundary of the last cell, however, must be adjusted to offset the one digit subtraction started at the first cell. Just add 1 to the last digit (even though this is not technically correct, it still works). For our example, the upper boundary of the ninth cell is

$$1.087 + 0.005 + 0.001 = 1.093.$$

8. Tally the data; determine the frequency of each cell (it may be helpful to first arrange the data in ascending or descending order). This step is shown in Table 3.2.
9. List the cell boundaries in order from low to high, along with their associated midpoints and frequencies, as in Table 3.2.

Grouping by Individual Values

If the individual values are small in number (less than 20), grouping by cells is impractical. In this case, each individual value (measurement or count) becomes the equivalent of a cell midpoint and there are no cell boundaries. The steps to organizing this type of data are quite simple.

1. List the values from low to high.
2. Tally the data for each value (measurement).
3. List the frequency for each data value.
4. Table the data.

Example 3.1 Determine the frequency distribution of the following data: 3, 2, 1, 3, 2, 1, 3, 4, 4, 3 (number of failures in ten samples tested for 100 hours).

Solution

X	f	Tally
1	2	11
2	2	11
3	4	1111
4	2	11

Frequency Groupings

Three main methods are used to illustrate a distribution—all are related to the frequency (number of times that a particular value occurs in the sample).

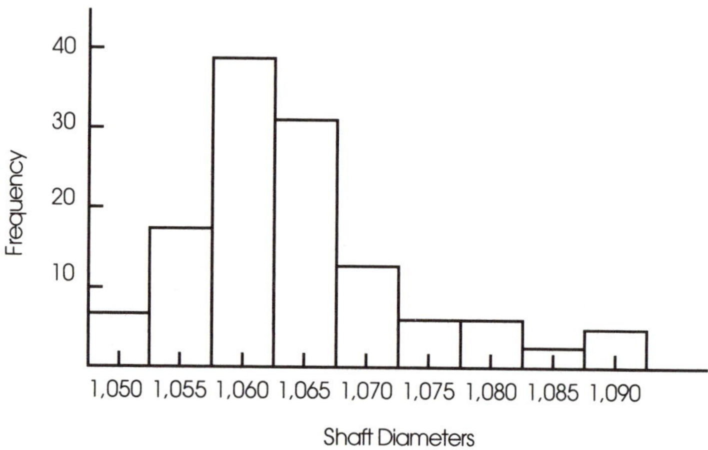

Figure 3.1. Histogram of shaft diameters.

1. **Table.** List of values with their associated frequencies (Table 3.2—midpoints and frequencies only).
2. **Histogram.** Frequencies arranged as bars on a chart (Figure 3.1).
3. **Curve.** A line drawn between the highest points on each bar as if there were an infinite number of bars, or an infinite number of possible points (or cells) theoretically between each value (Figure 3.2).

3.2 Discrete versus Continuous

Discrete data are those types of data which cannot have values between successive measurements or counts (cannot have half a failure,

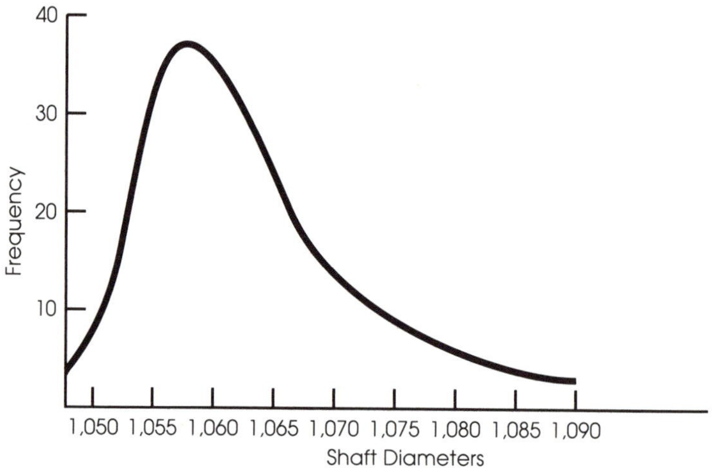

Figure 3.2. Curve of shaft diameters.

for instance). Since they are successive, the distance between individual values is always the same. When one discrete value is known, therefore, all values within that group can be deduced (the counting numbers starting with zero are 0, 1, 2, etc.; the group of even numbers starting with zero are 0, 2, 4, etc.; the group of odd numbers starting with zero are 1, 3, 5, etc.; the group of half values starting with zero are $^1/_2$, $1^1/_2$, $2^1/_2$, etc.). Thus, discrete data are discontinuous—they have gaps. The best example of discrete data in statistical process control (or anything else for that matter) is the counting of defective units in a sample (or number of defects on one unit). This is, normally, the only type of discrete data used in SPC. Since these types of data are characterized by a counting procedure, they will be termed "countable" data, and will be considered synonymous with the term "discrete" in this text. Obviously, "countable" data uses only the counting numbers; 1, 2, 3, etc. (Example 3.1).

Continuous data are those types of data which can be, theoretically, infinitely divisible between each pair of cell values or measurements. The best example of this type of data is the actual measurement of a dimension of a part (Tables 3.1 and 3.2). The difference between any two actual measurements can contain, theoretically, an infinite number of possible measurements, assuming that the measuring instrument has the capacity for infinite discrimination. In other words, there are theoretically an infinite number of possible measurements between 1 and 2 inches, between 1 and 1.5 inches, between 1 and 1.000005 inches, etc. This is normally the only type of continuous data used in SPC. Since these types of data are characterized by a measuring procedure, they will be termed "measurable" data and will be considered synonymous with the term "continuous" in this text.

Both continuous and discrete data can be grouped into cells (if the discrete data have many values of more than 20). However, most data grouped by cells are usually continuous in nature.

Both continuous and discrete data can also be grouped by individual values, if the number of individual data values is less than 20. However, most data grouped by individual values are usually discrete in nature.

3.3 The Universe versus a Sample

A universe (or a population) is a collection of all possible values, while a sample is just a small number of these values collected at random. For example, all 200 million American adults is a universe, while a group of 100 of these adults, chosen at random, is a sample. In statistical inference, the measure of a characteristic of this universe is inferred from the measurement of the same characteristic of the sample.

Suppose we wanted to know the average height of American adults. One way to determine this would be to measure all adults, sum the heights, and divide by the number of American adults. This would, of course, be a very expensive (and probably impossible) task. A more reasonable method would be to sample the universe (say 100 adults chosen at random), measure the sample characteristic, and then infer the mean from the sample mean. Of course, such a procedure is always subject to error, but various statistical procedures have been devised to minimize this possibility.

Bias

One of the most important rules in statistical sampling is that the sample must be unbiased. Three conditions must be present to ensure this situation.

1. The sample must be chosen at random. This means that every item in the universe has an equal chance of being chosen for the sample.
2. The sample must be homogeneous. This means that all groups in the sample must be represented in the same proportion in which they occur in the universe. In actual practice, this is accomplished by ensuring that each group in the universe has an equal chance of being chosen in the same proportion that they occur in the universe (the sample does not have to actually contain the different groups in the same proportion). An excellent example of this type of error occurred in the presidential election of 1948. The polls had incorrectly predicted that President Truman would lose the election. What happened was that the opinions were taken by telephone which did not permit the possibility of nontelephone users being included in the opinion (of which there were still a great number at that time). In SPC, homogeneity is usually not a problem, except in the case where identical product from two or more similar processes (machines) have been inadvertently mixed together.
3. The sample must be independent. This means that the selection of any one item does not affect the probability that any other item will be chosen. However, some types of sampling are deliberately chosen for dependence. For instance, when a sample of two or more from a lot are chosen, the resultant measurement of the probabilities involved is *not* independent (see Chapter 6). In this case, special statistical techniques must be used to properly calculate the probabilities.

A biased sample, then, is any sample that is *not* random, homogeneous, and/or independent.

Ensuring Randomality

There are several methods used by SPC and QC analysts to ensure that a reasonable chance for randomality exists in a sampling procedure. Some of the most important are listed below (for complex universes, random sampling procedures can be very complex and require the services of an accomplished statistician). Some of these procedures are not totally random, but are used to reduce the cost of ensuring total randomality and because the results are close enough for all practical purposes anyway, at least as far as quality control is concerned. Fortunately, SPC seldom works with complex universes, and therefore seldom needs complex randomality procedures (as is the case with political polls, for instance). Quality control and SPC usually work with lots of identical products where homogeneity is not a problem (it is the lack of homogeneity that adds complexity to randomality procedures). There are times, of course, in acceptance sampling especially, when two different lots of the same product are mixed together causing homogeneity and randomality problems. However, this problem is usually readily identifiable from a cursory examination of the control chart (patterns of successive high points, for instance).

1. The simplest method for ensuring randomality is to write the name or number of each unit on a slip of paper, mix them up thoroughly, and draw the required number of slips at random from the container. Obviously, due to practical considerations, this procedure is limited to small universes or lots.
2. A variant of method 1 above is to assign a number to each possible unit in the universe and then choose the sample from a table of random numbers. Random numbers can also be generated as desired on a hand calculator or computer. This is the method used by most computerized statistical procedures.
3. In quality control, especially in acceptance or receiving inspection, lots are frequently packaged so that a stratified random sampling procedure can be utilized. Although this is not a totally random procedure, it is close enough for this purpose. In stratified random sampling, the various layers and rows are first chosen randomly, then the units in the layers and rows are chosen randomly. Once again, this can be done, at each stage, with slips of paper or with random numbers from a table, hand calculator, or computer.

Parameters versus Statistics

A parameter is a measure of a characteristic of the universe (the average height of all American adults, for instance). A statistic is a measure of a characteristic of a sample of the universe (the average height of 100 American adults chosen at random, for instance). Ideally, statistics should resemble and closely approximate the universe parameters they represent.

In statistics, symbols are used to represent desirable characteristics, mostly for ease of calculation. In order to distinguish between the universe parameters and the sample statistics, different symbols are usually assigned to each. In quality control, the most important characteristics are the mean (arithmetic average) and the standard deviation (these values will be more precisely defined in a later section of this chapter).

The symbols shown below have been standardized—by ASQC (American Society for Quality Control)—and are the ones most used in quality control literature. The universe and sample symbols for mean and standard deviation are as follows.

1. Mean:
   a. Universe—μ (Greek letter mu)
   b. Sample—$\overline{X}$.
2. Standard Deviation:
   a. Universe—σ (lower case Greek letter sigma)
   b. Sample—s.

Why Sample?

Since sampling procedures are inherently error prone (there is always a chance for error), the question often asked is "why sample?" Why not, for instance, measure everything 100%? There are five main reasons why sampling is usually preferred over 100% inspection.

1. The universe, or population, may be too large, or of such a nature that 100% sampling is impossible or too costly (the height of all American adults, for instance).
2. The measurement itself may be too costly in relation to the product worth (chemical analysis of a casting, for instance).
3. The measurement may destroy the product (tensile tests, for instance).
4. The products or the measurement may be dangerous (radiation or toxic chemicals, for instance).
5. The boredom and fatigue of 100% inspection may cause more errors, and thus be less reliable, than sampling (an unfortunate psychological factor involved in most 100% inspections). Through the years, quality control practitioners have proved that this factor is very potent indeed; and this amply justifies the use of sampling procedures over 100% inspection (in most cases).

The above analysis does not infer that 100% inspection should never be used. Some products and/or characteristics must be inspected 100%. However, 100% inspection should be limited to expensive items or extremely important characteristics where measurement boredom is minimized.

Unfortunately, the lack of statistical training and/or the misunderstanding of sampling principles and procedures can lead to some rather bizarre errors. For instance, it has been estimated that over 30% of all chickens sold commercially in the United States (1987) harbor *Salmonella* bacteria (which can cause an unpleasant but usually not fatal disease), even though they are all subjected to 100% inspection. Proper quality control and sampling procedures would almost certainly reduce this percentage substantially (probably to less than 5%). A major stumbling block to initiating such procedures is the resistance of the public.

Their ignorance of statistical and sampling theory leads them to demand 100% inspection.

3.4 Measures of Central Tendency

Another means of arranging data for better understanding is to summarize them. In SPC and quality control, the most frequent types of summary are measures of central tendency, measures of dispersion, and control charts. Control chart principles, procedures, construction, and analysis will be studied in detail in Chapters 4 and 5. The remainder of this chapter will examine the different measures of central tendency and dispersion and their methods of calculation, and then these measures will be used to analyze data and certain types of production problems.

There are two great opposites in the universe—two opposing forces—which make all motion and life possible. They are the tendency to be the same and the tendency to be different. All objects exhibit these two tendencies to varying degrees. Most large groups of similar objects vary in some set pattern that can be formulated for prediction purposes. Although it is never possible to predict the actions of any single one of these objects, it is usually possible to predict how the entire group will respond to various forces, on the average. This principle can be used, therefore, to predict and control the production process. Before this control can be accomplished, however, the various measures of these forces must be calculated. First, the measures of central tendency will be presented, and then the measures of dispersion will be discussed.

The central tendency is the tendency to be the same. It is a central or midway value from which other values deviate in some set pattern. If that tendency is strong, the values or measurements will group closely about the central value. If that tendency is weak, the values or measurements will not group closely about the central value; more values will be at a greater distance. The three main types of central values are:

1. arithmetic mean or average
2. mode
3. median.

Arithmetic Average

This type of central value is also called the arithmetic mean; it is frequently called just the mean, although there are other mean values that are not arithmetic averages. The arithmetic average is the most common and most useful of all central values. It is the sum of all values (or measurements) divided by the number of values.

There are two main formulas, depending on the form of the data presentation (how it is organized), although there are several versions of each:

1. the general formula
2. the grouped data formula.

The General Formula

There are three forms of the general formula.

1. The basic formula is:

$$\overline{X} = (X_1 + X_2 + X_3 + \cdots X_n)/n$$

where

$\overline{X}$ = the arithmetic mean
n = the number of observation or measurements
X_1, etc. = the value of each individual observation.

2. The mathematical shorthand version is:

$$\overline{X} = \sum_{j=1}^{n} X_j/n$$

where

Σ = "the sum of" (the upper case Greek letter sigma)
X_j = the jth measurement.

This can be interpreted as: the arithmetic average equals the sum from $j=1$ to n of the individual values ($X_1 + X_2$, etc.) divided by n. The j in the above formula can also be changed to i. The only difference is in the way the data are presented (or visualized as being presented). If presented in column form, the i is used; if in a row, the j is used. Both are identical as far as computation is concerned.

3. The abbreviated form of the shorthand version is:

$$\overline{X} = \Sigma X/n.$$

This is the version of the general formula that will be used in this book. The formal jth (or ith) notation will be omitted from all formulas from now on.

Example 3.2 Find the mean of the values: 3, 2, 1, 3, 2, 1, 3, 4, 4, 3.

Solution

$$\overline{X} = (3+2+1+3+2+1+3+4+4+3)/10 = 26/10 = 2.6.$$

The Grouped Data Formula

It is usually much more useful to summarize large volumes of data by grouping them into cells; the calculations then become more manageable, and the data presentation is more understandable (see Section 3.1).

The grouped data formula is:

$$\overline{X} = \Sigma(fX)/n$$

where

$\overline{X}$ = the arithmetic mean

X = an individual value

$n = \Sigma f$ = the total number of observations

f = the number of observations within each cell

Σ = the sum of (the upper case Greek letter sigma).

The grouped data formula can be used for either discrete or continuous data (as long as they are grouped—either into cells or by individual values).

Example 3.3 Find the mean of Example 3.1 using the grouped data formula. (Note that this is an example of discrete data where the data values are counts of number of failures. There can be no division between 2 and 3; we cannot have 2½ failures, for instance.)

X	f	(fX)
1	2	2
2	2	4
3	4	12
4	2	8
	$\Sigma f = n = 10$	$\Sigma(fX) = 26$

Solution

$$\overline{X} = \Sigma(fX)/n = 26/10 = 2.6.$$

Example 3.4 Find the mean of Table 3.2 using the grouped data formula. This is an example of continuous data.

X	f	(fX)
1.050	3	3.150
1.055	15	15.825
1.060	36	38.160
1.065	28	29.820
1.070	9	9.630
1.075	3	3.225
1.080	3	3.240
1.085	1	1.085
1.090	2	2.180
	$\Sigma f = n = 100$	$\Sigma(fX) = 106.315$

Solution

$$\overline{X} = \Sigma(fX)/n = 106.315/100 = 1.06315.$$

Mode

The mode is that value which occurs the most often, i.e., has the highest frequency (f). In Example 3.3, the mode is 3. In Example 3.4, the mode is 1.060.

Median

The median is that value which is halfway between the high and low values. With discrete data, arrange the values from low to high, and count up and down simultaneously until both counts meet at the center.

1. For an odd number of values, the median is that value where the two counts meet.
2. For an even number of values, the median is determined by adding the two center numbers and dividing by two. For Example 3.3, the median is 3 $(3+3/2)$.

For continuous data arranged in cells, the calculations are somewhat complicated. The formula is:

$$Md = L_m + i(n/2 - cf_m)/f_m$$

where

Md = the median
n = total number of observations
cf_m = cumulative frequency of all cells below L_m
f_m = frequency of the middle cell
i = cell interval
L_m = lower boundary of the middle cell.

The median of Example 3.4 is:

$$Md = 1.058 + 0.005((100/2) - 18)/36 = 1.06244.$$

3.5 Measures of Dispersion

Dispersion refers to the principle that causes the values to vary about the central value. It is the variability of the distribution or the tendency to be different. If this tendency is strong, the spread of values will be greater and the average distance from the central value will be greater.

There are three main types of variability measures:

1. range
2. standard deviation
3. variance.

Range

The range is the difference between the high and low values. Since the range uses only two values—the lowest and the highest—a lot of information is lost (the values in between are ignored). Although used extensively in SPC and quality control to approximate the standard deviation, the range is really an inefficient means of measuring dispersion. The range can be used effectively in quality control and SPC only because of the special way the data are captured and utilized. The formula is:

$$R = X_h - X_l.$$

Example 3.5 Find the range of the distribution in Example 3.3.

Solution

$$R = 4 - 1 = 3.$$

Example 3.6 Find the range of the distribution in Example 3.4.

Solution

$$R = 1.090 - 1.050 = 0.040.$$

Standard Deviation

The standard deviation is the most useful and most used measure of dispersion in all statistics. It is defined as follows.

1. "The square root of the sum of the squares of the differences between the individual values and the mean divided by the number of values" (ASQC).
2. A measure of the average distance that the values deviate from the mean, or arithmetic average.

To illustrate the standard deviation, assume a mean of 3 and a standard deviation of 2. Now construct a number line from minus infinity to plus infinity, with the mean ($\overline{X}$) at the number 3.

$$\begin{array}{cccccccccccccccc} -\infty & -5 & -4 & -3 & -2 & -1 & 0 & 1 & 2 & 3 & 4 & 5 & 6 & 7 & 8 & +\infty \\ \hline & & & & & & & & & \overline{X} & & & & & & \end{array}$$

Standard deviations can then be shown as distances on the number line: 1 standard deviation can be measured from 2 to 4, 2 standard deviations can be measured from 1 to 5, 3 from 0 to 6, 2.6 from 0.4 to 5.6, etc. The illustrations could continue with any number of desired decimal points (such as 1.1, 2.45, etc.). Later on, the standard deviations will be divided into hundredths, to two decimal points, for precise calculation of areas under the curve. Tables of these divisions, with their associated areas, are available (Table A1).

Although the above standard deviation values are represented by distances on the number line, they are never to scale. In fact, many of the numbers may represent the type of units (pounds, failures, etc.) that are impossible to represent schematically to scale.

There are three main formulas for the standard deviation:

1. the basic formula
2. the "sum of squares" formula
3. the grouped data formula.

The Basic Formula

$$s=\sqrt{\Sigma(X-\overline{X})^2/(n-1)}$$

where

s = the standard deviation
X = an individual value
$\overline{X}$ = the arithmetic mean
n = the number of observations (or measurements)
Σ = "the sum of."

Example 3.7 Find the standard deviation of Example 3.3.

X	$-$	$\overline{X}$	$=$	$(X-\overline{X})$	$(X-\overline{X})^2$
3	−	2.6	=	0.4	0.16
2	−	2.6	=	−0.6	0.36
1		2.6		−1.6	2.56
3		2.6		0.4	0.16
2		2.6		−0.6	0.36
1		2.6		−1.6	2.56
3		2.6		0.4	0.16
4		2.6		1.4	1.96
4		2.6		1.4	1.96
3		2.6		0.4	0.16
$\Sigma X=46$				$\Sigma(X-\overline{X})=0.0$	$\Sigma(X-\overline{X})^2=10.40$

Solution

$$s=\sqrt{\Sigma(X-\overline{X})^2/(n-1)}=\sqrt{10.40/(10-1)}=1.075.$$

Note that the sum of $(X-\overline{X})$ is equal to zero and therefore cannot be used in further calculations. This is why $\Sigma(X-\overline{X})^2$ is used to find the variation.

The Sum of Squares Formula

Using basic algebra, a formula for the standard deviation can be derived that does not require the calculation of the mean. This is called the "sum of squares" and is extremely useful in advanced analysis techniques such as analysis of variance (ANOVA) and analyses using experimental designs. The derivation is:

$$(X-\overline{X})^2 = X^2 - 2X\overline{X} + \overline{X}^2$$

summing

$$\Sigma X^2 - 2\Sigma X\overline{X} + n\overline{X}^2$$

substituting

$$\Sigma X^2 - 2\Sigma X(\Sigma X/n) + n(\Sigma X/n)^2$$

$$= \Sigma X^2 - 2(\Sigma X)^2/n + (\Sigma X)^2/n$$

$$= \Sigma X^2 - (\Sigma X)^2/n.$$

Substituting into the basic formula yields:

$$s = \sqrt{[\Sigma X^2 - (\Sigma X)^2/n]/(n-1)}.$$

This formula is used almost exclusively in place of the "basic formula." It is ideally suited for a computer or hand calculator. Only three running totals need to be maintained:

1. ΣX (just add each new value to the previous sum)
2. ΣX^2 (just add the square of each new value to the previous sum)
3. n (add 1 for each new value entered).

Thus, a running value for the standard deviation, and arithmetic average, can be computed at any time (say, weekly or monthly).

Example 3.8 Compute the standard deviation of Example 3.3 using the "sum of squares" formula.

X	X^2
3	9
2	4
1	1
3	9
2	4
1	1
3	9
4	16
4	16
3	9
$\Sigma X = 26$	$\Sigma X^2 = 78$

Solution

$$s = \sqrt{[\Sigma X^2 - (\Sigma X)^2/n]/(n-1)}$$

$$s = \sqrt{[78 - (26)^2/10]/(10-1)} = 1.075.$$

Note that the mean can still be computed from this method by using ΣX and n ($\overline{X} = \Sigma X/n$).

The Grouped Data Formula

When data are organized into cells or groups, the "sum of squares" formula must be modified slightly; each value must be multiplied by its respective frequency. The formula is:

$$s = \sqrt{[\Sigma(fX^2) - (\Sigma fX)^2/n]/(n-1)}.$$

Example 3.9 Find the standard deviation for Example 3.3 using the grouped data formula.

X	f	(fX)	X^2	(fX^2)
1	2	2	1	2
2	2	4	4	8
3	4	12	9	36
4	2	8	16	32
	$\Sigma f = n = 10$	$\Sigma(fX) = 26$		$\Sigma(fX^2) = 78$

Solution

$$s = \sqrt{[78 - (26)^2/10]/(10-1)} = 1.075.$$

Example 3.10 Find the standard deviation of Example 3.4 using the grouped data formula.

X	f	(fX)	X^2	(fX^2)
1.050	3	3.150	1.1025	3.3075
1.055	15	15.825	1.1130	16.6954
1.060	36	38.160	1.1236	40.4496
1.065	28	29.820	1.1342	31.7583
1.070	9	9.630	1.1449	10.3041
1.075	3	3.225	1.1556	3.4669
1.080	3	3.249	1.1664	3.4992
1.085	1	1.085	1.1772	1.1772
1.090	2	2.180	1.1881	2.3762
	$\Sigma f = n = 100$	$\Sigma(fX) = 106.315$		$\Sigma(fX^2) = 113.0344$

Solution

$$s = \sqrt{[113.0344 - (106.315)^2/100]/(100-1)}$$

$$= 0.0075.$$

Variance

The variance (s^2) is just the square of the standard deviation. It can be computed by using any of the standard deviation formulas and omitting the radical, or by just squaring the standard deviation. In the two examples above, the variance is 1.1556 (1.075^2) and 0.0000562 (0.0075^2).

3.6 Characteristics of the Normal Curve

Earlier in this chapter, the differences between a universe and a sample were explained, along with the various symbols and uses. The formulas for the means of a sample and for a universe are basically identical, except that all the individual universe values must be used for determining the universe mean, and only a sample of these values are used for determining the sample mean. Therefore,

$$\overline{X} = \mu = \Sigma X/n \quad \text{(for an unbiased sample).}$$

Actually, in real life, X-bar seldom exactly equals μ, due to the differences in the number of measurements used to calculate the two values. It is assumed, however, that in an unbiased (random) sample of enough values (100 or more), X-bar will usually be close enough to μ so that it can be used as if it equals μ. In general, the larger the sample size, the closer X-bar is likely to be to μ. (X-bar becomes a better "estimator" of μ as the sample size increases.)

X-bar is an example of what is called, in statistics, a *random variable*. This refers to the fact that the measurements are usually different (that is, they vary), and that these differences are caused by chance alone (that is, random). One of the most important functions of statistics is to determine just how close these two values are likely to be, even though the universe from which the sample was drawn is so large, or of such a nature, that its mean (μ) can never be calculated accurately.

The formulas for the two standard deviations, however, are not the same. The formula for the universe standard deviation is

$$\sigma = \sqrt{\Sigma(X-\mu)^2/n}$$

while the formula for the sample standard deviation is

$$s = \sqrt{\Sigma(X-\overline{X})^2/(n-1)}.$$

Since $\mu = \overline{X}$ (assuming the universe and the sample are both normally distributed and that the sample is unbiased), the only real difference between the two formulas is that one is divided by n while the other (the sample) is divided by $n-1$. The reason for this is to offset the normal bias of small sample sizes. When the sample size becomes large (100 or more), there is little difference between the formulas. (Dividing by 100 gives almost identical results as dividing by 99, while dividing by 10 will give quite different results than dividing by 9.)

Shape Characteristics

The normal curve is quite distinctive in its shape. It is symmetrical, unimodal, and bell-shaped with the mean, mode, and median being equal to each other. A symmetrical object, when folded along its center line (the mean in this case), will have the outline of one side exactly cover the outline of the other. Unimodal means there is only one high spot in the curve. The characteristic shape of the normal curve is the reason it is so often called the bell-shaped curve.

The series of pictures in Figure 3.3 gives a graphical illustration of these relationships. The first picture shows a normal, symmetrical, bell-shaped curve. The next picture shows a distribution that is skewed to the right. Skewedness always refers to the direction of the long tail. This curve is also positively skewed (positive to the right, negative to the left). The third picture shows a negatively skewed curve (skewed to the left) with the long tail to the left. Pictures (d) and (e) show the leptokurtic-type distribution with its high peak and narrow dispersion (strong central tendency) and the platykurtic-type distribution with its low central peak and wide distribution (weak central tendency). (Kurtic comes from the word kurtosis which means peakedness.) Leptokurtic curves have small standard deviations, while platykurtic standard deviations are quite large in comparison. The last picture shows a bimodal distribution with two humps. Data that were used to construct this curve probably came from two separate universes (such as two different machines).

Figure 3.4 illustrates the relationship between the mean and the shape. Notice that changes in the mean have no effect on the shape of

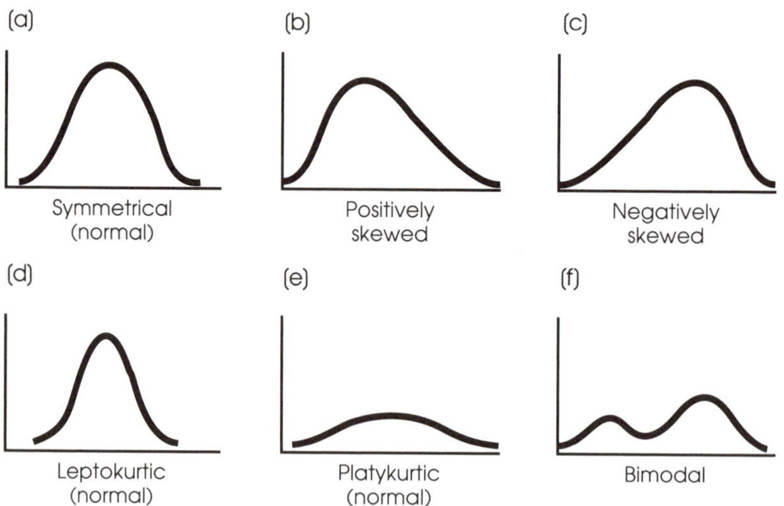

Figure 3.3. Characteristics of frequency distributions.

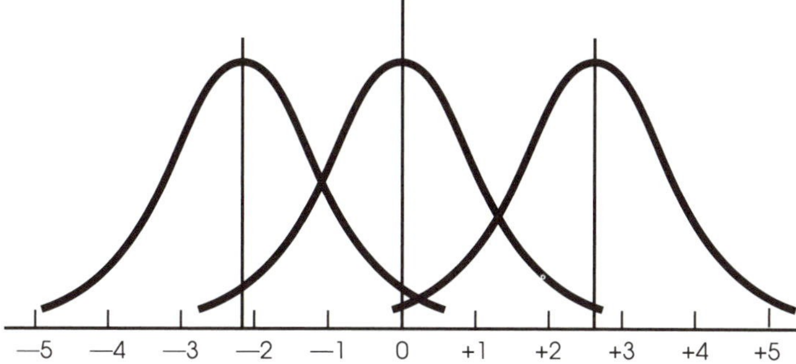

Figure 3.4. Normal curves with identical standard deviations but different means.

the curve. These changes affect only the position of the curve on the number line. Theoretically, there can be an infinite number of curves of the same shape, each having a different mean but the same standard deviation.

In Figure 3.5, the relationship of standard deviation to shape is illustrated. The standard deviation definitely affects the shape of the curve. There can be, theoretically, an infinite number of curves with the same mean (at the same location on the number line), but with each having a different standard deviation.

Figure 3.6 illustrates the relationship of mean, mode, and median for different types of curves. The first curve in the figure is a normal curve. In this curve, the mean = the mode = the median. This will

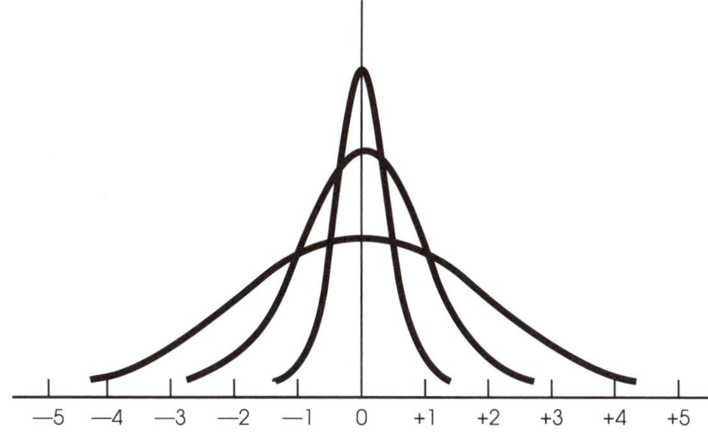

Figure 3.5. Normal curves with identical means but different standard deviations.

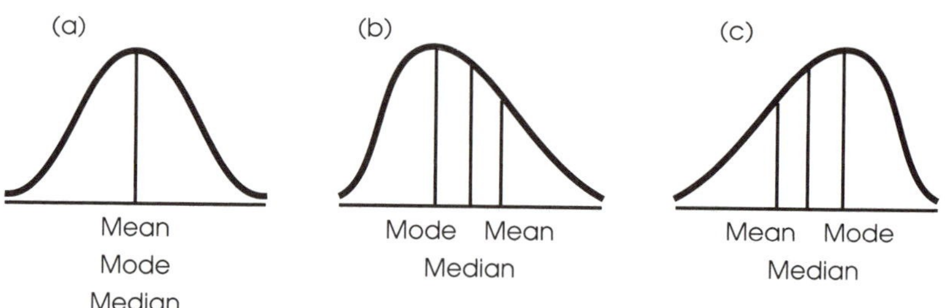

Figure 3.6. Relationship among mean, mode, and median.

always be true for all normal curves. The second curve is positively skewed (not normal). Note that in a positively skewed curve, the mode and median are shifted to the left, opposite to the long tail. The final curve is negatively skewed (also not normal) with the mode and median shifted to the right (once again opposite the long tail).

3.7 Area Under the Curve

Equations can be developed for any curve, and the normal curve is no exception. The equation (formula) for the normal curve is

$$f(X) = [1/\sigma\sqrt{2\pi}]\{\exp[-(X-\overline{X})^2/2\sigma^2]\}.$$

Thus, the area under this curve can be found by the techniques of integral calculus (actually numerical analysis). This area can be directly related to the percent of items in the distribution. Thus, the area under the curve from $-\infty$ to $+\infty$ represents 100% of all items in the distribution. The area under the curve from $-\infty$ to the mean (and from the mean to $+\infty$) represents 50% of all the items in the distribution. This can be verified by actually calculating the total area under a curve and dividing it into the area under the curve from $-\infty$ to the mean. Similarly, any area from any value to another value can be calculated, and the total area divided into it to get the percent (area or ratio $\times$ 100) of items in the distribution between the two values. Then, if the total number of items in the distribution is known, this total can be multiplied by the area (ratio) between the two values to get the actual number of items that lie between these two values.

This process is quite tedious and time-consuming, so a table of these ratios has been calculated called the table of areas under the normal curve (see the Appendix, Table A1). This table is also called the table of Z scores because the calculated Z value is used to find the desired ratio (or probability). The ratios (probabilities) in the table were calculated using numerical analysis from the standard normal curve. The numbers in the body of this table are ratios (numbers between 0 and

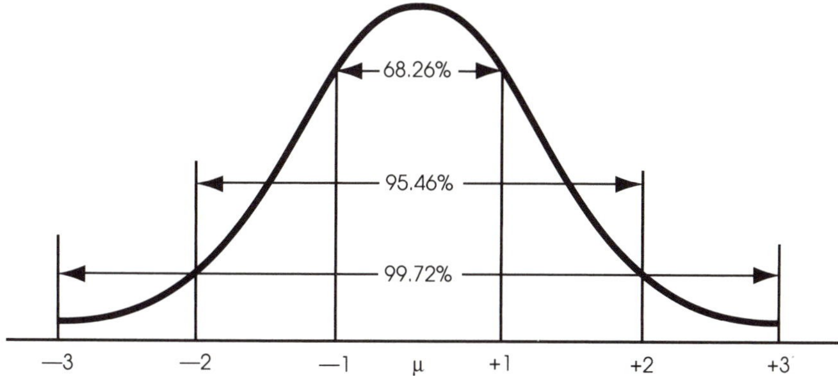

Figure 3.7. Percentage of items between 1, 2, and 3 standard deviations from the mean.

1), and as such represent probabilities. They become percentages when multiplied by 100.

All normal curves are symmetrical, so the percent area under the curve from the mean to 1, 2, or 3 standard deviations from the mean is always the same for all normal curves. Thus, the percent area under the curve from the mean to plus 1 standard deviation (to the right) is always 34.13% for all normal curves. The standard deviation (and the mean) may be different, but the percent area from the mean to 1 standard deviation is always the same for any normal curve. This also holds true, of course, for 2 or 3 standard deviations, or any other value (such as 1.5, 2.14, etc.). The area also refers to a probability value, that is, the probability that any one measurement will be below or above a certain value or will be between two values. Figure 3.7 illustrates these concepts showing the percent areas for 1, 2, and 3 standard deviations above and below the mean.

Standard Normal Curve

Since the percent area under the curve is the same for any normal curve, or all normal curves, for the same number of standard deviations from the mean, only one normal curve needs to be used to calculate these areas (Table A1). Therefore, it would be best to use the curve that is easiest to calculate. Such a curve is available and is called the standard normal curve (or standard normal distribution). It is a special normal curve with a mean of 0 and a standard deviation of 1. In this curve, the area equals 1.00, eliminating the need to divide by the total area to find the percentage. (Just find the desired area for this curve for various values of the standard deviation.)

The use of this standard normal curve, then, in conjunction with the Z score formula, allows the use of a simplified normal curve formula to

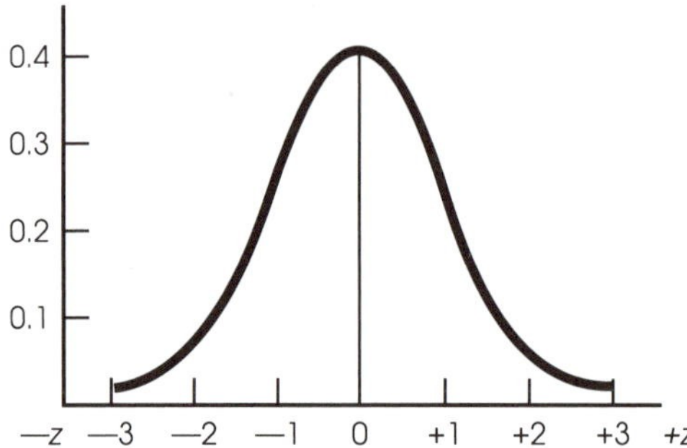

Figure 3.8. Normal curve with a mean of 0 and a standard deviation of 1.0.

find the values in Table A1. Since the mean is equal to 0, any term multiplied by or divided into this value becomes 0 and can be eliminated from the formula. Also, any term multiplied or divided by the standard deviation is unchanged (because the standard deviation is 1.00). Therefore, these values can be eliminated from the formula, making it much easier to calculate. The new, simplified, normal curve formula (called the standard normal deviate) is

$$f(Z) = [1/\sqrt{2\pi}][\exp(-Z^2/2)].$$

The standard normal curve, and the Z formula, is used extensively in statistics as a transformation vehicle to determine the area under the curve (or percent items, or probability). Since the numbers to the left of the mean of this distribution are always negative (the mean of this particular curve = 0), standard deviations to the left of the mean are always considered to be moving in the negative direction and, therefore, Z scores to the left of the mean are considered to be negative. Of course, Z scores to the right are considered to be positive (Figure 3.8). This is the reason that curves skewed to the left (with the long tail to the left) are called negatively skewed curves, and curves skewed to the right are called positively skewed curves. All normal curve analyses follow this convention.

3.8 Z Scores

As previously stated, a Z value is needed in order to use Table A1 to find a percentage (or probability). The Z value is simply the number of standard deviations from the mean, and is found by using the following formula:

$$Z = (X - \mu)/\sigma$$

where

Z = the standardized normal value, or number of standard deviations from the mean

X = an individual observation or measurement; or a desired value, or a specification

μ = the arithmetic mean of the universe

σ = the standard deviation of the universe.

If the mean and standard deviation had been derived from a sample, the t distribution must be used. The t distribution is a special normal with the tails extended to offset the normal bias from small sample sizes. The t becomes almost identical to the Z when the sample size increases to 30 or more (especially above 100). Since most control chart analyses use samples of 100 or more, the Z is more than adequate for this use. (The t and other distributions are used for experimental design where the sample sizes are almost always quite small. Procedures for using the t distribution will be explained in Chapter 7.)

The procedure for using the Z tables is as follows.

1. Calculate the Z value using the formula given previously. (Sometimes the Z value may be inferred or estimated by engineering or management.)
2. Enter the table of Z scores (Table A1) at the Z value along the side of the table and read the corresponding P value (probability value, which when multiplied by 100 becomes the percentage) from the body of the table. Each Z value has its own distinctive P value. Remember that positive and negative Z values are different and are read from different pages of the table. For example, a Z of 2.00 has a P value of 0.9773, while a Z of -2.00 has a P of 0.0228. The first two digits of the Z value are read from the far left column, while the third is read from the top. If the Z value has more than two decimals, the P value must be interpolated. Interpolation techniques are presented in the Appendix. (A summary version is used at the end of Step 3, which follows.) When using the normal curve for quality control analysis, rounding the Z value to two decimal points is usually adequate. The following is a list of P values from respective Z values:

   if $Z = 0.56$; $P = 0.7123$
   if $Z = 1.56$; $P = 0.9406$
   if $Z = -0.56$; $P = 0.2877$
   if $Z = -1.56$; $P = 0.0594$.

   Notice that the P values for $Z = 0.56$ and $Z = -0.56$ sum to 1.00. All P value pairs derived from negative/positive Z value pairs will always sum to 1.00. (Figure 3.8 illustrates this concept.) The P value from the table always corresponds to the area under the curve from $-\infty$ to the Z value. The area from $-\infty$ to a Z of -0.56 is 0.2877, while the area from a Z of 0.56 to $+\infty$ is also 0.2877 ($1-0.7123$ – the total area under the curve is always equal to 1 or 100%). This is due to the symmetrical nature of the curve and because the distance from the mean to a Z of -0.56 is identical to the distance from the mean to $+0.56$.

3. Sometimes a P value is known or can be inferred from other information (from similar products produced on similar processes, or just desired by management, engineering, and/or the customer). In this case, an associated Z value might be desired to calculate important control information. Finding this Z value from the given P is called the inverse use of the normal. Simply enter the body of the table and find the P value (interpolation is often necessary); then read the associated Z value from the side (and top) of the table. The following are several P values with their associated Z values:

   if $P=0.9900$; $Z=2.327$ (interpolating)
   if $P=0.9000$; $Z=1.282$ (interpolating)
   if $P=0.0228$; $Z=-2.000$ (no interpolation needed)
   if $P=0.1000$; $Z=-1.282$ (interpolating).

   To find the Z for 0.9900, note that this value falls between 0.9898 and 0.9901 in the body of Table A2 (see the Appendix). A P of 0.9898 corresponds to a Z of 2.32, while a P of 0.9901 corresponds to a Z of 2.33. The distance between 0.9898 and 0.9900 is 2/3 the distance between 0.9898 and 0.9901. Thus, the distance between 2.32 and the required Z value for a P of 0.9900 is 2/3 the distance between 2.32 and 2.33 (or 0.007): $2.32+0.007=2.327$.

3.9 Applications of the Normal Curve

The normal curve can be used to determine a percent of items below a certain value, above a certain value, or between two values. It can also be used inversely to determine a desired value or mean from a given percent of items (percent $\div$ 100 = probability or area). Remember that when the problem asks for a percent of items, this is the same as asking for the probability that any one item is below or above a value. Also, the answer from the body of Table A1 is a probability value and must be multiplied by 100 to change it to a percentage. (Or, if a percentage is given and a Z value is needed, the percentage must first be divided by 100 before entering the table.) Seven types of production problems can be solved using the normal curve.

1. Find a percent of items below a given value.
2. Find a percent of items above a given value.
3. Find a percent of items between two values.
4. Find a value given a maximum percent of items desired to be below that value. (What must the specification be, for example, if no more than a certain percentage is allowed to be below that specification?)

5. Find a value given a maximum percent of items desired to be above that value.
6. Find the new mean given a maximum percent of items desired to be below a certain value. (To what mean value must we produce our product, for example, given that no more than a certain percent of our product is to measure below a given lower specification?)
7. Find the new mean given a maximum percent of items desired to be above a certain value.

Problems 4 through 7 are examples of what is known as the inverse use of the normal (solving for Z from a given P). Note that pictures of the normal curve are used in every problem. Pictures simplify the thought processes involved in these types of analyses enormously, and act as excellent guides in directing the solution to the problem. These seven types of problems will now be explored in detail.

Find the Percent of Items Below a Given Value

The steps are as follows.

1. Draw the normal curve.
2. Locate all given and calculated values on the drawing.
3. Calculate Z.
4. Get the P value from Table A1. (This is the answer.)

Example 3.11 The mean weight of a product is 30 oz., with a standard deviation of 2 oz. Find the percent of product likely to weigh less than 27.5 oz.

Solution (See Figure 3.9)

$$Z = \frac{(27.5 - 30)}{2} = -2.5/2 = -1.25$$

$$P(Z \leq -1.25) = 0.1057 = 10.57\%$$

This can be interpreted as follows: the probability that Z is less than or equal to -1.25 is 0.1057, or 10.57%. It also means any one of the following three equivalent statements (they mean the same thing):

1. 10.57% of the items are below 27.5 oz., *or*
2. the chance of any one item being below 27.5 oz. is 10.57%, *or*
3. out of 10,000 items, 1057 will weigh less than 27.5 oz., while 10,000 − 1057 or 8943 will weigh more.

Find the Percent of Items Above a Certain Value

The steps are as follows.

1. Draw the normal curve.
2. Locate all values on the curve.
3. Calculate Z.

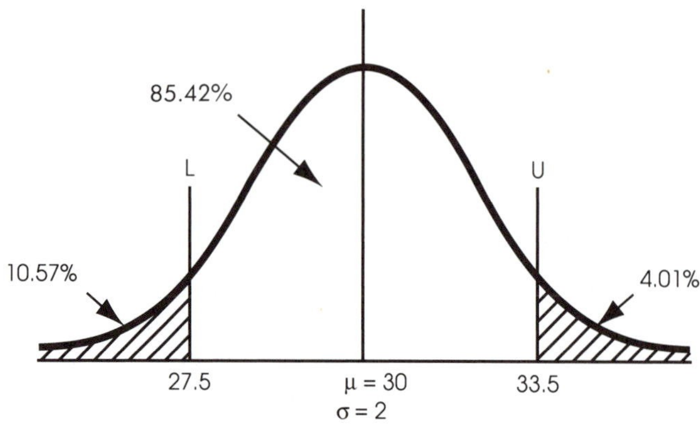

Figure 3.9. Curve illustrating Examples 3.11, 3.12, and 3.14.

4. Get the *P* value from Table A1.
5. Subtract the *P* value from 1.00.

Example 3.12 The mean weight of a product is 30 oz., with a standard deviation of 2 oz. Find the percent of product likely to weigh more than 33.5 oz.

Solution (See Figure 3.9)

$$Z = (33.5 - 30)/2 = 3.5/2 = 1.75$$

$$P(Z > 1.75) = 1 - P(Z \leq 1.75) = 1 - 0.9599 = 4.01\%.$$

Find the Percent of Items Between Two Values

The steps are as follows.

1. Draw the curve.
2. Locate all values on the curve.
3. Calculate *Z* for each given value.
4. Find the *P* value for each *Z* from Table A1.
5. Subtract the smaller table value from the larger.

Example 3.13 The mean weight of a product is 30 oz., with a standard deviation of 2 oz. Find the percent of product likely to weigh between 27.5 and 33.5 oz.

Solution (See Figure 3.9)

$$Z_{27.5} \text{ (from Example 2.5-1)} = -1.25$$

$$Z_{33.5} \text{ (from Example 2.5-2)} = 1.75$$

$$P(-1.25 \leq Z \leq 1.75) = 0.9599 - 0.1057 = 85.42\%$$

Another way to calculate this area (percent items) is to subtract the sum of the areas in the tails from one $[1-(0.1057+0.0401)=0.8542]$.

Find the Lower Limit Given a Maximum Desired Percent of Items Below that Limit

The steps are as follows.

1. Draw the curve.
2. Locate all values on the curve.
3. Find the Z score from Table A1 using the given percentage.
4. Calculate the limit from the Z formula.

Example 3.14 The mean weight of a product is 30 oz., with a standard deviation of 2 oz. Find what the lower specification must be to ensure that, on the average, no more than 5% of the items will weigh less than that specification. (Remember to divide the 5% by 100 before beginning the calculations.)

Solution (See Figure 3.10)

$$Z_{0.05}=-1.645 \text{ (from Table A1)}$$

$$Z_{0.05}=-1.645=(X-\mu)/\sigma=(X-30)/2$$

$$X=30-1.645(2)=26.71 \text{ oz.}$$

Find the Upper Limit Given a Maximum Desired Percent of Items Above that Limit

The steps are as follows.

1. Draw the curve.
2. Locate all values on the curve.
3. Find the Z score from Table A1 using the given percentage.
4. Calculate the limit from the Z formula.

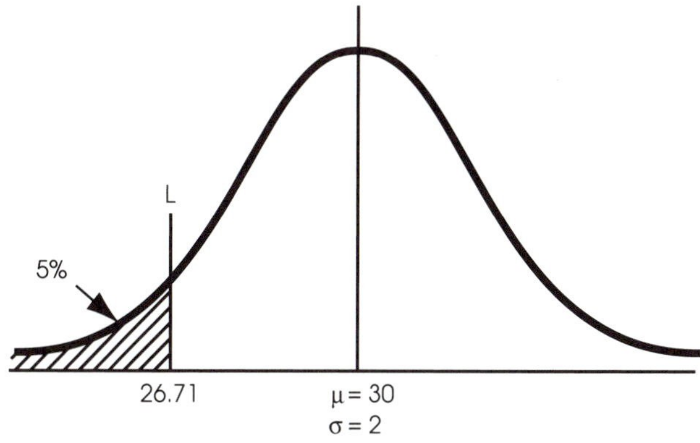

Figure 3.10. Curve illustrating Example 3.14.

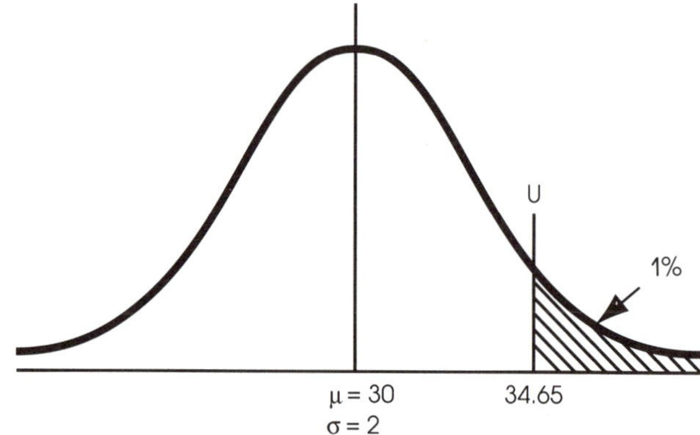

Figure 3.11. Curve illustrating Example 3.15.

Example 3.15 The mean weight of a product is 30 oz., with a standard deviation of 2 oz. Find what the upper specification must be to ensure that no more than 1% of the items will weigh more than that specification.

Solution (See Figure 3.11)

$$Z_{1-0.01} = Z_{0.99} = 2.327 \text{ (Table A1)}$$

$$Z_{0.99} = 2.327 = (X - \mu)/\sigma = (X - 30)/2$$

$$X = 30 + 2.327(2) = 34.654 \text{ oz.}$$

Find the New Mean Given a Maximum Desired Percent of Items Below a Given Lower Specification Limit

The steps are as follows.

1. Draw the curve.
2. Locate all values on the curve.
3. Find the Z score from Table A1 using the given percentage.
4. Calculate the mean from the Z formula.

Example 3.16 The standard deviation of a certain product is expected to be 2 oz. (Similar products from the same process have that standard deviation, or that product has had that same standard deviation when run before.) Find what the mean value must be (what the machine setting must be) to ensure that no more than 5% of the items will weigh less than the lower specification of 27.5 oz.

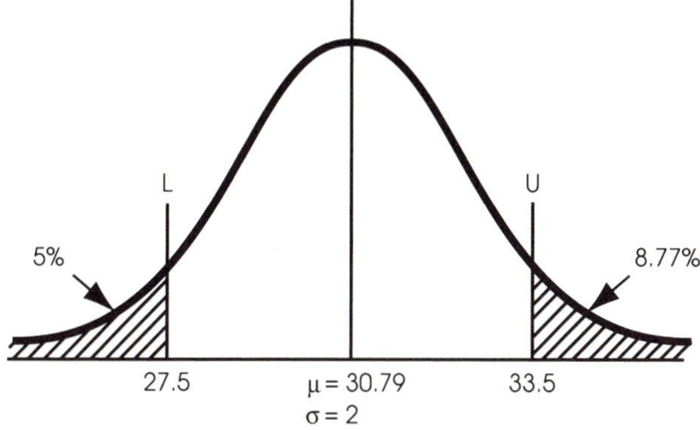

Figure 3.12. Curve illustrating Examples 3.16 and 3.17.

Solution (See Figure 3.12)

$$Z_{0.05} = -1.645 \text{ (from Table A1)}$$

$$Z_{0.05} = (X - \mu)/\sigma = (27.5 - \mu)/2$$

$$\mu = 27.5 + 1.645(2) = 30.79 \text{ oz.}$$

Example 3.17 How does this new mean (30.79 oz.) affect the percent of items above the upper specification limit of 33.5 oz.?

Solution (See Figure 3.12)

$$Z = (33.5 - 30.79)/2 = 2.71/2 = 1.355$$

$$P(Z > 1.355) = 1 - P(Z \leq 1.355) = 1 - 0.9123 = 8.77\%$$

Find the New Mean Given a Maximum Desired Percent of Items Above a Given Upper Specification Limit

The steps are as follows.

1. Draw the curve.
2. Locate all values on the curve.
3. Find the Z score from Table A1 using the given percentage.
4. Calculate the mean from the Z score.

Example 3.18 The standard deviation of a certain product is expected to be 2 oz. Find what the mean value must be (what the machine setting must be) to ensure that no more than 1% of the items will weigh more than 33.5 oz.

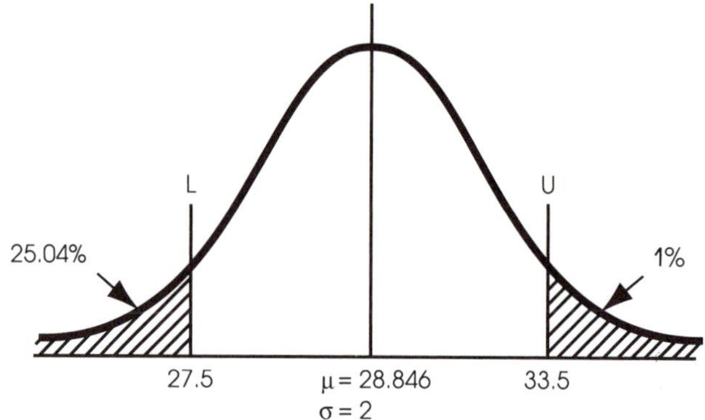

Figure 3.13. Curve illustrating Examples 3.18 and 3.19.

Solution (See Figure 3.13)

$$Z_{1-0.01} = Z_{0.99} = 2.327 \quad \text{(from Table A1)}$$

$$Z_{0.99} = 2.327 = (X - \mu)/\sigma = (33.5 - \mu)/2$$

$$\mu = 33.5 - 2.327(2) = 28.846 \text{ oz.}$$

Example 3.19 How does this new mean of 28.846 affect the percent below the lower limit of 27.5 oz?

Solution (See Figure 3.13):

$$Z = (X - \mu)/\sigma = (27.5 - 28.846)/2 = -0.673$$

$$P(Z \leq -0.673) = 25.04\%$$

Example 3.20 Using the data from Table 3.1, and assuming that the mean of 1.06315 and the standard deviation of 0.0075 are universe values, solve the seven normal curve analysis questions for an upper limit of 1.082 and a lower limit of 1.054. Although, technically, the student's t is the correct distribution to use here (when a sample size is available), at a sample size of 100, the t and Z distributions are essentially identical.

Solution

1. The percent of items likely to be below 1.054 is (see Figure 3.14)

$$Z = (X - \mu)/\sigma = (1.054 - 1.06315)/0.0075 = -1.22$$

$$P(Z \leq -1.22) = 0.1112 \text{ or } 11.12\% \quad \text{(Table A1).}$$

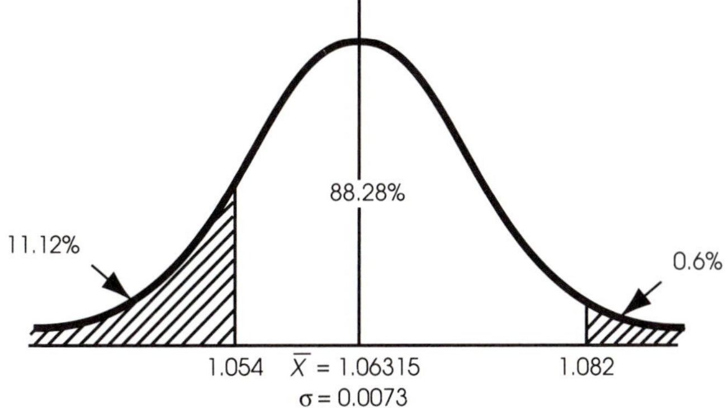

Figure 3.14. Curve illustrating Example 3.20, parts 1, 2, and 3.

2. The percent of items likely to be above 1.082 is (see Figure 3.14)

$$Z = (X - \mu)/\sigma = (1.082 - 1.06315)/0.0075 = 2.51$$

$$P(Z > 2.51) = 1 - P(Z \leq 2.51) = 1 - 0.9940 = 0.6\%$$

3. The percent of items likely to be between the two limits is (see Figure 3.14)

$$0.9940 - 0.1112 = 88.28\%$$

or

$$1 - (0.1112 + 0.006) = 88.28\%$$

4. The new lower limit needed to have no more than 5% of the items measure less than that limit is (see Figure 3.15):

$$Z_{0.05} = -1.645 \quad \text{(Table A1)}$$

$$Z_{0.05} = -1.645 = (X - \mu)/\sigma = (X - 1.06315)/0.0075$$

$$X = 1.06315 + 0.0075(-1.645) = 1.051.$$

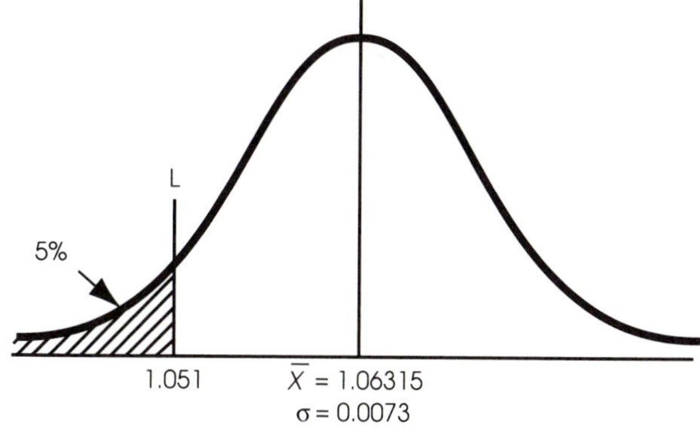

Figure 3.15. Curve illustrating Example 3.20, part 4.

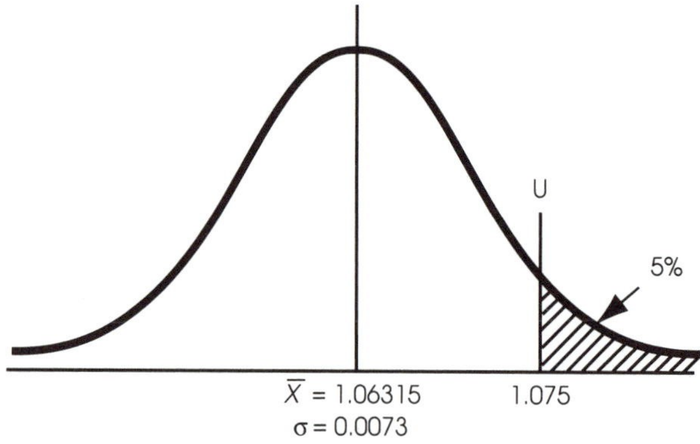

Figure 3.16. Curve illustrating Example 3.20, part 5.

5. The new upper limit needed to have no more than 5% of the items measure more than that limit is (see Figure 3.16)

$$Z_{1-0.05} = Z_{0.095} = +1.645 \quad \text{(Table A1)}$$

$$Z_{0.95} = +1.625 = (X - \mu)/\sigma = (X - 1.06315)/0.0075$$

$$X = 1.06315 + 0.0075(+1.645) = 1.075.$$

6. The new mean needed (the new machine setting) to ensure that no more than 5% of the items will measure less than 1.054 inches is (see Figure 3.17)

$$Z_{0.05} = -1.645 \quad \text{(Table A1)}$$

$$Z_{0.05} = -1.645 = (X - \mu)/\sigma = (-1.054 - \mu)/0.0075$$

$$\mu = 1.054 - 0.0075(-1.645) = 1.066.$$

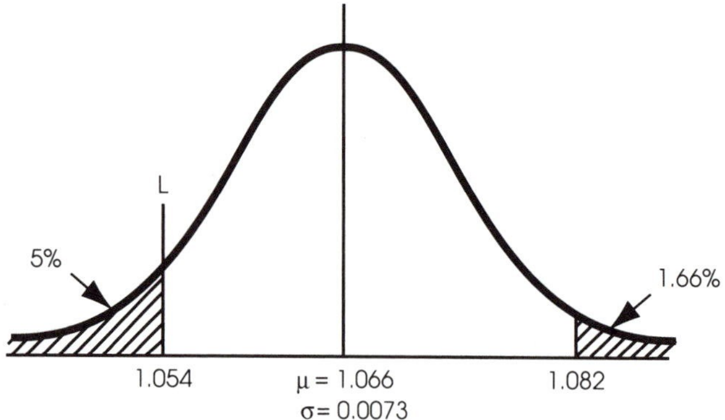

Figure 3.17. Curve illustrating Example 3.20, part 6.

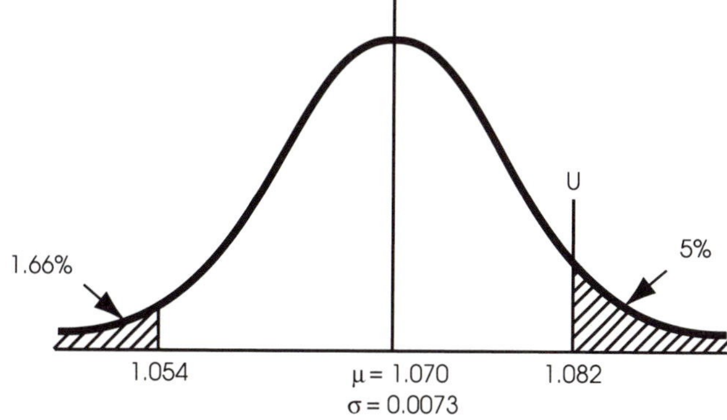

Figure 3.18. Curve illustrating Example 3.20, part 7.

The new percent area above the upper limit of 1.082, with the new mean of 1.066, is

$$Z = (X - \mu)/\sigma = (1.082 - 1.066)/0.0075 = 2.13$$

$$P(Z \leq 2.13) = 0.0166 \text{ or } 1.66\% \text{ (Table A1).}$$

7. The new mean needed (the new machine setting) to ensure that no more than 5% of the items will measure more than 1.082 inches is (see Figure 3.18)

$$Z_{1-0.05} = Z_{0.95} = +1.645 \quad \text{(Table A1)}$$

$$Z_{0.95} = +1.645 = (X - \mu)/\sigma = (1.082 - \mu)/0.0075$$

$$\mu = 1.082 - 0.0075(+1.645) = 1.070.$$

The new percent area below the lower limit of 1.054, with the new mean of 1.070, is

$$Z = (X = \mu)/\sigma = (1.054 - 1.070)/0.0075 = -2.13$$

$$P(Z > -2.13) = 1 - P(Z \leq -2.13) = 1 - 0.9834.$$

$$= 1.66\%$$

3.10 The Normal Curve and Quality Control Charts

All quality control charts are derived from the normal curve. Attributes charts are related to other distributions (the normal curve approximation to the binomial for *p*-type charts and the normal curve approximation to the Poisson for *u* and *c* charts), but are still based on the normal curve theory. Quality control charts are actually just upended normal curves with the center at the mean (μ) of the process and the limits at $\pm 3\sigma$. (In the basic *X*-bar, *R* chart, the real mean of μ is closely

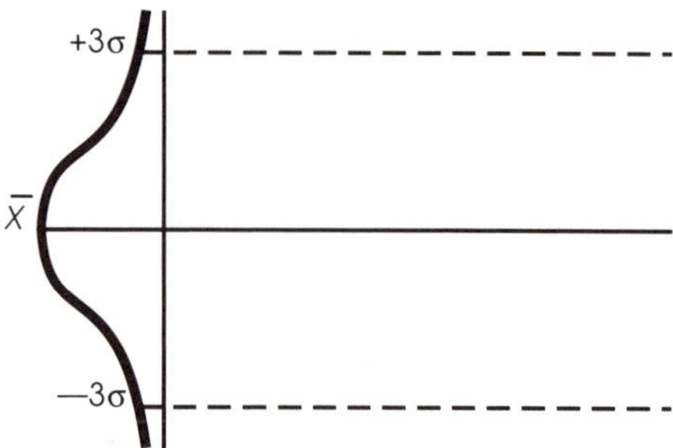

Figure 3.19. Curve illustrating the normal curve relationship to quality control charts.

approximated by X-double-bar, while σ is closely approximated by 3R-bar.) The chart standard deviation is derived from process data, not from engineering specification information. The center and limit lines are extended to form the chart (Figure 3.19). In actual practice, however, the curve is not shown on the charts.

The limit lines in quality control charts, unlike the limits used so far in this chapter, are not specification limits. Control chart limits represent what the process is capable of, and they have no relationship to engineering specification limits. Statistically, control chart limits define an area under the curve within which 99.73% of all subgroup averages (not individual measurements) are supposed to measure. There is such a small probability that a unit will measure outside these lines that it is assumed, for purposes of control, that any subgroup average which does measure outside of these lines shows a possible out-of-control condition (a possible assignable, or special, cause).

Therefore, if the mean and limits have been properly determined, and if the process is operating properly, 99.73% of all subgroup (subsample) averages will fall between the limits (only subgroup averages, not individual measurements), and only 0.27% will fall outside of these limits (0.135% above the upper limit and 0.135% below the lower limit). Averages outside these limits are usually assumed to have "assignable," or special, causes (because of the very small chance that they will not).

Only the first three of the seven normal curve analysis questions are needed to derive the control charts (areas above, below, and between the limits). Control charts limits are placed at ± 3 standard deviations from the mean. Thus, there are 6 sigmas (6σ) total between the limits. This is an arbitrary decision based on experience. The area under the curve below the upper limit, at $+3\sigma$, is 0.99865 (from Table A1). The area under the curve below the lower limit, at -3σ, is 0.00135 (from

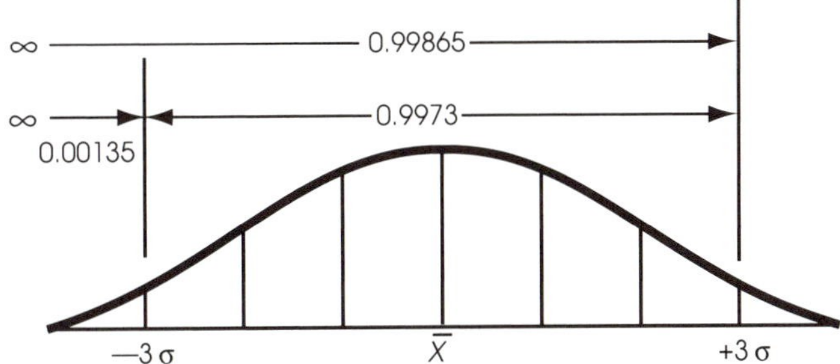

Figure 3.20. Curve illustrating the 6σ relationship to quality control chart limits.

Table A1). Therefore, the area between the two limits is 0.9973, or 99.73% (Figure 3.20).

Control Charts and Normal Curve Analysis

The seven normal curve analyses just performed assume that the information (measurements) used is normally distributed. For most large groups of measurements, this is usually the case, but not always. Unfortunately, there are many times during manufacturing problems when the measurements do not form a normal distribution. In this case, the normal curve analyses just shown will not work, but will provide erroneous answers.

The best way to overcome this problem is to use the distribution of means of small subsamples as explained in the next chapter (in relation to control charts). This distribution (the means of small subsamples of the entire group of measurements) is always normal (or close enough), so that normal curve analyses using this distribution will always give reasonably correct answers. The procedures are identical except that a new mean and standard deviation are used. The mean is now the average of the subsample means (X-double-bar) and the standard deviation is R-bar (the averages of the ranges of the subsamples) divided by d_2 (from the Appendix, Table A3).

One of the best uses of this procedure is to find the optimum mean value (the best machine setting) that will minimize the total cost of defectives (total of scrap and rework). An example of this type of calculation is presented in Chapter 6, "Normal Curve Economic Analysis."

Practice Problems

3–1 From the following list of 100 cereal box weights:

a. construct a frequency distribution showing the number of cells, cell boundaries, cell midpoints, and frequencies;

b. construct a frequency histogram;
c. calculate the mean and standard deviation of the distribution.

1.12	0.81	1.30	1.22	1.00	1.46	1.19	0.72	1.32	1.36
1.81	1.81	1.44	1.69	1.90	1.52	1.66	1.76	1.61	1.55
1.02	2.03	1.67	1.55	1.62	1.79	1.62	1.54	1.48	1.73
1.88	1.43	1.54	1.29	1.37	1.65	1.77	1.43	1.71	1.66
1.94	1.67	1.43	1.61	1.55	1.73	1.42	1.66	1.79	1.77
2.17	1.55	1.12	1.63	1.43	1.63	1.36	1.58	1.79	1.41
1.77	1.44	1.61	1.43	1.61	1.74	1.67	1.72	1.81	1.65
0.82	1.52	1.33	1.57	1.98	1.85	1.63	1.44	1.87	1.69
1.25	1.43	1.55	1.68	1.77	1.68	1.54	1.76	1.64	1.57
1.65	2.15	1.90	1.18	1.60	1.45	1.63	1.85	1.67	1.36

Answers

$C=11$; $i=0.15$; $\overline{X}=1.567$; $s=0.261$; lowest boundary of lowest cell $=0.62$.

3–2 The following table lists the number of failures in 120 samples of a certain electronic component tested for 100 hours each.

a. construct a frequency distribution showing the number of cells, cell boundaries, cell midpoints, and frequencies;
b. construct a frequency histogram;
c. calculate the mean and standard deviation of the distribution.

10	13	13	11	13	8	16	18	13	15
12	13	14	12	13	15	14	13	11	9
13	15	11	13	14	17	10	12	5	15
11	14	12	10	13	11	13	8	14	18
14	13	14	11	14	12	13	11	13	16
13	14	13	14	13	12	14	12	11	15
13	14	11	14	13	10	9	12	11	15
14	11	12	13	14	13	12	13	17	7
12	13	14	13	12	17	13	11	15	16
10	4	8	12	11	7	9	10	6	9
11	15	14	16	17	12	13	16	16	15
15	16	16	13	14	16	6	13	14	16

Answers

$C=14$; $i=1$; $\overline{X}=12.7$; $s=2.6$; lowest boundary of lowest cell = there are no boundaries, individual values only.

3–3 The tensile strength of 100 castings was tested, and the results are listed in the table below.

a. construct a frequency distribution showing the number of cells, cell boundaries, cell midpoints, and frequencies;

b. construct a frequency histogram;
c. calculate the mean and standard deviation of the distribution.

15.1	11.0	5.3	13.3	13.0	10.9	9.4	4.2	12.3	13.0
10.6	6.0	10.6	7.0	10.8	8.0	10.8	8.0	10.9	6.7
9.4	4.8	8.9	9.0	10.1	11.0	10.5	5.7	7.6	16.6
6.0	10.7	7.8	8.9	9.2	12.6	16.7	7.9	9.5	15.8
8.6	6.6	16.7	7.1	11.5	15.9	9.5	15.8	8.4	14.2
12.3	13.9	9.3	13.7	7.0	10.8	8.7	7.6	6.5	15.4
14.9	9.3	13.0	10.0	10.1	11.2	12.0	10.9	9.2	12.6
16.1	11.5	15.2	12.6	16.4	14.0	10.1	11.2	12.6	16.5
9.6	6.3	16.8	6.1	10.5	15.5	11.5	9.8	11.4	14.2
12.1	13.1	11.3	10.7	8.2	10.8	8.7	9.6	7.1	13.7

Answers

$C=11$; $i=1.3$; $\overline{X}=10.81$; $s=3.12$; lowest boundary of lowest cell $=3.4$.

3–4 A worker makes 12 trips to load a truck. The time of each trip, in minutes, is: 12.6, 13.7, 18.2, 8.3, 8.1, 10.0, 11.9, 14.0, 12.6, 12.6, 9.7, and 14.5. What is the mean and standard deviation?

Answers

12.2; 2.87

3–5 What is the mean and standard deviation of: 12, 11, 10, 12, 17, 21, 13, 13, 12, and 9?

Answer

13; 3.53

3–6 The following table shows the number of failures in 19 tests of a certain product.

a. construct a frequency distribution;
b. construct a frequency histogram;
c. calculate the mean and standard deviation of the distribution.

NUMBER OF FAILURES

3, 3, 5, 6, 7, 9, 6, 5, 6, 5, 6, 9, 7, 6, 7, 7, 6, 7, and 9.

Answers

$C=5$; $\overline{X}=6.26$; $s=1.69$

3–7 What is the mean and standard deviation of the following data?

X	f
2.4	7
2.7	11
3.0	20
3.3	15
3.6	14
3.9	6

Answer
3.148; 0.428

3–8 What is the mode of the data in 2–4? 2–5?

Answer
12.6; 12

3–9 What is the median of the data in 2–1? 2–3?

Answer
12.6; 12

3–10 What is the median of the data in 2–4? 2–5?

Answer
12.25; 12

3–11 The mean is 1.567 and the standard deviation is 0.261. Find:
a. the percentage of items expected to measure below 1.20;
b. the percentage of items expected to measure above 2.10;
c. the percentage of items expected to measure between 1.20 and 2.10.

Answers
7.99%; 2.06%; 89.95%

3–12 The mean is 12.7 and the standard deviation is 2.6. Find:
a. the percentage of items expected to measure below 10;
b. the percentage of items expected to measure above 20;
c. the percentage of items expected to measure between 10 and 20.

Answers
14.96%; 0.25%; 84.79%

3–13 The mean is 10.81 and the standard deviation is 3.12. Find:
a. the percentage of items expected to measure below 5.0;
b. the percentage of items expected to measure above 15.0;
c. the percentage of items expected to measure between 5.0 and 15.0.

Answers
8.96%; 3.13%; 87.91%

3–14 The mean is 3.148 and the standard deviation is 0.428. Find:
a. the percentage of items expected to measure below 2.3;
b. the percentage of items expected to measure above 4.1;
c. the percentage of items expected to measure between 2.3 and 4.1.

Answers
2.37%; 1.30%; 96.33%

3–15 The mean is 1.567 and the standard deviation is 0.261. Find:
a. the necessary lower specification limit if no more than 5% of the items can measure below that limit;
b. the necessary upper specification limit if no more than 2% of the items can measure above that limit.

Answers
1.14; 2.10.

3–16 The mean is 12.7 and the standard deviation is 2.6. Find:
a. the necessary lower specification limit if no more than 3% of the items can measure below that limit;
b. the necessary upper specification limit if no more than 1% of the items can measure above that limit.

Answers
8; 19.

3–17 The mean is 10.81 and the standard deviation is 3.12. Find:
a. the necessary lower specification limit if no more than 1% of the items can measure below that limit;
b. the necessary upper specification limit if no more than 4% of the items can measure above that limit.

Answers
3.6; 16.3.

3–18 The mean is 3.148 and the standard deviation is 0.428. Find:
a. the necessary lower specification limit if no more than 5% of the items can measure below that limit;
b. the necessary upper specification limit if no more than 5% of the items can measure above that limit.

Answers
2.4; 3.9.

3–19 The mean is 1.567 and the standard deviation is 0.261. Find:
a. the new mean needed for no more than 5% to measure below the lower specification limit of 1.2;
b. the percent above the upper specification of 2.1, for the new mean of part (a) of this problem.

Answers
1.629; 3.55%

3–20 The mean is 1.567 and the standard deviation is 0.261. Find:
a. the new mean needed for no more than 2% to measure above the upper specification limit of 2.1;
b. the percent below the lower specification of 1.2, for the new mean of part (a) of this problem.

Answers
1.564; 8.14%

3–21 The mean is 12.7 and the standard deviation is 2.6. Find:
a. the new mean needed for no more than 3% to measure below the lower specification limit of 10;
b. the percent above the upper specification of 20, for the new mean of part (a) of this problem.

Answers
14.89; 2.47%

3–22 The mean is 1.27 and the standard deviation is 2.6. Find:
a. the new mean needed for no more than 1% to measure above the upper specification limit of 20;
b. the percent below the lower specification of 10, for the new mean of part (a) of this problem.

Answers
13.95; 6.44%

3–23 The mean is 10.81 and the standard deviation is 3.12. Find:
a. the new mean needed for no more than 1% to measure below the lower specification limit of 5;
b. the percent above the upper specification of 15, for the new mean of part (a) of this problem.

Answers
12.26; 18.99%

3–24 The mean is 10.81 and the standard deviation is 3.12. Find:

a. the new mean needed for no more than 4% to measure above the upper specification limit of 15;
b. the percent below the lower specification of 5, for the new mean of part (a) of this problem.

Answers

9.53; 7.32%

3–25 The mean is 3.148 and the standard deviation is 0.428. Find:

a. the new mean needed for no more than 5% to measure below the lower specification limit of 2.3;
b. the percent above the upper specification of 4.1, for the new mean of part (a) of this problem.

Answers

3.00; 0.51%

3–26 The mean is 3.148 and the standard deviation is 0.428. Find:

a. the new mean needed for no more than 5% to measure above the upper specification limit of 4.1;
b. the percent below the lower specification of 2.3, for the new mean of part (a) of this problem.

Answers

3.40; 0.51%

CHAPTER 4 BASIC CONTROL CHARTS

In this chapter, the theory and use of quality control charts (in general) and the basic control charts (in particular) are developed. Special control charts—for short production runs, nonmanufacturing, etc.—will be covered in Chapter 5.

Objectives

1. Understand the basic theory of, and the steps in construction and use of, the various types of control charts.
2. Be able to select a proper control chart quality characteristic.
3. Be able to develop a proper control chart quality plan.
4. Be able to select a proper control chart.
5. Be able to choose a proper control chart sample (or subgroup) size.
6. Be able to collect the proper control chart data.
7. Be able to determine the trial control limits and chart midpoint (or chart centerline).
8. Be able to determine the revised control limits and chart midpoint (or chart centerline).
9. Be able to construct the revised control chart.
10. Be able to continue to use the chart.
11. Construct and interpret the basic X-bar, R control chart.
12. Construct and interpret the basic X-bar, s control chart.
13. Construct and interpret the run chart.
14. Construct and interpret the basic p chart.
15. Construct and interpret the basic u chart.
16. Construct and interpret the basic c chart.

4.1 Control Chart Theory and Use

A control chart is a graphical display of a measure of a quality characteristic (weight, length, temperature, waiting time, etc.) over time. The measurement of the characteristic is plotted on the vertical axis, with the sample number (also called subgroup, subsample, or just sample number) on the horizontal axis. The time that the sample was taken should also be recorded so that the sample number can give information to the operator and management about problems as they occur. A central value—the process mean—is usually plotted as a horizontal solid line and upper and lower control limits as horizontal dotted lines (see Figure 3.17). Some analysts like to reverse this procedure and plot the limit lines as solid with the central line dotted. Patterns in the chart-plotted values are used to evaluate the process (see Chapter 6).

All quality control charts have a midpoint (or centerline) which corresponds to the process average (the mean of the normal distribution; the μ of Chapter 3), and an upper and lower limit which correspond to $\pm$ three standard deviations ($\pm\ 3\sigma$) from this midpoint. How these chart values are determined will be explained later in this chapter for each basic chart, and in Chapter 5 for each specialized chart.

Symbols are used in the charts as a shorthand means of conveying information. A bar above a symbol, such as $\overline{X}$ (pronounced "X-bar") means "the average of" (X-bar, then, means the average of the X's). Two bars above a symbol, such as $\overline{\overline{X}}$, (pronounced "X-double-bar") means the average of the averages (X-double-bar, then, means "the average of the X-bars"). Other symbols, for each chart, will be explained as each chart is presented.

Control charts are usually used quite extensively at the beginning of a new program, process, or product for all important operations and/or product characteristics, and are then removed as they are found to be unnecessary (sometimes control charts are maintained far past their normal usefulness for the psychological effect on the operators—they like to see tangible evidence of their good work). The number of control charts usually decreases until the process stabilizes. As process knowledge increases, the number of variables control charts tends to increase while the number of attributes control charts tends to decrease. Also, control information on number and types of control charts being used should be maintained by quality management.

There are at least 27 different types of control charts, divided into two categories: control charts for variables and control charts for attributes. Attributes control charts are further divided into two categories: attributes control charts for defective units, and attributes control charts for defects (per unit). This chapter will present the basic control charts (the ones that are used the most, and from which all other charts are derived), while Chapter 5 will analyze the specialized control charts (for special applications).

In quality control, a variable refers to a continuous characteristic (length, width, temperature, hardness, etc.), while an attribute is a discrete characteristic (number of items not in conformance to specifications). A continuous characteristic can, theoretically, take on any value (there can be, theoretically, an infinite number of possible measurements between 1 and 2, 2 and 3, etc.), while a discrete characteristic, as far as quality control is concerned, is a counting number only (1, 2, 3, etc.). It is the actual measurements (actually, averages of subgroups of these measurements) or some coded variation of them that are plotted on the variables charts. In attributes charts, it is the average number of nonconforming items or nonconformances that are charted (in manufacturing, a nonconformance is usually called a defective).

All variables charts, except for zero-base coding charts, must chart only one quality characteristic of one product on the same chart (even with zero-base coding charts, the same characteristic must be measured for the different products charted). Any of the attributes charts (p, u, c, or any variation of these three) can chart a single characteristic, many characteristics, a single characteristic of many products, many characteristics of many products, an entire plant, or labor or administration performance. Attributes charts are much more versatile than variables charts, but variables charts can provide much more definitive information than can any attributes chart. Attributes charts can only provide nonconformance information, i.e., information outside the specification limits, while variables charts can show patterns within the specification limits (see Chapter 6 for a discussion on pattern analysis for quality and process improvement).

In quality control, a defective quality characteristic is called a "defect" or nonconformance. A unit which has at least one defective quality characteristic (at least one defect) is called a "defective," or nonconforming, unit (examples of quality characteristics are: length, weight, color, hardness, etc.). Therefore, a defective (a defective unit) can have many defects. (The terms nonconformance and nonconforming unit are much more meaningful when quality is applied to nonmanufacturing.)

Variables data, or a measurement, can easily be converted into attributes data just by comparing it to the specification limits (any measurement outside the tolerance spread, or specification limits, is defective or nonconforming). It is also possible to convert attributes into variable data (by judging on a scale of 1 to 5, 1 to 10, etc.), but this is much more difficult—so difficult, in fact, that it is almost never done (some nonmanufacturing data are handled this way).

A fundamental principle of SPC (statistical process control) is that the emphasis is on controlling the process, not the product (that is the reason for the word "process" rather than "quality"). If the process is in control, it is much more probable that products produced from that process will also be in control. Thus, application of these charts, as well as all other principles of SPC, requires thorough knowledge and understanding of the processes involved in producing the product. The relationship between product and process, and the way this is used to control product quality, is explained in Chapter 6.

The basic purpose of all quality control charts is to reduce variation. The way they do this is to provide information on the causes of variation so that these causes can be eliminated (or, at least, their effects can be substantially reduced). The first way that variation is reduced is to correct quality problems—to eliminate causes of outside measurements (measurements outside the limits). The second way that variation is reduced is to improve the process—to reduce variation within the control limits so that the limits get closer and closer to the chart central value. The correction of problems, the first variation reduction, is usually accomplished by the operator and/or the immediate supervisor. In process improvement, which is the second variation reduction scheme, where the limits are moved closer and closer to the center, top management must get involved (top management can also get involved in correcting problems, but usually doesn't). The relation between control charts and these two variation reduction activities (corrective action and process improvement) is thoroughly examined in Chapter 6.

In addition to reducing variation, attributes charts can also be used to supply control information to management (percent defectives per process, per product, per plant, etc.). Attributes control charts, then, have two broad purposes. The first is to provide overall quality information to management (percent defectives for a particular process, for an entire product line, for an entire plant, etc.). If this is the purpose of the chart, it can record any kind of defect and/or defective for as many products as desired. No (or very little) breakdown of the information would be required (types and kinds of defects, etc.).

The second purpose of attributes control charts, however, is much more definitive; it is to provide information for the correction of problems and the improvement of quality. When this purpose is paramount, the charts must be much more carefully designed. Careful breakdowns of defectives and defects by type and causes must be designed into the procedures and into the charts (see Figure 4.7). In fact, in this type of approach, the attributes chart would be used more like a variables chart—with one chart covering only one operation of one process, and types of defects that caused the defective shown on the chart (to provide information for analysis, correction and improvement). This type of chart (see Figure 4.7) contains an organized type of information that allows for an almost automatic Pareto analysis (see Chapter 2 for a discussion of Pareto analyses). Corrective action type attributes charts are usually limited to those characteristics that either cannot be measured or are too costly to measure.

Long process times present an especially difficult problem for attributes charts. When process times are long, it just takes too long for an attributes chart to signal a possible out-of-control situation. Also, when process times are very long, each subgroup may take more than one day to complete. In this case, it is preferable, if possible, to use one day's production as the subgroup size (people usually have a difficult time remembering what happened more than one day at a time).

There are two problems with using one day's production as the sample size. First, a variable subgroup size, or average subgroup size, will have to be used (it would be very rare that one day's production would be the same size every day). Second, one day's production may not be large enough to constitute an acceptable subgroup size, so that too many of the samples would be likely to have zero defectives (and thus destroy the statistical viability of the chart). However, the nature of attributes charts is such that they can usually still be effectively used (still indicate problems and often even the nature of the problems) even though they are violating statistical theory. However, they must be used, in such situations, with the utmost care.

Usually, when the charts are started, the process average (% defective) will be so high that one day's production will constitute an acceptable subgroup size. Then, as the chart progresses, the process average reduces to such an extent that one day's production is no longer adequate. However, by that time, the process average is usually so low that, in order to continue process improvement activities, every defective must now be examined. At that point, the chart becomes more a recording device for defectives and their causes than a true statistical chart. Thus, it can be continued with the one day's production as the sample size, even though it violates statistical theory. Actually, according to theory, the chart may even be able to be removed at this point, although it is usually best to keep it up so that production personnel can have a visible reminder, and proof, of their good work (in the improvement of quality).

When using one day's production as a sample (or subgroup) size, all production for that day is inspected (100% inspection). Thus, at the start of such a chart, the chart would not really be a statistical sampling chart (see Section 5.11). Instead, it would record the results of a 100% inspection (although all statistical chart procedures would be used as if it were a regular statistical control chart). Later, as the process improves and the percent defective decreases, a sampling procedure using MIL-STD-105E can be instituted (one company has done quite well inspecting 25% or 13, whichever is higher, every time a lot reaches the inspector; even though the *p* charts quickly reduced to mostly zeros). At this point, most of the samples would show zero defectives, and the chart would record mostly zero percent defective. This would not be a statistically viable chart, of course, but it can still be useful as a visible record of accomplishment. Also, whenever too many defectives are recorded, too many in accordance to MIL-STD-105E (see Chapter 9), 100% inspection would have to be resumed until the process is brought back into control.

The nine steps in constructing control charts are as follows.

1. Select the quality characteristic.
2. Develop a quality plan.
3. Select the type of control chart.
4. Choose the proper subgroup size.
5. Collect the data.
6. Determine the trial control limits and chart midpoint.
7. Determine the revised control limits and chart midpoint.
8. Construct the revised control chart.
9. Continue to use the chart.

4.2 Step 1: Select the Quality Characteristic

Quality characteristics are chosen for control chart analysis because they are important ones that can affect the performance of the product (critical or major characteristics); or because they are causing, or are central to, a manufacturing or quality problem; or because of contract requirements.

Control charts can be placed at any point where inspections are being performed. These points should be precisely defined by manufacturing flowcharts (see Chapter 2 for flowchart design and use) and the production work order. (Normally, the production work order contains all the details of the production plan and the quality plan. However, each of these plans can be separate documents.) These inspection points are determined, in part at least, by the following important considerations.

- Inspect after operations that are likely to produce defective items to ensure that no more work will be performed on faulty items.
- Inspect before costly operations so that the costly work will not be performed on defective parts.
- Inspect prior to those operations where faulty items are likely to cause production problems (such as breaking or jamming the machine).
- Inspect before operations that might cover up a defect (such as painting, assembly, etc.).
- Inspect before assembly operations that can't be undone (such as welding).
- Inspect first and last pieces on automatic and semiautomatic machines, but rarely in between.

- Inspect before storage.
- Inspect finished products. Remember that the customer is the next inspector, and that a satisfied customer is the best job insurance.
- Use engineering and/or operator judgment to determine when, where, and how to inspect and to use the charts.

4.3 Step 2: Develop the Quality Plan

The purpose of quality planning should be to establish an economic balance between the cost of measurement and the value of the measurement to product acceptance and customer satisfaction. The general rule should be to inspect as little as possible while still ensuring product quality. Quality plans define the inspection/testing points and methods, and they reference specific inspection instructions and acceptance criteria.

Quality plans, along with production plans, are primarily documented on the work order (although they can be separate documents). The work order lists all production steps and inspection points, and references the drawings, specifications, procedures, instructions, and standards that contain information required for production and inspection.

Quality plans should contain as many of the following elements as possible (usually on the work order).

- Identification of the various points in the process flow where the measurements should be taken (see Section 4.2). These "inspection points" should be shown on flowcharts (see Chapter 2 for an explanation of flowchart and use) as well as listed on the work order (or separate quality plan, if used). Control charts are frequently associated with these inspection points.
- The type of measurement to be made and the method used to make the measurement. This can range from a simple visual inspection (for surface defects, color, etc.) to a sophisticated measuring machine with computer interface. Most measurements, however, are made with special measuring tools called gauges. The selection of the proper gauge is important and usually takes special engineering and/or gauge selection training and experience.
- The sample size or, in control chart language, the subgroup or subsample size. This usually refers to the number of individual units to be measured at any one time. Sample size determination will be covered in Section 4.5.
- How often the measurements are to be taken (hourly, every 100 units, four times per day, etc.).
- The mechanism (tool, gauge, etc.) to be used for making the measurement.
- Who makes the measurement (operator, inspector, etc.).

4.4 Step 3: Choose the Type of Control Chart

This step is divided into two sections, i.e., two substeps. Step 3a is concerned with determining which category of chart to use—variables or attributes. In Step 3b, the type of chart is chosen (which variables chart or which attributes chart).

Step 3a: Determine the Category of Chart (Variables or Attributes)

This choice will depend on the nature of the measurement and the cost involved. If the characteristic to be controlled is unmeasurable, such as color, surface defects, etc., only an attributes chart can be used. If a great many characteristics need control, it may be too costly to use variables charts because each variables chart can normally be used with only one characteristic at a time and, therefore, each characteristic must have its own variables chart. A single attributes chart can be used in place of all the possible variables charts because each measurement can be classified as good or bad, with the unit being rejected if any one of the characteristics is found to be nonconforming. This can greatly reduce the cost of controlling all of these characteristics.

However, attributes charts have several disadvantages not shared by variables charts. First, although they can provide hints and even fairly strong evidence of possible causes of nonconformance, they seldom provide the detailed information often needed for a complete solution. They can never, for instance, provide information on the process patterns that occur between the specification limits; it takes a variables chart to do this. Second, they do not react to process changes until after the changes occur and the process is out of control. Variable charts, on the other hand, indicate shifts and potential problems before defects are actually produced, i.e., before the process deteriorates to an out-of-control status (see Chapter 6). Finally, they seldom provide the definitive information needed for good process improvement programs. Mostly this is because of the lack of in-control patterns from measurements that fall between the specification limits (which are, of course, provided by variables charts only).

In general, variables data can easily be converted into attributes data (any item that measures outside the specifications is defective), but it is much more difficult to convert attributes data into variables data. Attributes can be converted into variables by use of an interval scale (judge the effectiveness, or "degree" of quality, on a scale of 1 to 10, for instance); but this practice is seldom necessary or useful (except occasionally in the use of SPC for nonmanufacturing or service processes). Even when used, its effectiveness is suspect because of the subjective "judgment" that must be employed. Interval scale "judgments" require a great deal of training so that all inspectors involved will be judging from the same base, i.e., the same perspectives and understandings. Definitions of each scale interval (for instance, what constitutes a 1, a 2, a 3, etc.) must be understood the same way by all (see Section 5.4 for an example of a variables chart using attributes data).

The following summary presents some general guidelines for determining what type of chart to use.

1. The variables chart.
   - Installing a new process or product or changing an old process or product.
   - The process is obviously in trouble; it cannot produce to the tolerances on a consistent basis.
   - Destructive or expensive testing is being used.
   - Sampling further along in the manufacturing process can be reduced by a more positive control at an earlier stage.
   - Attributes control charts have shown a problem to exist but the solution is difficult or unknown.
   - There are difficult problem processes with tight specifications, overlapping assembly tolerances, expensive materials, etc.
   - When large subgroup sizes are desired (greater than 8) and a variables chart is indicated, use X-bar,s. When a variables chart is indicated but the characteristic is not critical enough to warrant a large subsample size, use X-bar,R.
   - The critical characteristic is measurable.
   - Customer and/or contract requirements.
2. The attributes chart.
   - Operators have a high degree of control over assignable causes.
   - Assembly operations are complex.
   - Quality can only be measured in terms of good or bad, or measurement data are otherwise unobtainable.
   - Historical information is needed for management review (an overall management control device).
   - Many characteristics must be measured at one time.
   - Cost of measurement is high.
   - Production runs are large.

Step 3b: Choose the Type of Chart to Use (Type of Variables Chart or Type of Attributes Chart)

Once it is determined which category of chart to use (variables or attributes), the actual chart to be used must be chosen (which variables chart or which attributes chart, as the case may be). This requires a knowledge and understanding of what each chart is, what it can do, and where it can be used. Frequently, more than one chart can be effectively used in any one situation, and the choice of which one to finally use is often due as much to individual taste as to any theoretical consideration.

Variables Control Charts

Following is a list of the different types of variables control charts, along with a description of the chart and an explanation of the conditions under which each one may be used.

1. ***X*-bar,*R* charts** (see Section 4.11). The average (*X*-bar) and range *(R)* of periodic small samples are plotted and evaluated. Each small sample consists of successive units produced. This variables chart is used to control characteristics where small sample sizes (4 to 10, but usually 4 or 5) can be used so that sample cost can be minimized. This is probably the most used of all variables charts. It is the most basic of all variables charts, and thus forms the model for most other charts. (It is recommended that a subgroup size of 4 be used.)
2. ***X*-bar,*s*** (see Section 4.12). Identical to *X*-bar,*R* except that the standard deviation *(s)* of each sample is used in place of the range *(R)*. This variables chart is used to control critical characteristics where the cost of sample error is large. Larger sample sizes (greater than 10) must be chosen, and the choice must be carefully made to balance the cost of sampling with the cost of possible sample error.
3. ***X*-bar,*R* charts using zero-base coding** (see Section 5.1). The same as *X*-bar,*R* except that a coded value is plotted in place of each *X*-bar and each *R* (the averages and ranges of the differences between each measurement and its specification midpoint are plotted and evaluated, instead of the averages and ranges of the actual measurements). This procedure allows for the use of more than one product per chart for evaluating processes where the run sizes are small (quality control charts evaluate and control "processes," not products—it is assumed that products produced from properly controlled processes are most likely to be in conformance with specifications). This chart is probably the best one to use for short production runs. (It is recommended that the subgroup size be 4.)
4. **Moving average** (see Section 5.2). The same as the *X*-bar,*R* chart except that, instead of using individual subgroups of successive units produced, a moving average (*X*-bar) and a moving range *R* are calculated from individual measurements (only one measurement is made periodically instead of 4 or more successive ones). This chart is used where measurement of successive units produced would be impractical (chemical processes, for instance), or where variation in successive measurements are so tiny they are unmeasurable (bottling plants, for instance), or where run sizes are small or process times are large, or where automated testing is used, or where most errors are likely to be test errors. Although, theoretically, any subgroup size may be used, in actual practice only a subgroup size of three is used, in order to preserve the observed variation (the larger the subgroup size used to calculate the moving averages, the more the variations in the process are smoothed over by the moving averaging procedure). The subgroup is the present measurement plus the two previous ones.

5. **Moving average using zero-base coding** (see Section 5.3). This chart is identical to the zero-base chart explained above (in the zero-base coding with X-bar,R chart), except that moving averages are used in place of X-bar,R. It is used for very small run sizes, or where measurements of successive units are impractical. The subgroup is the present measurement plus the two previous ones.
6. **Charts using converted attributes data** (see Section 5.4). Both X-bar,R and moving average charts can be used for attributes data which have been converted to variables data (estimate the degree of nonconformance on a scale of 1–10, 1–100, etc., using the judgment of the inspector). The possible effectiveness of these kinds of charts for production data is dubious (due to the need for judgment on the part of the inspector). However, converted attributes data have been used with some success in controlling nonmanufacturing processes. Only converted moving average charts will be shown.
7. **Pre-Control** (see Section 5.5). The tolerance band on this chart is divided into five zones: a central target zone bounded by two cautionary zones, which in turn are bounded by two reject zones. The chart center is the specification midpoint, and the specification (tolerance) spread determines the location and extent of the five zones (the center, target, area is one-half the specification spread and the specification limits form the boundaries of the two cautionary zones). The chart is frequently colored for ease of analysis, with the center portion (target area) colored green, the two cautionary areas colored yellow, and the two reject zones colored red (in this form, it is called a stop-light chart). Special rules are used to determine when the process needs adjusting. This allows a control procedure to be instituted immediately without waiting for data to be gathered. This chart can be used for short production runs, or for ongoing, long-run, products where the worker has a great deal of control. Although great for control, this variables chart cannot be used for process analysis and improvement.
8. **Trend charts** (see Section 5.6). Used for processes where wear is an integral part of the process (such as tool wear). The center and limit lines slope up (or down), necessitating the use of regression formulas for their computation. In the case of tool wear, the chart can also be used for determining optimum tool replacement policies. It is recommended that only a subgroup size of 4 be used.
9. **Charts using individual values** (see Section 5.7). Only one measurement is made at a time, and each individual measurement is used, and plotted, as if it were a subgroup average. This variables chart can be used in situations where only one measurement at a time can be done (certain chemical processes, for instance), where most errors are likely to be measurement errors, where automated measurement is used, or where production run times are long (days, weeks, etc.). It cannot be used if the process is not normally distributed (other charts control on sample averages, instead of only single measurements, and thus assure a relatively normal distribution).
10. **Charts using specification limits** (see Section 5.8). In this variables

chart, the specification limits are used as control limits, so that charting can begin at the start of the process. Although this chart has the advantage of instantaneous start-up, it also has two serious disadvantages. First, if the process is not centered on the specification midpoint, the chart can be misleading, i.e., it can show a problem where none exists, or not show one that does exist. Second, the limits do not show process improvements. This chart can be useful at the beginning of a product run but should be replaced as soon as possible with one of the more traditional charts (such as the zero-base chart for short production runs, or the basic X-bar,R chart for longer runs). This chart can also be used for short production runs, although the zero-base coding charts are usually more effective for short runs. A subgroup size of 4 is recommended.

11. **Run charts** (see Section 4.13). This is not a statistical chart like all the others. It is just a chart with the sample means plotted to show trends—the central value and limits are *not* calculated (although a central value of sorts can be approximated by drawing a horizontal line through the center of the plotted points with an equal number of points on either side). This chart is used at the start of a process, product, or measurement in order to show trends and to provide for a measure of control until regular statistical charts can be constructed. (The run chart can also be used with individual measurements.)
12. **Constant limit X-bar** (not covered in this book). Plots the number of average deviations from the mean (X-bar) rather than the average measurements (using a rather complex formula for each plot). The limits are constants that are determined solely by the sample size. Used for short production runs and for charting more than one product on the same chart, as in the zero-base charts. However, this chart has disadvantages that the zero-base charts do not, including: complex calculations for each plot, no way to calculate process capability indices, and the chart limits do not show process improvements. Because of these disadvantages, it is not included in this book.
13. **Charts for large sample sizes** (not covered in this book). Used when the sample size is greater than 30. Special procedures are used to determine the control limits. This chart has such limited use that it is not included in this book (see Montgomery, 1985 for a description of this chart).
14. **Multivariate charts.** Used for controlling two or more interrelated characteristics at the same time, and on the same chart. It is for very complex and difficult calculations. This chart has such limited use, and is so difficult to use, that it is not included in this book (see Montgomery, 1985 for a description of this chart).

Attributes Control Charts for Defectives

Following is a list of the different types of attributes control charts for defectives (defective units), along with a description of the chart and an explanation of the conditions under which each one may be used.

These kinds of charts are called *p* charts, or some kind of *p*. Subgroup sizes for *p* charts must be calculated (see Section 4.5, step 4).

1. **The constant sample size *p* chart—The basic *p* chart** (see Section 4.14). Also called the fraction defective chart, this chart is used to control defective units, not defects per unit. The *p* is the fraction defective, or process average, and is the plotted value. This is the basic attributes chart that is used the most. It is used to control ongoing, long-term production and is usually difficult to use with short production runs, long process times, or other special cases. Most special cases require one or more of the special *p* chart adaptations listed below (or found in Chapter 5).
2. **The 100*p* chart.** This is not an actual chart of its own, but is just the *p* chart converted to percentages. The central value, control limits, and each plotted value *(p)* are multiplied by 100. This is the form of the *p* chart that is used most because most people understand percentages so much better than they do decimal fractions. This "percentage" chart can be used with any of the *p* charts (and is the form of the *p* chart that is used in the examples in this text). The 100*p*—the percentage—is usually limited to the closest decimal point.
3. **The *np* chart** (see Section 5.9). The actual number of defectives in the sample (a whole number) is plotted, rather than a fraction or percentage. Used mostly to facilitate operator understanding.
4. **The variable sample size *p* chart** (see Section 5.10). In this chart, the subgroup (sample) sizes are not constant (not the same for every sample). Therefore, the control limits do not form a straight line as they do in constant sample size charts. Each sample (subgroup) has its own control limits. The variable *p* chart is good for short production runs and long process times where only counted data are available. Subgroup sizes are usually determined by production runs or by the amount available to count.
5. **The average *p* chart** (see Section 5.11). This chart is identical to the variable *p* chart, except that an average sample size is used to determine the control limits so that the limits will form a straight line. Theoretically, this chart can only be used if the various sample sizes (subgroup sizes) are within 10% of each other, although this limit is often exceeded in actual practice (the chart is often used quite successfully even when the sample size, subgroup size, differences are considerably greater than 10%).
6. **The weighted *p* chart; using a constant sample (subgroup) size** (see Section 5.12). The counts of each type of defective are adjusted by weights, so that more important types of defectives are given special consideration. Used for constant subgroup sizes. Especially useful for nonmanufacturing applications.
7. **The weighted average *p* chart; using a variable sample (subgroup) size** (see Section 5.12). Identical to the weighted *p* chart, except that an average subgroup (sample) size is used in the computations. Used with vari-

able subgroup sizes. Especially useful for nonmanufacturing applications.

8. **The constant limit *p* chart** (not covered in this book). Plots the number of standard deviations from the mean, instead of the actual counts. The limits are always constant at +3 and −3. The sample (subgroup) sizes must also be constant. However, it has two big disadvantages: complex calculations for each plot, and the chart limits do not show process improvements. This chart is not included in this book.

Attributes Control Charts for Defects

Following is a list of the different types of attributes control charts for defects (defects per unit), along with a description of the chart and an explanation of the conditions under which each one may be used. These types of charts are called *u* charts, except when the subgroup size is 1 (then it is called a c chart). The sizes of *u* chart subgroups are determined by calculation (see Section 4.5, step 4). Of course, c charts *always* use a subgroup size of 1.

1. **The constant sample size *u* chart—The basic *u* chart** (see Section 4.15). Also called the average defect per unit chart, this chart is used to control defects (or errors) per unit, not defective units. The *u* is the average defects per unit and is the plotted value. Just like the *p* chart, this chart is used to control ongoing, long-term production and, like the *p* chart, is usually difficult to use with short production runs, long process times, and other special cases. These cases require one or more of the special *u* chart adaptations listed below (and in Chapter 5).
2. **The variable sample size *u* chart** (see Section 5.13). As in all variable sample size charts, the subgroup (sample) sizes in this chart are not constant (not the same for every sample). Therefore, the control limits do not form a straight line as they do in constant sample size charts; each sample (subgroup) has its own control limits. This chart can be used for short production runs and long process times where measurements are not possible, nor desirable. Variable sample sizes (variable subgroup sizes) depend mostly on the production run and/or the amount available to count.
3. **The average sample size *u* chart** (see Section 5.14). The same as the variable *u* chart (sample sizes are not constant), except that an average sample size is used to determine the control limits so that the limits will form a straight line. Theoretically, the sample sizes must be within 10% of each other but, as with the average *p* chart, this 10% limit is often successfully exceeded in actual practice.
4. **The weighted *u* chart; using a constant sample (subgroup) size** (see Section 5.15). The counts of each type of defect are adjusted by weights, so that more important defect types are given more attention. It is used with constant subgroup sizes only; and it is especially useful for nonmanufacturing applications.
5. **The weighted average *u* chart; using a variable sample (subgroup) size**

(see Section 5.15). Identical to the weighted *u* chart, except that an average subgroup (sample) size is used in the computations. It is used with variable subgroup sizes only; and it is especially useful for nonmanufacturing applications.

6. **The constant limit *u* chart** (not covered in this book). Plots the number of standard deviations from the mean, instead of the actual counts. The limits are always constant at +3 and −3. The sample (subgroup) sizes must also be constant. However, it has two big disadvantages: complex calculations for each plot, and chart limits that do not show process improvements (in the other charts, the limits get closer and closer to the chart midpoint as the process improves). This chart is not included in this book.
7. **The basic *c* chart** (see Section 4.16). The *c* chart is a special case of the *u* chart, where the sample (subgroup) size is always one (one unit). Also called the defect per unit chart (there can be no average size sample when the sample size is always 1), it is used for very large and very critical products. The *c* is the defects per unit and is the plotted value.
8. **The weighted *c* chart** (see Section 5.16). The counts of each type of defect are adjusted by weights, so that more important types of defects are given special attention. It is especially useful for nonmanufacturing applications.
9. **The constant limit *c* chart** (not covered in this book). Plots the number of standard deviations from the mean, instead of the actual counts. The limits are always constant at +3 and −3. Its one big advantage is that it can be used for short production runs. However, it has two big disadvantages: complex calculations for each plot, and chart limits that do not show process improvements. This chart is not included in this book.

4.5 Step 4: Choose the Rational (Proper) Sample Size

Actually, there are two sample sizes involved in control charts: the total sample size needed to start up the chart, and the subgroup size. The total start-up sample size normally used is 25 subgroups. Thus, if the subgroup size is 4, the total start-up sample size is 100. In order to be statistically viable, the start-up sample size should consist of 100 or more measurements or observations (some special charts do use less, which is one reason they should be used with care).

The subgroup size is the amount measured at one time, and should be measured consecutively as produced, if possible (if this is not possible, the period-of-time method can be used). Subgroups are also statistical samples but are called subgroups (and sometimes subsamples) so as not to confuse them with the total start-up sample. The actual size of the sample depends on the analysis method being used, the production run size, the amount available to count, and/or on cost and time considerations. In actual practice, the subgroup is usually called just the sample or sample size after the initial start up is completed.

Sampling Frequency

A good rule of thumb to use for determining sample size and sampling frequency for variables data is adapted from MIL-STD-414. In general, the number to be inspected per lot is as follows:

Lot Size	Percentage
1. 60–300	10%
2. 301–1000	5%
3. 1001–5000	2%
4. Over 5000	1%

Normally, a lot size is considered to be one day's production; however, this can be expanded to as much as one week under special circumstances. The main reason for limiting the lot size to one day's production is to facilitate process analysis and assignable cause identification. People tend to forget the details of what happened after more than one day has transpired.

For a daily production of 200 (using the above rule of thumb), 20 units should be inspected each day. If the subgroup size is to be 4, there should then be a minimum of 5 samples of 4 measured and recorded per day. The 5 subgroups, of course, must be taken at random, or as random as possible. Remember, however, that the subgroup sample (in this case, 4) should be measured consecutively as produced, not randomly (if this is not possible, of course, the samples can then be measured using the period-of-time method). The reason for this is that the sampling time is often critical to correction and/or improvement procedures. The conclusions reached via this logic can, and often should, be adjusted by management to satisfy other considerations (inspection and product cost, product worth, product and characteristic importance, production schedules, degree of production disruption caused by the measurement process, etc.).

Variables Charts Sample Sizes

The following list shows the total start-up sample size and subgroup size normally used with each type of variables chart.

1. ***X*-bar,*R*** (see Section 4.11). Normally, 25 subgroups of 4 or 5 are used (usually 4) for a total start-up sample size of 100 or 125. Although it is possible to use larger subgroup sizes than 4 or 5 (the tables actually go from 2 to 25), it is dangerous to do so. The reason for this is that range calculations ignore all data between the high and low values. For small subgroup sizes, this is not too important because there are not too many in-between values to ignore (for a subgroup of 4, for instance, only 2 measurements per subgroup are ignored in the determination of the standard deviation; while in a subgroup of 20, 18 measurements are ignored). Although there are good theoretical reasons for not using a subgroup of less than 4, subgroup sizes of 2 are used when inspection

costs are extremely high and/or inspection destroys the product (tensile strength, for instance). Actually, a good rule of thumb for X-bar,R charts is to always use subgroup size 4 (except for the special cases already explained). A subgroup size of 5 has been used extensively in the past because certain mathematical tricks can be used to simplify manual calculations (hand calculators and computers now make this unnecessary). This is the most often used variables control chart.

2. **X-bar,s** (see Section 4.12). For a very critical characteristic, it may be desirable to use larger subgroup sizes for control (the larger the sample, the less chance of sample error). In this case, the X-bar,s chart is more desirable. The X-bar,s chart will usually be used for subsample sizes of 8 or more, depending on tradeoffs between sample cost and desired quality (this is a management decision, of course). The total start-up sample size will then be 25 subgroups. For a subgroup size of 10, the total start-up sample size will be 250 (10×25); for a subgroup size of 20, the start-up sample size will be 500 (20×25). A good rule of thumb for X-bar,s charts is to always use the largest subgroup size that is not too costly to inspect. Because of excessive inspection costs, the X-bar,s chart is seldom used.
3. **Zero-base coding with X-bar,R** (see Section 5.1). Identical to the X-bar,R chart, as far as sample size is concerned.
4. **Moving average** (see Section 5.2). In order to keep the moving average from smoothing out the variation too much (variation is, after all, what we are trying to measure), the subgroup size must be three. The minimum start-up sample size is then $3 \times 23 = 66$ (23 subgroups are constructed out of 25 individual measurements).
5. **Zero-base coding with moving average** (see Section 5.3). Identical to the moving average chart.
6. **Charts using attributes data** (see Section 5.4). Identical to the chart being used (either X-bar,R or moving average).
7. **Pre-Control** (see Section 5.5). See the discussion on pre-control charts in Section 4.8 for start-up sample size. Subgroup size is usually 1 (it can be 2 if the first falls in the warning area).
8. **Trend charts** (see Section 5.6). Identical to X-bar,R.
9. **Chart for individual values** (see Section 5.7). The subgroup size is 1. Therefore, the minimum start-up sample size is 25 (obviously, with such a small sample size, it is easy for this chart to make errors; therefore, it must be watched carefully).
10. **Charts using specification limits** (see Section 5.8). Since the limits do not have to be calculated, there is no start-up sample size. Subgroup sizes are identical to X-bar,R.
11. **Run** (see Section 4.13). Only individual measurements, or subgroup averages, are plotted.

Attributes Charts Sample Sizes (see Sections 4.5–4.7 and 5.9–5.16)

As with variables charts, the start-up sample size for attributes charts should be 25 subgroups. However, the subgroup size must be determined by using the process average (p-bar or u-bar, depending on which chart is being used). In general, attribute charts are ineffective as control devices unless most of the subgroups have some defectives. Therefore, some prior knowledge of the process average is needed in order to know what the subgroup size must be. If this information is not available, the subgroup size must be estimated. This is why attributes chart sampling must sometimes be repeated with different subgroup sizes until the proper size is determined.

If the subgroup size is too large, unnecessary cost is incurred. If it is too small, too many subgroups of zero defectives will occur, destroying the predictive nature of the chart. Also, as the process is perfected, the process average tends to decrease, which means that the subgroup size must then be increased. Ongoing, steady-state, attributes charts tend to have fairly large subgroup sizes. Subgroup sizes of 300 to 3000 are common for p charts, and 20–100 are common for u charts (c charts always have a subgroup size of 1).

For example, suppose that a process normally runs about 1% defective (1 in 100 are, on the average, outside the specification limits), or that a pre-chart sample showed a probable 1% defective rate. A subgroup size of 100 would then have an average of 1 defective for each subgroup. However, some subgroups would have many defectives, while some would have none at all. The probability here is that a very large percentage of the first 25 subgroups would have zero defectives. The chart constructed from these subgroups would be useless. In this case, a subgroup size of about 500 would be needed. The same logic is also true of u charts. The subgroup size for c charts is always 1 (and, therefore, the start-up sample size is 25).

For u and p charts, then, the subgroup size should be that amount that will have a very low probability (likelihood) of zero nonconformances. This will come from a knowledge of the process, similar products run on the same process, or a special pre-chart assessment (say, an average of the averages of 10 subgroups). For p charts, many practitioners use the following rule-of-thumb formula for determining practical subgroup sizes:

$$\text{Subgroup size} = 5/p\text{-bar or } 5/\text{process average.}$$

For the example where $\bar{p} = 1\%$, the subgroup size $= 5/0.01 = 500$.

Constant versus Variable Subgroup Size

For variable control charts, a constant subgroup size is assumed (always measure the next 4 consecutive units produced, for instance), even though it is possible to vary the subgroup sizes (4 one time, 6 the next, 4 the next, 8 the next, etc.). The reasons for this are threefold. First, variable subgroup sizes require the calculation of control limits for each subgroup and are quite difficult to use, leading to an increased likelihood of errors. More important, however, is the fact that variable subgroup size chart limits cannot be determined ahead of time, thus destroying the predictive nature of the chart. Finally, for variables charts, at least, the nature of the situation is such that there is almost never a time when a constant subgroup cannot be used, so that the difficulties inherent in variable subsampling need never be confronted. This is not true for many attributes charts, however, because of the large sample sizes required.

Actually, control limits will vary in relation to the sample size (see Figure 6.12 and the accompanying discussion in Chapter 6). The larger the sample size, the closer the limits will be to the central value. If this kind of close control is desired, a larger subgroup size must be chosen. However, the range (R) is not an accurate measure of dispersion with larger subgroup sizes, and becomes less and less accurate as the subgroup size increases (see Montgomery, 1985, p. 174). The standard deviation is much more accurate for large subgroup sizes (for variables data), and becomes even more accurate as the subgroup size is increased. For large variables subgroup sizes, therefore, the standard deviation chart should be used, instead of the R chart.

4.6 Step 5: Collect the Data

Any sample, in order to properly represent the population characteristics, must be unbiased (random, independent, and homogeneous). In meeting this criteria, subgroups can be selected from product produced at one time or over a period of time. The instant-time method is usually preferred because it provides a time reference for pinpointing assignable causes, and because it is more sensitive to process changes. However, some products and/or characteristics, by their nature, may demand the period-of-time method (long production cycles). The rule here is to use the instant-time method unless circumstances make this impossible.

If the instant-time method is used, the inspector measures several subgroups of parts at random times during the day (that is, each subgroup is randomly chosen, but the subgroup itself consists of consecutive units produced at the random time chosen). If the period-of-time method is used, each subgroup unit is chosen randomly from all the parts produced during that period of time. After the measurements (called observations) are made, the mean of the subgroup is calculated and graphed. Because of the Central Limit Theorem (Section 1.2), only the averages are graphed, never the individual values (except for some specialized charts).

If the purpose is to gather enough data for construction of the control chart, the measurements are recorded until enough observations are made, after which the chart is made and then the subgroup averages recorded. Data are usually gathered by the inspection function as a normal part of their regular duties, or by the operators themselves if a complete SPC program is in effect.

The data are collected and tabled either vertically or horizontally (the examples in this book are mostly horizontally tabled). In actual practice, the data are usually entered directly onto the chart in a space provided (see Figure 4.2 as an example).

Data Categorization

Statisticians usually categorize data into four types. The first three can be used in variables charts. Only the fourth can be used in attributes charts.

1. **Continuous** (in quality control, this type of data is the measurable data used in most variables charts).
2. **Ranked** (list from high to low). Each ranking is assigned a value that is then treated, in the variables charts, as if it were an actual measurement. Usually these values are just the ranking positions (1, 2, 3, etc.), but they do not have to be; they can also reflect varying degrees of difference in importance (such as 1, 3, 7, 15, etc.). This is one method of converting attributes data into variables data.
3. **Interval** (judgment, or weighting, on a scale of 1 to 5, 1 to 10, etc.: how good is it, or how bad is it). In this case, the weighted values are used, in variables charts, as if they were actual measurements. This is the most used method of converting attributes data into variables data (see Section 5.4).
4. **Discrete.** In quality control, all discrete data are countable; count the number of defects or defectives. This is the only type of data that can be used in attributes charts. Discrete (attributes) data can be converted into ranked or interval data which can then be used in a variables (X-bar,R or moving average) chart. Interval data are most commonly used in this type of conversion. However, since judgment is involved (judge the degree of nonconformance on a scale of 1 to 5, 1 to 10, etc.), this method is not recommended except for some nonmanufacturing processes and other special cases. Clearly defined standards must be available for each rating level, and everyone must be carefully trained to these standards so that they will be able to make essentially the same judgment as to the rating level for the same item. Even so, the judgments will seldom be the same, although they are often quite close (if training has been efficient and effective). In order to minimize these differences, an average of several analysts' assessments (judgments) can be used (the assessments must be completely independent in order to eliminate any possibility of bias). If any one assessment is grossly different than all the others, it would be discarded before the averaging is done. This "team approach" is, of course, quite expensive and should probably be used only on critical processes.

4.7 Step 6: Determine the Trial Control Limits and Chart Midpoint

Control limits are values that are plus and minus three sigmas (σ's) from the central value, or midpoint (special formulas and tables are used to make the calculations from the observations). Therefore, if the midpoint and limits have been properly determined and the process is properly operating, 99.73% of all subgroup averages will fall between these control limits. Any one average, in other words, has only a 0.27% chance (100–99.73%) of being outside of these limits (actually, the chance is ½ of 0.27 or 0.135% that the measurement will be above the upper limit, and 0.135% that it will be below the lower). Because of this small chance, any values above the upper limit or below the lower limit are assumed to have assignable (special) causes (the process is assumed to be out of control), and a search is instituted to find them.

All statistical quality control charts have a midpoint (centerline) which corresponds to the process average (the μ of Chapter 3) and an upper and lower limit which correspond to $\pm$ three standard deviations (the σ of Chapter 3) from this midpoint or centerline. How these chart values are determined will be explained in the remainder of this chapter and in Chapter 5.

Although a trial X-bar,R chart can now be constructed, it really serves no useful purpose—only revised control charts are actually kept and used at the job site (although technically incorrect, some systems use only the trial control chart; revised limits are never calculated). Trial control limit values are only needed for comparison to the subsample means: to determine which subsample means are outside the limits.

4.8 Step 7: Determine the Revised Control Limits and Chart Midpoint

Trial control limits are calculated first for the entire sample, after which the out-of-control subgroup means (those that are either above the upper limit or below the lower limit) are discarded and the limits recalculated. Before any values (subgroup means) can be discarded, however, they must first be proved to be out-of-control (have assignable causes). If not, they should not (theoretically) be discarded for revised limit calculation.

However, please note that only 27 subgroup means out of 10,000 ($1-0.9973=0.0027$ or 27 out of 10,000) can be outside of the control limits of Section 4.11 by chance alone. If several subgroup means are outside the limits and no assignable causes can, at first, be found, it is far more likely that the search for assignable causes has been flawed. Under these conditions, the search should probably be expanded and continued.

For instance, the probability that two outside values in a row would occur by chance alone is $0.0027 \times 0.0027 = 0.0000072$ (or about 7 out of 1,000,000). The chance that they would occur on the same side of the chart is $0.00135 \times 0.00135 = 0.0000018$ (or about 2 out of 1,000,000). The chance that the five outside values of Figure 4.1 are all outside the limits by chance alone is 7.2 in one trillion (these probabilities were calculated using the binomial distribution of Chapter 7). It is for this reason that many analysts (when constructing the revised chart) automatically assume an out-of-control condition when more than two (or two in a row) high and/or low points are present, even though no assignable cause can, at first, be found.

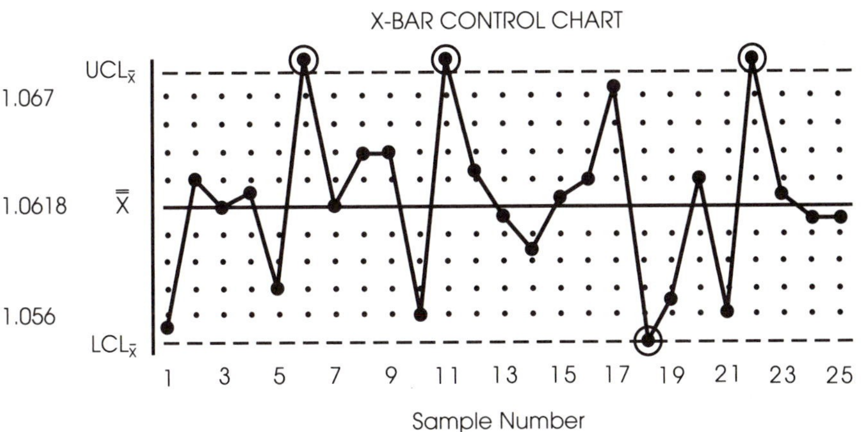

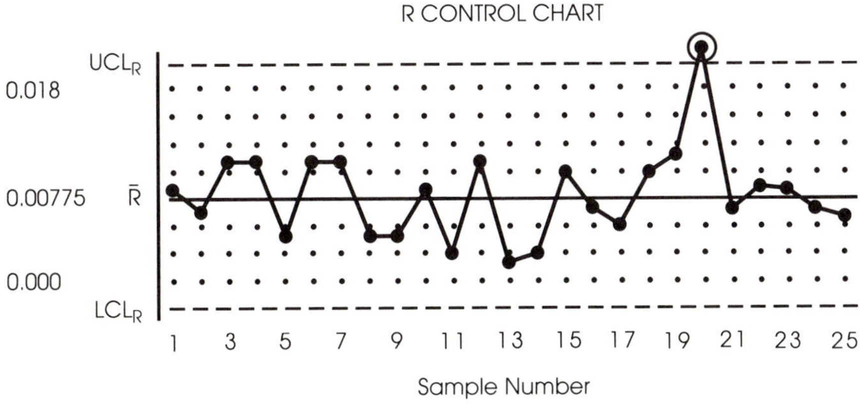

Figure 4.1. Revised *X*-bar, *R* control charts for Table 4.1.

4.9 Step 8: Construct the Revised Control Chart

Control charts are just graphs of the subgroup means (averages), with the central value shown as a solid line and each limit shown as a dotted line. Actually, control charts are just upended normal curves with the mean and 6 sigma limits extended ($+3\sigma$, or +3 standard deviations, above the mean for the upper control limit, and -3σ below the mean for the lower control limit) (see Figure 3.17).

All quality control charts are constructed from the basic normal curve model (Gaussian). Control charts for variables (X-bar,R, X-bar,s, etc.) use the normal curve model direct, while attributes charts use the normal curve approximation to the binomial (p charts) and the normal curve approximation to the Poisson (u and c charts). Special formulas and tables have been derived to simplify these calculations.

Control charts are normally constructed for revised limits only. Trial control limits are used only to determine which, if any, of the subsample means to discard. However, some quality systems, even some computer programs, use only the initial trial control chart—revised charts are never determined or used. Although, in actual practice, this appears to work (at least most of the time), it is technically incorrect (revised control limits are closer to the chart midpoint and could, therefore, show a point outside the revised limit that would not be outside the trial limit).

4.10 Step 9: Continue to Use the Charts

Once the revised control chart is constructed, all subgroup means (even the out-of-control values) are entered on the chart, and the chart is displayed conspicuously at the job site. Samples of the same size (the subgroup size) are measured periodically and charting is continued. Thus, the chart presents a continuous picture of the process improvement. The means of accomplishing this—called Process Analysis—will be explained in Chapter 6.

4.11 Variables Control Charts: The Basic *X*-Bar,*R* Chart

This is the most basic, and most used, of all variables charts. It is used for ongoing, long-run products where sample cost is high and the risk of sample error is low. Periodic random samples (usually 4) are taken of successive units produced.

The formulas are

$$\overline{X} = X\text{-bar} = \Sigma X/n$$

$$R = X_h - X_l$$

$$\overline{\overline{X}} = X\text{-double-bar} = \Sigma\overline{X}/m$$

$$\overline{R} = R\text{-bar} = \Sigma R/m$$

$$\text{UCL}_{X\text{-Bar}} = \overline{\overline{X}} + A_2\overline{R}$$

$$\text{LCL}_{X\text{-Bar}} = \overline{\overline{X}} - A_2\overline{R}$$

$$\text{UCL}_R = D_4\overline{R}$$

$$\text{LCL}_R = D_3\overline{R}$$

where

X = an individual value or measurement

X_h = the highest value or measurement

X_l = the lowest value or measurement

$\overline{X}$ = X-bar = a subgroup average

R = a subgroup range

$\overline{\overline{X}}$ = X-double-bar = the mean of the subgroup averages and the X-bar chart midpoint

$\overline{R}$ = R-bar = the mean of the subgroup ranges and the R chart midpoint

n = the subgroup size

m = the number of subgroups.

$\text{UCL}_{X\text{-Bar}}$ = upper control limit of the $\overline{X}$ chart

$\text{LCL}_{X\text{-Bar}}$ = lower control limit of the $\overline{X}$ chart

UCL_R = upper control limit of the R chart

LCL_R = lower control limit of the R chart

A_2, D_3, *and* D_4 = factors from Table A4 (used for converting subsample ranges to 3σ limits).

X-double-bar in the formulas is equivalent to the mean of the normal curve (μ of Chapter 3). A_2R-bar is equivalent to 3 standard deviations (3σ of Chapter 3) from the mean. Therefore, the area between the limits is equal to 0.9973 (or there is a 99.73% probability that any one measurement, from a process in control, will fall between the limits).

Example 4.1 Use the data in Table 4.1 to construct an X-bar,R chart (see Fig. 4.2). Use a subgroup of four.

Table 4.1. Shaft Diameters (in.)

Sample No.	Measurements (observations) X_1	X_2	X_3	X_4	Mean $\overline{X}$	Range R
1	1.055	1.062	1.054	1.055	1.0565*	0.008
2	1.060	1.061	1.065	1.067	1.0633	0.007
3	1.058	1.068	1.059	1.062	1.0618	0.010
4	1.057	1.065	1.067	1.061	1.0625	0.010
5	1.058	1.062	1.056	1.057	1.0583	0.005
6	1.091	1.085	1.089	1.081	1.0865*	0.010
7	1.060	1.056	1.066	1.062	1.0610	0.010
8	1.064	1.063	1.065	1.068	1.0650	0.005
9	1.066	1.063	1.063	1.068	1.0650	0.005
10	1.055	1.063	1.060	1.058	1.0590	0.008
11	1.070	1.074	1.071	1.073	1.0720*	0.004
12	1.069	1.065	1.058	1.064	1.0640	0.011
13	1.060	1.063	1.061	1.060	1.0610	0.003
14	1.059	1.059	1.063	1.059	1.0600	0.004
15	1.062	1.060	1.069	1.057	1.0620	0.012
16	1.060	1.062	1.067	1.064	1.0633	0.007
17	1.064	1.070	1.067	1.065	1.0665	0.006
18	1.055	1.057	1.051	1.061	1.0560*	0.010
19	1.063	1.063	1.057	1.051	1.0585	0.012
20	1.065	1.060	1.050	1.080	1.0638	0.030*
21	1.055	1.054	1.059	1.060	1.0570	0.006
22	1.077	1.078	1.067	1.070	1.0730*	0.011
23	1.062	1.060	1.067	1.059	1.0620	0.008
24	1.061	1.057	1.062	1.064	1.0610	0.007
25	1.061	1.064	1.061	1.058	1.0610	0.006
	Totals (Σ) =				26.5800	0.216

*Indicates a possible out-of-control condition.

Solution

1. Determine the individual subgroup averages and ranges. This has already been done in Table 4.1, but an example calculation will be shown for subgroup 1.

$$\overline{X}_1 = \Sigma X/n = (1.055 + 1.062 + 1.054 + 1.055)/4 = 1.0565$$

$$R_1 = X_h - X_l = 1.062 - 1.054 = 0.008.$$

2. Calculate trial limits and midpoints for both X-bar and R charts.

$$\overline{\overline{X}} = \Sigma\overline{X}/m = 26.58/25 = 1.0632$$

$$\overline{R} = \Sigma R/m = 0.216/25 = 0.00864$$

$$\text{UCL}_{X\text{-Bar}} = \overline{\overline{X}} + A_2\overline{R} = 1.0632 + 0.729(0.00864) = 1.069$$

$$\text{LCL}_{X\text{-Bar}} = \overline{\overline{X}} - A_2\overline{R} = 1.0632 - 0.729(0.00864) = 1.057$$

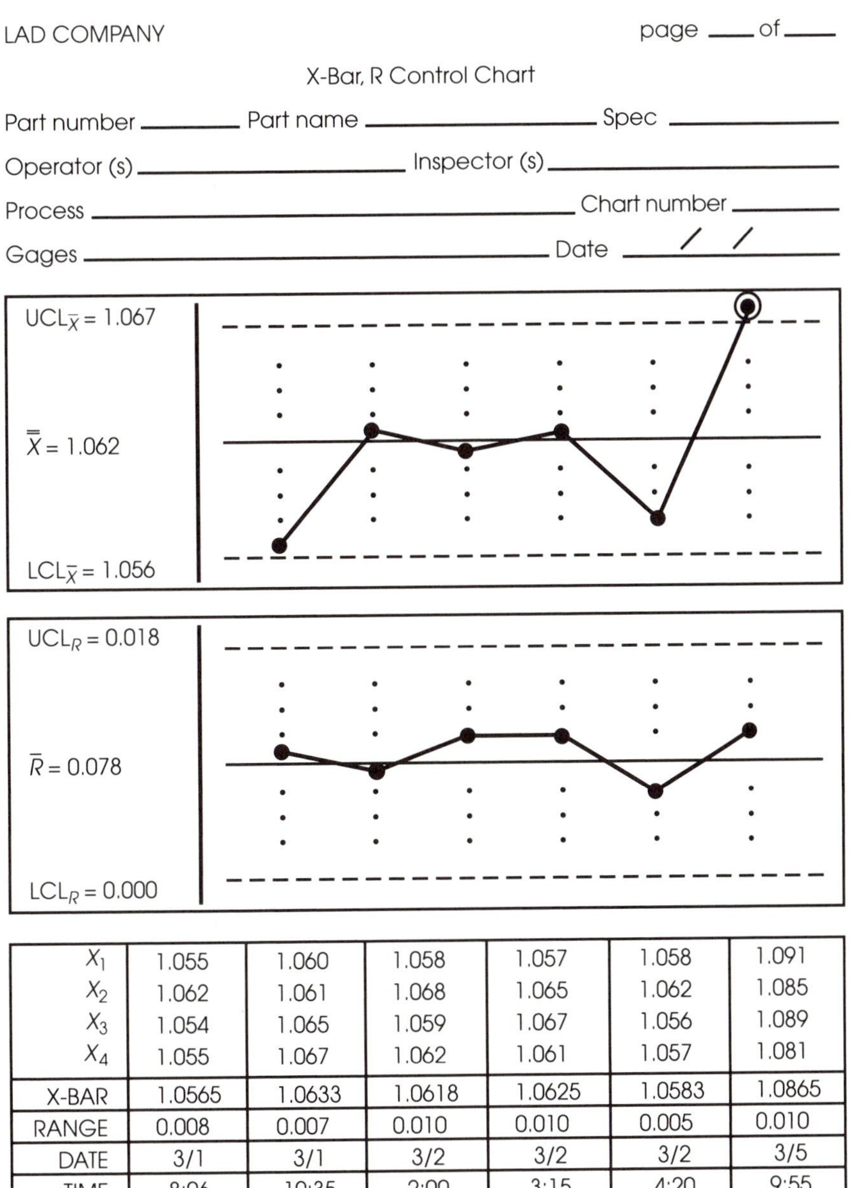
LAD COMPANY page ___ of ___

X-Bar, R Control Chart

Part number ______ Part name ______ Spec ______

Operator (s) ______ Inspector (s) ______

Process ______ Chart number ______

Gages ______ Date / /

X_1	1.055	1.060	1.058	1.057	1.058	1.091
X_2	1.062	1.061	1.068	1.065	1.062	1.085
X_3	1.054	1.065	1.059	1.067	1.056	1.089
X_4	1.055	1.067	1.062	1.061	1.057	1.081
X-BAR	1.0565	1.0633	1.0618	1.0625	1.0583	1.0865
RANGE	0.008	0.007	0.010	0.010	0.005	0.010
DATE	3/1	3/1	3/2	3/2	3/2	3/5
TIME	8:06	10:35	2:00	3:15	4:20	9:55

Figure 4.2. Sample X-bar, R control chart for Table 4.1.

$$\text{UCL}_R = D_4\overline{R} = 2.282(0.00864) = 0.020$$

$$\text{LCL}_R = D_3\overline{R} = 0(0.00864) = 0.000.$$

3. Calculate the revised central values (chart midpoints) and control limits. Compare the X-bar limits to the X-bar values in Table 4.1, and the R limits to the R values of this table. Note that five average values (X-bars) and one range value (R) are outside of the limits (denoted by an asterisk (*) in Table 4.1). The five average values are, therefore, greater than 1.069 or less than 1.057, while the one range value is greater than 0.020. Since there is a very small probability that this could happen by chance alone, they can be assumed to have assignable causes (and a search should be instituted to find these causes). If no assignable causes are found, these values can then be assumed to be part of the normal pattern of chance causes—part of the 0.27% of the values that would normally be outside of the control limits (this is extremely unlikely, however, since the probability that all 5 could occur by chance alone is 0.0000000072, or 7.2 in one trillion!). If causes are found, these subsample means would be omitted from the calculations, and new, revised, limits calculated. The revised control limits for the data of Table 4.1, assuming that all outside values have assignable causes, are determined as follows (note that the A_2, D_4, and D_3 values do not change since the subgroup size stays the same).

$$\overline{\overline{X}} = \Sigma\overline{X}/m = [26.58 - (1.0565 + 1.0865 + 1.072 + 1.056 + 1.073)]/(25 - 5) = 1.0618$$

$$\overline{R} = \Sigma R/m = (0.216 - 0.03)/(25 - 1) = 0.00775$$

$$\text{UCL}_{X\text{-Bar}} = \overline{\overline{X}} + A_2\overline{R} = 1.0618 + 0.729(0.00775) = 1.067$$

$$\text{LCL}_{X\text{-Bar}} = \overline{\overline{X}} - A_2\overline{R} = 1.0618 - 0.729(0.00775) = 1.056$$

$$\text{UCL}_R = D_4\overline{R} = 2.282(0.00775) = 0.018$$

$$\text{LCL}_R = D_3\overline{R} = 0(0.00775) = 0$$

4. Construct the control chart and plot the values (all X-bars and Rs, even those that are outside the limits). Figure 4.1 shows the revised control chart for Table 4.1 with the 25 subgroup averages and ranges entered. Figure 4.2 shows a portion of this chart as designed for actual use, with measurements and calculations entered onto the chart.
5. Continue to use the chart; sample, plot and analyze patterns (see Chapter 6 for a discussion on chart analysis).

4.12 Variables Control Charts: The Basic *X*-Bar, *s* Chart

This chart is identical to the X-bar,R chart, except that sample standard deviations (s) are used for the dispersion value rather than the range (R). Thus, larger subgroup sizes should be used—as large as pos-

Table 4.2. Shaft Diameters (in.)

Sample No.	Measurements (observations) X_1	X_2	X_3	X_4	Mean $\overline{X}$	Std. Dev. s
1	1.055	1.062	1.054	1.055	1.0565*	0.0037
2	1.060	1.061	1.065	1.067	1.0633	0.0033
3	1.058	1.068	1.059	1.062	1.0618	0.0045
4	1.057	1.065	1.067	1.061	1.0625	0.0044
5	1.058	1.062	1.056	1.057	1.0583	0.0026
6	1.091	1.085	1.089	1.081	1.0865*	0.0044
7	1.060	1.056	1.066	1.062	1.0610	0.0042
8	1.064	1.063	1.065	1.068	1.0650	0.0022
9	1.066	1.063	1.063	1.068	1.0650	0.0025
10	1.055	1.063	1.060	1.058	1.0590	0.0034
11	1.070	1.074	1.071	1.073	1.0720*	0.0018
12	1.069	1.065	1.058	1.064	1.0640	0.0046
13	1.060	1.063	1.061	1.060	1.0610	0.0014
14	1.059	1.059	1.063	1.059	1.0600	0.0020
15	1.062	1.060	1.069	1.057	1.0620	0.0051
16	1.060	1.062	1.067	1.064	1.0633	0.0030
17	1.064	1.070	1.067	1.065	1.0665	0.0027
18	1.055	1.057	1.051	1.061	1.0560*	0.0042
19	1.063	1.063	1.057	1.051	1.0585	0.0057
20	1.065	1.060	1.050	1.080	1.0638	0.0125*
21	1.055	1.054	1.059	1.060	1.0570	0.0029
22	1.077	1.078	1.067	1.070	1.0730*	0.0054
23	1.062	1.060	1.067	1.059	1.0620	0.0036
24	1.061	1.057	1.062	1.064	1.0610	0.0029
25	1.061	1.064	1.061	1.058	1.0610	0.0025
				Totals (Σ) =	26.5800	0.0953

*Denotes a possible out-of-control condition.

sible, but not so large that the measurement costs become prohibitive. This chart should only be used for very critical characteristics where the measurement costs are not too great.

Table 4.2 uses the same observations from Table 4.1, except that the standard deviation is computed from each sample rather than the range (in this way, a comparison can be made of the two methods). Summation, calculation, and graphing procedures from then on are the same. Even the control limit formulas are similar, except for the conversion values from Table A4.

The formulas are:

$$\overline{X} = \Sigma X/n$$

$$s = \sqrt{[\Sigma X^2 - (\Sigma X)^2/n]/(n-1)}$$

$$\overline{\overline{X}} = \Sigma\overline{X}/m$$

$$\bar{s} = \Sigma s/m$$

$$UCL_{X\text{-Bar}} = \overline{\overline{X}} + A_3\bar{s}$$

$$LCL_{X\text{-Bar}} = \overline{\overline{X}} - A_3\bar{s}$$

$$UCL_s = B_4\bar{s}$$

$$LCL_s = B_3\bar{s}$$

where

X = an individual value or measurement

$\overline{X}$ = a subsample mean

s = a subsample standard deviation

$\overline{\overline{X}}$ = the central X-bar chart value = the mean of the subsample averages

$\bar{s}$ = the central s chart value = the mean of the subsample standard deviations

n = the subsample size

m = the number of subgroups.

$UCL_{X\text{-Bar}}$ = upper control limit of the $\overline{X}$ chart

$LCL_{X\text{-Bar}}$ = lower control limit of the $\overline{X}$ chart

UCL_s = upper control limit of the s chart

LCL_s = lower control limit of the s chart

A_3, B_3, and B_4 = factors from Table A4 (used for converting subsample s's to 3σ limits)

X-double-bar in the formulas is equivalent to the mean (μ) of Chapter 3. A_3 s-bar is equivalent to 3 standard deviations (the standard deviation is the σ of Chapter 3) from the mean. Therefore, the area between the limits is equal to 0.9973 (or there is a 99.73% probability that any one measurement, from a process in control, will fall between the limits).

Example 4.2 Use the data in Table 4.2 to construct an X-bar,s chart. Use a subgroup of four (so that the completed chart can be compared to the X-bar,R chart of Section 4.11).

Solution

1. Determine the individual subgroup averages and ranges. This has already been done in Table 4.2, but an example calculation will be shown for subgroup 1.

$$\overline{X}=(1.055+1.062+1.054+1.055)/4=1.0565$$

$$s=\sqrt{[4.46481-(4.226)^2/4]/(4-1)}=0.0037.$$

2. Calculate the trial limits and midpoints for both the X-bar and s charts.

$$\overline{\overline{X}}=\Sigma\overline{X}/m=26.58/25=1.0632$$

$$\bar{s}=\Sigma s/m=0.0953/25=0.0038$$

$$UCL_{X\text{-Bar}}=\overline{\overline{X}}+A_3\bar{s}=1.0632+1.628(0.0038)=1.069$$

$$LCL_{X\text{-Bar}}=\overline{\overline{X}}-A_3\bar{s}=1.0632-1.628(0.0038)=1.057$$

$$UCL_s=B_4\bar{s}=2.266(0.0038)=0.0086$$

$$LCL_s=B_3\bar{s}=0(0.0038)=0.$$

3. Calculate the revised central value (chart midpoint) and control limits. As in Section 4.11 for X-bar,R charts, the same five average values (X-bars) and one standard deviation value (s) are outside of the limits (denoted by an asterisk (*) in Table 4.2). Also, as in the X-bar,R chart, a search for assignable causes must be instituted. All values with an assignable cause should be discarded from the calculations, and revised values recalculated. Values with no assignable causes are retained in the revised calculations. The revised control limits for the data of Table 4.2, assuming that all outside values have assignable causes, are determined as follows (note that the A_2, B_4, and B_3 values do not change since the subgroup size stays the same):

$$\overline{\overline{X}}=\Sigma\overline{X}/m=[26.58-(1.0565+1.0865+1.072+1.056+1.073)]/(25-5)=1.0618$$

$$\bar{s}=\Sigma s/m=(0.0953-0.0125)/(25-1)=0.00345$$

$$UCL_{X\text{-Bar}}=\overline{\overline{X}}+A_3\bar{s}=1.0618+1.628(0.00345)=1.068$$

$$LCL_{X\text{-Bar}}=\overline{\overline{X}}-A_3 s=1.0618-1.628(0.00345)=1.056$$

$$UCL_s=B_4\bar{s}=2.266(0.00345)=0.0078$$

$$LCL_s=B_3\bar{s}=0(0.00345)=0.$$

4. Construct the control chart and plot the values (all X-bars and s's, even those that are outside the limits). Figure 4.3 shows the revised control chart for Table 4.2 with the 25 subgroup averages (X-bars) and standard deviations (s's) entered. Figure 4.4 shows a portion of this chart as designed for actual use, with measurements and calculations entered onto the chart.

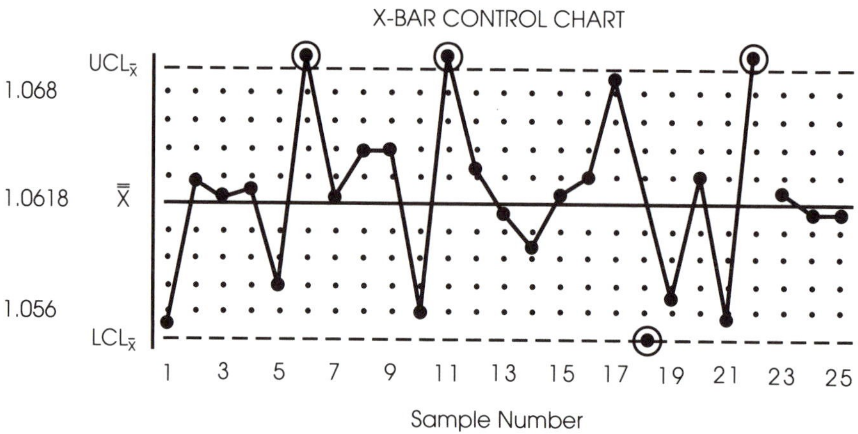

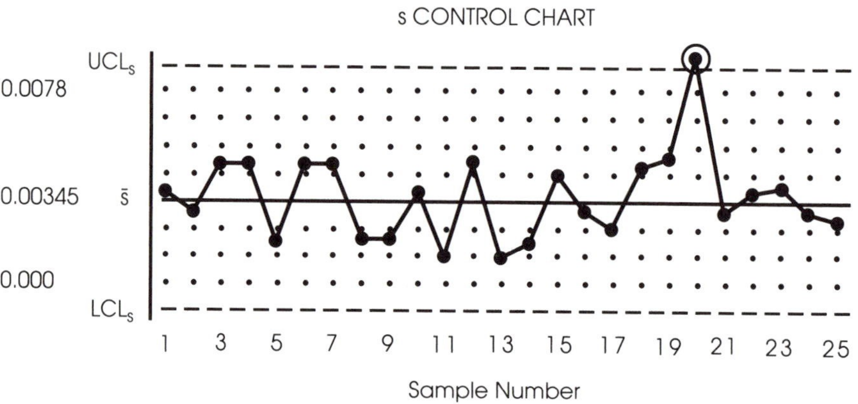

Figure 4.3. Revised *X*-bar, *s* control charts for Table 4.2.

5. Continue to use the chart: sample, plot, and analyze patterns (see Chapter 6 for a discussion on chart analysis).

4.13 Run Charts

The run chart is not a statistically derived chart like the others in this chapter. It is just a simple graph of the measured values as they occur. The purpose of the run chart is to keep track of the process characteristic prior to actual statistical charting. Valuable process information may therefore become apparent early in the control procedure. Run charts are usually used in conjunction with other, statistical, chart procedures to provide a measure of control until the desired statistical

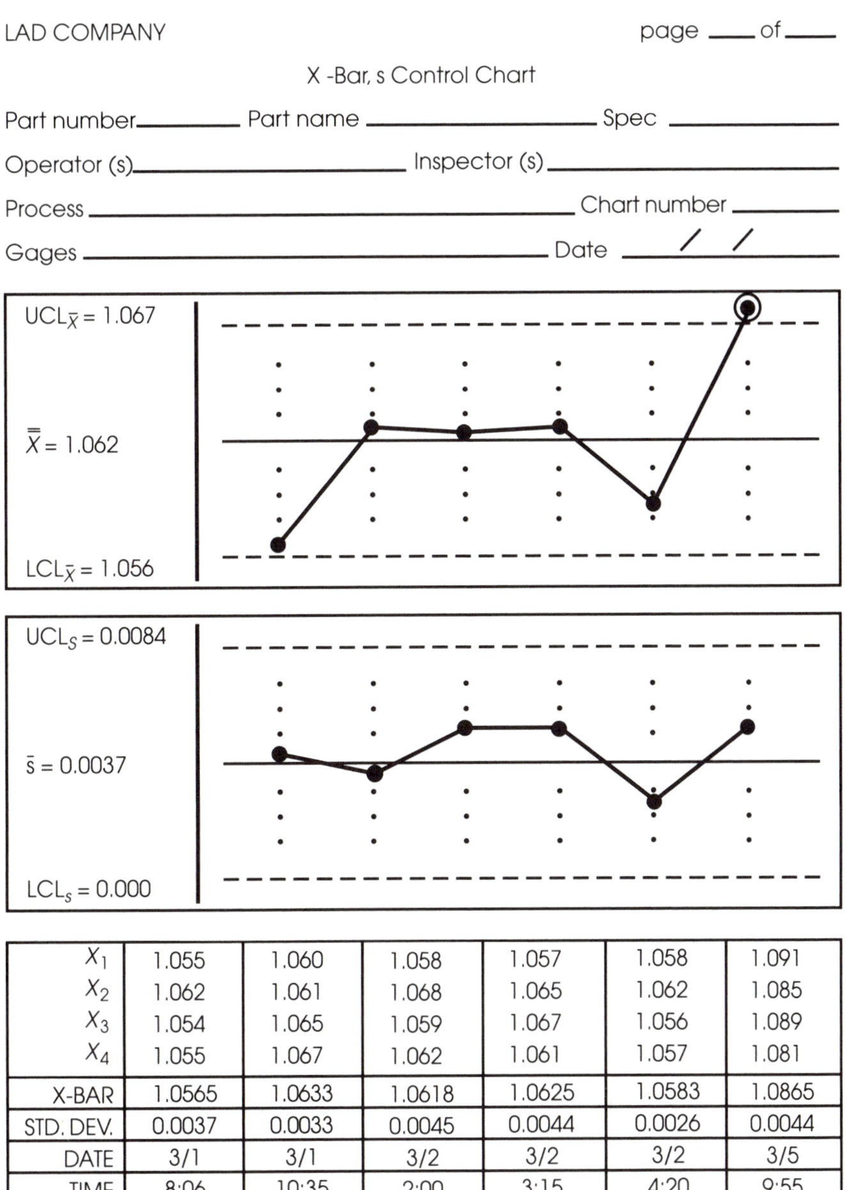

X_1	1.055	1.060	1.058	1.057	1.058	1.091
X_2	1.062	1.061	1.068	1.065	1.062	1.085
X_3	1.054	1.065	1.059	1.067	1.056	1.089
X_4	1.055	1.067	1.062	1.061	1.057	1.081
X-BAR	1.0565	1.0633	1.0618	1.0625	1.0583	1.0865
STD. DEV.	0.0037	0.0033	0.0045	0.0044	0.0026	0.0044
DATE	3/1	3/1	3/2	3/2	3/2	3/5
TIME	8:06	10:35	2:00	3:15	4:20	9:55

Figure 4.4. Sample *X*-bar, *s* control chart for Table 4.2.

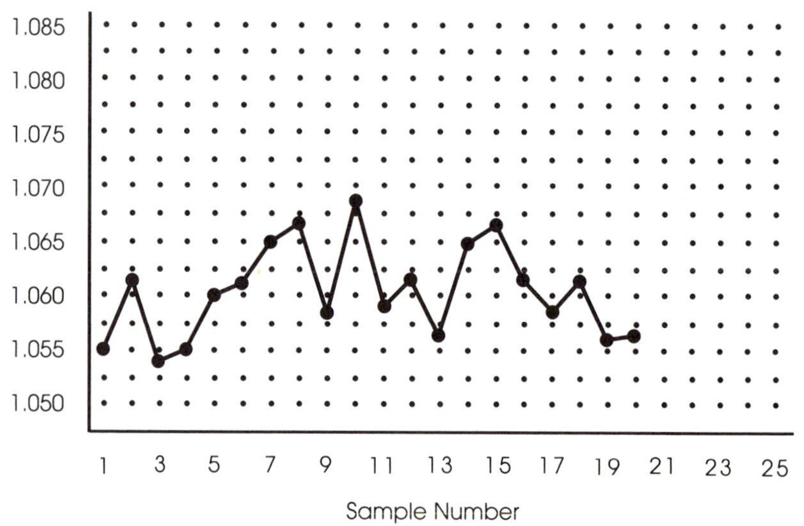

Figure 4.5. Run chart for Table 4.1.

chart can be implemented. Figure 4.5 shows the data from Table 4.1 (the first 20 measurements only are shown).

4.14 Attributes Control Charts for Defectives: The Constant Sample Size *p* Chart (the Basic *p* Chart)

This chart controls on defective units, not defects per unit. The plotted value is the fraction defective (p)—determined by dividing the number of defective units in the sample by the total number of units in the sample. Because of the way p is measured (part of the whole divided by the whole), it is also a probability value—the probability that any one unit in the sample is defective.

To be effective in control charts, p must be smaller than 0.15 (or 15%). The normal curve approximation that makes the p chart work, i.e., that makes it theoretically correct, does not apply to p values greater than 0.15. However, as far as quality control is concerned, this is no problem because p values greater than 0.15 indicate a process so far out of control that it should not need a control chart to show it (it should be obvious just from observing the process).

There are four types of p charts: constant subgroup size, variable subgroup size, average subgroup size, and the np chart. In addition, any one of these types can be used with weighting procedures (multiply by a weighting factor to reflect different levels of importance of different kinds of defects or defectives). Only the basic, constant subgroup size, *p* chart is shown in this chapter. All others are covered in Chapter 5.

An excellent way of determining the appropriate subgroup size is by using the following formula:

$$n = 5/p\text{-bar}.$$

n is the subgroup size (the sample size). The *p*-bar can be the *p*-bar from other similar products run on the same process (called the process average), or a $\bar{p}$ calculated from a sample run prior to charting, or even an informed estimate of the process average.

In almost all *p* chart applications, percentages are used on the chart instead of the fraction defective (in this form it is called the 100*p* chart). The reason for this is that most people are much more comfortable with percentages than with fractions or decimals. Only the final values (central value, limits, and plotted *p*'s) are actually changed to percentages (multiplied by 100). Of course, percentages are never used in the actual calculations. All *p* charts used in this book follow this convention.

Note that when the lower control limit (LCL) calculates to a negative number, it is changed to zero (there cannot be a negative number of defectives).

The *p* chart formulas are:

$$p = np/n$$

$$\bar{p} = \Sigma np/\Sigma n$$

$$UCL_p = \bar{p} + 3\sqrt{[\bar{p}(1-\bar{p})/n]}$$

$$LCL_p = \bar{p} - 3\sqrt{[\bar{p}(1-\bar{p})/n]}$$

where

$\bar{p} = p$-bar = the average fraction defective, of all samples

$p =$ the fraction defective of a sample

$n =$ the number of units in a sample

$3 =$ the number of σ from the mean

$UCL_p =$ the upper limit for a *p* chart

$LCL_p =$ the lower limit for a *p* chart.

The *p*-bar in the formula approximates the μ or midpoint of the normal distribution); and $\sqrt{[\bar{p}(1-\bar{p})/n]}$ approximates the standard deviation (σ) of the normal distribution. The "3" in the formulas refers to 3 standard deviations from the mean.

Example 4.3 Construct a *p* chart using the data from Table 4.3.

Table 4.3. Number of Defective Parts

Sample Number	Number Inspected n	Number Defective np	Fraction Defective p
1	500	14	0.028*
2	500	4	0.008
3	500	10	0.020
4	500	5	0.010
5	500	0	0.000
6	500	6	0.012
7	500	6	0.012
8	500	3	0.006
9	500	8	0.016
10	500	12	0.024
11	500	5	0.010
12	500	14	0.028*
13	500	8	0.016
14	500	3	0.006
15	500	0	0.000
16	500	5	0.010
17	500	8	0.016
18	500	7	0.014
19	500	18	0.036*
20	500	2	0.004
21	500	5	0.010
22	500	6	0.012
23	500	0	0.000
24	500	3	0.006
25	500	2	0.004
	Totals 12,500	153	

*Denotes out-of-control subgroups (higher than the upper limit).

Solution

1. Collect the samples (subgroups) and calculate the subgroup averages. This has already been done in Table 4.3. The following calculation of the first subgroup average will be used as an example of these calculations.

$$p_1 = np/n = 14/500 = 0.028.$$

2. Calculate the trial control limits and central value.

$$\bar{p} = \Sigma np/\Sigma n = 153/12{,}500 = 0.01224$$

$$\text{UCL}_p = \bar{p} + 3\sqrt{[\bar{p}(1-\bar{p})/n]} = 0.01224$$

$$+ 3\sqrt{0.01224(1-0.01224)/500} = 0.027$$

$$\text{LCL}_p = \bar{p} - 3\sqrt{[\bar{p}(1-\bar{p})/n]} = 0.01224$$
$$-3\sqrt{0.01224(1-0.01224)/500} = -0.0025;\ \text{use } 0.$$

3. Calculate the revised control limits. Compare the trial limits to each of the 25 p's, search for assignable causes for each nonconforming p (those above the upper limit), and omit from the revised calculations those nonconforming p's that have assignable causes. The revised control limits, assuming that all outside values have assignable causes, are:

$$\bar{p} = \Sigma np/\Sigma n = (153 - 14 - 14 - 18)/(12{,}500 - 1500) = 0.0097$$
$$\text{UCL}_p = \bar{p} + 3\sqrt{[\bar{p}(1-\bar{p})/n]} = 0.0097$$
$$+3\sqrt{0.00097(1-0.0097)/500} = 0.023$$
$$\text{LCL}_p = \bar{p} - 3\sqrt{[\bar{p}(1-\bar{p})/n]} = 0.0097$$
$$-3\sqrt{0.00097(1-0.0097)/500} = -0.0034;\ \text{use } 0.$$

4. Construct the chart and plot all 25 p values (see Figures 4.6 and 4.7). Remember to convert the central value (p-bar), the limits, and all plotted values to percentages (multiply by 100).
5. Display the chart in a conspicuous place, and continue to measure and plot.

4.15 Attributes Control Charts for Defects: The Constant Sample Size *u* Chart (the Basic *u* Chart)

Defectives are controlled by the p chart and its adaptations. Defects are controlled by the u and the c chart and their adaptations. The u chart controls on the average number of defects per unit for small sample sizes (average number of defects are charted), and is therefore

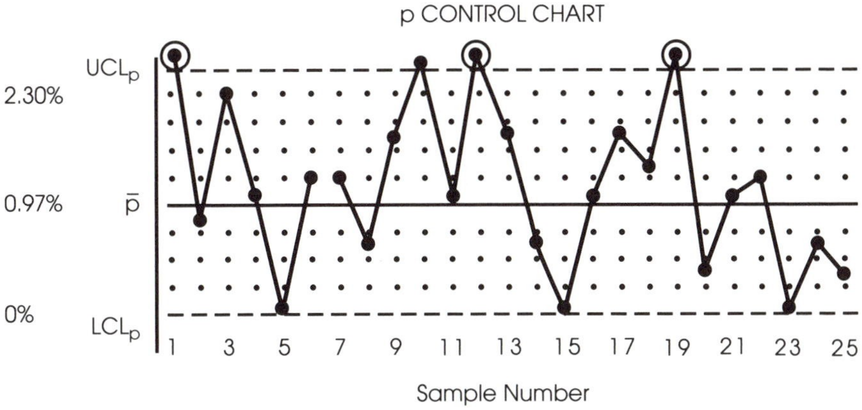

Figure 4.6. ***p*** **control chart for the data of Table 4.3.**

LAD COMPANY page ____ of ____

p Control Chart

Part number ________ Part name ________________ Spec __________

Operator (s) ________________ Inspector (s) ________________

Process ________________________ Chart number ________

Gages ________________________ Date ___ / / ___

REVISED VALUES 3.0
2.6
UCL = 2.3%
2.0
1.6
$\bar{P}$ = 0.97% 1.0
0.6
LCL = 0 0.2

DATE:	3/1	3/2	3/3	3/4	3/5	3/8	3/9	TOTAL CHART TOTALS
# DEFECTS	16	5	13	6	0	9	10	183
1. Oversize	2		2	2		3	2	34
2. Undersize	10	4	8	3		3	7	109
3. Rough	4	1	3	1		3	1	40
4.								
5.								
# DEFECTIVES	14	4	10	5	0	6	6	153
# CHECKED	500	500	500	500	500	500	500	12,500
% DEFECTIVES	2.8	0.8	2.0	1.0	0.0	1.2	1.2	1.2

Figure 4.7. Partial *p* control chart for Table 4.3.

called the "average" defects per unit chart. The *c* chart, on the other hand, controls on the actual number of defects for a single unit, and is therefore called just the defects per unit chart (the subgroup size is a single unit only and, therefore, the actual number of defects are charted, not the average number).

The central value for the *u* chart is *u*-bar, or average number of defects per unit. As in the other control chart systems, the data are gathered and tabled, and the u value, defects per unit, is calculated for each of the 25 subgroups. When the lower control limit (LCL) calculates to a negative number, it is changed to zero (there cannot be a negative number of defects).

Only the basic, constant subgroup size, u chart is presented here. All others are shown in Chapter 5.

The u chart formulas are:

$$u = c/n$$

$$\bar{u} = \Sigma c/\Sigma n = \Sigma c/nm$$

$$\text{UCL}_u = \bar{u} + 3\sqrt{\bar{u}/n}$$

$$\text{LCL}_u = \bar{u} - 3\sqrt{\bar{u}/n}$$

where

u = average defects per unit for a subgroup

$\bar{u}$ = u-bar = average defects per unit for the entire chart, and midpoint of the chart

c = number of defects per unit

n = subgroup size

m = number of subgroups

UCL_u = upper control limit for a u chart

LCL_u = lower control limit for a u chart.

Because we are using the Poisson approximation to the normal, the u-bar is equivalent to the mean (μ of Chapter 3), while the square root of u-bar divided by n is equivalent to σ of the same chapter. The 3 in the formula refers to ± 3 standard deviations (σ) from the mean (u-bar).

Example 4.4 Construct a u chart from the data in Table 4.4.

1. Collect the samples (subgroups) and calculate the subgroup averages. This has already been done in Table 4.4. The following calculation of the first subgroup average will be used as an example of these calculations.

$$u_1 = c/n = 48/100 = 0.48.$$

2. Calculate the trial control limits and chart midpoint.

$$\bar{u} = c/n = 1746/2500 = 0.70$$

$$\text{UCL}_u = \bar{u} + 3\sqrt{\bar{u}/n} = 0.70 + 3\sqrt{0.70/100} = 0.95$$

$$\text{LCL}_u = \bar{u} - 3\sqrt{\bar{u}/n} = 0.70 - 3\sqrt{0.70/100} = 0.45.$$

Table 4.4. *u* Chart Data

	Number Inspected n	Number of Defects c	Defects per Unit u
	100	48	0.48
	100	58	0.58
	100	53	0.53
	100	78	0.78
	100	89	0.89
	100	68	0.68
	100	77	0.77
	100	49	0.49
	100	86	0.86
	100	79	0.79
	100	69	0.69
	100	69	0.69
	100	62	0.62
	100	62	0.62
	100	67	0.67
	100	74	0.74
	100	75	0.75
	100	89	0.89
	100	69	0.69
	100	56	0.56
	100	47	0.47
	100	76	0.76
	100	71	0.71
	100	66	0.66
	100	117	1.17*
Totals =	2500	1746	

*Denotes possible out-of-control values.

3. Calculate the revised control limits. Compare the trial limits to each of the 25 u's, search for assignable causes for each nonconforming u (those above the upper limit), and omit from the revised calculations those nonconforming u's that have assignable causes. Assuming all have assignable causes, the revised limits are:

$$\bar{u} = c/n = (1746 - 117)/(2500 - 100) = 0.68$$

$$UCL_u = \bar{u} + 3\sqrt{\bar{u}/n} = 0.68 + 3\sqrt{0.68/100} = 0.93$$

$$UCL_u = \bar{u} - 3\sqrt{\bar{u}/n} = 0.68 - 3\sqrt{0.70/100} = 0.43.$$

4. Construct the chart and plot all 25 u values (see Figures 4.8 and 4.9). Do not change to percentages.

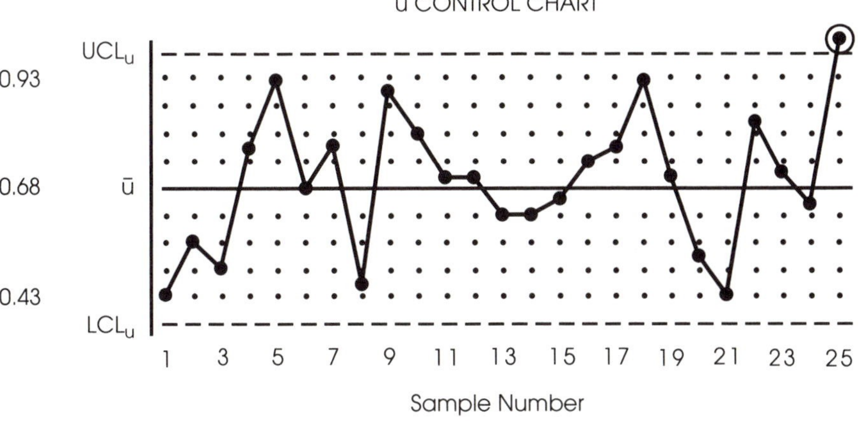

Figure 4.8. ***u*** **control chart for the data of Table 4.4.**

4.16 Attributes Control Charts for Defects: The Basic *c* Chart

Defects are controlled by the *u* and the c chart. The *u* chart controls the average number of defects per unit (and so is called the "average" defects per unit chart), while the c chart controls the actual number of defects for a single unit (and is therefore called just the defects per unit chart). The subgroup size is a single unit only and, therefore, only the actual number of defects are charted.

Actually, the c chart is just a special case of the *u* chart for large units where it is more practical to use a single unit as the subgroup size. The formulas are identical to those of the *u* chart except that dividing by *n* is no longer necessary, as *n*, the subsample size, is now equal to 1 (also c is substituted for *u* in the c chart formulas). Since the subgroup size is 1, *m* (the number of subgroups) equals Σn. When the lower control limit (LCL) calculates to a negative number, it is changed to zero (there cannot be a negative number of defects).

The c chart formulas are:

$$\bar{c} = \Sigma c / \Sigma n = \Sigma c / m$$

$$UCL_c = \bar{c} + 3\sqrt{c}$$

$$LCL_c = \bar{c} - 3\sqrt{c}$$

where

$\bar{c}$ = c-bar = number of defects per unit

UCL_c = upper control limit for a c chart

LCL_c = lower control limit for a c chart

LAD COMPANY page ____ of ____

u Control Chart

Part number ________ Part name ________________ Spec ____________

Operator (s) ________________ Inspector (s) ________________

Process ________________________ Chart number ________

Gages ________________________ Date ____/____/____

DATE:	3/1	3/2	3/3	3/4	3/5	3/8	3/9	TOTAL CHART TOTALS
REVISED VALUES; UCL = 0.93; $\bar{u}$ = 0.679; LCL = 0.43; scale 0–1.20								
DEFECT TYPE								
1. Oversize	8	10	2	12	10	13	12	243
2. Rough	35	35	38	53	51	43	57	1133
3. Undersize	5	13	13	13	28	12	18	370
4.								
5.								
# DEFECTS	48	58	53	78	89	68	77	1746
# CHECKED	100	100	100	100	100	100	100	2,500
DEFECTS/UNIT	0.48	0.58	0.53	0.78	0.89	0.68	0.77	0.6984

Figure 4.9. Partial basic *u* control chart for Table 4.4.

n = subsample size of 1

m = number of subsamples (units inspected).

The $\bar{c}$ in the formula is equivalent to the mean (μ) of Chapter 3. The $\sqrt{c}$ of the formula is equivalent to the standard deviation (σ) of

Chapter 3. The 3 refers to the number of standard deviations from the mean.

Example 4.5 Construct a c chart from the data in Table 4.5.

Solution

1. Calculate the trial control limits (note that subgroup averages do not have to be calculated since the subgroup size is 1).

$$\bar{c} = \Sigma c/\Sigma n = \Sigma c/m = 159/25 = 6.36$$

$$UCL_c = \bar{c} + 3\sqrt{\bar{c}} = 6.36 + 3\sqrt{6.36} = 13.9$$

$$LCL_c = \bar{c} - 3\sqrt{\bar{c}} = 6.36 - 3\sqrt{6.36} = -1.31; \text{ use } 0.$$

Table 4.5. *c* Chart Data

Subsample No.	Number of Defects (*c*)
1	8
2	7
3	6
4	4
5	3
6	9
7	1
8	5
9	0
10	0
11	23*
12	3
13	15*
14	8
15	5
16	7
17	3
18	0
19	12
20	3
21	4
22	18*
23	7
24	4
25	4
Total	159

*Denotes sample above upper limit.

2. Calculate the revised control limits. Compare the trial limits to each of the 25 c's, search for assignable causes for each nonconforming c (those above the upper limit), and omit from the revised calculations those nonconforming c's that have assignable causes. Assuming that all outside values have assignable causes, the revised limits are:

$$\bar{c} = \Sigma c/\Sigma n = \Sigma c/m = [159 - (23 + 15 + 18)/(25 - 3) = 103/22 = 4.68$$

$$UCL_c = \bar{c} + 3\sqrt{c} = 4.68 + 3\sqrt{4.68} = 11.2$$

$$LCL_c = \bar{c} - 3\sqrt{c} = 4.68 - 3\sqrt{4.68} = -1.8; \text{ use } 0.$$

3. Construct the chart and plot all 25 c values (see Figures 4.10 and 4.11). Do not change to percentages. Continue to measure and plot.

Practice Problems

4–1 From the following list of 100 cereal box weights, construct the revised control chart and plot all values (all subsample means), even those outside the limits. Use a subsample (subgroup) size of four.

Sample No.	Observation (Measurement) 1	2	3	4	Sample No.	Observation (Measurement) 1	2	3	4
1.	1.12	0.81	1.30	1.22	14.	1.12	1.63	1.43	1.63
2.	1.00	1.46	1.19	0.72	15.	1.36	1.58	1.79	1.41
3.	1.32	1.36	1.81	1.81	16.	1.77	1.44	1.61	1.43
4.	1.44	1.69	1.90	1.52	17.	1.61	1.74	1.67	1.72
5.	1.66	1.76	1.61	1.55	18.	1.81	1.65	0.82	1.52
6.	1.02	2.03	1.67	1.55	19.	1.33	1.57	1.98	1.85
7.	1.62	1.79	1.62	1.54	20.	1.63	1.44	1.87	1.69
8.	1.48	1.73	1.88	1.43	21.	1.25	1.43	1.55	1.68
9.	1.54	1.29	1.37	1.65	22.	1.77	1.68	1.54	1.76
10.	1.77	1.43	1.71	1.66	23.	1.64	1.57	1.65	2.15
11.	1.94	1.67	1.43	1.61	24.	1.90	1.18	1.60	1.45
12.	1.55	1.73	1.42	1.66	25.	1.63	1.85	1.67	1.36
13.	1.79	1.77	2.17	1.55					

Answers

X-bar chart: 1.25, 1.608, 1.96;
R chart: 0.00, 0.487, 1.37

4–2 From the following list of observations, construct the revised control chart and plot all values (all subsample means), even those outside the limits. Use a subsample size of six.

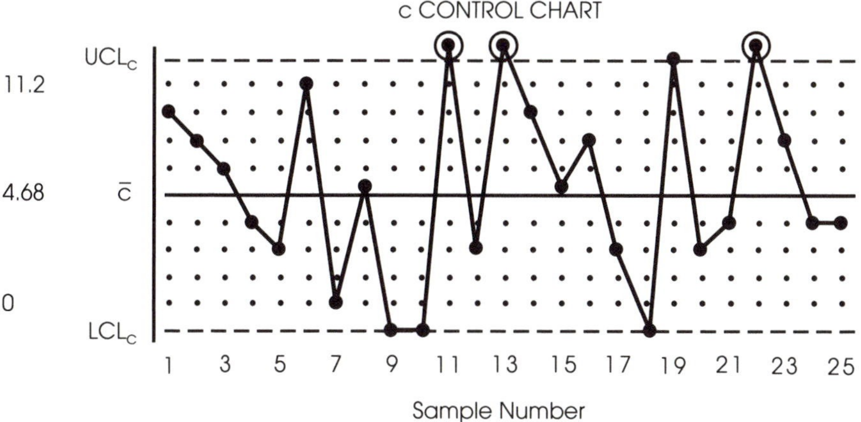

Figure 4.10. ***c*** **control chart for the data of Table 4.5.**

Sample No.	Observation (Measurement) 1	2	3	4	5	6
1.	10	13	13	11	13	8
2.	16	18	13	15	12	13
3.	14	12	13	15	14	13
4.	11	9	13	15	11	13
5.	14	17	10	12	5	15
6.	11	14	12	10	13	11
7.	13	8	14	18	14	13
8.	14	11	14	12	13	11
9.	13	16	13	14	13	14
10.	13	12	14	12	11	15
11.	13	14	11	14	13	10
12.	9	12	11	15	14	11
13.	12	13	14	13	12	13
14.	17	7	12	13	14	13
15.	12	17	13	11	15	16
16.	10	4	8	12	11	7
17.	9	10	6	9	11	15
18.	14	16	17	12	13	16
19.	16	15	15	16	16	13
20.	14	16	6	13	14	16

Answers

X-bar chart: 10, 12.9, 16

R chart: 0, 5.6, 11

LAD COMPANY page ____ of ____

c Control Chart

Part number ________ Part name ________________ Spec __________

Operator (s) ________________ Inspector (s) ________________

Process ____________________________ Chart number ________

Gages ____________________________ Date ____ / / ____

DATE:	3/1	3/2	3/3	3/4	3/5	3/8	3/9	

DEFECT TYPE								
1. Oversize	1		2	1		3		30
2. Rough	7	6	4	2	2	6	1	117
3. Undersize		1		1	1			12
4.								
5.								
# DEFECTS	8	7	6	4	3	9	1	159
# CHECKED	1	1	1	1	1	1	1	25
DEFECTS/UNIT								6.36

Figure 4.11. Partial *c* control chart for Table 4.5.

4–3 Determine the X-bar,s control limits for problem 4–1, construct the revised control chart, and plot all values (all subsample means), even those outside the limits. Use a subsample size of four.

Answers

X-bar chart: 1.26, 1.608, 1.96

s chart: 0.00, 0.214, 0.49

4–4 Determine the X-bar,s control limits for problem 4–2, construct the revised control chart, and plot all values (all subsample means), even those outside the limits. Use a subsample size of six.

Answers
X-bar chart: 10, 12.9, 16
s chart: 0, 2.0, 4

4–5 Construct a p chart for a constant sample size of 140. Assume all values outside of the upper trial control limit have assignable causes. The number of defectives for the first 20 subsamples were: 8, 3, 2, 2, 7, 7, 11, 4, 3, 6, 5, 14, 0, 4, 1, 5, 8, 13, 6, and 5.

Answers
0.0345, 0.081

4–6 Construct a p chart for a constant subsample size of 2000. Assume all values outside of the upper trial control limit have assignable causes. The number of defectives for the first 20 subsamples were: 215, 115, 115, 171, 110, 165, 142, 155, 154, 171, 210, 110, 143, 72, 206, 99, 163, 143, 203, and 234.

Answers
0.0676, 0.0844

4–7 Construct a u chart for a constant subsample size of 12. Assume all values outside of the upper trial control limit have assignable causes. The number of defects for the first 20 subsamples were: 30, 40, 41, 27, 25, 31, 35, 17, 35, 40, 32, 43, 34, 55, 45, 37, 28, 34, 28, and 58.

Answers
2.787, 4.23

4–8 Construct a c chart for the defects listed below. Assume all values outside of the upper trial control limit have assignable causes. The number of defects for the first 20 subsamples were: 1, 2, 3, 1, 1, 0, 1, 0, 1, 6, 2, 1, 3, 1, 1, 0, 0, 2, 1, and 1.

Answers
1.16, 4

4–9 Construct a run chart from the data from Practice Problem 4–1.

4–10 Construct a run chart from the data from Practice Problem 4–2.

CHAPTER 5 SPECIALIZED CONTROL CHARTS

This chapter is actually a continuation of Chapter 4, where basic charts are explained. All the charts in this chapter are adaptations of these basic charts, and are presented here to complete the data. The principles are identical to those used in Chapter 4; the differences are mostly in the way the data are presented and charted. Note that Sections 5.12 and 5.15 each cover two charts. Almost all charts can be used in more than one type of situation so that the actual chart used often becomes a matter of individual taste, based on chart knowledge.

The principles involved in the theory and construction of control charts have been thoroughly explained in Sections 4.1 through 4.10. The reader is strongly urged to review that material before continuing with this chapter.

Objectives

1. Be able to construct and interpret the *X*-bar, *R* control chart using zero-base coding.
2. Be able to construct and interpret the moving average control chart.
3. Be able to construct and interpret the moving average control chart using zero-base coding.
4. Be able to construct and interpret the moving average control chart using attributes data.
5. Be able to construct and interpret the pre-control chart.
6. Be able to construct and interpret the trend chart.
7. Be able to construct and interpret the *X*-bar,*R* chart using individual values (the individuals chart).
8. Be able to construct and interpret the specifications chart.

9. Be able to construct and interpret the *np* chart.
10. Be able to construct and interpret the variable sample size *p* chart.
11. Be able to construct and interpret the average sample size *p* chart.
12. Be able to construct and interpret the weighted *p* chart and the weighted average *p* chart.
13. Be able to construct and interpret the variable sample size *u* chart.
14. Be able to construct and interpret the average sample size *u* chart.
15. Be able to construct and interpret the weighted *u* chart and the weighted average *u* chart.
16. Be able to construct and interpret the weighted c chart.

5.1 Variables Control Charts: The *X*-Bar,*R* Chart Using Zero-Base Coding

The coding procedure of this chart makes it possible to chart more than one product on the same chart (remember that control charts control the process, not the product). This is one of the few variables charts where this is possible. This makes it an excellent chart to use for short production runs—probably the best one.

This chart is identical to the *X*-bar,*R* chart except that all measurements are coded and the plotted values, the averages (*X*-bars) and ranges (*R*'s), are calculated from these coded values. The coded values represent distances from the respective specification midpoints rather than the actual measurements, which is why many similar products can be charted on the same chart (the coding puts them all on the same footing, as far as charting is concerned).

There are several requirements, as follows.

1. The products must be similar.
2. The plotted characteristics must be identical (although the engineering specifications do not need to be). Each chart is for one characteristic on one process. If the chart is designed to control a turning process on a lathe, for instance, no other lathe process, such as drilling, can be plotted on the same chart as the turning process. Even different turning procedures may not be able to be charted on the same chart if different enough, and especially if the process variations (*R*) are too different. Actually, it is possible to chart any number of different processes on this chart, as well as products, but the chart would then lose its ability to provide information for problem correction and process improvement. Without this ability, any chart is essentially worthless (see Chapter 6).
3. Only variables data can be used.
4. The materials must be similar. Two different types of metals, for instance, would probably have different causes for any one nonconformance problem.
5. The dispersions of the data (*R*), from one product to another, must be similar (although similar products on the same process should almost guarantee this condition).

The coding formula is:

coded value = measurement − specification midpoint.

The specification in the formula refers to the engineering specification for the particular product characteristic being measured, so the specification midpoint is almost certain to be different for each product being charted.

In some coding procedures, the above coding formula is further divided by a "unit of measurement." The unit of measurement refers to the measurement discrimination, the number of decimal units (0.1, 0.01, 0.001, etc.). Division by this unit of measurement makes the coded values a whole number. This adds unnecessary complexity to the calculations, and results in a plotted value that has no real meaning. The plotted value (coded value) used in this book, on the other hand, is not only simple to calculate, it also results in a more meaningful figure—the distance (variation) from its own, respective, specification midpoint (which is the ideal, or desired, measurement).

The only problem with this method is that some people are uncomfortable with the negative numbers thus generated. Although it is possible to choose a zero base that will generate only positive numbers, other calculation problems result that are much more serious and much more difficult to handle (it also results in a much less meaningful plotted value). Therefore, this book will use only specification midpoints as the zero base.

Once the coded values are determined, the remainder of the procedures and formulas are identical to those of the X-bar,R chart.

Example 5.1 Construct a zero-base X-bar,R chart using the data from Table 5.1, and using the specification midpoint as the zero base. Plot the coded values on the revised charts. Note that Tables 5.1 and 5.1a contain only one sample (of 5 measurements each) for each product. This is because each product run was so small that only one sample (of 5 measurements) could be obtained. If any of the runs had been longer, more than one sample (of 5 measurements each) might have been possible. For instance, suppose that Product A run had been long enough for two samples. The table then would have shown Sample number 1 and 2 under Product A, Sample number 3 under Product B, Sample number 4 under Product C, etc. In this case, the upper specification limit (USL), lower specification limit (LSL), and the specification midpoint (MIDPT) would not have been repeated for the second sample of Product A. These three values only need to be shown once for each product.

In actual practice, only the final chart (see Figure 5.1) need be used. In this chart, the actual measurement can be determined (if necessary) by adding the coded value algebraically to its respective midpoint.

Table 5.1. Shaft Diameters (in.)

Sample No.	Measurements (observations) X_1	X_2	X_3	X_4	X_5	USL	LSL	MIDPT
				Product A				
1	1.424	1.430	1.438	1.435	1.428	1.438	1.425	1.4315
				Product B				
2	1.563	1.550	1.557	1.561	1.554	1.563	1.547	1.555
				Product C				
3	1.611	1.610	1.626	1.602	1.618	1.625	1.606	1.6155
				Product D				
4	1.730	1.745	1.749	1.744	1.732	1.750	1.728	1.739
				Product E				
5	1.790	1.800	1.808	1.805	1.803	1.800	1.788	1.794
. . .								
. . .								
. . .								
25								

Table 5.1a. Coded Values for Table 5.1

Sample No.	X_1	Coded Measurements X_2	X_3	X_4	X_5	X-Bar	R
			Product A				
1	−0.0075	−0.0015	0.0065	0.0035	−0.0035	−0.0005	0.014
			Product B				
2	0.008	−0.005	0.002	0.006	−0.001	0.002	0.013
			Product C				
3	−0.0045	−0.0055	0.0105	−0.0135	0.0025	−0.0021	0.024
			Product D				
4	−0.009	0.006	0.010	0.005	−0.007	0.001	0.019
			Product E				
5	−0.004	0.006	0.014	0.011	0.009	0.072	0.018
. . .							
. . .							
. . .							
25						. . . . .	. . . . .
Totals (Σ)						0.043	0.440

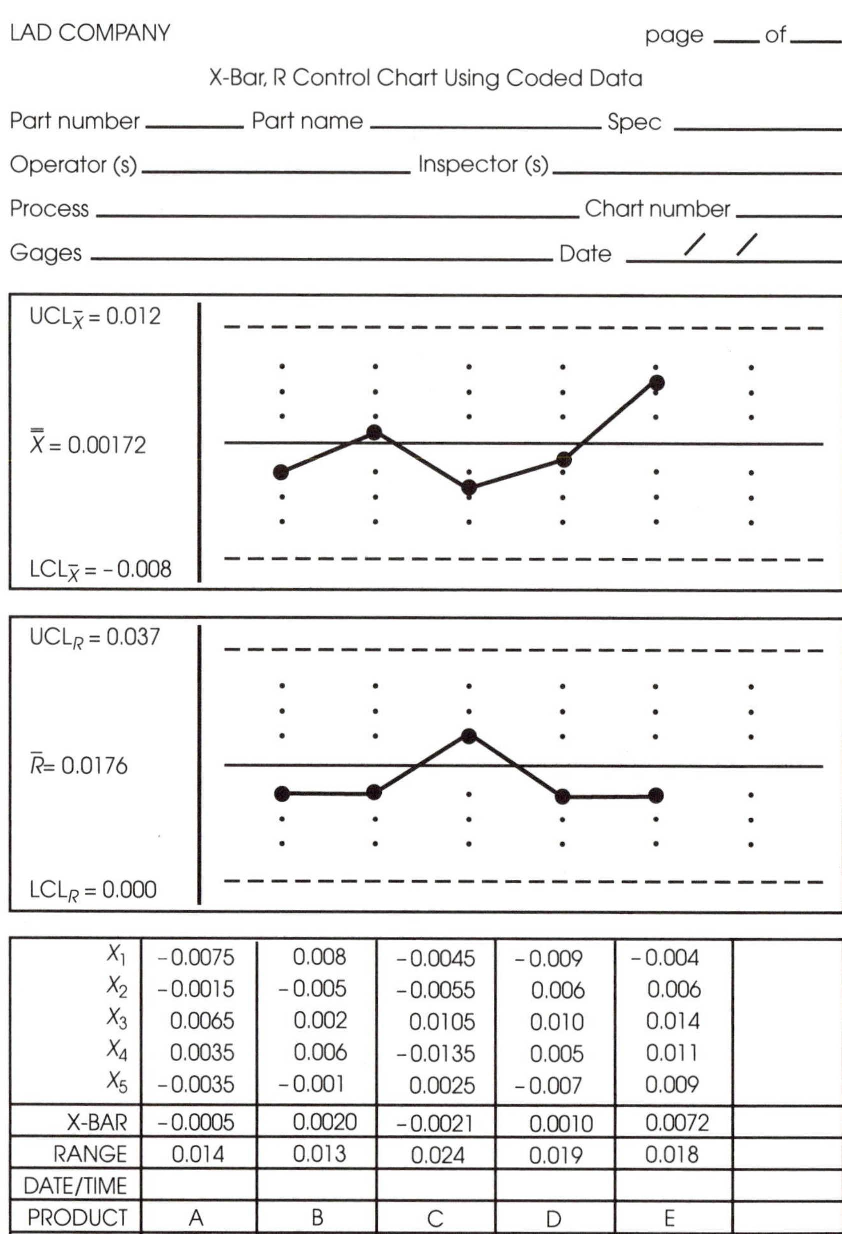

LAD COMPANY page ____ of ____

X-Bar, R Control Chart Using Coded Data

Part number ________ Part name ________________ Spec ________

Operator (s) ________________ Inspector (s) ________________

Process ________________________ Chart number ________

Gages ________________________ Date ____/____/____

X_1	-0.0075	0.008	-0.0045	-0.009	-0.004	
X_2	-0.0015	-0.005	-0.0055	0.006	0.006	
X_3	0.0065	0.002	0.0105	0.010	0.014	
X_4	0.0035	0.006	-0.0135	0.005	0.011	
X_5	-0.0035	-0.001	0.0025	-0.007	0.009	
X-BAR	-0.0005	0.0020	-0.0021	0.0010	0.0072	
RANGE	0.014	0.013	0.024	0.019	0.018	
DATE/TIME						
PRODUCT	A	B	C	D	E	
MIDPOINT	1.4315	1.555	1.6155	1.739	1.794	

Figure 5.1. Sample *X*-bar, *R* control chart using coded data.

Solution

1. Code the measurements, calculate X-bar and R for each subsample, and total. This has already been done in Table 5.1a. Measurement 1 (X_1), and X-bar and R, of Sample 1 shall be used as an example of how these calculations are made.

$$\text{Coded } X_1 = \text{measurement} - \text{specification midpoint}$$
$$= 1.424 - 1.4315 = -0.0075$$

$$\overline{X}_1 = \Sigma X/n = (-0.0075 + -0.0015 + 0.0065 + 0.0035 + -0.0035)/5 = -0.0005$$

$$R_1 = X_h - X_1 = 0.0065 - -0.0075 = 0.014.$$

2. Calculate the trial limits.

$$\overline{\overline{X}} = \Sigma\overline{X}/m = 0.043\backslash 25 = 0.00172$$

$$\overline{R} = \Sigma R/m = 0.440\backslash 25 = 0.0176$$

$$\text{UCL}_{X\text{-bar}} = \overline{\overline{X}} + A_2\overline{R} = 0.00172 + 0.577(0.0176) = 0.012$$

$$\text{LCL}_{X\text{-bar}} = \overline{\overline{X}} - A_2\overline{R} = 0.00172 - 0.577(0.0176) = -0.008$$

$$\text{UCL}_R = D_4\overline{R} = 2.115(0.0176) = 0.037$$

$$\text{LCL}_R = D_3\overline{R} = 0(0.0176) = 0.$$

3. Calculate the revised control limits. There are no points outside the limits. Therefore, the trial limits are the revised limits.
4. Construct the control chart and plot the coded values (see Figure 5.1).
5. Continue to use the chart. C_p values (see Chapter 6) are constructed using the coded values only.

5.2 Variables Control Charts: The Moving Average/ Moving Range Chart

This chart is the same as the X-bar,R chart, except that the measurements are collected individually (one measurement every hour instead of four each hour, for instance); X-bar is determined by using a moving average of three (average the first three, then 2, 3, and 4, then 3, 4, and 5, etc.); and the range is determined by subtracting the low from the high of each set of three. The subgroup size is always three; larger subgroup sizes smooth out the variation too much. In start-up, the first two measurements are not charted (because no average or range is available), so that there are always two less plotted values than the number of measurements.

One problem with this procedure is that it uses much less than the usual 100 or more measurements to start the chart. Even so, it still essentially maintains normality, mainly because the normal curve is "robust" in this situation (fairly large deviations from normal will not materially affect the outcome).

Although this chart can be used for short production runs and/or long process times, it is especially useful for processes where it is not practical to take successive samples, such as chemical processes and processes where very little variation occurs from piece to piece, so that more time and units are needed for a significant variation to accumulate (such as in bottling plants).

Example 5.2 Construct an X-bar,R chart using the moving average procedure and using the data from Table 5.2.

Table 5.2 Shaft Measurements (in.)

Subsample No.	Measurements X	Average $\bar{X}$	Range R
1	1.055	—	—
2	1.062	—	—
3	1.054	1.0570	0.008
4	1.055	1.0570	0.008
5	1.060	1.0563	0.006
6	1.061	1.0587	0.006
7	1.065	1.0620	0.006
8	1.067	1.0643	0.006
9	1.058	1.0633	0.006
10	1.068	1.0643	0.010
11	1.059	1.0617	0.010
12	1.062	1.0630	0.009
13	1.057	1.0593	0.005
14	1.065	1.0613	0.008
15	1.067	1.0630	0.010
16	1.061	1.0643	0.006
17	1.058	1.0620	0.009
18	1.062	1.0603	0.004
19	1.056	1.0587	0.006
20	1.057	1.0583	0.005
21	1.075	1.0627	0.019
22	1.071	1.0677	0.018
23	1.068	1.0713*	0.007
24	1.050	1.0630	0.021
25	1.059	1.0590	0.009
	Totals (Σ)	24.4185	0.220

*Denotes possible out-of-control values (higher than the upper limit or lower than the lower limit).

Solution

1. Calculate X-bar and R for each measurement. This has already been done in Table 5.2. Note that there are no X-bars nor R's at measurements 1 and 2. This occurs only on the first (start-up) chart, and only because there are no earlier measurements with which to average. The calculations of the first two X-bars and R's are:

$$\overline{X}_3 = \Sigma X/n = (1.055 + 1.062 + 1.054)/3 = 1.057$$

$$R_3 = X_h - X_1 = 1.062 - 1.054 = 0.008$$

$$\overline{X}_4 = (1.062 + 1.054 + 1.055)/3 = 1.057$$

$$R_4 = 1.062 - 1.054 = 0.008.$$

2. Calculate the trial midpoint (X-double-bar), the trial range (R-bar), and the trial control limits. Once the moving averages and ranges are determined, the remaining chart procedures and formulas are identical to those of the X-bar,R charts of Section 4.2. Note that the conversion factors from Table A4 (for a sample of 3) have been entered into the formulas as constants (1.023 for A_2, 2.575 for D_4, 0 for D_3). This is because the subgroup size never changes—it is always 3.

$$\overline{\overline{X}} = \Sigma \overline{X}/m = 24.4185/23 = 1.0617$$

$$\overline{R} = \Sigma R/m = 0.220/23 = 0.0096$$

$$UCL_{X\text{-Bar}} = \overline{\overline{X}} + 1.023\overline{R} = 1.0617 + 1.023(0.0096) = 1.071$$

$$LCL_{X\text{-Bar}} = \overline{\overline{X}} - 1.023\overline{R} = 1.0617 - 1.023(0.0096) = 1.052$$

$$UCL_R = 2.575\overline{R} = 2.575(0.0096) = 0.025$$

$$LCL_R = 0.000.$$

3. Calculate the revised limits and central values. The next step is to compare the X-bar limits to the moving average (X-bar) values in Table 5.2, and the R limits to the R values of this table. There is only one plotted value in this table that is outside the limits—an X-bar at the 23rd measurement. A search should be conducted to determine if there is an assignable cause. If none is found, the trial control limits become the revised limits. If so, the outside value is omitted from the revised calculations. Remember that outside values are plotted on the chart, they are *not* omitted from the chart as they are from the limit calculations. The revised control limits for the data of Table 5.2, assuming that all outside values have assignable causes, are:

$$\overline{\overline{X}} = \Sigma \overline{X}/m = [24.4185 - 1.0713]/(23 - 1) = 1.0612$$

$$\overline{R} = \Sigma R/m = 0.220/23 = 0.0096$$

$$UCL_{X\text{-Bar}} = \overline{\overline{X}} + 1.023\overline{R} = 1.0612 + 1.023(0.0096) = 1.071$$

$$LCL_{X\text{-Bar}} = \overline{\overline{X}} - 1.023\overline{R} = 1.0612 - 1.023(0.0096) = 1.051$$

$$UCL_R = 2.575\overline{R} = 2.575(0.0096) = 0.025$$

$$LCL_R = 0.$$

4. Construct the revised chart and plot all values. Figure 5.2 shows a partial revised control chart with the values (X-bars and ranges) charted. This chart can be compared to Figure 4.1 (since the data of Table 5.2 consist of 25 measurements from Table 4.1). Note that the limits are

LAD COMPANY page ____ of ____

Moving Average/Moving Range Control Chart

Part number ______ Part name ____________ Spec ________

Operator (s) ____________ Inspector (s) ____________

Process ____________________ Chart number ______

Gages ____________________ Date ___ / ___ / ___

$UCL_{\overline{X}} = 1.071$

$\overline{\overline{X}} = 1.0612$

$LCL_{\overline{X}} = 1.051$

$UCL_R = 0.025$

$\overline{R} = 0.0096$

$LCL_R = 0.000$

X	1.055	1.062	1.054	1.055	1.060	1.061
X-BAR	—	—	—	1.0570	1.0570	1.0563
RANGE (R)	—	—	—	0.008	0.008	0.006
DATE						
TIME						

Figure 5.2. Partial moving average control chart.

fairly close, although not identical. If all 100 measurements from Table 4.1 had been used, the limits would have been essentially the same.

5.3 Variables Control Charts: The Moving Average Control Chart Using Zero-Base Coding

This chart is identical to the moving average chart (of Section 5.2), except that the measurements are coded prior to plotting (as in Section 5.1). The coding procedures and formula are identical to those in Section 5.1:

$$\text{coded value} = \text{measurement} - \text{specification midpoint}.$$

Once the coded values (plotting values) are determined, the chart construction and use proceeds as in the moving average chart of Section 5.2.

This chart is useful for short runs in processes where successive measurements are impractical, such as in bottling plants where the differences in successive measurements are so small that the only practical approach is to measure once each 20 or 30 minutes (or longer, if necessary), after variations have time to accumulate to measurable amounts.

Example 5.3 Determine the trial and revised control limits for the coded data of Table 5.3 (coding procedures are identical to those explained in Section 5.1, "X-Bar,R Chart Using Zero-Base Coding"). Cal-

Table 5.3. Coded Values for Example 5.3

Subsample No.	Coded Measurement X	Average $\bar{X}$	Range R
	Product A		
1	−0.0075	—	—
2	−0.0015	—	—
3	0.0065	−0.0008	0.0140
4	0.0035	0.0028	0.0080
5	−0.0035	0.0022	0.0100
	Product B		
6	0.0080	0.0027	0.0115
7	−0.0050	−0.0002	0.0130
8	0.0020	0.0017	0.0130
...	...	...	...
...	...	...	...
25	...	...	...
	Totals (Σ)	0.0337	0.2945

culate X-bar and R for each subgroup and plot on the charts (see Figure 5.3).

Notice that there are no X-bars or R's for the first two X's. Also notice that the X-bars and R's for the first measurement of product B (sixth X; sixth measurement; sixth subgroup) are derived using the last two measurements from the previous product (Product A). This is acceptable only if Product B directly follows Product A in the production cycle. If Product B had been produced after substantial delay (say, a week or more after Product A), or if other products had been produced between Products A and B that were not included on the chart, the chart would have had to have been restarted at Product B. Control charts lose much of their analytical power unless each subgroup follows each other sequentially in time (as produced).

Solution

1. Code the measurements and calculate the subgroup averages (X-bars) and the subgroup ranges (R's), and then total. This has already been done in Table 5.3. The coded values shown here were derived exactly as was done in Section 5.2. Averages and ranges for subgroups 3, 4, and 6 are shown below as examples.

$$\overline{X}_3 = \Sigma X/n = (-0.0075 + -0.0015 + 0.0065)/3 = -0.0008$$

$$\overline{X}_4 = \Sigma X/n = (-0.0015 + 0.0065 + 0.0035)/3 = 0.0028$$

$$\overline{X}_6 = \Sigma X/n = (0.0035 + -0.0035 + 0.0080)/3 = 0.0027$$

$$R_3 = X_h - X_l = (0.0065 - -0.0075) = 0.0140$$

$$R_4 = X_h - X_l = (0.0065 - -0.0015) = 0.0080$$

$$R_6 = X_h - X_l = (0.0080 - -0.0035) = 0.0115.$$

2. Calculate the trial limits.

$$\overline{\overline{X}} = \Sigma \overline{X}/m = 0.0337/23 = 0.001465$$

$$\overline{R} = \Sigma R/n = 0.2945/23 = 0.0128$$

$$UCL_{X\text{-bar}} = \overline{\overline{X}} + 1.023\overline{R} = 0.001465 + 1.023(0.0128) = 0.0146$$

$$LCL_{X\text{-bar}} = \overline{\overline{X}} - 1.023\overline{R} = 0.001465 - 1.023(0.0128) = -0.0116$$

$$UCL_R = 2.575\overline{R} = 2.575(0.0128) = 0.0330$$

$$LCL_R = 0.$$

4. Calculate the revised limits and central value. Since there are no out-of-control values, the trial limits and central value are the revised limits and central value.
5. Construct the control charts and plot the coded values. Figure 5.3 presents a partial control chart for this example. Continue to use the chart to control and improve the process (see Chapter 6).

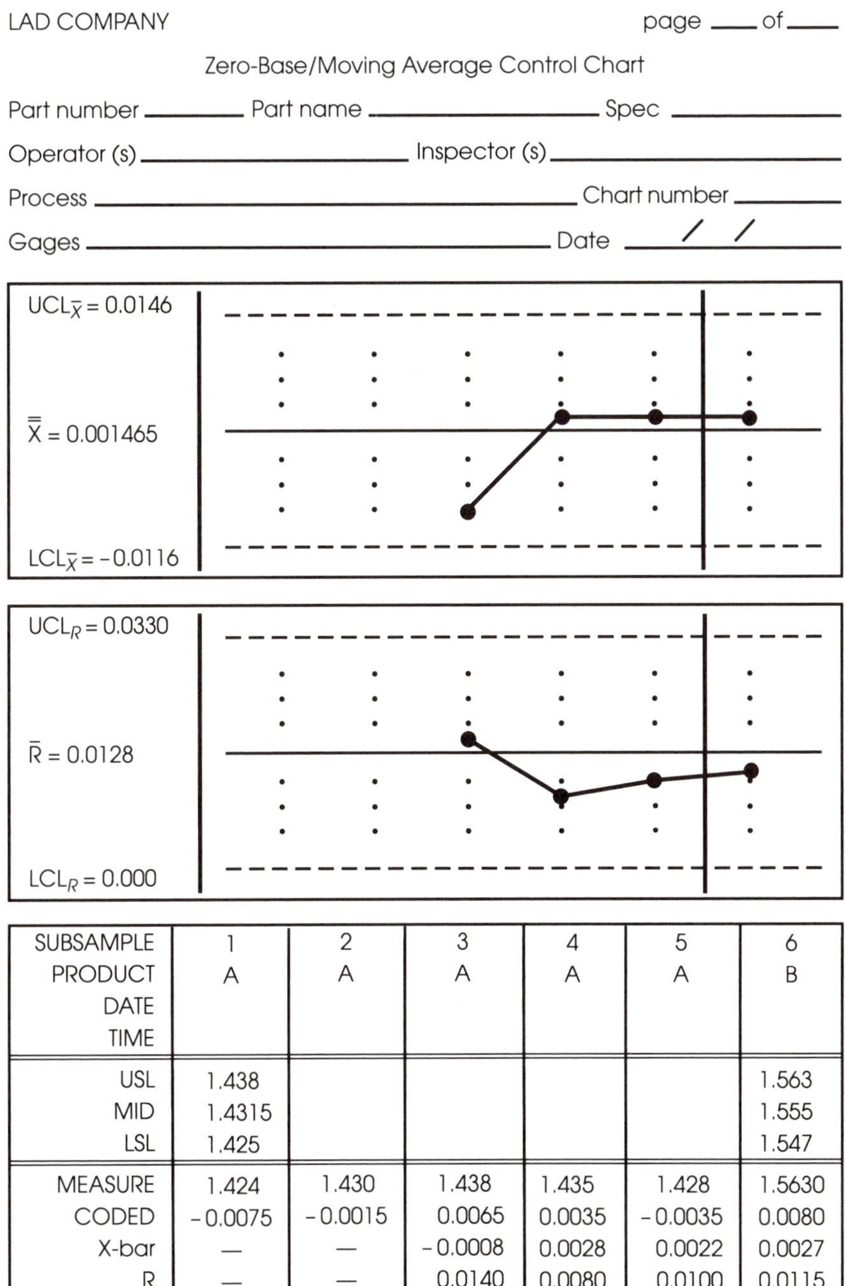

LAD COMPANY page ____ of ____

Zero-Base/Moving Average Control Chart

Part number ________ Part name ________________ Spec ____________

Operator (s) ________________ Inspector (s) ________________

Process ______________________________ Chart number ________

Gages ______________________________ Date ____/____/____

$UCL_{\bar{X}} = 0.0146$

$\bar{\bar{X}} = 0.001465$

$LCL_{\bar{X}} = -0.0116$

$UCL_R = 0.0330$

$\bar{R} = 0.0128$

$LCL_R = 0.000$

SUBSAMPLE	1	2	3	4	5	6
PRODUCT	A	A	A	A	A	B
DATE						
TIME						
USL	1.438					1.563
MID	1.4315					1.555
LSL	1.425					1.547
MEASURE	1.424	1.430	1.438	1.435	1.428	1.5630
CODED	-0.0075	-0.0015	0.0065	0.0035	-0.0035	0.0080
X-bar	—	—	-0.0008	0.0028	0.0022	0.0027
R	—	—	0.0140	0.0080	0.0100	0.0115

Figure 5.3. Partial moving average chart using zero-base coding.

5.4 Variables Control Charts: The Moving Average Chart Using Attributes Data

In general, attributes data should not be used for variables charts, unless necessary (which is often the case for nonmanufacturing). The reason for this is the necessary "judgment" that must be employed, and the near impossibility of getting everyone to "judge" the same way. Therefore, when attributes data are converted into variables data, a great deal of judgmental variation is usually created, as well as the normal process variation. This "judgmental variation" is, of course, extremely undesirable. Nevertheless, there are a few circumstances when this type of chart can be profitably used—mostly in conjunction with nonmanufacturing processes.

Attributes data can be used (when converted into variables data) with either the basic X-bar,R chart or the moving average chart. However, the nature of attributes data is such that the moving average chart is almost always preferable (especially with nonmanufacturing processes). Therefore, the moving average chart shall be used to illustrate the technique. Actually, the only difference in using either chart is in the conversion procedure. After that, the chart construction and use continues as already explained (for either the basic X-bar,R chart or the moving average chart).

The best method of converting attributes data into variables data is to use a weighting procedure and assess the value of the observation on a predetermined scale (such as: a scale of 1 to 5, 1 to 10, etc.). It is vitally important, with this method, that each weight be completely described, and that all evaluators be thoroughly trained in what the descriptions mean.

The best evaluation method is to use a team evaluation. Each member of the team does an individual assessment (without the others knowing what the assessment is), and the several assessments (evaluations or weights) are then averaged. Usually, with the team procedure, any extreme evaluations (either very high or very low) would be discarded from the averaging procedure. However, the team approach is costly and probably should not be used except for critical processes.

Example 5.4 Use the attributes data from Table 5.4 to construct a moving average chart.

Solution

As each error was observed, the analyst made an instant assessment of degree of nonconformance (weighting) on a scale of 1 to 20, and recorded the weighting as well as the error and time of error (time is often important in later analysis and corrective activities). Even though there are not quite enough data (22 observations instead of 25) for a

Table 5.4. Data Entry Errors (Weighted on a Scale of 1–20)

Error No.	Weighting X	Average X-Bar	Range R
1 (8:46 AM)	5	—	—
2 (9:33 AM)	12	—	—
3 (9:42 AM)	4	7.0	8
4 (9:45 AM)	5	7.0	8
5 (9:49 AM)	10	6.3	5
6 (9:53 AM)	11	8.7	6
7 (9:57 AM)	15	12.0	5
8 (11:08 AM)	17	14.3	6
9 (11:23 AM)	8	13.3	9
10 (11:35 AM)	18	14.3	10
11 (11:46 AM)	9	11.7	10
12 (11:52 AM)	12	13.0	9
13 (11:53 AM)	7	9.3	5
14 (11:55 AM)	15	11.3	8
15	17	13.0	10
16	11	14.3	6
17	8	12.0	9
18	12	10.3	4
19	6	8.7	6
20	7	8.3	6
21	10	7.7	4
22	11	9.3	4
	Totals	211.8	138

completely viable (statistically viable) chart, they must still be used in order to analyze the process. Any conclusions reached from this chart, therefore, must be carefully examined before application. This is often the case with this type of data—emphasizing again the need for care in the use of these charts.

The weighted data in Table 5.4 are all individually rated (no team was used). With this type of data, it is almost impossible to use the team approach because the characteristic occurs only momentarily (while being observed). Teams are used most successfully for evaluating products with characteristics that endure for a while, such as cosmetic problems (scratches, blemishes, etc.).

Once the weighted values are determined, the chart construction proceeds exactly as does the moving average chart of Section 5.2. Figure 5.4 shows a partial chart using data from Table 5.4. The calculations are as follows.

1. Calculate X-bar and R. This has already been done in Table 5.4. Subgroups 3 and 4 are presented as examples of the calculation procedures.

$$\overline{X}_3 = \Sigma X/3 = (5 + 12 + 4)/3 = 7.0$$

$$R_3 = X_h - X_1 = 12 - 4 = 8$$

LAD COMPANY

page ___ of ___

Moving Average/Moving Range Control Chart

Part number ______ Part name ______________ Spec __________

Operator (s) ______________ Inspector (s) ______________

Process ______________________________ Chart number ______

Gages ______________________________ Date ___ / / ___

X	5	12	4	5	10	11
X-BAR	—	—	7.0	7.0	6.3	8.7
RANGE	—	—	8	8	5	6
DATE	3/1	3/1	3/2	3/2	3/2	3/5
TIME	8:06	10:35	2:00	3:15	4:20	9:55

Figure 5.4. Partial moving average control chart using attributes data.

$$\overline{X}_4 = \Sigma X/3 = (12+4+5)/3 = 7.0$$

$$R_4 = X_h - X_1 = 12 - 4 = 8.$$

2. Calculate the trial limits.

$$\overline{\overline{X}} = \overline{X}/m = 211.8/20 = 10.59$$

$$\overline{R} = R/m = 138/20 = 6.9$$

$$UCL_{X\text{-bar}} = \overline{\overline{X}} + 1.023\overline{R} = 10.59 + 1.023(6.9) = 17.6$$

$$LCL_{X\text{-bar}} = \overline{\overline{X}} - 1.023\overline{R} = 10.59 - 1.023(6.9) = 3.5$$

$$UCL_R = 2.575\overline{R} = 2.575(6.9) = 17.8$$

$$LCL_R = 0 = 0.$$

3. The chart has no out-of-control values, so use the trial values to complete the chart. Figure 5.4 presents a partial chart of this procedure.

5.5 Variables Control Charts: The Pre-Control Chart

This chart, also called the "target" or "stoplight" control chart, is one of the two charts that use specification limits instead of control limits. The advantages of this chart are that it is very easy to construct and use, and that it provides excellent product control. Its one big disadvantage is that it cannot be used for process analysis and improvement (see Chapter 6); it can only indicate when and how often to adjust (the basis of its excellent product control features).

Because of these problems, the pre-control chart can only be used safely when the process is producing well within the specifications, when approximately 86% of the measurements fall within the center "target" area. Obviously, prior knowledge about the process capability must be available: from experience with other, similar, products and/or from prior process capability analyses.

Construction

The steps in constructing a pre-control (P-C) chart are as follows (see Figure 5.5).

1. Construct a chart with the mean at the center of the tolerance, and the tolerance limits (specifications) at equal distances from this mean (this corresponds to + and − 3σ on the normal curve).
2. Construct "pre-control" (P-C) limits within the tolerances limits at half the tolerance, and centered about the mean (the center of the tolerance).
3. Label the center portion, between the P-C limits, as the "target area." Some people color the center portion *green,* the two intermediate areas (between the P-C limits and the tolerance limits) *yellow,* and the outside area (outside the tolerance limits) *red,* and call it a "stoplight chart."

Procedure (Use)

The step-by-step procedures for using the chart are as follows.

1. Obtain a set-up approval by inspecting 100% until five pieces in a row (or more, if management desires) are found acceptable (within the center *(green)* target area).
2. Measure a unit periodically according to a predetermined sampling plan. This plan should be based on process needs, but an excellent starting point would be a frequency of 1 in 10 for lot sizes to 200; 1 in 20 for lot sizes from 201 to 1000; and 1 in 30 for lot sizes over 1000. Sampling tables can also be constructed using MIL-STD-105E. At the beginning of the run, this plan would have to develop from prior experience first: either from similar product run on the same process, or from prior experience with the product being run. Then, during the run, the plan can be adjusted to fit the measurement data. A "rule of thumb" is to adjust about every 25 measurements. If adjustments start occurring more often than this, the sampling frequency should be increased (say, from 1 in 30 to 1 in 20); if less often, the sampling frequency should be decreased (say, from 1 in 30 to 1 in 40). Sampling frequency is a management decision and should be based on:
   a. cost—process, product, and/or measurement;
   b. process difficulty;
   c. processing time;
   d. scheduling needs;
   e. product importance;
   f. reliability requirements.
3. Whenever a single unit measures outside the specification limits (the red area), adjust; return to step 1 and start over.
4. If a unit measures between the specifications and the P-C limits (in the *yellow* area), measure a second consecutive piece. If the second piece measures in the center *(green)* area, continue sampling. If not, adjust; return to step 1 and start over. Two units measuring in the same *yellow* area (on the same side of the chart) indicate a shift in the process average; so recenter. One unit in one *yellow* area and one in the other *yellow* area indicate problems with the process variation, and may require management and/or engineering assistance.

Statistics

The statistics, i.e., the mathematical justification, of the P-C chart are as follows.

1. Since the tolerance spread is equated to + and − 3σ, the target spread is half that or + and − 1.5σ. The area under the curve between the P-C limits (the target, or *green*, area) is:

$$P(Z \leq 1.5) = 0.9332$$

$$P(Z \leq -1.5) = 0.0668.$$

$$\text{Target area} = 0.9332 - 0.0668 = 0.8664 \text{ (or } 86.64\%).$$

2. The area between each tolerance limit and its respective P-C limit (the *yellow* area) is:

$$P(Z \leq 3.0) = 0.99865$$

$$P(Z \leq 1.5) = 0.9338.$$

Each *yellow* area $= 0.99865 - 0.9338 = 0.065$ (or 6.5%).

3. Each area outside the specifications (tolerance limits) or each *red* area is:

$$P(Z \leq 3.0) = 0.99865.$$

Each *red* area $= 1 - 0.99865 = 0.00135$ (or 0.135%).

4. The probability that a unit will measure outside the specifications, in one of the *red* areas, is 0.135% for the lower *red* area and 0.135% for the upper *red* area, or 0.27% for both (much less than the 1% rule of Chapter 6).
5. The probability that two consecutive units will measure in the *yellow* area is:

$$0.065 \times 0.065 = 0.004225$$

which is obviously less than 1%.

Example 5.5 Construct a pre-control (P-C) chart for Table 5.5. Use specification limits of 1.082/1.054. Figure 5.5 shows an example of this chart.

Solution

1. The central value is:

$$(1.082 + 1.054)/2 = 1.068.$$

2. The lower P-C limit (P-C_l) is:

$$(1.054 + 1.068)/2 = 1.061.$$

3. The upper P-C limit (P-C_u) is:

$$(1.082 + 1.068)/2 = 1.075.$$

Table 5.5. Shaft Diameters (in.)

1. 1.065	6. 1.062	11. 1.054	16. 1.055
2. 1.070	7. 1.061	12. 1.065	17. 1.067
3. 1.068	8. 1.068	13. 1.059	18. 1.062
4. 1.067	9. 1.065	14. 1.067	19. 1.061
5. 1.068	10. 1.062	15. 1.066	20. 1.067

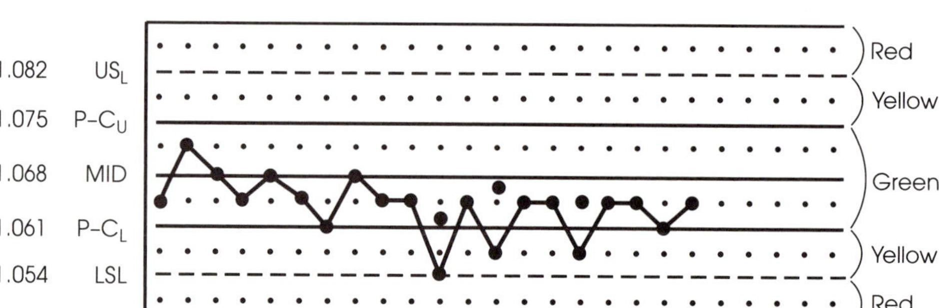

Figure 5.5. P-C chart for Example 5.5.

4. Plot the measurements from Table 5.5. The entries only need be placed in the area in which they belong, not to an exact location. This is another simplification of this chart.

5.6 Variables Control Charts: Control Chart for Trends

This type of chart controls the normal wear and tear of tools, assists in determining and predicting tool wear characteristics, and provides information for optimizing tool design. The only difference between this and the basic X-bar, R chart is that the trend X-bar chart has upward, or downward, sloping limits and central value. All other chart activities are identical to those of the basic X-bar, R chart.

One note of warning: the formulas and procedures presented here for trend line calculations assume a linear relationship. If the tool wear characteristics are not linear with time, this chart will not work. In that case, nonlinear regression procedures must be used. However, a nonlinear tool wear characteristic would be a bad problem in itself, as it would cause the tool to wear exceptionally fast (a very undesirable situation). It is best, therefore, to design and control to linear wear characteristics as much as possible.

The specifications must be much broader than the control limits for this procedure to work (the tolerance must be much much greater than 6σ).

The trend line formula is:

$$\overline{\overline{X}}_n = a + bn$$

where

b = the slope of the line of best fit

a = the intercept, where the line of best fit crosses the Y or vertical axis (measurement axis)

m = the number of subgroups (# of X-bars)

n = a subgroup number (1, 2, 3, ..., m)

$\overline{\overline{X}}_n$ = the chart central value at the subgroup number (n) chosen

Σ = "the sum of."

This formula is used to calculate the central trend line. The central trend line constitutes the central value of the trend X-bar chart, the ideal measurement, the target value (a different central value, for each unit of time, or subgroup number). If all subgroup averages were to plot exactly on the line, the tool wear characteristics would be totally predictable—a highly desirable condition.

The formulas and procedures will be explained in conjunction with an example.

Example 5.6 Construct a trend control chart (Figure 5.6) using the data from Table 5.6. The subgroup size (n) is 4. The upper specification limit (USL) is 22, and the lower specification limit (LSL) is 8.

Solution

1. Calculate the trend line parameters (a and b). A computer or hand calculator programmed for regression analysis computations is very helpful here—almost essential (manual calculations are extremely difficult and time consuming, and quite apt to generate errors).

$$b = \frac{m\Sigma(n\overline{X}) - (\Sigma n)(\Sigma\overline{X})}{m\Sigma(n^2) - (\Sigma n)^2} = \frac{25(5332.2) - 325(383.5)}{25(5525) - (325)^2}$$

$$= 0.27$$

$$a = \Sigma\overline{X}/m - b(\Sigma n)/m = 383.5/25 - 0.27(325)/25 = 11.8.$$

2. Calculate two points on the central line (these two points define the central trend line).
   a. Use the intercept, the "a" value just determined, for the first point. This is the central value for $n = 1$ (the first subgroup).
   b. The second point must be calculated. Plug the a and b values just calculated into the trend line formula at a predetermined subgroup point (say, at subgroup number 20). The trend line formula calculates the central chart value associated with the subgroup number chosen.

$$\overline{\overline{X}}_{20} = a + bn = 11.8 + 0.27(20) = 17.2.$$

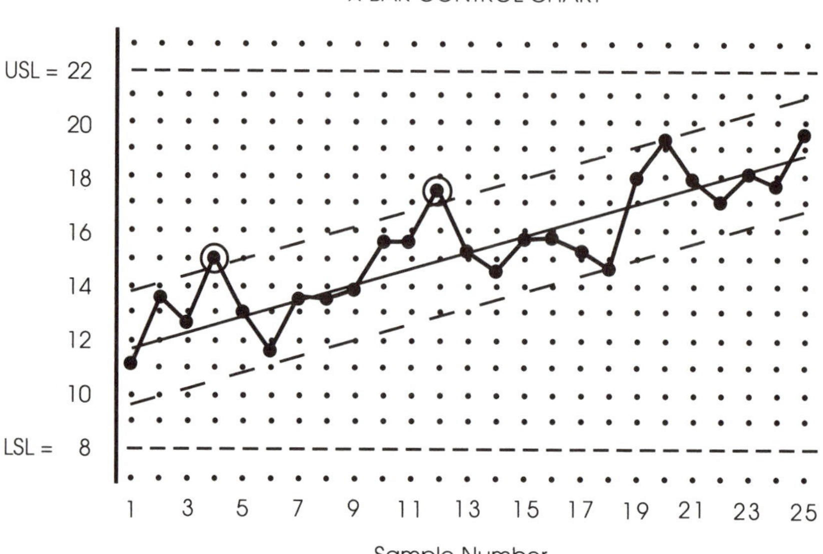

Figure 5.6. Trend control chart.

3. Draw a straight line, on the chart, through the two points just identified. This is the chart central trend line (it will slope up or down, depending on the type of product and/or process). This is the line that defines the ideal, or desired, measurement. Note that the desired measurement will be different at each subgroup number; it will get smaller, or larger, as time progresses. Thus, there is no single central value (X-double-bar) to the trend chart.

4. Calculate the X-bar control limits. These are also upward, or downward, sloping lines, at $\pm\ 3\sigma$ from the central trend line. Two points are also needed to define each of these lines. It is easiest to construct them above and below the same points (subgroup numbers) used to construct the central trend line. The formulas are the same as those used to calculate control limits for the basic X-bar, R chart. The control limit points at $n = 1$ are:

$$\overline{R} = \Sigma R/n = 72.51/25 = 2.9$$

$$\mathrm{UCL}_1 = \overline{\overline{X}} + A_2\overline{R} = 11.8 + 0.729(2.9) = 13.9$$

$$\mathrm{LCL}_1 = \overline{\overline{X}} - A_2\overline{R} = 11.8 - 0.729(2.9) = 9.7.$$

The control limit points at $n = 20$ are:

$$\mathrm{UCL}_{20} = \overline{\overline{X}} + A_2\overline{R} = 17.2 + 0.729(2.9) = 19.3$$

$$\mathrm{LCL}_{20} = \overline{\overline{X}} - A_2\overline{R} = 17.2 - 0.729(2.9) = 15.1.$$

Table 5.6. Least Squares Calculation Table

Subgroup Number n	Subgroup Average X-bar	Product of n Times X-bar n(X-bar)	n^2	Subgroup Range R
1	11.1	11.1	1	2.1
2	13.7	27.4	4	3.2
3	12.9	37.8	9	3.4
4	15.1	60.4	16	1.9
5	13.0	65.0	25	.
6	11.4	68.4	36	.
7	13.2	92.4	49	.
8	13.2	105.6	64	.
9	13.9	125.1	81	
10	15.5	155.0	100	
11	15.4	169.4	121	
12	17.3	207.6	144	
13	15.0	195.0	169	
14	14.3	200.2	196	
15	15.4	231.0	225	
16	15.7	251.2	256	
17	15.1	256.7	289	
18	14.8	266.4	324	
19	18.0	342.0	361	
20	19.2	384.0	400	
21	17.8	373.8	441	
22	17.2	378.4	484	
23	18.1	416.3	529	
24	17.9	429.6	576	
25	19.3	482.5	625	
325	383.5	5333.2	5525	72.51

$\overline{R} = 72.51/25 = 2.9.$

Note that the X-double-bar at the X-bar axis ($n=1$) is the "a" value calculated above, and that the X-double-bar used for $n=20$ is the one already calculated above for the central line at $n = 20$.

5. Construct the control chart. Draw straight lines through each set of points. Use dotted lines for the control limit lines (between 19.3 and 13.9, and 15.1 and 9.7) and a solid line for the central line (between 17.2 and 11.8). Plot the specification limits (USL and LSL) on the chart (these will be straight, horizontal lines). If desired, the chart can be re-centered to leave a larger gap (a safety margin) between the applicable specification limit and control limit (lower limits if the lines slope upwards, and upper limits if the lines slope downwards). However, this will shorten the tool life. Adjusting the process means that the three control lines are shifted up (if upward sloping), or down (if downward sloping),

for the distance of the adjustment. Now plot the X-bars on the control chart. Analyze for possible out-of-control (assignable causes), correct the assignable causes, and continue to use the chart to control the process.

A computer or calculator programmed to do least-squares or correlation analysis would make the last three columns of the above calculation table unnecessary. The first two columns contain the necessary data for construction of the chart.

5.7 Variables Control Charts: The Individuals Chart

Only one measurement is made at a time, and each individual measurement is used, and plotted, as if it were a subgroup average. This chart can be used in situations where only one measurement at a time can be done (certain chemical processes, for instance), where most errors are likely to be measurement errors, where automated measurement is used, or where production run times are long (days, weeks, etc.). It cannot be used if the process is not normally distributed (other charts control on sample averages, instead of only single measurements, and thus assure a relatively normal distribution). Individuals charts are very rarely used and, when used, should be used with extreme care.

Since the subgroup size of the individuals chart is only 1, the process variation (R-bar) cannot be determined in the traditional manner; a moving average procedure must be used instead. The individuals R chart uses a moving range of two ($n=2$), and so the limit conversion values for a subsample size of 2 from Table A4 are used as constants in the formulas. Moving range values are absolute values of the present measurement minus the previous measurement (or just simply subtract the smaller from the larger). Therefore, there is always one less moving range value than measurements (because the first measurement has nothing from which to subtract).

The control chart formulas are similar to those of the X-bar, R chart, except that the Table A2 values for a subgroup of 2 are incorporated into the formulas as constants, the actual individual measurements are used in place of subgroup averages, and X-bar is used in place of X-double-bar for the chart central value. In the formulas: 2.66 = 3/1.128 (where the 1.128 is d_2 from Table A2 for a subgroup of 2, and the 3 is the number of standard deviations from the chart mean, i.e., the X-bar); 3.267 is D_4 from Table A2 for a subgroup of 2, and 0 is D_3 from Table A2 for a subgroup of 2. The formulas are:

$$\overline{X} = \Sigma X / n$$

$$\overline{R} = \Sigma R / n$$

$$\text{UCL}_X = \overline{X} + 2.66\overline{R}$$

$$LCL_X = \overline{X} - 2.66\overline{R}$$

$$UCL_R = 3.267\overline{R}$$

$$LCL_R = (0)\overline{R}.$$

Example 5.7 Using the data from Table 5.7, construct an individuals control chart.

Solution

1. Calculate the ranges (R). These are given in Table 5.7. The first two range calculations will be shown here as examples:

$$R_2 = |1.062 - 1.055| = 0.007$$

$$R_3 = |1.054 - 1.062| = 0.008.$$

2. Calculate the trial control limits and midpoints.

$$\overline{X} = \Sigma X/n = 21.322/20 = 1.0661$$

$$\overline{R} = \Sigma R/n = 0.128/19 = 0.0067$$

Table 5.7. Shaft Diameters (in.)

Sample No.	Measurement X	Moving Range *MR*
1	1.055	—
2	1.062	0.007
3	1.054	0.008
4	1.055	0.001
5	1.060	0.005
6	1.061	0.001
7	1.065	0.004
8	1.067	0.002
9	1.058	0.009
10	1.068	0.010
11	1.059	0.009
12	1.062	0.003
13	1.057	0.005
14	1.065	0.008
15	1.067	0.002
16	1.061	0.006
17	1.091*	0.030*
18	1.085*	0.006
19	1.089*	0.004
20	1.081	0.008
Totals	21.322	0.128

*Denotes possible out-of-control values.

LAD COMPANY page ____ of ____

Individuals Control Chart

Part number ________ Part name ____________________ Spec ____________

Operator (s) ____________________ Inspector (s) ____________________

Process ______________________________ Chart number __________

Gages ______________________________ Date ____/____/____

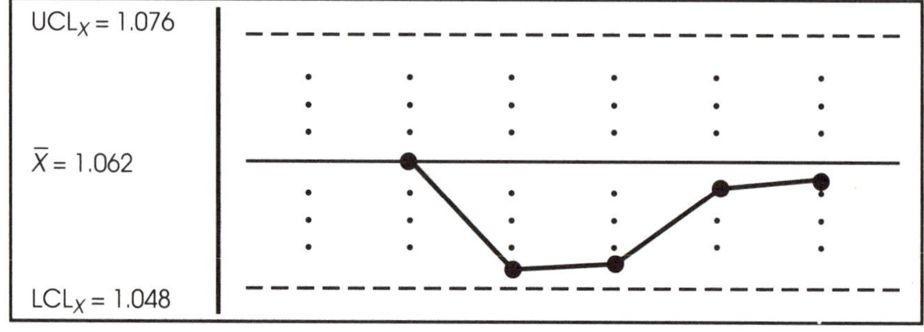

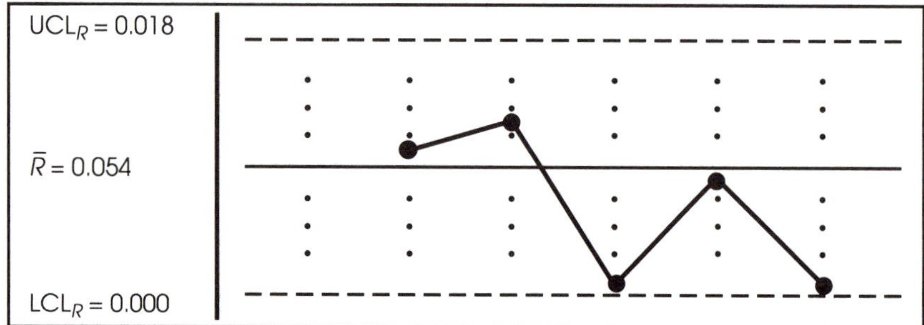

X	1.055	1.062	1.054	1.055	1.060	1.061
RANGE	—	0.007	0.008	0.001	0.005	0.001
DATE	3/1	3/1	3/2	3/2	3/2	3/5
TIME	8:06	10:35	2:00	3:15	4:20	9:55

Figure 5.7. Sample individuals control chart.

$$\mathrm{UCL}_X = \overline{X} + 2.66\overline{R} = 1.0661 + 2.66(0.0067) = 1.084$$

$$\mathrm{LCL}_X = \overline{X} - 2.66\overline{R} = 1.0661 - 2.66(0.0067) = 1.048$$

$$\mathrm{UCL}_R = 3.267\overline{R} = 3.267(0.0067) = 0.022$$

$$\mathrm{LCL}_R = 0 = 0.$$

3. Compare the trial limits to the X's and R's of Table 5.7, investigate all outside points (outside the control limits) for assignable causes, correct

the causes, and remove all out-of-control points from the revised calculations. There are three measurements (X's) and one moving range in Table 5.7 that are outside the limits (all higher than the upper limits of 1.084 and 0.022). Assuming that all of these values have assignable causes, calculate the revised limits and midpoint.

$$\overline{X} = (21.322 - 1.091 - 1.085 - 1.089)/(20-3) = 1.062$$

$$\overline{R} = \Sigma R/n = (0.128 - 0.030)/(19-1) = 0.0054$$

$$UCL_X = \overline{X} + 2.66\overline{R} = 1.062 + 2.66(0.0054) = 1.076$$

$$LCL_X = \overline{X} - 2.66\overline{R} = 1.062 - 2.66(0.0054) = 1.048$$

$$UCL_R = 3.267\overline{R} = 3.267(0.0054) = 0.018$$

$$LCL_R = 0 = 0.$$

4. Construct the chart and chart all X's and R's. (Some practitioners advocate charting the moving ranges in between the two measurements from which they are derived.) The user is cautioned that patterns on the moving range chart may not designate possible out-of-control conditions, as they do on other charts, due to possible correlations from one measurement to another caused by the moving average procedure. Figure 5.7 presents a partial chart of this example.

5.8 Variables Control Charts: Chart Using Specification Limits

This is another type of chart that uses specification limits in place of control limits (the other is the pre-control chart). These charts are basically designed for short production runs, although they can be used for long process times as well. The central value (midpoint or X-bar) and limits for this chart are established using the specifications (since there is never enough time to establish actual process control limits). This type of chart does not give the same measure of process control as do the basic X-bar, R charts, but it does provide a measure of control where none could exist otherwise.

Since these limits are derived from specifications, they represent what is desired for the process rather than what the process can do (as is the case in most other control charts). All chart analyses should be made with this limitation in mind. If the process is not centered on the chart midpoint (if the X-bar of the chart does not equal the process μ), it is possible for the chart to signal a possible out-of-control condition when, in fact, none exists. Thus, much valuable time could be lost trying to find an assignable cause that does not exist.

As in the basic X-bar, R chart, two charts are used for the μ (mu), σ (sigma) chart. The one for the central value (the μ or mu chart) takes the place of the X-bar chart, and the one for the dispersion (the σ or sigma chart) takes the place of the R chart. In this type of chart, the central value of the μ chart is the midpoint of the specification spread, and a standard deviation is determined at 1/6 the spread. The central value of the σ chart (R-bar) must be computed by multiplying sigma by d_2 (from Table A4).

The formulas are:

$$\mu = (\text{USL} + \text{LSL})/2$$

$$\sigma = (\text{USL} - \text{LSL})/6$$

$$\overline{R} = d_2\sigma$$

$$\text{UCL}_\mu = \mu + 3\sigma/\sqrt{n}$$

$$\text{LCL}_\mu = \mu - 3\sigma/\sqrt{n}$$

$$\text{UCL}_\sigma = D_2\sigma$$

$$\text{LCL}_\sigma = D_1\sigma$$

where

USL = the upper specification limit

LSL = the lower specification limit

μ = mu = the central value of the μ chart, the assumed mean of the distribution

σ = the assumed standard deviation

$\overline{R}$ = R-bar = the central value of the σ chart

d_2, D_1, D_2 = conversion values from Table A4

UCL_μ = the upper control limit for the μ chart

LCL_μ = the lower control limit for the μ chart

UCL_σ = the upper control limit for the σ chart

LCL_σ = the lower control limit for the σ chart.

Example 5.8 Construct a specifications chart for an upper specification limit (USL) of 1.082 and a lower specification limit (LSL) of 1.054. The sample size is 4.

Solution

1. Calculate the control limits and central values.

$$\mu = (\text{USL} + \text{LSL})/2 = (1.082 + 1.054)/2 = 1.068$$

$$\sigma = (\text{USL} - \text{LSL})/6 = (1.082 - 1.054)/6 = 0.00467$$

$$\overline{R} = d_2\sigma = 2.059(0.00467) = 0.0096$$

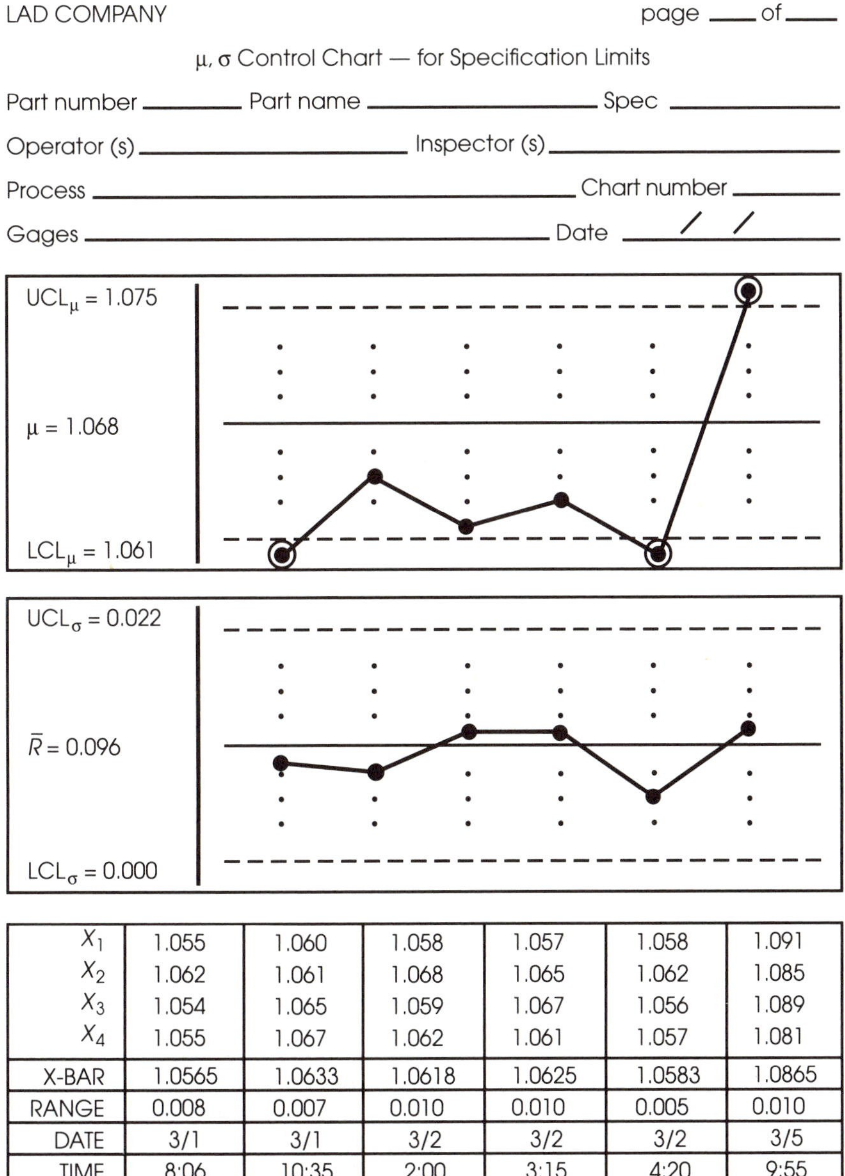

LAD COMPANY page ____ of ____

μ, σ Control Chart — for Specification Limits

Part number ________ Part name ________________ Spec ____________

Operator (s) ________________ Inspector (s) ________________

Process ________________________________ Chart number ________

Gages ________________________________ Date ____ / / ____

X_1	1.055	1.060	1.058	1.057	1.058	1.091
X_2	1.062	1.061	1.068	1.065	1.062	1.085
X_3	1.054	1.065	1.059	1.067	1.056	1.089
X_4	1.055	1.067	1.062	1.061	1.057	1.081
X-BAR	1.0565	1.0633	1.0618	1.0625	1.0583	1.0865
RANGE	0.008	0.007	0.010	0.010	0.005	0.010
DATE	3/1	3/1	3/2	3/2	3/2	3/5
TIME	8:06	10:35	2:00	3:15	4:20	9:55

Note: Specifications are 1.082/1.054

Figure 5.8. Sample μ, σ control chart—with specification limits.

$$UCL_\mu = \mu + 3\sigma/\sqrt{n} = 1.068 + 3(0.00467)/\sqrt{4} = 1.075$$

$$LCL_\mu = \mu - 3\sigma/\sqrt{n} = 1.068 - 3(0.00467)/\sqrt{4} = 1.061$$

$$UCL_\sigma = D_2\sigma = 4.698(0.00467) = 0.022$$

$$LCL_\sigma = D_1\sigma = 0(0.00467) = 0.$$

2. Construct the chart, measure the samples (of 4 each), calculate the sample averages (X-bars) and ranges (R's), and plot the X-bars and R's on the chart as the samples are measured. The X-bars are charted on the μ chart and the R's on the σ chart. Figure 5.8 presents a partial control chart using the data from Table 5.8. Since these charts are not derived from sample measurements, there is no need for revised limit calculations.

Table 5.8. Shaft Diameters (in.)

Sample No.	Measurements (observations) X_1	X_2	X_3	X_4	Mean X-bar	Range R
1	1.055	1.062	1.054	1.055	1.0565*	0.008
2	1.060	1.061	1.065	1.067	1.0633	0.007
3	1.058	1.068	1.059	1.062	1.0618	0.010
4	1.057	1.065	1.067	1.061	1.0625	0.010
5	1.058	1.062	1.056	1.057	1.0583	0.005
6	1.091	1.085	1.089	1.081	1.0865*	0.010
7	1.060	1.056	1.066	1.062	1.0610	0.010
8	1.064	1.063	1.065	1.068	1.0650	0.005
9	1.066	1.063	1.063	1.068	1.0650	0.005
10	1.055	1.063	1.060	1.058	1.0590	0.008
11	1.070	1.074	1.071	1.073	1.0720*	0.004
12	1.069	1.065	1.058	1.064	1.0640	0.011
13	1.060	1.063	1.061	1.060	1.0610	0.003
14	1.059	1.059	1.063	1.059	1.0600	0.004
15	1.062	1.060	1.069	1.057	1.0620	0.012
16	1.060	1.062	1.067	1.064	1.0633	0.007
17	1.064	1.070	1.067	1.065	1.0665	0.006
18	1.055	1.057	1.051	1.061	1.0560*	0.010
19	1.063	1.063	1.057	1.051	1.0585	0.012
20	1.065	1.060	1.050	1.080	1.0638	0.030*
21	1.055	1.054	1.059	1.060	1.0570	0.006
22	1.077	1.078	1.067	1.070	1.0730*	0.011
23	1.062	1.060	1.067	1.059	1.0620	0.008
24	1.061	1.057	1.062	1.064	1.0610	0.007
25	1.061	1.064	1.061	1.058	1.0610	0.006
			Totals (Σ)		26.5800	0.216

*Indicates a possible out-of-control condition.

5.9 Attributes Control Charts for Defectives: The *np* Chart (Number Defective Chart)

This chart is an adaptation of the basic *p* chart, where the actual number of nonconformities is plotted instead of the percentage. The purpose of this chart is to provide better understanding to the operator, who may understand whole numbers of actual nonconformities better than percentages. This chart requires a constant subgroup size. Actual nonconformities from variable subgroup sizes cannot be compared—one nonconformity from a sample of 10 shows a much higher rate of problems (10%) than does one from a sample of 100 (1%).

The formulas are:

$$\bar{p} = \Sigma np/\Sigma n$$

$$\text{UCL}_{np} = n\bar{p} + 3\sqrt{[n\bar{p}(1-\bar{p})]}$$

$$\text{LCL}_{np} = n\bar{p} - 3\sqrt{[n\bar{p}(1-\bar{p})]}.$$

Example 5.9 Construct an *np* chart for the data in Table 5.9.

Solution

1. Collect the samples (subgroups). This has already been done in Table 5.9. Note that the *p*'s have not been calculated here as they were in the previous two *p* charts (they are not needed in this chart).

2. Calculate the trial control limits.

$$\bar{p} = \Sigma np/\Sigma n = 153/12{,}500 = 0.01224$$

$$n\bar{p} = 500(0.01224) = 6.12$$

$$\text{UCL}_{np} = n\bar{p} + 3\sqrt{[n\bar{p}(1-\bar{p})]}$$

$$= 6.12 + 3\sqrt{6.12(1-0.01224)} = 13.5$$

$$\text{LCL}_{np} = n\bar{p} - 3\sqrt{[n\bar{p}(1-\bar{p})]}$$

$$= 6.12 - 3\sqrt{6.12(1-0.01224)} = -1.256\text{; use } 0.$$

3. Calculate the revised control limits. Compare the trial limits to each of the 25 *np*'s, search for assignable causes for each nonconforming *np* (those above the upper limit), and omit from the revised calculations those nonconforming *np*'s that have assignable causes. Assuming all outside values have assignable causes, the revised limits are:

$$\bar{p} = \Sigma np/\Sigma n = (153 - 14 - 14 - 18)/(12{,}500 - 1500) = 0.0097$$

$$n\bar{p} = 500(0.0097) = 4.85$$

$$\text{UCL}_{np} = n\bar{p} + 3\sqrt{[n\bar{p}(1-\bar{p})]}$$

$$= 4.85 + 3\sqrt{4.85(1-0.0097)} = 11.4$$

Table 5.9. Number of Defective Parts

Sample Number	Number Inspected n	Number Defective np
1	500	14*
2	500	4
3	500	10
4	500	5
5	500	0
6	500	6
7	500	6
8	500	3
9	500	8
10	500	12
11	500	5
12	500	14*
13	500	8
14	500	3
15	500	0
16	500	5
17	500	8
18	500	7
19	500	18*
20	500	2
21	500	5
22	500	6
23	500	0
24	500	3
25	500	2
Totals	12,500	153

*Denotes a possible out-of-control subgroup (higher than the upper limit).

$$\text{LCL}_{np} = n\bar{p} - 3\sqrt{[n\bar{p}(1-\bar{p})]} = 0.021$$

$$= 4.85 - 3\sqrt{4.85(1-0.0097)} = -1.7\text{; use } 0.$$

4. Construct the chart and plot all 25 *np* values (see Figure 5.9). In this chart, the chart values are not converted to percentages.

5.10 Attributes Control Charts for Defectives: Variable Subgroup Size *p* Charts

This chart is identical to the constant subgroup size chart, except that limits must be calculated for each subgroup. Actually, this is also true of constant subgroup size charts. It is just that the limits are the

LAD COMPANY page ___ of ___

np Control Chart

Part number ______ Part name ______ Spec ______

Operator (s) ______ Inspector (s) ______

Process ______ Chart number ______

Gages ______ Date __/__/__

								CHART TOTALS
# DEFECTS	16	5	13	6	0	9	10	183
1. Oversize	2		2	2		3	2	34
2. Undersize	10	4	8	3		3	7	109
3. Rough	4	1	3	1		3	1	40
4.								
5.								
# DEFECTIVES	14	4	10	5	0	6	6	153
# CHECKED	500	500	500	500	500	500	500	12,500
% DEFECTIVES								1.2

Figure 5.9. Partial *np* control chart.

same for each subgroup when the sample size is constant, making the resultant line a straight line, and making it unnecessary to calculate the limits for each subgroup. The formulas are identical for both charts—they are just used more often (for each subgroup instead of just once). This chart should only be used when constant subgroup sizes are either impossible, unavailable, or unrealistic. Note that in Figure 5.10 the

LAD COMPANY page ___ of ___

p Control Chart

Part number ______ Part name __________ Spec ________

Operator (s) __________ Inspector (s) __________

Process __________________ Chart number ______

Gages __________________ Date / /

DATE:	3/1	3/2	3/3	3/4	3/5	3/8	3/9	TOTALS
REVISED VALUES: 6.0, 5.2, 4.4, UCL 3.6, 2.8, $\bar{p}$ = 2.1% 2.0, 1.2, 0.4, LCL 0.0								
# DEFECTS	40	8	29	13	4	14	15	422
1. Fill	12	2	9	3		7	5	77
2. Burnt	20	6	13	7	2	6	8	178
3. Cold	8		7	3	2	1	1	37
# DEFECTIVES	30	8	21	9	1	12	5	292
# CHECKED	450	400	560	510	430	470	490	11,220
% DEFECTIVES	6.7	2.0	3.8	1.8	0.2	2.6	1.0	2.6
UCL	4.1	4.3	3.9	4.0	4.2	4.1	4.0	
LCL	0.1	0.1	0.3	0.2	0.1	0.1	0.2	

Note: The LCL lines are not shown because they are so close to zero.

Figure 5.10. Sample variable *p* control chart.

number of defects provide a kind of automatic Pareto for further analysis.

Example 5.10 Construct a variable *p* chart using the data in Table 5.10.

Table 5.10. Number of Defective Parts, Variable Subgroup Size

Subgroup No.	Number Inspected n	Number Defective np	Fraction Defective p	UCL_p	LCL_p
1.	450	30	0.067*	0.049	0.003
2.	400	8	0.020	0.050	0.002
3.	560	21	0.038	0.046	0.006
4.	510	9	0.018	0.047	0.005
5.	430	1	0.002	0.049	0.003
6.	470	12	0.026	0.048	0.004
7.	490	5	0.010	0.048	0.004
8.	470	8	0.017	0.048	0.004
9.	570	15	0.026	0.046	0.006
10.	500	25	0.050*	0.047	0.005
11.	500	10	0.020	0.047	0.005
12.	520	22	0.042	0.047	0.005
13.	500	0	0.000	0.047	0.005
14.	500	6	0.012	0.047	0.005
15.	500	10	0.020	0.047	0.005
16.	380	16	0.042	0.050	0.001
17.	350	14	0.040	0.052	0.000
18.	300	29	0.097*	0.054	−0.002
19.	490	4	0.008	0.048	0.004
20.	600	11	0.018	0.045	0.007
21.	390	10	0.026	0.050	0.002
22.	300	0	0.000	0.054	−0.002
23.	400	15	0.038	0.050	0.002
24.	340	5	0.015	0.052	0.000
25.	300	11	0.037	0.054	−0.002
Totals	11,220	292			
Revised limits for the first seven subgroups.					
1.				0.041	0.0007
2.				0.043	0.0005
3.				0.039	0.003
4.				0.040	0.002
5.				0.042	0.0003
6.				0.041	0.0012
7.				0.040	0.0016

*Denotes possible out-of-control subgroups (higher than the upper limit).

Solution

1. Collect the samples (subgroups) and calculate the subgroup averages. This has already been done in Table 5.10. The following calculation of

the first subgroup average will be used as an example of these calculations.

$$p_1 = np/n = 30/450 = 0.067.$$

2. Calculate the trial control limits for all 25 subgroups. This has already been done in Table 5.10, but the calculations for subgroup 1 shall be shown as an example.

$$\bar{p} = \Sigma np/\Sigma n = 292/11{,}220 = 0.026$$

$$\text{UCL}_{p1} = \bar{p} + 3\sqrt{\bar{p}(1-\bar{p})/n} = 0.026 + 3\sqrt{0.026(1-0.026)/450} = 0.049$$

$$\text{LCL}_{p1} = \bar{p} - 3\sqrt{\bar{p}(1-\bar{p})/n} = 0.026 - 3\sqrt{0.026(1-0.026)/450} = 0.003.$$

3. Calculate the revised control limits. Compare the trial limits of each subgroup to its own p, search for assignable causes for each nonconforming p (those above the upper limit), and omit from the revised calculations those nonconforming p's that have assignable causes. Assuming that all outside values have assignable causes, the revised central value (p-bar) and the limits for subgroup 1 are given below. Table 5.10 gives the limits for the first seven subgroups.

$$\bar{p} = \Sigma np/\Sigma n = (292-30-25-29)/(11{,}220-450-500-300) = 0.021$$

$$\text{UCL}_{p1} = \bar{p} + 3\sqrt{\bar{p}(1-\bar{p})/n} = 0.021 + 3\sqrt{0.021(1-0.021)/450} = 0.041$$

$$\text{LCL}_{p1} = \bar{p} - 3\sqrt{\bar{p}(1-\bar{p})/n} = 0.021 - 3\sqrt{0.021(1-0.021)/450} = 0.0007.$$

Calculate control limits for all 25 subgroups.

4. Construct the chart and plot all 25 p values (see Figure 5.10). Remember to convert the central value (p-bar), the limits, and all plotted values to percentages (multiply by 100). Note the uneven limit lines on the chart.

5.11 Attributes Control Charts: Average Sample Size *p* Chart

This chart (also called the stabilized p chart) is the same as the variable p chart, with variable subgroup sizes, except that an average subgroup size is used to calculate the limit lines. Thus, the limits can be represented as straight lines, restoring the predictive nature of the chart. Theoretically, the variation in subgroup sizes should be no greater than 25% in order to use the stabilized chart. However, in actual practice, the sizes can usually vary much more than this and still provide reasonable and effective control—just investigate all high values, whether inside or outside the limit. After all, the purpose of control charts is to reduce nonconformities. Since all entries on a p chart represent nonconformities, any investigation into causes, whether inside or outside the limits, should contribute to that goal.

This is probably the best chart for long production times, where the sample size (at least when the chart is started) is one day's production. Long production times present a special problem to quality professionals, but this problem can be solved and controlled (see Section 4.5).

The formulas are still the same, except that one more formula is added to determine the average subgroup size. That formula is: $n_a = \Sigma n/m$, where n_a is the average subgroup size.

Example 5.11 Construct an average p chart from the data of Table 5.11.

Solution

1. Collect the samples (subgroups) and calculate the subgroup averages. This has already been done in Table 5.11. The following calculation of the first subgroup average will be used as an example of these calculations:

$$p_1 = np/n = 30/450 = 0.067.$$

2. Calculate the trial control limits.

$$\bar{p} = \Sigma np/\Sigma n = 292/11{,}220 = 0.026$$

$$n_a = \Sigma n/m = 11{,}220/25 = 448.8$$

$$\begin{aligned} UCL_p &= \bar{p} + 3\sqrt{\bar{p}(1-\bar{p})/n_a} = 0.026 \\ &\quad + 3\sqrt{0.026(1-0.026)/448.8} = 0.049 \\ LCL_p &= \bar{p} - 3\sqrt{\bar{p}(1-\bar{p})/n_a} = 0.026 \\ &\quad - 3\sqrt{0.026(1-0.026)/448.8} = 0.003. \end{aligned}$$

3. Calculate the revised control limits. Compare the trial limits to each of the 25 p's, search for assignable causes for each outside p (those above the upper limit), and omit from the revised calculations those outside p's that have assignable causes. Assuming that all outside values have assignable causes, the revised limits are:

$$\bar{p} = \Sigma np/\Sigma n = (292 - 30 - 25 - 29)/(11{,}220 - 450 - 500 - 300) = 0.021$$

$$n_a = \Sigma n/m = (11{,}220 - 450 - 500 - 300)/(25 - 3) = 453.2$$

$$\begin{aligned} UCL_p &= \bar{p} + 3\sqrt{\bar{p}(1-\bar{p})/n_a} \\ &= 0.021 + 3\sqrt{0.021(1-0.021)/453.2} = 0.041 \end{aligned}$$

Table 5.11. Number of Defective Parts, Variable Subgroup Size

Subgroup No.	Number Inspected n	Number Defective np	Fraction Defective p
1.	450	30	0.067*
2.	400	8	0.020
3.	560	21	0.038
4.	510	9	0.018
5.	430	1	0.002
6.	470	12	0.026
7.	490	5	0.010
8.	470	8	0.017
9.	570	15	0.026
10.	500	25	0.050*
11.	500	10	0.020
12.	520	22	0.042
13.	500	0	0.000
14.	500	6	0.012
15.	500	10	0.020
16.	380	16	0.042
17.	350	14	0.040
18.	300	29	0.097*
19.	490	4	0.008
20.	600	11	0.018
21.	390	10	0.026
22.	300	0	0.000
23.	400	15	0.038
24.	340	5	0.015
25.	300	11	0.037
Totals	11,220	292	

*Denotes possible out-of-control subgroups (higher than the upper limit).

$$\begin{aligned} \mathrm{LCL}_p &= \bar{p} - 3\sqrt{\bar{p}(1-\bar{p})/n_a} \\ &= 0.021 - 3\sqrt{0.021(1-0.021)/453.2} = 0.001. \end{aligned}$$

4. Construct the chart and plot all 25 p values (see Figure 5.11). Remember to convert to percentages.

5.12 Attributes Control Charts: The Weighted *p* Chart and the Weighted Average *p* Chart

These are the same as the basic p chart, except that the various types of defectives are categorized and weighted, i.e., multiplied by a weighting factor. Each weighting factor is applied as a portion of 100% (to keep the resultant weighted p value below 1.00, because the p chart

LAD COMPANY page ____ of ____

p Control Chart

Part number ________ Part name ________________ Spec ________

Operator (s) ________________ Inspector (s) ________________

Process ________________________ Chart number ________

Gages ________________________ Date ___/___/___

DATE:	3/1	3/2	3/3	3/4	3/5	3/8	3/9	

REVISED VALUES 6.0, 5.2, 4.4, UCL = 4.1%, 3.6, 2.8, $\bar{p}$ = 2.1% 2.0, 1.2, 0.4, LCL = 0.1% 0.0

								TOTALS
# DEFECTS	40	8	29	13	4	14	15	422
1. Fill	12	2	9	3		7	5	77
2. Burnt	20	6	13	7	2	6	8	178
3. Cold	8		7	3	2	1	1	37
4.								
5.								
# DEFECTIVES	30	8	21	9	1	12	5	292
# CHECKED	450	400	560	510	430	470	490	11,220
% DEFECTIVES	6.7	2.0	3.8	1.8	0.2	2.6	1.0	2.6

Figure 5.11. Sample average p control chart.

will not work for p values greater than 1.00). For instance, in Figure 5.12, defective type A has a weighting of 0.05 (5%). Also, the sum of all the weighting factors must equal 100% (there cannot be more defectives than 100%). Note that in Figure 5.12, the weighting factors sum to 1.00 (100%).

LAD COMPANY page ___ of ___

Weighted p Control Chart

Part number ________ Part name ________________ Spec ____________

Operator (s) ________________ Inspector (s) ________________

Process ______________________________ Chart number ________

Gages ______________________________ Date ___/___/___

DATE:	3/1	3/2	3/3	3/4	3/5	3/8	3/9

0.08

UCL = 0.075

0.07

0.06

0.05

M = 0.0425

0.04

0.03

0.20

LCL = 0.01

0.10

ITEM	WEIGHT	DEFECTS PER SUBSAMPLE PER ITEM							TOTALS
A	0.05	1	2	3	3	2	5	1	40
B	0.15	2	3	4	5		8		60
C	0.30	3	4	5	7		9	1	80
D	0.50	4	5	6	3	1	8	2	100
# CHECKED		90	110	100	150	120	120	70	2000
p_i (Plot)		0.036	0.039	0.053	0.030	0.005	0.068	0.019	0.0425

$p_i = \Sigma(W_j E_{i\,j})/n_i$

Figure 5.12. Sample weighted average *p* control chart.

Some important weighting characteristics are:

- customer satisfaction;
- production, schedule, amount;
- safety;
- product liability;
- cost;

- contribution to profit;
- combinations of any of the above.

This chart can be used with either a constant or variable subgroup size. As with any control chart, it is always best to use a constant subgroup size, if possible. Weighted attribute charts are most often used with nonmanufacturing applications, and 100% inspection is often necessary in nonmanufacturing situations.

Basic attributes charts (or average subgroup size charts, if the subgroup sizes cannot be kept constant) are normally recommended over weighted charts. Weighted charts tend to obscure (hide or lose) the reasons for errors in the weighting procedure. Note that weighted charts always use a constant subgroup size, while a weighted average chart (p or u) always uses a variable subgroup size (different size subgroup sizes, so that the subgroup average has to be calculated and used). Weighted charts are mostly used in nonmanufacturing situations and, in these situations, it is very common to see weighted variable charts (different subgroup sizes).

Note that the only difference between the weighted p and the weighted average p charts is the extra calculation for the average sample size ($n_a = \Sigma n_i/m$) in the weighted average p chart. Only weighted average p charts will be illustrated here.

The formulas are:

$$\bar{p}_j = (\Sigma E_{ij})/\Sigma n_i \qquad \text{(sum from } i=1 \text{ to } m \text{ for each } \bar{p}_j\text{)}$$

$$M = \Sigma(W_j p_j) \qquad \text{(sum from } j=1 \text{ to } q\text{)}$$

$$n_a = \Sigma n_i/m \qquad \text{(sum from } i=1 \text{ to } m\text{).}$$

(When constant subgroup sizes are used, omit the n_a formula.)

$$C = \Sigma[W_j^2 \bar{p}_j(1-\bar{p}_j)]$$

$$\text{UCL}_{pW} = M + 3\sqrt{C/n_a}$$

$$\text{LCL}_{pW} = M - 3\sqrt{C/n_a}.$$

(For constant subgroup sizes, use n instead of n_a.)

$$p_i = \Sigma(W_j E_{ij})/n_i \text{ (sum from } j=1 \text{ to } q \text{ for each } p_i\text{)}$$

where

M = the weighted average % defective for all subgroups

W_j = the weighted factor for the jth type of item

p_j = the average fraction defective for the jth type of item

E_{ij} = the number of defective items of each type in each subgroup

m = the number of subgroups

n_i = the number of items inspected in the ith subgroup

n_a = the average number of items inspected per subgroup (omit when constant subgroup sizes are used)

n = subgroup size for constant subgroup formula

q = the number of types of items

j = the type of item

i = subgroup number

C = an interim value used to simplify the limit calculations

UCL_{pW} = the upper control limit for the weighted p chart

LCL_{pW} = the lower control limit for the weighted p chart.

Example 5.12 Construct a weighted average p chart for the data of Table 5.12.

Solution

1. Form a team (a single individual *can* be used, but this procedure works best with teams).
2. List the different types of items, errors, and/or instruments (reports, line items, assemblies, etc.).
3. Weight each type of item, error, or instrument found. Use teams, and brainstorm.
4. Count the errors and/or defectives. Sampling should be used if possible, but 100% inspection can be used if necessary.
5. Calculate the mean. There will be a p-bar for each type (j) item, which will then be summed in the M equation. The first p-bar will be shown as an example.

$$\bar{p}_j = (\Sigma E_{ij})/\Sigma n_i = \bar{p}_A = (\Sigma E_{iA})/\Sigma n_i = 40/2000 = 0.02$$

$$M = \Sigma(W_j \bar{p}_j) = 0.05(0.02) + 0.15(0.03)$$
$$+ 0.3(0.04) + 0.5(0.05) = 0.0425.$$

6. Calculate the limits.

$$n_a = \Sigma n_i / m = 2000/20 = 100$$

$$C = \Sigma[W_j^2 \bar{p}_j(1 - \bar{p}_j)] = 0.05^2(0.02)(1 - 0.02)$$
$$+ 0.15^2(0.03)(1 - 0.03) + 0.3^2(0.04)(1 - 0.04)$$
$$+ 0.5^2(0.05)(1 - 0.05) = 0.0119$$

Table 5.12. Data for Weighted p Chart Example

Subgroup Number (i)	Number of Defective Items for Type of Item (j) A	B	C	D	Subgroup Size (n_i)	p_i
1	1	2	3	4	90	0.036
2	2	3	4	5	110	0.039
3	3	4	5	6	100	0.053
4	3	5	7	3	150	0.030
5	2	0	0	1	120	0.005
6	5	8	9	8	120	0.068
7	1	0	1	2	70	0.019
.	.	.	.	.	.	.
.	.	.	.	.	.	.
.	.	.	.	.	.	.
20	2	2	2	3	100	0.025
Totals	40	60	80	100	2000	
Weighting (W_j) for each item	0.05	0.15	0.30	0.50		
Weighted average ($\bar{p}_j$) for each item	0.02	0.03	0.04	0.05		

$$UCL_{pW} = M + 3\sqrt{C/n_a} = 0.0425 + 3\sqrt{0.0119/100} = 0.075$$

$$LCL_{pW} = M - 3\sqrt{C/n_a} = 0.0425 - 3\sqrt{0.0119/100} = 0.010.$$

7. Calculate plotting points for each of the subgroups. This is the weighted average of all defective items from each subgroup. There will be one plotted point for each subgroup (m number of p's, or plotted points, for the initial chart). Note that for a constant subgroup size, the n_i will always be the same for all subgroups. These p's are given in the last column of Table 5.12. The calculation for the first plotted point will be shown as an example.

$$p_1 = \Sigma(W_j E_{1j})/n_1 = [0.05(1) + 0.15(2) + 0.3(3) + 0.5(4)]/90 = 0.036.$$

8. Check for out-of-control points, remove out-of-control data, and recalculate (for the revised chart). There are no out-of-control points (above the upper limit), so use the trial limits as the revised limits.
9. Construct the revised chart and plot the points, the p_i (see Figure 5.12).
10. Continue to measure and plot.

5.13 Attributes Control Charts: The Variable Sample Size *u* Chart

This chart is identical to the basic, constant subgroup size, *u* chart in Chapter 4 (Section 4.6), except that the subgroup sizes are not constant. As with the constant *u* chart, when the lower control limit (LCL) calculates to a negative number, it is changed to zero (there cannot be a negative number of defects). The same formulas apply to this chart as to the basic, constant subgroup size, chart. The only difference is that the limit formulas are applied to each subgroup (just as in the variable *p* chart, and for exactly the same reasons). Basic attributes charts, with constant sample sizes, are normally recommended over variable charts.

Example 5.13. Construct a *u* chart from the data in Table 5.13.

Solution

1. Collect the samples (subgroups) and calculate the subgroup averages. This has already been done in Table 5.13. The following calculation of the first subgroup average will be used as an example of these calculations.

$$u_1 = c/n = 48/100 = 0.48.$$

2. Calculate the chart midpoint (*u*-bar).

$$\bar{u} = \Sigma c/\Sigma n = 1746/2565 = 0.68.$$

3. Calculate the trial control limits for each subgroup. This has already been done in Table 5.13, but the calculations for subgroup 1 will be presented as an example.

$$\text{UCL}_{u1} = \bar{u} + 3\sqrt{\bar{u}/n} = 0.68 + 3\sqrt{0.68/100} = 0.93$$

$$\text{LCL}_{u1} = \bar{u} - 3\sqrt{\bar{u}/n} = 0.68 - 3\sqrt{0.68/100} = 0.43.$$

4. Calculate the revised control limits for all 25 subgroups. Compare the trial limits to each of the 25 *u*'s, search for assignable causes for each nonconforming *u* (those above the upper limit), and omit from the revised calculations those nonconforming *u*'s that have assignable causes. Assuming all have assignable causes, the revised limits for subgroup 1 are given below (the revised limits for the first seven subgroups are given in Table 5.13):

$$\bar{u} = \Sigma c/\Sigma n = (1746 - 117)/(2500 - 100) = 0.66$$

$$\text{UCL}_{u1} = \bar{u} + 3\sqrt{\bar{u}/n} = 0.66 + 3\sqrt{0.66/100} = 0.90$$

$$\text{UCL}_{u1} = \bar{u} - 3\sqrt{\bar{u}/n} = 0.66 - 3\sqrt{0.66/100} = 0.42.$$

Table 5.13. *u* Chart Data—Variable Subsample Size

Subgroup No.	Number Inspected *n*	Number of Defects *c*	Defects per Unit *u*	UCL	LCL
1.	100	48	0.48	0.93	0.43
2.	110	58	0.53	0.92	0.44
3.	120	53	0.44	0.91	0.45
4.	140	78	0.56	0.89	0.47
5.	100	89	0.89	0.93	0.43
6.	80	68	0.85	0.96	0.40
7.	95	77	0.81	0.94	0.43
8.	85	49	0.58	0.96	
9.	90	86	0.96	0.94	
10.	130	79	0.61	0.90	
11.	110	69	0.63	0.91	
12.	100	69	0.69	0.93	
13.	110	62	0.56	0.91	
14.	120	62	0.52	0.89	
15.	75	67	0.89	0.97	
16.	100	74	0.74	0.93	
17.	100	75	0.75	0.93	
18.	100	89	0.89	0.93	
19.	75	69	0.92	0.96	
20.	95	56	0.59	0.94	
21.	110	47	0.43	0.91	
22.	110	76	0.69	0.91	
23.	110	71	0.65	0.91	
24.	100	66	0.66	0.93	
25.	100	117	1.17*	0.93	
Totals =	2565	1746			

Revised limits for the first seven subgroups.

Subgroup No.				UCL	LCL
1.				0.90	0.42
2.				0.89	0.43
3.				0.88	0.44
4.				0.87	0.45
5.				0.90	0.42
6.				1.00	0.32
7.				0.91	0.41

*Indicates a possible out-of-control condition.

5. Construct the chart and plot all 25 *u* values and all 25 limits (see Figure 5.13). Do not change to percentages.
6. Display the chart in a conspicuous place and continue to measure and plot.

LAD COMPANY page ___ of ___

u Control Chart

Part number ______ Part name ____________ Spec ________

Operator (s) ____________ Inspector (s) ____________

Process ____________________ Chart number ______

Gages ____________________ Date / /

DATE:	3/1	3/2	3/3	3/4	3/5	3/8	3/9	
REVISED VALUES 1.20								
1.04								
UCL 0.88								
0.72								
$\bar{u}$ = 0.66 0.56								
LCL 0.40								
0.24								
0.08								
.0								TOTALS
TYPE DEFECT								
1. Scratches	12	15	15	23	21	19	25	460
2. Oversize	28	34	30	43	44	41	35	1064
3. Welds	8	9	8	12	24	8	17	222
# DEFECTS	48	58	53	78	89	68	77	1746
# CHECKED	100	110	120	140	100	80	95	2565
DEFECTS/UNIT	0.48	0.53	0.44	0.56	0.89	0.85	0.81	0.68
UCL	0.90	0.89	0.88	0.87	0.90	1.00	0.91	
LCL	0.42	0.43	0.44	0.45	0.42	0.32	0.41	

Figure 5.13. Sample variable *u* control chart.

5.14 Attributes Control Charts: The Average Sample Size *u* Chart

This chart, also known as the stabilized *u* chart, is the same as the variable *u* chart, with variable subgroup sizes, except that an average subgroup size is used to calculate the limit lines. Thus, the limits can be represented as straight lines, restoring the predictive nature of the chart. Theoretically, the variation in subgroup sizes should be no greater than 25% in order to use the stabilized chart. However, in actual practice, the sizes can usually vary much more than this and still provide reasonable and effective control—just investigate all high values, whether inside or outside the limit. After all, the purpose of control charts is to reduce nonconformities. Since all entries on a *u* chart represent nonconformities, any investigation into causes, whether inside or outside the limits, should contribute to that goal.

The formulas are still the same, except that one more formula is added to determine the average subgroup size:

$$n_a = \Sigma n/m$$

where n_a is the average subgroup size.

Example 5.14 Construct an average *u* chart from the data of Table 5.14.

Solution

1. Collect the samples (subgroups) and calculate the subgroup averages. This has already been done in Table 5.14. The following calculation of the first subgroup average will be used as an example of these calculations:

$$u_1 = c/n = 48/100 = 0.48.$$

2. Calculate the chart midpoint (*u*-bar).

$$\bar{u} = \Sigma c/\Sigma n = 1746/2565 = 0.68.$$

3. Calculate the trial control limits.

$$n_a = \Sigma n/m = 2565/25 = 102.6$$

$$\text{UCL}_u = \bar{u} + 3\sqrt{\bar{u}/n_a} = 0.68 + 3\sqrt{0.68/102.6} = 0.92$$

$$\text{LCL}_u = \bar{u} - 3\sqrt{\bar{u}/n_a} = 0.68 - 3\sqrt{0.68/102.6} = 0.44.$$

3. Calculate the revised control limits. Compare the trial limits to each of the 25 *u*'s, search for assignable causes for each outside *u* (those above the upper limit), and omit from the revised calculations those outside *u*'s that have assignable causes. Assuming that all outside values have assignable causes, the revised limits are:

$$\bar{u} = \Sigma c/\Sigma n = (1746 - 117)/(2565 - 100) = 0.66$$

$$n_a = \Sigma n/m = (2565 - 100)/(25 - 1) = 102.7$$

$$\text{UCL}_u = \bar{u} - 3\sqrt{\bar{u}/n_a} = 0.66 + 3\sqrt{0.66/102.7} = 0.90$$

$$\text{LCL}_u = \bar{u} - 3\sqrt{\bar{u}/n_a} = 0.66 - 3\sqrt{0.66/102.7} = 0.42.$$

Table 5.14. *u* Chart Data—Variable Subgroup Size

Subgroup No.	Number Inspected n	Number of Defects c	Defects per Unit u
1.	100	48	0.48
2.	110	58	0.53
3.	120	53	0.44
4.	140	78	0.56
5.	100	89	0.89
6.	80	68	0.85
7.	95	77	0.81
8.	85	49	0.58
9.	90	86	0.96
10.	130	79	0.61
11.	110	69	0.63
12.	100	69	0.69
13.	110	62	0.56
14.	120	62	0.52
15.	75	67	0.89
16.	100	74	0.74
17.	100	75	0.75
18.	100	89	0.89
19.	75	69	0.92
20.	95	56	0.59
21.	110	47	0.43
22.	110	76	0.69
23.	110	71	0.65
24.	100	66	0.66
25.	100	117	1.17*
Totals =	2565	1746	

*Indicates a possible out-of-control condition.

4. Construct the chart and plot all 25 u values (see Figure 5.14). Do not convert to percentages.

5.15 Attributes Control Charts: The Weighted *u* Chart and the Weighted Average *u* Chart

This chart is similar to the basic u chart, except that the various types of defectives are categorized and weighted, i.e., multiplied by a weighting factor. (Note that the p chart weighted values must be kept below one; these must sum to one. This is not true of the weighted u value.) Each weighting factor is applied on a scale of some kind (1 to 5, 1 to 10, etc.). For instance, medication on time might be judged on a scale of 1 to 10 (judge the severity, possible adverse effects of being

LAD COMPANY page ____ of ____

Average u Control Chart

Part number ________ Part name ____________________ Spec ______________

Operator (s) ______________________ Inspector (s) ________________________

Process ____ Chart number ________

Gages ______________________________________ Date ____/____/____

REVISED VALUES

UCL = 0.90

$\bar{u}$ = 0.66

LCL = 0.42

1.20, 1.04, 0.88, 0.72, 0.56, 0.40, 0.24, 0.08, 0.0

DATE:	3/1	3/2	3/3	3/4	3/5	3/8	3/9	TOTALS
TYPE DEFECT								
1. Scratches	12	15	15	23	21	19	25	460
2. Oversize	28	34	30	43	44	41	35	1064
3. Welds	8	9	8	12	24	8	17	222
4.								
5.								
# DEFECTS	48	58	53	78	89	68	77	1746
# CHECKED	100	110	120	140	100	80	95	2565
DEFECTS/UNIT	0.48	0.53	0.44	0.56	0.89	0.85	0.81	0.68

Figure 5.14. Sample average *u* control chart.

late, of that particular late medication on that particular patient), while an incorrect operating procedure might be judged on a scale of 1 to 10,000.

Some important weighting characteristics are:

- customer satisfaction;
- production, schedule, amount;

- safety;
- product liability;
- cost;
- contribution to profit;
- combinations of any of the above.

This chart can be used with either a constant or variable subgroup size. As with any control chart, it is always best to use a constant subgroup size, if possible. Weighted attributes charts are most often used with nonmanufacturing applications, and 100% inspection is often necessary in nonmanufacturing situations.

Basic attributes charts (or average subgroup size charts, if the subgroup sizes cannot be kept constant) are normally recommended over weighted charts. Weighted charts tend to obscure (hide or lose) the reasons for errors in the weighting procedure. Note that weighted charts always use a constant subgroup size, while a weighted average chart (*p* or *u*) always uses a variable subgroup size (different size subgroup sizes, so that the subgroup average has to be calculated and used). Weighted charts are mostly used in nonmanufacturing situations and, in these situations, it is most usual to see weighted variable charts (different subgroup sizes).

Note that the only difference between the weighted *u* and the weighted average *u* charts is the extra calculation for the average sample size ($n_a = \Sigma n_i/m$) in the weighted average *u* chart. Only weighted average *u* charts will be illustrated here.

The formulas are:

$$\bar{u}_j = (\Sigma E_{ij})/\Sigma n_i \qquad \text{(sum from } i=1 \text{ to } m \text{ for each } j)$$

$$M = \Sigma(W_j \bar{u}_j) \qquad \text{(sum from } j=1 \text{ to } q)$$

$$n_a = \Sigma n_i/m \qquad \text{(sum from } i=1 \text{ to } m).$$

(When constant subgroup sizes are used, omit this step.)

$$C = \Sigma(W_j^2 \bar{u}_j)$$

$$\text{UCL}_{uW} = M + 3\sqrt{C/n_a}$$

$$\text{UCL}_{uW} = M - 3\sqrt{C/n_a}.$$

(For constant subgroup sizes, use *n* instead of n_a.)

$$u_i = \Sigma(W_j E_{ij})/n_i.$$

(This is the weighted average of all defective items from each subgroup; there will be one plotted point (u_i) for each subgroup (*m* number of *u*'s, or plotted points) for the initial chart.)

M = the weighted average % defective for all subgroups

W_j = the weighting factor for the jth type of item

$\bar{u}_j$ = the average number defective for the jth type of item

E_{ij} = the number of defective items of each type in each subgroup

m = the number of subgroups

n_i = the number of items inspected in the ith subgroup

n_a = the average number of items inspected per subgroup (omit when constant subgroup sizes are used)

n = subgroup size for constant subgroup size

q = the number of types of items

j = type of item

i = subgroup number

C = an interim value used to simplify the limit calculations

UCL_{uW} = the upper control limit for the weighted u chart

LCL_{uW} = the lower control limit for the weighted u chart.

Example 5.15 Construct a weighted average u chart for the data of Table 5.15.

Solution

1. Form a team (a single individual can be used, but this procedure works best with teams).
2. List the different types of items, errors, and/or instruments (reports, line items, assemblies, etc.).
3. Weight each type of item, error, or instrument found. Use teams, and brainstorm.
4. Count the errors and/or defectives. Sampling should be used if possible, but 100% inspection can be used if necessary.
5. Calculate the mean. There will be a u-bar for each type (j) item, which will then be summed in the M equation.

$$\bar{u}_A = (\Sigma E_{iA})/\Sigma n_i = 325/2000 = 0.16$$

$$\bar{u}_B = (\Sigma E_{iB})/\Sigma n_i = 400/2000 = 0.20$$

$$\bar{u}_C = (\Sigma E_{iC})/\Sigma n_i = 450/2000 = 0.23$$

$$\bar{u}_D = (\Sigma E_{iD})/\Sigma n_i = 520/2000 = 0.26$$

$$M = \Sigma(W_j \bar{u}_j) = 2(0.15) + 6(0.19) + 12(0.21) + 20(0.25) = 9.0.$$

Table 5.15. Data for Weighted u Example

Subgroup Number (i)	Number of Defects by Type (j)				Subgroup Size (n)	u_i
	A	B	C	D		
1	11	20	23	14	90	8.4
2	22	23	14	25	110	7.7
3	33	24	25	6	100	6.3
4	3	5	17	23	150	4.7
5	12	0	0	10	120	1.9
6	25	8	9	8	120	3.1
7	11	10	1	2	70	1.9
.	.	.	.	.	.	.
.	.	.	.	.	.	.
.	.	.	.	.	.	.
20	42	32	42	53	100	18.4
Totals	325	400	450	520	2000	

Weighting (W_j) for each item (on a scale of 1–20)

2	6	12	20

Weighted average ($\bar{u}_j$) for each item

0.16	0.20	0.23	0.26

6. Calculate the limits.

$$n_a = \Sigma n_i/m = 2000/20 = 100$$

$$C = 2^2(0.16) + 6^2(0.20) + 12^2(0.23) + 20^2(0.26) = 145.0$$

$$\text{UCL}_{uW} = M + 3\sqrt{C/n_a} = 9.0 + 3\sqrt{145.0/100} = 12.6$$

$$\text{LCL}_{uW} = M - 3\sqrt{C/n_a} = 9.0 - 3\sqrt{145.0/100} = 5.4.$$

7. Calculate plotting points for each of the subgroups. This is the weighted average of all defective items from each subgroup. There will be one plotted point for each subgroup (m number of u's, or plotted points, for the initial chart). Note that for a constant subgroup size, the n, will always be the same for all subgroups. These u's are given in the last column of Table 5.15. The calculation for the first plotted point will be shown as an example.

$$u_1 = \Sigma(W_j E_{ij})/n_i = [2(11) + 6(20) + 12(23) + 20(14)]/90 = 8.4.$$

8. One value (18.4) was higher than the upper control limit (do not delete values below the lower limits. Analyze the process for an assignable cause and, if one is found, delete and recalculate the limits. Assuming that all outside values have assignable causes, the revised limits are:

LAD COMPANY page ____ of ____

Weighted u Control Chart

Part number ________ Part name ____________ Spec ________

Operator (s) ____________ Inspector (s) ____________

Process ____________ Chart number ________

Gages ____________ Date / /

DATE:	3/1	3/2	3/3	3/4	3/5	3/8	3/9

REVISED VALUES

UCL = 12.5

$\bar{u}$ = 9.0

LCL = 5.5

ITEMS	WEIGHT	3/1	3/2	3/3	3/4	3/5	3/8	3/9	TOTALS
		DEFECTS PER SUBSAMPLE PER ITEM							
A	2	11	22	33	3	12	25	11	325
B	6	20	23	24	5	0	8	10	400
C	12	23	14	25	17	0	9	1	450
D	20	14	25	6	23	10	8	2	520
# CHECKED (Na)		90	110	100	150	120	120	70	2000
u_i (Plot)		8.4	7.7	6.3	4.7	1.9	3.1	1.9	9.4

$u_i = \Sigma(W_j E_{i\,j})/n_i$

Figure 5.15. Sample u_W control chart.

$$\bar{u}_A = (325 - 42)/(2000 - 100) = 0.15$$

$$\bar{u}_B = (400 - 32)/(2000 - 100) = 0.19$$

$$\bar{u}_C = (450 - 42)/(2000 - 100) = 0.21$$

$$\bar{u}_D = (420 - 53)/(2000 - 100) = = 0.25$$

$$M = 2(0.15) + 6(0.19) + 12(0.21) + 20(0.25) = 9.0$$

$$C = 2^2(0.15) + 6^2(0.19) + 12^2(0.21) + 20^2(0.25) = 137.7$$

$$n_a = (2000 - 100)(20 - 1) = 100$$

$$UCL_{uW} = 9.0 + 3\sqrt{137.7/100} = 12.5$$

$$LCL_{uW} = 9.0 - 3\sqrt{137.7/100} = 5.5.$$

9. Construct the chart and plot all 25 u_i values (see Figure 5.15).
10. Display the chart and continue to measure and plot.

5.16 Attributes Control Charts: The Weighted *c* Chart

This chart is similar to the basic c chart, except that the various types of defectives are categorized and weighted, i.e., multiplied by a weighting factor. Each weighting factor is applied on a scale of some kind (1 to 5, 1 to 10, etc.). For instance, medication on time might be judged on a scale of 1 to 10 (judge the severity, possible adverse effects of being late, of that particular late medication on that particular patient), while an incorrect operating procedure might be judged on a scale of 1 to 10,000.

This chart is also similar to the weighted *u* chart, except that the sample size *n* is one (1) and c is used in place of *u*.

Some important weighting characteristics are:

- customer satisfaction;
- production, schedule, amount;
- safety;
- product liability;
- cost;
- contribution to profit;
- combinations of any of the above.

This chart cannot be used with a variable subgroup size, as the subgroup for any c chart is always one (1). This chart can also be used with 100% inspection (as well as the normal sampling procedures used by most charts). Weighted attribute charts are most often used with nonmanufacturing applications, and 100% inspection is often necessary in nonmanufacturing situations.

Basic attributes charts are normally recommended over weighted charts, if possible. Weighted charts tend to obscure (hide or lose) the reasons for errors in the weighting procedure.

The formulas are:

$$\bar{c}_j = (\Sigma E_{ij})/m \qquad \text{(sum from } i = 1 \text{ to } m \text{ for each } j\text{)}$$

$$M = \Sigma(W_j c_j) \qquad \text{(sum from } j = 1 \text{ to } q\text{)}$$

$$C = \Sigma(W_j^{\,2} E_{ij})$$

$$\text{UCL}_{Wc} = M + 3\sqrt{C}$$

$$\text{LCL}_{Wc} = M - 3\sqrt{C}$$

$$c_i = \Sigma(W_j E_{ij})$$

where

M = the weighted average % defective for all subgroups

W_j = the weighting factor for the jth type of item

$\bar{c}_j$ = the average number defective for the jth type of item

E_{ij} = the number of defective items of each type in each subgroup

m = the number of subgroups

n_i = the number of items inspected in the ith subgroup

q = the number of types of items

j = type of item

i = subgroup number

C = an interim calculation to simplify the limit calculations

UCL_{Wc} = the upper control limit for the weighted c chart

LCL_{Wc} = the lower control limit for the weighted c chart

c_i = the chart plotted points.

Example 5.16 Construct a weighted c chart for the data of Table 5.16.

Solution

1. Form a team (a single individual can be used, but this procedure works best with teams).
2. List the different types of items, errors, and/or instruments (reports, line items, assemblies, etc.).
3. Weight each type of item, error, or instrument found. Use teams, and brainstorm.
4. Count the errors and/or defectives. Sampling should be used if possible, but 100% inspection can be used if necessary.
5. Calculate the mean. There will be a c-bar for each type (j) item, which will then be summed in the M equation.

$$\bar{c}_A = (\Sigma E_{iA})/m = 60/20 = 3.0$$

$$\bar{c}_B = (\Sigma E_{iB})/m = 70/20 = 3.5$$

$$\bar{c}_C = (\Sigma E_{iC})/m = 80/20 = 4.0$$

Table 5.16. Data for Weighted *c* Example

Subgroup Number (i)	Number of Defects by Type (j)				Subgroup Size	c_i
	A	*B*	*C*	*D*		
1	1	2	3	4	1	130
2	2	3	4	5	1	170
3	3	4	5	6	1	210
4	3	5	7	3	1	180
5	2	0	0	1	1	24
6	5	6	5	3	1	166
7	1	0	1	2	1	54
.	.	.	.	.	.	...
.	.	.	.	.	.	...
.	.	.	.	.	.	...
20	4	9	12	9	1	386
Totals	60	70	80	90	20	
Weighting (W_j) for each item (on a scale of 1–20)	2	6	12	20		

$$\bar{c}_D = (\Sigma E_{iD})/m = 90/20 = 4.5$$

$$M = \Sigma(W_j \bar{c}_j) = 2(3.0) + 6(3.5) + 12(4.0) + 20(4.5) = 165.$$

6. Calculate the limits.

$$C = \Sigma(W_j^2 E_j)$$

$$= 2^2(3.0) + 6^2(3.5) + 12^2(4.0) + 20^2(4.5) = 2514$$

$$\text{UCL}_{Wc} = M + 3\sqrt{C} = 165 + 3\sqrt{2514} = 315$$

$$\text{LCL}_{Wc} = M - 3\sqrt{C} = 165 - 3\sqrt{2514} = 15.$$

7. Calculate plotting points for each of the subgroups. This is the weighted average of all defective items from each subgroup. There will be one plotted point for each subgroup (m number of u's, or plotted points, for the initial chart). These plotting points, c's, are given in the last column of Table 5.16. The calculation for the first plotted point will be shown as an example.

$$c_1 = \Sigma(W_j E_{1j}) = 2(1) + 6(2) + 12(3) + 20(4) = 130.$$

8. One value (386) was higher than the upper control limit (do not delete values below the lower limit). Analyze the process for an assignable cause and, if one is found, delete and recalculate the limits. Assuming that all outside values have assignable causes, the revised limits are:

LAD COMPANY page ____ of ____

c Control Chart

Part number ________ Part name ____________ Spec ________

Operator (s) ____________ Inspector (s) ____________

Process ____________________ Chart number ________

Gages ____________________ Date / /

DATE:		3/1	3/2	3/3	3/4	3/5	3/8	3/9	
REVISED VALUES	350								
UCL = 300	300								
	250								
	200								
$\bar{c}$ = 154.2	150								
	100								
	50								
LCL = 8.3	0.0								
ITEMS	WEIGHT	DEFECTS PER SUBSAMPLE PER ITEM							TOTALS
A	2	1	2	3	3	2	5	1	325
B	6	2	3	4	5	0	6	0	400
C	12	3	4	5	7	0	5	1	450
D	20	4	5	6	3	1	3	2	520
# CHECKED		1	1	1	1	1	1	1	20
c_i (Plot)		130	170	210	180	24	166	54	165

$c_i = \Sigma(W_j E_{i\,j})$

Figure 5.16. Sample weighted *c* control chart.

$$\bar{c}_A = (60 - 4)/(20 - 1) = 2.9$$

$$\bar{c}_B = (70 - 9)/(20 - 1) = 3.2$$

$$\bar{c}_C = (80 - 12)/(20 - 1) = 3.6$$

$$\bar{c}_D = (90 - 9)/(20 - 1) = 4.3$$

$$M = 2(2.9) + 6(3.2) + 12(3.6) + 20(4.3) = 154.2$$

$$C = 2^2(2.9) + 6^2(3.2) + 12^2(3.6) + 20^2(4.3) = 2365.2$$

$$\text{UCL} = 154.2 + 3\sqrt{2365.2} = 300.0$$

$$\text{LCL} = 154.2 - 3\sqrt{2365.2} = 8.3.$$

9. Construct the chart and plot all 25 c_i values (see Figure 5.16).
10. Display the chart and continue to measure and plot.

Practice Problems

5–1 Construct an *X*-bar, *R* chart using a zero-base for the following data. Use a subsample of four. Use 1.10 and 1.80 as the engineering specifications.

Sample No.	Observation (Measurement) 1	2	3	4	Sample No.	Observation (Measurement) 1	2	3	4
1.	1.12	0.81	1.30	1.22	14.	1.12	1.63	1.43	1.63
2.	1.00	1.46	1.19	0.72	15.	1.36	1.58	1.79	1.41
3.	1.32	1.36	1.81	1.81	16.	1.77	1.44	1.61	1.43
4.	1.44	1.69	1.90	1.52	17.	1.61	1.74	1.67	1.72
5.	1.66	1.76	1.61	1.55	18.	1.81	1.65	0.82	1.52
6.	1.02	2.03	1.67	1.55	19.	1.33	1.57	1.98	1.85
7.	1.62	1.79	1.62	1.54	20.	1.63	1.44	1.87	1.69
8.	1.48	1.73	1.88	1.43	21.	1.25	1.43	1.55	1.68
9.	1.54	1.29	1.37	1.65	22.	1.77	1.68	1.54	1.76
10.	1.77	1.43	1.71	1.66	23.	1.64	1.57	1.65	2.15
11.	1.94	1.67	1.43	1.61	24.	1.90	1.18	1.60	1.45
12.	1.55	1.73	1.42	1.66	25.	1.63	1.85	1.67	1.36
13.	1.79	1.77	2.17	1.55					

Answers

X-bar chart: 1.25, 1.608, 1.96
R chart: 0.00, 0.487, 1.37

5–2 Construct a moving average chart using the following data. 15.1, 11.0, 5.3, 13.3, 13.0, 10.9, 9.4, 4.2, 12.3, 13.0, 10.6, 6.0, 10.6, 7.0, 10.8, 8.0, 10.8, 8.0, 10.9, 6.7, 9.4, 4.8, 8.9, 9.0, and 10.1.

Answers

X-chart: 14.4; 9.47; 4.5
R chart: 12.7; 4.813; 0.0

5–3 Construct a moving average chart using a zero-base for the data of Problem 5-2. The engineering specifications are 13.1 and 5.8.

Answers

X-bar chart: 4.9; 0.02; −4.9
R chart: 18.7; 7.26; 0.0

5–4 Construct a moving average chart using attributes data for the following data. 8, 3, 2, 2, 7, 7, 11, 4, 3, 6, 5, 14, 0, 4, 1, 5, 8, 13, 6, 8, 3, 18, 12, 8, and 5.

Answers

X-bar chart: 14.0; 6.61; 0.0
R chart: 18.7; 7.26; 0.0

5–5 Construct a pre-control chart for an engineering specification of 2.10 and 1.20. What happens if an entry is made for 1.7? for 1.23?

Answers

1.88; 1.65; 1.43

5–6 Construct an individuals chart for the following data. The first two values in the first line (1.12 and 0.81) form the first sample, the next two (1.30 and 1.22) form the next sample, etc.

1.12 0.81 1.30 1.22 1.00 1.46 1.19 0.72 1.32 1.36
1.81 1.81 1.44 1.69 1.90 1.52 1.66 1.76 1.61 1.55

Answers

X chart: 2.12; 1.4125; 0.71
R chart: 0.87; 0.266; 0.00

5–7 Construct a specifications chart (μ, σ chart) for the specifications of 2.10 and 1.20 and with a subgroup size of 4.

Answers

μ chart: 1.87, 1.65, 1.43
σ chart: 0.70, 0.31, 0.00

5–8 Construct an *np* chart for a constant sample size of 140. Find the central value and the upper control limit for the revised chart. Assume all values outside of the upper trial control limit have assignable causes. The number of defectives for the first 20 subsamples were: 8, 3, 2, 2, 7, 7, 11, 4, 3, 6, 5, 14, 0, 4, 1, 5, 8, 13, 6, and 5.

Answers

4.83, 11

5–9 Construct a variable subsample size p chart from the following data. Find the central p value and control limits (assuming a future constant subsample size of 100) and plot the data.

Number Inspected	Number Defective
120	9
110	7
90	8
130	18
130	11
70	3
100	0
80	9
80	10
80	2
70	9
60	12
90	8
110	8
100	8
80	7
120	2
70	0
70	6
110	13

Answers

0.076, 0.155, 0.00

5–10 Construct an average subsample size p chart from the data of Practice Problem 5-10. Find the central p value and control limits assuming an average subsample size, and plot the data.

Answers

0.076, 0.157, 0.00

CHAPTER 6 PROCESS ANALYSIS AND CONTROL

The statistical analysis and control chart procedures explained in the previous chapters are worthless unless used for a purpose. That purpose must be the control of the process so that quality products can be produced consistently. This control is exercised by meeting the following objectives.

Objectives

1. Understand the nature of control chart use in providing superior products and services.
2. Use control charts to correct the process.
3. Use control charts to improve the process.
4. Compare control chart limits to specification limits to control the process.
5. Calculate the capability ratios to determine the process capability (ability to produce to specifications consistently).
6. Use normal curve analyses to compare the limits and to determine the optimum mean.

6.1 Using Control Charts

It must never be forgotten that the main purpose of a company, its reason for being, is to produce a product to satisfy the customer. This product can be a physical unit, such as a refrigerator or an automobile; a service, such as the delivery of bottled water, nursing, or fire protection; the disseminating of information, such as newspapers, television programs, or college courses; the giving of advice, such as in psychiatry, business consulting, or financial and investment assistance; or anything that people need or desire.

The first step in the process of satisfying the customer is to design the product to customer needs. This may take the form of a drawing depicting the form and specifications of the product, or a prospectus showing the type and extent of the offered service. In manufacturing firms this is called design engineering.

The purpose of SPC is to assist in the manufacturing of the product or the delivery of the service, so that design specifications are achieved or surpassed. It does this by assisting the production group in correcting and improving the process. The process can be a machine or a group of machines, a truck and a delivery route, a classroom and a teaching methodology, an investing procedure, or whatever it takes to produce the product or service.

"Correcting" the process and "improving" the process should be thought of as two separate procedures, although each uses many of the same tools in meeting its objectives. Correcting the process refers to the use of control charts to identify and correct assignable causes so that the process can be brought back into statistical control, that is, so that the process can do what it was designed to do. Improving the process refers to those activities that concentrate on changing the process parameters so that the process can be made better than it was, that is, to redesign the process.

A process, therefore, is "perfected" and "in-control" when it has zero variation over time—all measurements are identical, day in and day out. Of course, this is impossible to actually achieve in real life, but it can usually be achieved in a practical sense, that is, close enough for all practical purposes. This should always be the goal and is the foundation of the SPC concept of continuous improvement, never stop trying to improve.

Although both approaches (correction and improvement) use identical tools and procedures most of the time—the main difference is in the use of more complex analysis procedures such as DOE (design of experiments) for the "improving" procedure—it is important to distinguish between them because of the change in managerial emphasis that occurs. The correction of assignable causes can usually be accomplished by operators and first-line managers alone (and process engineers where the process is complex), often without top management even being aware of the correction activities (except in reports). Changing process parameters, however, requires the total involvement of top management, as it often requires more complex analysis procedures (such as DOE) and the commitment of funds. It is also important that design engineering be made aware of the new process capabilities.

6.2 Use Control Charts to Correct the Process

Correcting the process involves the control and/or removal of assignable causes, the stabilization of the process, the use of the chart as a "dynamic" picture of the quality over time, and a psychological effect on the operator.

The whole process of using control charts to gain finer and finer control, to identify and correct assignable causes, and to perfect procedures and attitudes that ensure the maximum utilization of the process capabilities, depends on the process being stable. An unstable process, by its nature, cannot be dependable. When least expected it may suddenly become out-of-control, usually for no apparent reason. (Of course, analysis of assignable causes usually uncovers the reason eventually.) Although process parameter factors, unique to the process, may affect the stability (showing the need for in-depth process knowledge and understanding on the part of the analyst), the fact that the control charts exhibit closer and closer control limits over time is a strong indication of process stability.

Control charts are used in several ways to gain finer and finer control over the process. First, there is a psychological effect on the operator. The very existence of the chart, placed in a conspicuous place at the workplace, motivates the operator to be extra careful. Experience gained from this extra care tends to lead to long-term increases in quality.

The control chart also provides a picture of quality that assists the operator in finding new ways to produce the part better and to add precision and accuracy to the old methods. Control charts should not be static but should be used dynamically to picture the quality improvements as they occur. As quality improves, control limits must be revised continuously (usually monthly) so that they get closer and closer to the central value. In other words, the variability is reduced (the standard deviation becomes smaller and smaller) and the sample means group closer and closer about the central mean. In this way, the operator and others (production manager, quality engineer, maintenance engineer, manufacturing engineer, etc.) get a visual picture of their quality improvement efforts (Figure 6.1).

As the variations decrease, smaller and smaller assignable causes are uncovered and corrected. Eventually, the variations get so small they are indistinguishable from chance causes and the process settles down into a virtual steady-state condition where no more improvements and control limit revisions are possible (at least from correction activities alone; the changing of limits through perfection activities, that is, the changing of process parameters, is still possible). At this time the

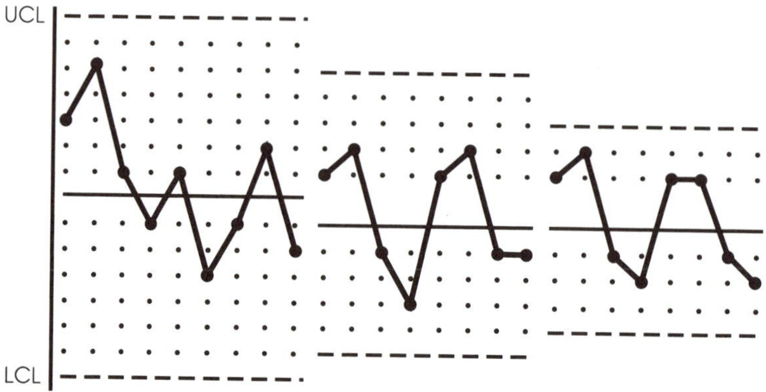

Figure 6.1. Control chart showing improvement over time.

process is nearly perfected and the control charts may no longer be needed. As they may be somewhat expensive to continue, they may now be removed, except where automatic monitoring and data collection systems are being used. Sometimes *p* charts are used by management as a continuous check on the overall product quality. In this case, since *p* charts are relatively inexpensive to use, they would not be removed, even though the overall quality had settled into a steady-state condition.

The final way control charts are used to control quality is to identify assignable causes. This is done, essentially, through pattern analysis, the analysis of control chart patterns, using the 1% rule. The 1% rule states that any control chart pattern that has greater than a 1% probability of occurring by chance alone indicates a probable out-of-control process. When any of these patterns occur, a search for an assignable cause should be instituted and the assignable cause corrected when found.

Control Chart Patterns

There are several patterns that identify possible out-of-control conditions. Although many of these patterns may occur within the control limits, they still indicate possible out-of-control conditions. Something in the process may be causing this condition, and should be found and controlled. A process that can be more closely controlled usually leads to higher quality in the long run. Also, some of these patterns may indicate assignable causes of "superior" quality. Control of these kinds of causes often leads to parameter changes and permanent quality improvements. These patterns are as follows:

1. Any subsample mean that falls outside of the control limits (Figures 4.1 and 4.2). Since control limits are set at + and -3σ, the probability that any in-control value (caused by chance alone) will be outside of these limits is 0.27% (1 − .9973). Since the distribution is symmetrical (control charts are derived from the normal curve), the probability that a value will fall above the upper control limit from chance causes only is half of 0.27%, or 0.135%. The same is true for values below the lower control limit. The probability that more than one value will fall outside the control limits from chance alone quickly becomes astronomical, in other words, almost a certainty that something is wrong. (The chance that five of 25 subsamples will be outside the limits, for example, is 75 out of 10 billion!) Note that this pattern clearly satisfies the 1% rule (the probability is less than 1% that it could occur by chance alone). In fact, control limits can be set considerably below + and -3σ and still satisfy this rule (actually at + and −2.327 or above). However, it has become customary for many years (since 1924) to use 6σ limits, due to the ease of calculation.
2. Seven subsample means in a row (Figure 6.2). This can be 7 in a row above the mean, 7 below the mean, 7 in a row alternating above and below the mean, 7 in a row going up, or 7 in a row going down. The mathematics of this pattern rule is as follows: Since, by chance alone, it is equally likely that any one value (subsample mean) will either be part of the pattern or not, the probability that any one value is part of a pattern is 0.50 or 50%. The probability that any two values are part of a pattern then is $0.5 \times 0.5 = 0.25$. (This is the product rule of probability that says that the probability of both is the product of their individual probabilities. See Chapter 7.) If this logic is continued for 7 values in a row, the probability that all 7 are part of a pattern is $0.5^7 = 0.0078$ or 0.78%, obviously less than 1% (6 in a row $= 0.5^6 = 0.0156$, obviously greater than 1%).
3. Ten of 11 subsample means in a row (Figure 6.3). This can be 10 of 11 in a row above the mean, 10 of 11 below the mean, 10 of 11 in a row alternating above and below the mean, 10 of 11 in a row going up, or 10 of 11 in a row going down. The mathematics of this pattern rule is

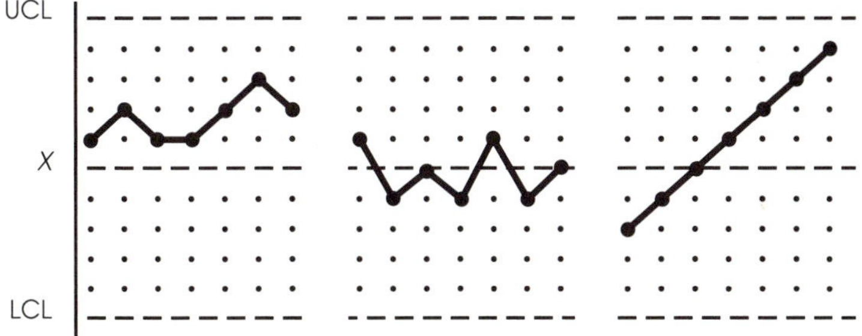

Figure 6.2. Control chart showing seven out-of-control patterns in a row.

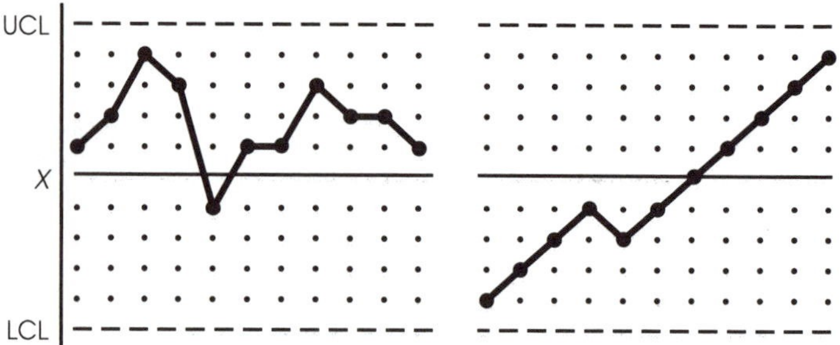

Figure 6.3. Control chart showing 10 of 11 out-of-control patterns in a row.

rather complex and requires the use of the binomial probability distribution. It will be explained in Chapter 7.

4. Twelve of 14 subsample means in a row (Figure 6.4). This can be 12 of 14 in a row above the mean, 12 of 14 below the mean, 12 of 14 in a row alternating above and below the mean, 12 of 14 in a row going up, or 12 of 14 in a row going down. The mathematics of this pattern rule also requires the use of the binomial probability distribution, and will be explained in Chapter 7.
5. Patterns between + or −1 standard deviation from the mean (Figure 6.5). These patterns are: (1) 5 in a row, and (2) 6 of 7 in a row. Since control chart limits are set at + and −3 standard deviations (6σ), the chart can be divided into six equal parts, each one corresponding to the distance of a single standard deviation. The probability that any one value will fall within the first of these areas from the mean, either above or below the mean, is 0.3413 (Chapter 3). The probability that 5 in a row will occur is $0.3413^5 = 0.00463$. This clearly meets the 1% rule's criteria for out-of-control (4 in a row = 0.0136 and, thus, fails the 1% rule). The mathematics for 6 of 7 in a row is, once again, somewhat complex and will be explained in Chapter 7.
6. Patterns between +1 and +2 standard deviations from the mean or −1 and −2 (Figure 6.6). These patterns are: (1) 3 in a row, and (2) 4 of 5 in a row. The probability that any one value will fall within either

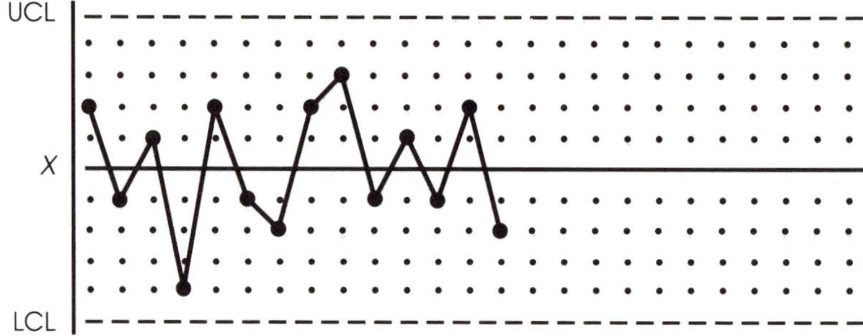

Figure 6.4. Control chart showing 12 of 14 out-of-control patterns in a row.

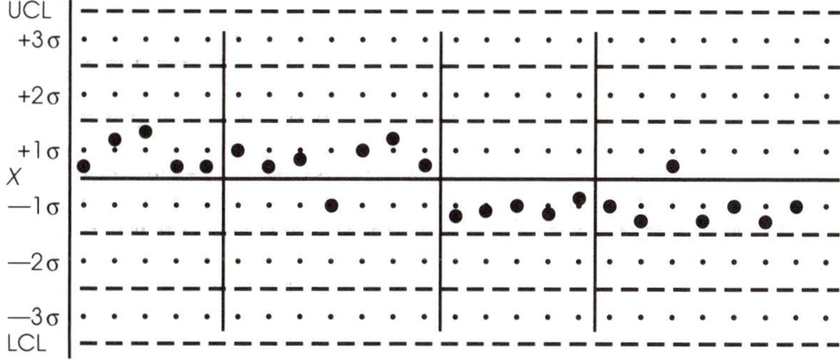

Figure 6.5. Control chart showing out-of-control patterns within + or − 1 standard deviation from the mean.

one of these areas is 0.136 (0.9773 at $+2\sigma - 0.8413$ at $+1\sigma$). The probability that there will be 3 in a row, therefore, is $0.136^3 = 0.0025$ (which clearly satisfies the 1% rule). The mathematics for 4 of 5 is, once again, somewhat complex and will be given in Chapter 7.

7. Two values in a row between +2 and +3 standard deviations from the mean or between −2 and −3 (Figure 6.7). The probability that any one value will fall within either one of these areas is 0.02135 (0.99865 at $+3\sigma - 0.9773$ at $+2\sigma$). The probability that there will be 2 in a row, therefore, is $0.02135^2 = 0.0004558$ (which clearly satisfies the 1% rule).
8. Groupings and long-term trends. Any pattern where the probability of it being caused by chance is less than 1%. This includes any long-term trend (up, down, alternating, etc.) that has an obvious pattern, or if too many of the values group too close to the mean (more than 68.26% within + and − 1 standard deviation) with few or no values close to the limits, or too many values close to the limits, or too many values spread all over the chart (even if all are still inside the control limits).

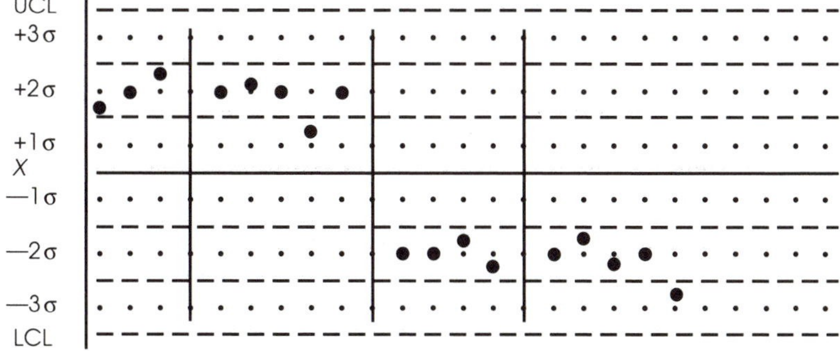

Figure 6.6. Control chart showing out-of-control patterns between 1 and 2 standard deviations from the mean.

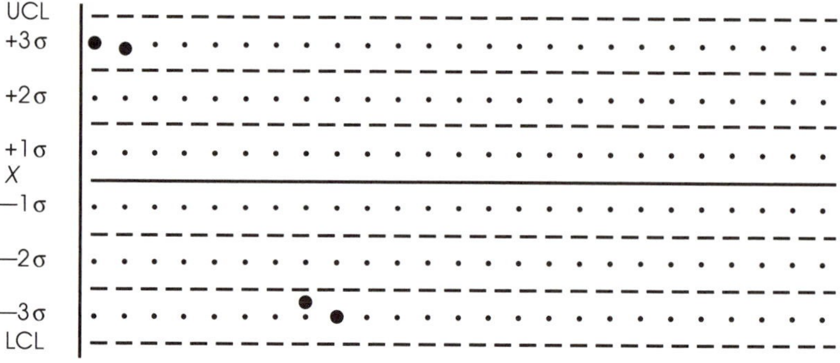

Figure 6.7. Control chart showing out-of-control patterns between 2 and 3 standard deviations from the mean.

Causes of Patterns

When analyzing control chart patterns, always be aware of the ten categories of out-of-control causes (the same as the ten causes of variation listed in Section 1.4). Each type of pattern often has essentially the same cause, especially in the same environment. Thus, once the cause of a particular type of pattern has been identified, it should be noted and then used as a guide in finding causes of similar pattern in the future. Eventually a checklist of patterns and probable causes could be prepared that would greatly enhance pattern analysis activities.

Although checklists of patterns and their probable causes should be prepared separately for each installation, there are some general guidelines that may be helpful. When analyzing control charts, the general rule is to first correct the R chart (get it in-control) before analyzing the X-bar chart.

1. Freaks (points outside the 3σ limits). Look first for a possible measurement error and then for a sudden change in raw material.
2. Zone patterns (between the mean and 1σ, 1σ and 2σ, or 2σ and 3σ). Once again look first for a measurement error and then for a sudden change in raw material. These patterns are also frequently caused by incomplete or missing operations.
3. Shifts (seven in a row above or below the center or any long-term change in the process center). If the shift occurs in the X-bar chart, look first for changes in materials or suppliers, and then for shift changes, changes in machine speed, or measurement error. If it occurs in the R chart, look for operator problems or poor maintenance.
4. Cycles (seven in a row up and down or any long-term up and down trend). Look for the same things happening over and over again, usually at the same time. (Time is often a dead giveaway for cycles.) Look for such things as shift changes, new hires, defective equipment, fluctuating power, weather changes, and fatigue occurring at about the same time (most common cause of cycles in the R chart).

5. Trends (seven in a row up or down or any long-term trend up or down or straight). Trends in the X-bar chart are usually interpreted quite differently than trends in the R chart. Any up or down trend in the X-bar chart is bad while a straight trend is good (especially at the center). However, an up trend in the R chart is bad while a down trend is good. A straight trend in the R is mediocre. Good trends are usually caused by increased training and/or morale, better maintenance, increased experience, and better process controls. Bad trends are often caused by tool wear (X-bar), tired operators, and poor maintenance.
6. Grouping and bunching. When this occurs in the R chart it usually means that several distributions are represented (such as a mixture from two or more machines). In the X-bar chart, any of the ten causes may be operating. It is especially important when analyzing groupings and bunchings that the R chart be in-control first.
7. Chart relationships. Sometimes a chart at one location on the line is related to another at an earlier location. They could be measuring the same characteristic, or a different one that is related in some way. This relationship can be positive (both charts go up and down together) or negative (one chart goes up when the other goes down). Analyzing both charts together can often give clues to the problem when a single chart analysis will not. Remember that the charts are often displaced in time so that a positive relationship may appear to be negative, and vice versa (because the earlier operation occurred before the latter). In this case, time must be factored into the analysis.

6.3 Using Control Charts to Improve the Process (to Change the Parameters)

The goal of this procedure is to improve the process by changing the process parameters (temperature, pressure, time, etc.); by redesigning the process. The results of this change, of course, are identical to those of the "correction" procedure: to reduce the process variation and to move the control limits closer to the process center.

Accomplishing this goal includes the same methods used in the correction procedure, except that now the emphasis is on finding clues that lead to parameter changes that improve the process. For the most effective use of resources, these two procedures (correction and improvement) are carried out simultaneously. Both concepts should be kept in mind when analyzing the charts so that the different kinds of clues, when noted, can be properly utilized. Although many good process improvements can be accomplished this way, improvements often require more complex analysis procedures (including DOE) than corrections.

Control charts, when used properly, are powerful analysis tools for both correction and improvement. As discussed, the improvement activities should proceed in concert with the correction activities. However, once the process achieves stability the correction activities can end, but the improvement activities can continue depending on need and availability of funds. These further activities are usually somewhat more expensive than the earlier combination correction and improvement procedures. They also require the involvement of and the decision-making function of top management. This requires a critical change in management emphasis. Another powerful ability of the chart is to signal when this change in emphasis becomes necessary. This is done when the chart signals that the process has settled into its steady-state condition, that is, when no more readily available corrections and/or improvements can be identified.

6.4 Control Charts and Specifications

Control chart limits can be compared to specification tolerances to determine the process capability. In fact, it is imperative that this be done for good control. Since specification limits refer only to measurable characteristics, this use is limited to control charts for variables. There are several procedures that can be used. The most important are:

1. *Direct comparison.* Specifications are imposed upon the control chart to compare them with the control limits.
2. *Normal curve analysis.* The techniques of Chapter 3 are used to determine whether a process that is in-control can produce to specifications effectively.
3. C_p *analysis.* A ratio is calculated for use as a control value. This procedure will be explained in Section 6.5.
4. *P-C chart.* Using control chart and C_p theory, a special control chart is constructed that uses specifications as control limits. This procedure was explained in Chapter 5.
5. *Experimental design.* Process capability studies can also be made by various types of industrial experiments using advanced statistical design. The basic theory of experimental design, and some of the more simplistic designs, will be explained in Chapter 10.

Direct Comparison

There are three main types of conditions, each requiring a different type of solution:

1. The control chart central value does not match the specification central value. This is the easiest of all process capability problems to solve since one of the central values can be changed to match the other one. Specifications, by their nature, cannot easily be changed since they are determined by product and customer requirements. Therefore, it is the control chart central value that usually must be changed. In most cases, this is a simple matter of changing a machine setting. This might not be necessary, though, if the specification limits are outside the control limits. When patterns are offset this way, however, there is always a poten-

tial for interference problems to develop, and it should be corrected, unless the central values have been deliberately offset to minimize scrap and rework costs (see Chapter 3—this special problem will be expanded on in Section 6.6). If specification limits are inside the control limits, the solutions in condition 2 must also be applied. In other words, two problems must be solved simultaneously: first the central values must be matched and then the process must be brought under control, as explained in condition 2.

2. Specification limits lie inside the control limits and the central values are equal (Figure 6.8). The farther the specifications limits lie inside the control limits, the higher the number of rejects that will be produced. For example, suppose that the specifications lie at exactly + and −2 standard deviations from the mean. About 95% of the parts will be acceptable and 5% will not. At + and −1 standard deviation, only 68% of the parts will be usable. This situation presents a difficult problem for management. Sometimes the specifications can be relaxed but this is rarely possible. Usually something has to be done to the process to reduce the variability (in other words, reduce the standard deviation), such as the following:
   a. Better operator training
   b. Better maintenance (tighten the machine, replace worn parts, etc.)
   c. Correction of assignable causes
   d. Methods changes and improvements
   e. Combinations of any or all of these

   If these actions are not adequate, an entire new process and/or machine may have to be designed or purchased. It is obvious that the solution to this condition can be quite expensive.
3. Specification limits lie outside the control limits. This condition is usually not a problem (Figure 6.9). Sometimes it is a good idea to keep the specifications far enough outside of the control limits to take care of any contingencies that might develop. Just how far out-

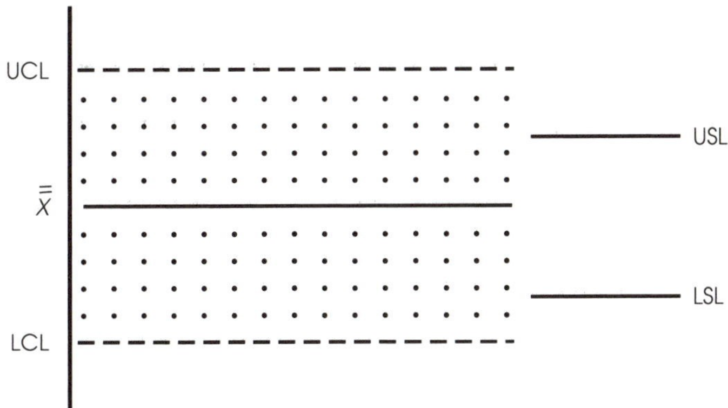

Figure 6.8. Control chart with specification limits inside the control limits.

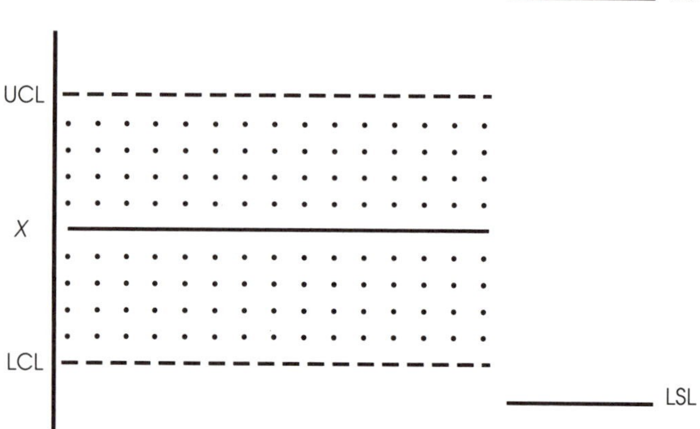

Figure 6.9. Control chart with specification limits outside the control limits.

side depends on many factors, primarily product and production costs. A good rule of thumb is to have the specification limits extend the 6σ limits about one third beyond the control limits. This can be better controlled by calculating a capability ratio as explained in Section 6.5, and/or by using the normal curve analysis techniques explained in Chapter 3 and in Section 6.6.

6.5 Process Capability Ratios

Another way to analyze the process is to calculate a process capability ratio. There are four types. The formulas are:

$$C_p = \text{tolerance}/6\sigma = (\text{USL} - \text{LSL})/6\sigma$$

$$C_{pl} = (\overline{\overline{X}} - \text{LSL})/3\sigma$$

$$C_{pu} = (\text{USL} - \overline{\overline{X}})/3\sigma$$

$$C_{pk} = C_p\{1 - [(2|m - \overline{\overline{X}}|)/(\text{UCL} - \text{LCL})]\}$$

$$= \text{lower of } C_{pl} \text{ or } C_{pu}$$

where

C_p = the basic capability ratio

C_{pl} = the lower one-sided capability ratio

C_{pu} = the upper one-sided capability ratio

C_{pk} = the lower of C_{pl} or C_{pu}

UCL = the upper control limit

LCL = the lower control limit

USL = the upper specification limit

LSL = the lower specification limit

$\overline{\overline{X}}$ = the process mean

m = the specification mean

σ = the process standard deviation = $\overline{R}/d_2$

$|\,|$ = the absolute value of

The C_{pl} and C_{pu} are used when only one direction from the mean is important. The C_{pk} factors can be used to locate the process center, the $\overline{\overline{X}}$. It measures the distance of the process average $\overline{\overline{X}}$ from the closest specification. Therefore, the C_{pk} can be used in place of the other three. If any one of the capability ratios is below 1.00, the process is not capable of consistently producing product within the specification. A capability ratio above 1 is desirable. Only ratios above 1.33 are considered to be acceptable and provide the most efficient control. For example, the four capability ratios for Example 4.1 are:

$$C_p = (\text{USL} - \text{LSL})/6\sigma = (\text{USL} - \text{LSL})/[\sqrt{n}(\text{UCL} - \text{LCL})]$$
$$= (1.082 - 1.054)[\sqrt{4}(1.067 - 1.056)] = 1.27$$
$$C_{pl} = (\overline{\overline{X}} - \text{LSL})/3\sigma = (\overline{\overline{X}} - \text{LSL})/[1/2\sqrt{n}(\text{UCL} - \text{LCL})]$$
$$= (1.062 - 1.054)/[1/2\sqrt{4}(1.067 - 1.056)] = 0.73$$
$$C_{pu} = (\text{USL} - \overline{\overline{X}})/3\sigma = (\text{USL} - \overline{\overline{X}})/[1/2\sqrt{n}(\text{UCL} - \text{LCL})]$$
$$= (1.082 - 1.062)/[1/2\sqrt{4}(1.067 - 1.056)] = 1.82$$
$$C_{pk} = \text{lower of } C_{pl} \text{ or } C_{pu} = 0.73.$$

C_p Ratios Using Coded Data

When using coded data (such as in the zero-base models of Sections 5.1 and 5.3), the C_p ratios must be calculated using the coded data only. For instance, in Section 5.1, for Product A, the coded USL is 0.0065, the coded LSL is −0.0065, n is 5, UCL is 0.012, and the LCL is −0.008. So:

$$C_p = (\text{USL} - \text{LSL})/[\sqrt{n}(\text{UCL} - \text{LCL})]$$
$$= [0.0065 - (-0.0065)]/[\sqrt{5}(0.012 - (-0.008))] = 0.291$$
$$C_{pl} = (\overline{\overline{X}} - \text{LSL})/1/2\sqrt{n}(\text{UCL} - \text{LCL})]$$
$$= [0.00172 - (-0.0065)]/[1/2\sqrt{5}(0.012 - (-0.008))] = 0.368$$

$C_{pu} = (\text{USL} - \overline{\overline{X}})/1/2\sqrt{n}(\text{UCL} - \text{LCL})]$

$= [0.0065 - (-0.00172)]/[1/2\sqrt{5}(0.012 - (-0.008))] = 0.368$

$C_{pk} = \text{Lower of } C_{pl} \text{ or } C_{pu} = 0.368.$

Please note that this is far short of the needed 1.33 C_{pk} ratio.

Process Capability Analysis Using Attribute Data

The formulas just shown for process capability ratios obviously require measurable data. The only way to calculate a capability ratio for attribute data is to evaluate the data on a scale of one to 10 (or one to five, etc.). This type of measurement, however, almost always requires a great deal of independent judgment on the part of the person doing the measuring, thus causing great measurement differences between analysts. Also, it is almost impossible to set specifications with this type of arbitrary measurement system. Therefore, capability ratios are quite difficult for attribute data.

The only practical way to do capability analysis with attribute data is to determine a desirable central value (*p*-bar, *u*-bar, or c-bar) and compare this to the actual central value achieved by the process and shown on the chart. Upper limits cannot be compared this way because they can be changed arbitrarily by changing the subsample size (as the subsample size increases, the upper limit decreases, all else equal).

Parts per Million Analysis

Process capability analysis can also assist in another modern production problem. Modern high technology requires such a high degree of quality and reliability that 6σ control limits are frequently inadequate. A *parts per* million (*ppm*) of under 100 is now often being required. When compared to the *ppm* of 2700 for the basic control chart with 6σ limits ($1 - 0.9973 = 0.0027 = 27$ parts per $10{,}000 = 2700$ ppm) it is obvious that something better is needed. A high C_p ratio can help offset this deficiency (pre-control can also help). In general, a capability ratio of 1.33 or greater comes fairly close to providing this protection. (Many are advocating 1.50 or greater; the P-C chart uses 2.0.)

A C_p ratio of 1.33 means that the tolerance limits (specifications) represent 7.98σ ($1.33 \times 6\sigma$), or ± 3.99 standard deviations (3.99σ) from the mean. The Z table (Table A1b) extends from about 4σ to almost 6σ. A Z of 3.99, then, is equal to a P of 0.999967, or a *ppm* of 0.67 (less than 1 per million).

6.6 Normal Curve Analysis

The control and process analysis procedures explained in this chapter are excellent for controlling an ongoing process once the specification and control limit relationships are known. A process may occasionally settle into a steady-state condition, however, where no more process improvements are feasible, and end up with a low C_{pk} ratio (below 1.33). If the process cannot be improved any more, and if the specifications cannot be changed, the best and most positive method for determining the least cost relationship is through a normal curve analysis (explained at the end of this section).

Control limits are determined in relation to sample size. They are meant to be used as control vehicles and cannot be used to determine actual areas under the curve. For example, control limits (confidence limits in statistics) based on a sample size of 10,000 would have 1/50 the distance between them as would control limits based on a sample size of 4 (the difference between dividing by the square root of 4, or 2, and the square root of 10,000, or 100). However, they both have 6σ limits. We can be much more confident that our test answers are closer to the real universe value if our sample size is 10,000; thus, we can use control limits that are very close to the test central value. Control limits derived from a sample size of 4, on the other hand, must be much further apart due to the greater uncertainty involved.

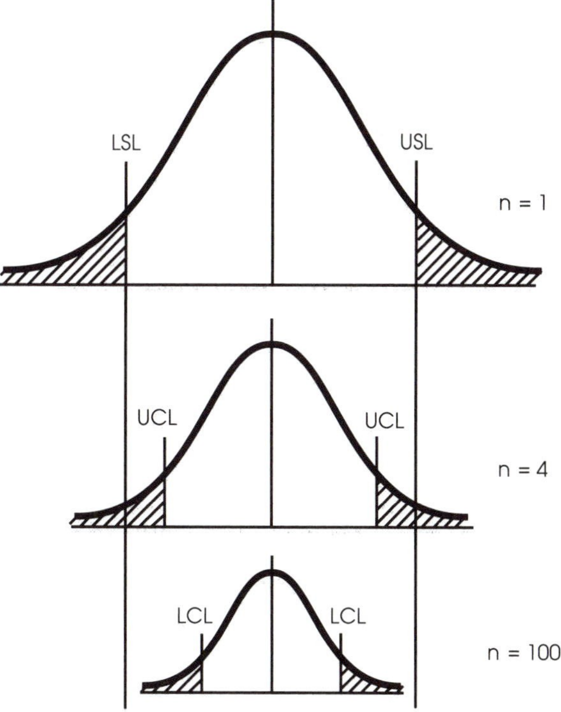

Figure 6.10. Comparison of control limits from different subsample sizes.

A control limit is a form of safety margin that changes as the incoming data change. The more data we have (the larger the sample size), the more certain we can be of our results and the less safety margin we need (the limits can be closer). Figure 6.10 illustrates this relationship. The distribution of individual values (where the subsample size, $n=1$) is compared to distributions derived from subsample sizes of 4 and 100. Note how the 6σ limits get closer to each other as the subsample size is increased. Obviously, we cannot use control limits to determine percent items below the specification limit. This must be done using the normal curve analysis procedures learned in Chapter 3 (basically using the distribution of individual values where $n=1$).

Economic Analysis

The normal curve analysis methods explained in Chapter 3 can also be used to determine the lowest cost alternative machine setting when the C_{pk} ratio is less than 1.33 and no further process changes can be made. (At a C_{pk} less than 1.33, a process will usually produce a significant amount of product outside of its specification limits, depending on just how low the ratio actually is.) This is an iterative procedure starting at the present mean value and working down or up one incremental value at a time until the lowest cost mean (machine setting) is found. The steps are as follows:

1. Calculate the present incremental cost of rework and scrap. The rework and scrap cost must be estimated using the resources of cost accounting, methods engineering, and/or cost estimating. Multiply the cost of reworking one unit by the rework ratio (the rework area), multiply the cost of scrapping one unit by the scrap ratio (the scrap area), and sum. Note that the scrap ratio may be the area below the lower limit in one problem (measuring a shaft diameter, for example), while in another it may be the area above the upper limit (such as the measurement of an inside diameter).
2. Subtract one incremental value from the mean (subtract 1 from the right-most digit) and recalculate the areas above the upper limit and below the lower limit. Then recalculate the incremental cost (as in step 1) using the new areas (new ratios). If the new incremental cost is lower than the previous one (the cost determined in step 1), go to step 3. If not lower (higher or equal) go to step 4.
3. Subtract another incremental value from the mean (subtract 2 from the right-most digit) and recalculate the areas and costs. Continue until a cost higher than the previous one is determined. The optimal mean value (machine setting) will be the one used in the previous calculation.
4. Add an incremental value to the mean (add 1 to the right-most digit of the present mean value) and recalculate the areas and costs above the upper limit and below the lower limit. If the new cost is again higher or equal to the previous cost, stop. The previous, present, mean value is optimal (provides the lowest cost). If the new cost is lower than the pre-

vious one (determined in step 1), add another incremental value to the mean (add 2 to the right-most digit), and recalculate the areas and costs. Continue until a cost higher than the previous one is determined. The optimal mean value (machine setting) will be the one used in the previous calculation.

It must be emphasized at this point that the normal curve analyses explained in Chapter 3 cannot be used for this type of economic analysis unless the data are known to be normal (Gaussian). Once these data are put into control chart form, however, as in Chapter 4, a normal curve economic analysis can be used because the data are now normal (because of the action of the central limit theorem). A special procedure is used to determine the equivalent universe standard deviation (σ). Sigma (σ) cannot be determined directly from the control chart (by dividing the distance between the limits by 6) because of the central limit theorem relationship as illustrated in Figure 6.10 (the control chart σ is related to universe σ by the ratio, $1/\sqrt{n}$). Therefore, the equivalent universe σ is determined by the following formula:

$$\sigma = \overline{R}/d_2 \ (d_2 \text{ is found in Table A4})$$

Example 6.1 Determine the optimal (least cost) machine setting (mean) for the outside diameter of a shaft if the average cost of a rework is \$1 and the average cost of a piece of scrap is \$10. The part is in-control (a control chart has been established and all assignable causes have been found and corrected), the mean is 1.062, R-bar is 0.00775, the subsample size is 4, the lower limit is 1.055, and the upper limit is 1.075. Sigma, therefore, is 0.00775/2.059 = 0.00376 in. Note that the scrap area is below the lower limit and the rework area is above the upper limit. In some problems the opposite is true.

Solution (see Figure 6.11)

1. The incremental cost of defective units produced at the present mean (1.062) is:
   a. The area below the lower limit is 0.0314. (See Chapter 3 for these calculation procedures.)

$$Z = (X - \mu)/\sigma = (1.055 - 1.062)/0.00376 = -1.86$$

$$P(Z \leq -1.86) = 0.0314$$

   b. The incremental scrap (IS) cost is:

$$\text{IS} = \text{Area} \times \text{Cost/Unit} = 0.0314 \times \$10 = \$0.314$$

   c. The area above the upper limit is 0.00027:

$$Z = (X - \mu)/\sigma = (1.075 - 1.062)/0.00376 = 3.46$$

$$P(Z > 3.46) = 1 - P(Z \leq 3.46) = 0.00027$$

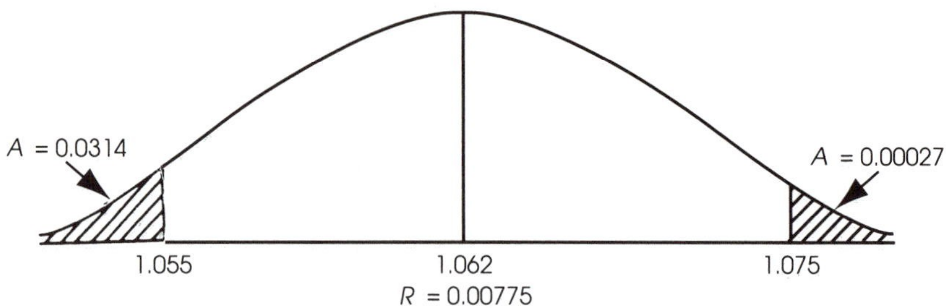

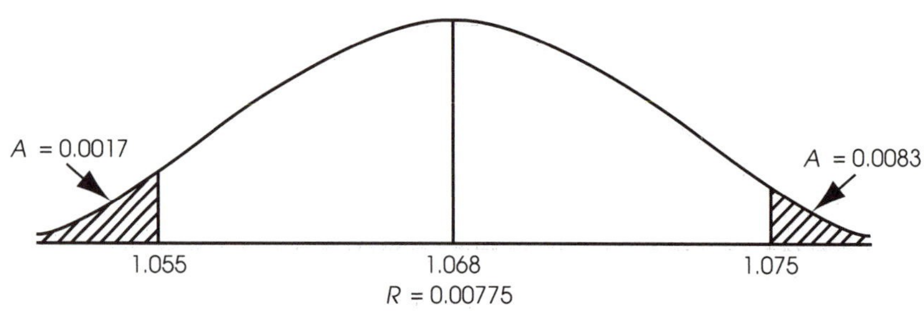

Figure 6.11. Curves illustrating Example 6.1.

d. The incremental rework (IR) cost is:

$$\text{IR} = \text{Area} \times \text{Cost/Unit} = 0.00027 \times \$1 = \$0.00027$$

e. The total incremental defective cost is:

$$0.314 + 0.00027 = \$0.31427$$

2. The incremental defective cost of one incremental subtraction is:
   a. The new mean value is:

$$1.062 - 0.001 = 1.061$$

   b. The area below the lower limit, the scrap area, is:

$$Z = (X - \mu)/\sigma = (1.055 - 1.061)/0.00376 = -1.60$$

$$P(Z \leq -1.60) = 0.0548$$

   c. The incremental scrap cost is:

$$\text{IS} = \text{Area} \times \text{Cost/Unit} = 0.0548 \times \$10 = \$0.548$$

d. The area above the upper limit, the rework area, is:

$$Z=(X-\mu)/\sigma=(1.075-1.061)/0.00376=3.72$$

$$P(Z>3.72)=1-P(Z\leq 3.72)=0.00007$$

e. The incremental rework cost is:

$$\text{IR}=\text{Area}\times\text{Cost/Unit}=0.00007\times\$1=\$0.00007$$

f. The total incremental defective cost is:

$$0.548+0.00007=\$0.54807$$

3. Since the incremental cost of an incremental subtraction (step 2) is greater than the original incremental cost (step 1), go to the incremental cost calculation procedure associated with incremental additions.
4. The incremental cost of an incremental addition is:

a. the new mean value is:

$$1.062+0.001=1.063$$

b. The area below the lower limit is:

$$Z=(X-\mu)/\sigma=(1.055-1.063)/0.00376=-2.13$$

$$P(Z\leq -2.13)=0.0166$$

c. The incremental scrap cost is:

$$\text{IS}=\text{Area}\times\text{Cost/Unit}=0.0166\times\$10=\$0.166$$

d. The area above the upper limit is:

$$Z=(X-\mu)/\sigma=(1.075-1.063)/0.00376=3.19$$

$$P(Z>3.19)=1-P(Z\leq 3.19)=0.00071$$

e. The incremental rework cost is:

$$\text{IR}=\text{Area}\times\text{Cost/Unit}=0.00071\times\$1=\$0.00071$$

f. The total incremental defective cost is:

$$0.166+0.00071=\$0.16671$$

5. The incremental defective cost of two incremental additions (1.062+ 0.002), or a mean of 1.064, is:

$$\$0.0857$$

6. The incremental cost of the next three means are:

	Incremental Cost		
Mean	**Total**	**Scrap**	**Rework**
1.065	\$0.0429	\$0.0390	\$0.0039
1.066	0.0253	0.0170	0.0083
1.067	0.0277	0.0071	0.0166

Conclusion: A mean (machine setting) of 1.066 is optimal, and will provide the least cost in rework and scrap.

The total optimal scrap and rework cost of a production run can be calculated from the incremental costs in step 6, as follows (assume a run of 1000 units):

1. The optimal scrap cost for the 1000 units is:

$$1000 \times \$0.017 = \$17$$

2. The optimal rework cost for the 1000 units is:

$$1000 \times \$0.0083 = \$8.30$$

3. The optimal total cost for defectives for the 1000 units is:

$$1000 \times \$0.0253 = \$25.30$$

This is a savings of 92% over the present mean [(\$314.27 − 25.30)/ \$314.27].

If, after this economic analysis is complete, one or both of the two tail areas are still too great, variation reduction procedures must be instituted. Unfortunately, reducing the variation is seldom as easy or as simple as adjusting the mean. It is usually a costly, often very costly, project. Some variation reduction procedures are:

1. Machine repair and/or adjustment.
2. Methods improvement.
3. Sorting (100% inspection)
4. New machine parts to reduce play, chatter, etc.
5. New machine or process.
6. Redesign of product and/or process.

Note that this comparison analysis was absolutely necessary to determine the optimum setting. None of the other control procedures in this text (with the possible exception of the experimental design techniques of Chapter 10) can do this. Once this determination is complete, the other methods can be used to continue control over time (with only an occasional check of the optimum setting). In fact, the C_{pk} ratio is an excellent control measure for this purpose, once the optimum setting has been found using normal curve analysis.

Practice Problems

6–1 Analyze the control chart patterns of Problems 4–1, 4–2, and 4–3 of Chapter 4.

6–2 Analyze the control chart patterns of Problems 4–13, 4–14, 4–15, 4–16, 4–17, and 4–18 of Chapter 4.

6–3 Compare the control limits of Problem 4–1 (1.25 and 1.96) to the specification limits of 1.20 and 2.10. The X-bar limits of Problem 4–1 are 1.25 and 1.96. Can the process manufacture the product to specifications?

6–4 Compare the control limits of Problem 4–2 (10 and 16) to the specification limits of 20 and 10. The X-bar limits of Problem 4–2 are 10 and 16. Can the process manufacture the product to specifications?

6–5 Compare the control limits of Problem 4–3 (6.8 and 14.8) to the specification limits of 15 and 5. The X-bar limits of Problem 4–13 are 6.8 and 14.8. Can the process manufacture the product to specifications?

6–6 For the data of Problem 3-1 (where the mean is 1.567 and the standard deviation is 0.261), the rework cost (below the lower limit) is $15 per part reworked and the scrap cost (above the upper limit) is $135 per part scrapped. Find:

a. The incremental cost for the mean of Problem 3–1.
b. The mean value needed to optimize (minimize) the incremental cost.
c. The incremental cost at the optimum mean value.
d. The percent of savings for part (d) over part (a).

Answers

$3.939; $5.543; $3.921; 1.49; $3.308

6–7 For the data of Problem 3–2 (where the mean is 12.7 and the standard deviation is 2.6), the rework cost (below the lower limit) is $45 per part reworked and the scrap cost (above the upper limit) is $300 per part scrapped. Find:

a. The incremental cost for the mean of Problem 3–2.
b. The mean value needed to optimize (minimize) the incremental cost.
c. The incremental cost at the optimum mean value.
d. The percent of savings for part (d) over part (a).

Answers

$7.482; $8.76; $5.94; 14; $5.94; 20.6%

6–8 For the data of Problem 3–3 (where the mean is 10.81 and the standard deviation is 3.12), the rework cost (below the lower limit) is $5 per part reworked and the scrap cost (above the upper limit) is $100 per part scrapped. Find:

a. The incremental cost for the mean of Problem 3–3.

b. The mean value needed to optimize (minimize) the incremental cost.
c. The incremental cost at the optimum mean value.
d. The percent of savings for part (d) over part (a).

Answers
$9.117; $19.04; $4.366; 7.1; $1.823; 80.0%

6–9 For the data of Problem 3–4 (where the mean is 3.148 and the standard deviation is 0.428), the rework cost (above the upper limit) is $50 per part reworked and the scrap cost (below the lower limit) is $200 per part scrapped. Find:

a. The incremental cost for the mean of Problem 3–4.
b. The mean value needed to optimize (minimize) the incremental cost.
c. The incremental cost at the optimum mean value.
d. The percent of savings for part (d) over part (a).

Answers
$5.39; $10.25; $3.52; 3.4; $3.48; 35.4%

6–10 Engineering specifications on the inside diameter of a certain bearing are 2.0000 in. + or − 0.0050 in. The process mean and standard deviation (estimated from similar bearings from the same process) are assumed to be 2.0019 and 0.0027, respectively. Find the expected percent of scrap and expected percent of rework (assume that all undersized bearings can be reworked).

Answers
0.53%; 12.55%

CHAPTER 7 OTHER PROBABILITY DISTRIBUTIONS

In this chapter, the various probability distributions that apply to SPC will be examined. Since the normal (Gaussian) has already been explained (Chapter 3), it will be omitted from this chapter. Sections 1, 3, and 4 of this chapter were derived from the author's book, *Reliability for the Technologies,* Industrial Press, 1985.

Objectives

1. Understand the basic probability rules that underlie all probability distributions and be able to use them to solve real life problems.
2. Understand and use the hypergeometric distribution.
3. Understand and use the binomial distribution.
4. Understand and use the Poisson distribution.
5. Understand and use the student's *t* distribution.

7.1 Basic Probability Rules

Probability can be defined as the chance that something will happen. Other terms (along with chance) that can be considered synonyms to probability are likelihood and tendency. Likelihood can be substituted for the word chance in the previous sentence, but tendency is used in a slightly different context. The tendency to be the same or the tendency to be different are both probability measures.

Probability is measured in terms of a ratio; that is, one value divided into part of that value. Therefore, probability values range between 0.00 and 1.00. The total of all possible chances in a situation is equal to 1.00. Probability is also frequently measured as a percent, but percent is simply the ratio multiplied by 100 (a ratio of 0.015 is equal to 1.5%). If an infinite number of objects are involved (or the possibility of infinite division between two measurements), the probability rules become virtually impossible to apply. Under these conditions, probability distributions, such as the normal curve, must be used.

There are only three types of symbols needed in probability theory. The first, $P(A)$ or P_A, are the symbols used for the probability of an event. These two symbols, $P(A)$ and P_A, mean the same thing and can be used interchangeably. Numbers can also be substituted for A [P_1 or $P(1)$] or other letters can be used (P_B, P_t, etc.). The second symbol, the lower case s, is used to denote a success, that is, a desirable event. Finally, the lower case n (identical in meaning to the sample size n used with the normal curve) is used to denote the total number of possibilities. The probability equation, then, is:

$$P(E) = P_E = s/n$$

where

$P_E = P(E) =$ the probability of an event

$s =$ the number of successes (or failures, depending on what is being evaluated)

$n =$ the total possible number of cases

Example 7.1 In the flip of a coin there are two possible cases: a head or a tail. Thus, $n=2$. There is one possible way of getting a head. Therefore, $s=1$. The probability of getting a head, then, on one flip of a coin is 1/2. $P(H) = s/n = 1/2$.

There are seven fundamental probability theorems, or rules. It is theoretically possible to solve any probability/statistical problem using one or more of these theorems. Most problems are so complex, however, it would take too long (years in some cases) if other methods were not used. The various probability distributions (normal, binomial, Poisson, t, etc.) are actually mathematical shorthand procedures for applying complex combinations of these theorems. Examples of how the probability theorems can be used to develop probability distributions will be given in Sections 7.2 and 7.3.

Theorem 1—Fundamental Property 1 The probability of an event lies between 0 and 1. Zero probability (000) is the certainty that event A will not occur. A probability of one (1.00) is the certainty that event A will occur.

Theorem 2—Fundamental Property 2 The sum of the probabilities of a situation is equal to 1.00. The equation is:

$$P_1 + P_2 + P_3 \ . \ . \ . \ + P_n = 1.00$$

Example 7.2 In the flip of a coin, the probability of a head is 1/2 and the probability of a tail is 1/2. The probability of a head or a tail (all possible cases) is equal to 1.00 (1/2 + 1/2) (neglecting the infinitesimal probability of the coin landing on its edge):

$$P(H \text{ or } T) = 1/2 + 1/2 = 1.00$$

Example 7.3 In the roll of a die, there are six faces and, therefore, six possible outcomes ($n = 6$). Each of the numbers (1 to 6) occur only once, therefore, $s = 1$ for each of the six numbers. The probability of any number from 1 to 6 on one roll of a die (all possibilities) is 1.00.

$$P(1, \text{ or } 2, \text{ or } 3, \text{ or } 4, \text{ or } 5, \text{ or } 6) = 1/6 + 1/6 + 1/6 + 1/6 + 1/6 = 1.00$$

This rule is used constantly in solving real life probability problems. However, it is critical in solving these problems to first determine what constitutes a set of all possible cases. For example, in a sample size of three where the number of defectives is being counted, the set of all possible cases would be 0, 1, 2, or 3 defectives in the sample. The sum of their probabilities must equal 1.000. In other words, when evaluating the probability of defectives in this type of sample, there are always $n + 1$ possible outcomes, not just n (because there is the probability of 0 defectives as well as 1, 2, or 3). This emphasizes the need for careful analysis when determining the size of a set of objects.

Theorem 3—The Complementary Law This rule states that if P is the probability that an event will occur, then $1 - P$ is the probability that the event will not occur. The probability of it occurring plus the probability of it not occurring always equals 1.00.

Example 7.4 In the roll of a die, the probability that a 1 will occur is 1/6. The probability that it will not occur is $1 - 1/6 = 5/6 = 83.3\%$.

Theorem 4—The Additive Law In this rule, the probability of either A or B is the sum of the probability of A and the probability of B. This rule is a special case (and an important one) of a more general rule, the combination law, which will be explained later. In this law, the two events must be mutually exclusive. (This is not true in the more general combination law.) Mutually exclusive means that the occurrence of one event makes the other impossible. (For example, there cannot be both a head and a tail on one toss of a coin.) The equation is:

$$P(A \text{ or } B) = P_A + P_B = P(A) + P(B)$$

The "or" is distinctive in this case and always means plus (or add) and never multiply (except in the case of the combination law where it can also mean minus). Where the additive law is applicable, the "or" will always occur in the statement of the problem (or be implied in the logic).

Example 7.5 The probability of a head or a tail in one toss of a coin is 1.00 (neglecting the infinitesimal probability that the coin will land on its edge).

$$P(H \text{ or } T) = P(H) + P(T) = 1/2 + 1/2 = 1.00$$

Example 7.6 What is the probability of a 1 or a 6 occurring on one roll of a die?

Solution

$$P(1 \text{ or } 6) = P(1) + P(6) = 1/6 + 1/6 = 2/6 = 0.333$$

Example 7.7 If the probability of finding 1 defective in a sample of 6 is 0.09 and the probability of finding 2 defectives in the sample is 0.04, what is the probability of finding 1 or 2 defectives in the sample?

Solution

$$P(1 \text{ or } 2) = P_1 + P_2 = 0.09 + 0.04 = 0.13 \text{ or } 13\%$$

Theorem 5—The Multiplicative Law or Product Rule (also called *joint* probability in statistics.) This law states that the mutual probability of two independent events is equal to the product of the probabilities of each event. If two events are independent, the occurrence of one does not affect the probability of the other occurring. (The occurrence of a head on the toss of one coin has no effect on the probability of a head or a tail occurring on a toss of a second coin.) Once again, this rule is a special case of another rule called the conditional law, or conditional probability, to be discussed later. The equation is:

$$P(A \text{ and } B) = P(A) \times P(B) = P_A \times P_B$$

The "and" in this case always refers to multiplying, never to addition or subtraction. Where the multiplicative law is applicable, the "and" will always occur in the statement of the problem (or be implied in the logic).

Example 7.8 What is the probability that, in two tosses of a coin, the first coin will be heads and the second tails?

Solution

$$P(H \text{ and } T) = P(H) \times P(T) = 1/2 \times 1/2 = 1/4$$

Example 7.9 What is the probability that, in two tosses of a coin, there will be a head and a tail (in any order)? Note that in this problem statement, an "or" is implied, in addition to an "and." Therefore, both the multiplicative and the additive laws apply. Two conditions will satisfy the solution of the problem: (1) a head on the first coin AND a tail on the second, OR (2) a tail on the first AND a head on the second.

Solution

$$P(H \text{ and } T \text{ or } T \text{ and } H) = [P(H) \times P(T)] + [P(T) \times P(H)]$$

$$= [(1/2 \times 1/2)] + [(1/2 \times 1/2)] = 1/4 + 1/4 = 1/2$$

Another way of analyzing this problem is to calculate the probabilities of all possible results. First, note that only four combinations are possible: (1) a head on the first toss and a tail on the second, (2) a head on the first toss and a head on the second, (3) a tail on the first toss and a head on the second, and (4) a tail on the first toss and a tail on the second. Since these four combinations include all possible results, the sum of their probabilities equals 1.00. These probability calculations and their results are summarized in Table 7.1.

Now the question asked in Example 7.9 can be answered by noting that two of the four combinations will solve the problem: case 2, the $P(H$ and $T)$ or case 3, the $P(T$ and $H)$. Since either one or the other will solve the problem, the solution is to add the two probabilities together $(1/4 + 1/4 = 1/2)$. This can also be answered by the use of the basic probability formula: $P = s/n$. Since there are two possible right answers (successes) in Table 7.1 $(s = 2)$ and four possible solutions in all $(n = 4)$, $P(H$ or $T) = sn = 2/4$ or $1/2$.

If, on the other hand, the question had been stated as in Example

Table 7.1 Probability Combinations for Tossing Two Coins

Case	First Coin	Second Coin	Calculations	Probability
1	H	H	$1/2 \times 1/2$	1/4
2	H	T	$1/2 \times 1/2$	1/4
3	T	H	$1/2 \times 1/2$	1/4
4	T	T	$1/2 \times 1/2$	1/4
				Total = 1.0

7.8 (that is, what is the probability that the first toss will be a head and the second will be a tail), only one of these combinations would have answered the problem: case 2, $P(H \text{ and } T)$. In this case, the answer would be 1/4 (or $P = 1/4$).

In these types of problems, it is imperative to analyze and apply the applicable rule or rules carefully. Note that an exhaustive analysis such as was just presented is seldom feasible except when the number of possible outcomes is small.

Example 7.10 The probability that an order of screws will be rejected is 0.12. The probability that a second order will be rejected is 0.30. What is the probability that they will both be rejected?

Solution

$$P(A \text{ and } B) = P(A) \times P(B) = 0.12 \times 0.30 = 0.36$$

Theorem 6—The Combination Law This law is used to find the probability of occurrence of either one or both of two events when the events are not necessarily mutually exclusive. As previously mentioned, this is actually the general rule of which the additive rule is only a special case (where the events are mutually exclusive). The equation is:

$$P(A \text{ or } B \text{ or both}) = P(A) + P(B) - P(A \text{ and } B)$$

Note that both the additive and the multiplicative laws are combined in this rule.

Example 7.11 In a deck of 52 playing cards, what is the probability of getting a king or a heart on one draw?

Solution

$$\begin{aligned} P(K \text{ or } H) &= P(K) + P(H) - (P_K \times P_H) \\ &= 4/52 + 13/52 - (4/52 \times 13/52) \\ &= 4/52 + 13/52 - 1/52 = 16/52 = 0.308 \end{aligned}$$

Note that the probability of getting a king includes the probability of one heart, while the probability of a heart includes the probability of one king. Therefore, when the two probabilities are added (P_K and P_H), the probability of getting a king of hearts is included twice. Therefore, one of them must be subtracted. Since the probability of a king of hearts is 1/52, this figure could have been deduced by this logic alone rather than calculated with the multiplicative law. In this case, the term subtracted would have been P_{KH} not $(P_K \times P_H)$.

An exhaustive analysis can also be made on this problem. Although this type of analysis is inefficient in this case (there are so many possible outcomes), it will nevertheless be presented for illustration and instructional purposes. Note that the probability of drawing a king or a heart is equal to the probability of drawing a king of hearts or a king of diamonds or a king of clubs or a king of spades or a two of hearts or a three of hearts or a four of hearts or a five of hearts or a six of hearts or a seven of hearts or an eight of hearts or a nine of hearts or a 10 of hearts or a jack of hearts or a queen of hearts or an ace of hearts. (Note that the king of hearts is included only once in this list.) The probability of a king or a heart, then, is the sum of the individual probabilities of each item on the list. But each item is just one card and the probability of drawing any one card from a deck of 52 cards is 1/52, therefore, the sum of these 16 items is 16/52, or:

$$P(K \text{ or } H) = 16/52 = 0.308$$

The subtracted term in the combination law ($P_K \times P_H$) is not always obvious or easy to derive. In fact, the term ($P_K \times P_H$) can only be used when all items are equal in amount. For example, there are four jacks, four queens, etc., and there are 13 of each of the four suits. If these variables were not equal (say only three jacks but four of each of the others), then the subtracted term must be determined by logic alone (as the P_{KH} was determined). This problem becomes especially difficult when the law is generalized to more than three events or occurrences.

Example 7.12 A box contains three cubes numbered 1 to 3, five prisms numbered 1 to 5, and eight spheres numbered 1 to 8. If one item is drawn at a time, what is the probability that it will be a cube or will be numbered 3? A prism or a number 3? A sphere or a number 3? A sphere or a number 7? A prism or a number 7?

Solution

1. $P(\text{c or } 3) = 3/16 + 3/16 - 1/16 = 5/16$
2. $P(p \text{ or } 3) = 5/16 + 3/16 - 1/16 = 7/16$
3. $P(s \text{ or } 3) = 8/16 + 3/16 - 1/16 = 10/16$
4. $P(s \text{ or } 7) = 8/16 + 1/16 - 1/16 = 8/16$
5. $P(p \text{ or } 7) = 5/16 + 1/16 - 0/16 = 6/16$

Theorem 7—The Conditional Law This is the general law from which the product rule is a special case. Unlike the product (multiplicative) rule, the conditional law applies to both dependent and independent events. Two events are dependent if the occurrence of one affects the probability of the second occurring; it doesn't necessarily affect the occurrence of the second event, just the probability that it will occur. The equation is:

$$P(A \text{ and } B) = P(A) \times P(B|A)$$

$P(B|A)$ means the probability of event B occurring given that event A has already occurred. $B|A$ is usually referred to as B given A. When A and B are dependent, special care must be taken to determine what the actual probabilities are. When they are independent, $P(B|A)$ degenerates into $P(B)$.

Example 7.13 A tote box contains 60 shafts, eight of which are defective. If a sample of two are removed, what is the probability that both will be defective? (Assume that neither shaft is replaced.) Note that after the first shaft is removed, the probabilities change, since there are only 59 shafts remaining. If the first one removed is a defective one, this again changes the probabilities since only seven defectives remain.

Solution

$$P(A \text{ and } B) = 8/60 \times 7/59 = 0.016$$

If the first shaft had been good, the probability of the second shaft being defective would have changed to 8/59. Therefore, the probability that the second shaft is defective (when measured this way) clearly depends on whether or not the first was defective. Thus, the probabilities are dependent.

Note that if each shaft had been measured and then replaced, the probability of getting a defective shaft on the second draw would have been independent of the first draw. The multiplicative law would have applied in this case and the answer would be:

$$P(A \text{ and } B) = 8/60 \times 8/60 = 0.18$$

Independence usually leads to higher probabilities.

These seven laws can all be generalized to more than two occurrences. Care must be taken, however, in applying them to more than two occurrences. This is especially true of the combination law and the conditional law. These laws when applied to three or more events can be very complex and require much thought and analysis. The laws can also be combined in problems, and often are (as in Example 7.9).

Counting Rules

It is often important in probability to determine the number of sets and subsets of objects. There are three main methods to do this, each having application to particular types of sets. They are:

1. Simple multiplication.
2. Permutations.
3. Combinations.

Simple Multiplication

When it is desired to know the total number of possible sets, the rule of simple multiplication usually applies. If event A can happen in any of n_1 ways and event B can happen in any of n_2 ways, the total number of ways that both can occur is $n_1 \times n_2$.

Example 7.14 There are five possible delivery routes in the morning and six possible routes in the afternoon. What is the total number of daily delivery routes possible?

Solution

$$\text{Total} = n_1 n_2 = 5 \times 6 = 30$$

Example 7.15 An electronic system has two components connected together in series. Component A has three different parallel circuits and component B has four. How many different ways can the current travel through the system?

Solution

$$n_1 n_2 = 3 \times 4 = 12$$

If component C with five parallel circuits is added to the system in series with components A and B, how many ways are there now?

Solution

$$n_1 n_2 n_3 = 3 \times 4 \times 5 = 60$$

Permutations

If the possible sets of objects are to be ordered (arranged in specific ways), then these sets are called permutations. A permutation is defined as an ordered arrangement of n objects taken d at a time. Suppose that three letters of the alphabet (A, C, and T) are chosen and it is desired to arrange them in definite order. In other words, the order of appearance of the letters is important. Permutations of these three letters are ACT, ATC, TAC, TCA, CAT, and CTA. There are six possible permutations of these three letters (even though only two make recognizable words). Note that our numbering and language systems are both permutations because the order of the digits or letters is important (changing the order changes the meaning). Of course, the language system does not use all possible permutations, as does the numbering system. The equation is:

$$P_d^n = n!/(n-d)!$$

(Note: The exclamation mark (!) means factorial.)

$$n! = (n)(n-1)(n-2)(n-3)\ldots(n-n)$$

$$0! \text{ always} = 1$$

Example 7.16 Find the permutation of five things, taken two at a time.

Solution

$$P_d^n = P_2^5 = 5!/(5-2)!$$
$$= (5\times4\times3\times2\times1\times1)/(3\times2\times1\times1) = 20$$

Combinations

If the way the objects are ordered is not important, the set is called a combination. Using the same three letters of the alphabet (A, C, and T), there is only one combination. Since the same three letters are used, and the order of arrangements does not matter, then (as far as combinations go) ACT = TAC = CAT, etc. There are always more permutations than combinations in the same set of objects (the letters A, C, and T have six permutations, but only one combination), except for the case of n things taken 0 at a time, in which case combinations = permutations = 1. The equation is:

$$C_d^n = \binom{n}{d} = n!/d!(n-d)!$$

Example 7.17 Find the combination of five things taken two at a time.

Solution

$$C_d^n = C_2^5 = 5!/[2!(5-2)!]$$
$$= (5\times4\times3\times2\times1)/[(2\times1)(3\times2\times1)] = 10$$

7.2 The Hypergeometric

The hypergeometric, along with the binomial, is the fundamental probability distribution for discrete values. Discrete means that the individual values are distinctive and do not blend into each other; they are attributes that cannot be divided (unlike continuous variables that can have an infinite number of possible divisions between any two measurements). In SPC, they are represented by the counting numbers 1, 2, 3, 4, etc. Discrete variables, in SPC, are counted while continuous variables are measured. The number of failures in a test is a discrete value as they are counted and are represented by whole numbers. (We cannot have half a failure or half a defect or half a defective.) The hypergeometric applies, then, to the finite case and requires that the random sample be taken without replacement from a known universe (such as a known lot size).

Derivation of the Hypergeometric

The hypergeometric can be derived from the basic probability rules. Suppose that a lot of 20 units has 5 defective units. If a sample of 4 is to be taken without replacement (the probabilities are then dependent), what is the probability that there will be exactly one defective part in the sample?

Since there are 5 defective parts in the lot, there are five ways of selecting 1 defective. Also, the order of the selection is unimportant (if 2 defectives were chosen, for example, it would only matter that they were defectives, not that they were chosen in any particular order). Therefore, the five ways of selecting the defective can be determined by calculating the combination of five things taken one at a time $\{5!/[1!(5-1)!]\}$. For each of these five combinations of defectives, there must be three good parts. Since there are 15 good parts in the lot, there are 455 ways of choosing the three good parts. This is determined by the combination of 15 things taken three at a time $\{15!/[3!(15-3)!]\}$. Each of the five ways of choosing a defective can occur in each of the 455 ways of choosing a good part making 2,275 ways (5 × 455) of matching the problem criteria (of succeeding). This is the *s* in the formula, $P = s/n$. The *n* is the total number of ways that four things can be selected from 20, or the combination of 20 things taken four at a time $\{20!/[4!(20-4)!] = 4{,}845\}$. Therefore, the probability that a sample of 4 will contain exactly 1 defective part is 2,275/4,845 = 0.47.

These calculations can be represented in formula form, as follows:

$$P(1) = C_1^5 C_4^{15} / C_5^{20} = 0.47$$

Which can be generalized to:

$$P(d) = C_d^D C_{n-d}^{N-D} / C_n^N$$

where

N = the lot size

D = the number of defectives in the lot

n = the sample size

d = the desired number of defectives in the sample.

Example 7.18 A lot of 50 objects has 10 defectives. What is the probability of getting exactly 2 defectives in a sample of 5?

Solution

$$P(2) = C_2^{10} C_{5-2}^{50-10} / C_5^{50}$$

$$= \frac{10!/[2!(10-2!] \times 40!/[3!(40-3)!]}{50!/[5!(50-5)!]} = 0.2098$$

If it were desired to know the probability of 2 or less, the probability of 0 ($d=0$) and the probability of 1 ($d=1$) would have to be calculated and added to the probability of 2. The probability of 2 or less = $P(0) + P(1) + P(2)$:

$$P(2 \text{ or less}) = 0.3106 + 0.4313 + 0.2098 = 0.9517$$

The probability of more than 2 is:

$$P \text{ (more than 2)} = 1 - P(2 \text{ or less})$$

$$= 1 - 0.9517 = 0.0483$$

Notice how useful the additive and complementary rules are in determining answers to complex hypergeometric problems.

Hypergeometric calculations can be quite difficult to make, even with modern calculators. Factorials of large numbers (like a lot of 1,200, for example) are too large for anything but a computer to handle. Tables of logs of factorials have been developed to assist in these types of calculations.

Example 7.19 A lot of 60 units has been received from a supplier whose defective rate is known to be 5%. What is the probability that a sample of 10 drawn at random will have exactly one defective? Less than one? More than one?

Solution

1. The probability of exactly one is:

$$P(1) = C_1^3 C_{10-1}^{60-3} / C_{10}^{60} = 0.358$$

2. The probability of less than one is:

$$P(0) = C_0^3 C_{10-0}^{60-3} / C_{10}^{60} = 0.573$$

3. The probability of more than one is:

$$P(\text{more than } 1) = 1 - P(1 \text{ or less})$$

$$= 1 - (0.358 + 0.573) = 0.069$$

7.3 The Binomial Distribution

The hypergeometric is the basic probability distribution when the lot size is known and sampling is accomplished without replacement.

(The probabilities are conditional or dependent; the probability that an event will occur depends on what happened in previous occurrences and preceding events.) If the lot size is unknown, however, and/or the values are independent (sampling occurs with replacement or by an equivalent procedure), the binominal becomes the basic distribution. Like the hypergeometric, the binomial is a discrete probability distribution.

The binomial is also a dichotomous distribution. Its two parts each represent an either/or situation such as good or bad, success or failure, pass or fail, etc. The two parts, or dichotomies, are represented by the symbols p and q, with p representing the probability of a success and q the probability of a non-success. A success, of course, can be any desired (or expected) condition, even a failure. Since only two conditions are possible (bi means two), the sum of the probabilities of the two conditions must equal to 1.00. Thus, $p+q=1$, and $q=1-p$.

The lower case p represents the probability of an event occurring. It is the probability, for instance, that any one part from a sample (or from the lot or the entire universe) is defective. q, or $1-p$, is the probability that the part will not be defective. The upper case P, on the other hand, is the probability that a certain number of defectives will occur in the sample. Even though these two terms are both probability values and have similar meanings, they are not the same thing. It is imperative that they be carefully defined in the problem statement. An excellent way of differentiating between these two symbols is to consider the lower case p a fraction defective or a process average rather than a probability value (even though a fraction defective is a probability value). A fraction defective (or percent defective), of course, is just another way of saying "the probability of an event occurring."

The Bernoulli Process

The binomial is also one of the distributions that evolves from what is known as the Bernoulli process. (Successive flipping of coins and rolling of dice are excellent examples of Bernoulli processes or Bernoulli trials.) In a Bernoulli process, three conditions must be present:

1. There must be only two possible outcomes and these outcomes are dichotomous, with their probabilities summing to 1.00 (a necessary condition from the second basic, or fundamental, property of probability).
2. The processes, and outcomes, are independent of each other; the probability of one event, or outcome, is not affected by previous outcomes.
3. The probabilities of the two possible outcomes (usually designated as p and q) must be constant; the process must be stable.

For example, the counting of defectives from a machine where the tool wears out quickly, and must be frequently replaced, is technically not a Bernoulli process, as the probability of a defective occurring increases over time. However, the binomial usually closely approximates even this type of process and so, due to practical considerations, is usually used in place of more complex models that apply more closely.

The binomial can approximate the normal curve and vice versa; when it does, the mean of the binomial is np and the standard deviation is the square root of npq:

$$\mu = np$$

$$\sigma = \sqrt{npq}$$

Derivation of the Binomial

The binomial, like the hypergeometric, can be derived from basic probability rules, and in this case, the product rule. For example, suppose that a lot of 20 parts, which is known to have 5 defective parts, is sampled. A sample of 4 is taken, with replacement. What is the probability that the sample of 4 will have exactly 1 defective part?

This is the same example used to develop the hypergeometric. In this case, however, each part in the sample is to be replaced as soon as it is measured, and prior to selecting the next part. Thus, the probabilities are independent (unlike in the hypergeometric example where the items were not replaced and were, therefore, dependent). Any sample that satisfies this condition will have one bad part and three good ones. There are four samples, out of all possible samples, that will satisfy the given conditions, as follows:

a. *B, G, G, G*
b. *G, B, G, G*
c. *G, G, B, G*
d. *G, G, G, B*

The probability that sample "a" will occur is:

$$5/20 \times 15/20 \times 15/20 \times 15/20 = (5/20)^1\ (15/20)^3 = 0.1055$$

Since any mixture of the same four fractions, multiplied together, will have the same result, the probability that any one of the four samples will occur is the same for each: 0.1055. Also, since any one of the four will satisfy the given conditions, the probability of getting exactly 1 bad part out of a sample of 4 taken at random with replacement is:

$$\begin{aligned} P(1) &= P(a) + P(b) + P(c) + P(d) \\ &= 0.1055 + 0.1055 + 0.1055 + 0.1055 \\ &= 4(0.1055) = 0.422\ (42.2\%) \end{aligned}$$

Note that the number of ways that the desired condition can occur is the combination of four things taken one at a time (the order of occurrence is unimportant). Also note that the probability of a bad part is always the same, as is the probability of a good part. Therefore, an equation for this problem can be generated as follows:

$$P(1)=C_1^4(5/20)^1(1-5/20)^{4-1}$$
$$=4!/[1!(4-1)!]\times(5/20)^1\times(15/20)^3=0.422$$

This can be generalized to the following formula (called the single-term binomial formula):

$$P(d)=C_d^n p^d(1-p)^{n-d}$$

In this example, the lot size does not have to be known. Suppose that the sample of four is to be drawn at random from a group of product from a production line known to produce 25% defective parts, on the average. Thus, $p=0.25$ and $q=1-p=1-0.25=0.75$. Then 0.25 can be substituted for 5/20 and 0.75 for 15/20, without even knowing the lot size (in this case the lot size is effectively infinite):

$$P(1)=C_1^4(0.25)^1(0.75)^{4-1}=0.422(42.2\%)$$

The Binomial Expansion

There are two formulas that can be used to calculate the binomial: the binomial expansion and the single-term formula (the same single-term formula previously derived). The equation for the binomial expansion is:

$$(p+q)^n=p^n+np^{n-1}q+n(n-1)/2!p^{n-2}q^2$$
$$+n(n-1)(n-2)/3!p^{n-3}q^3$$
$$+n(n-1)(n-2)(n-3)/4!p^{n-4}q^4+\ldots+q^n$$

where

p = the probability of an event

q = the probability of a non-event $(1-p)$

n = the number of trials, or the sample size

In the above expansion, each term represents the probability of a particular number of events (successes or failures, depending on what is desired or expected, that is, what is being measured). Thus, the first term p^n is the probability of n successes (or desired events, or expected defectives); the second term is the probability of $n-1$ successes (p^{n-1}), etc. There are always $n+1$ terms in the binomial expansion representing the probability of n, $n-1$, $n-2$, . . . 0 successes, respectively. Note that the final term is the probability of 0 successes. The number of successes in a term is dictated by the exponent of p. Thus, in a sample of five, the probability of five (n) successes is found from the first term (P^5), the probability of four ($n - 1$) successes is found from the second term (P^4), etc. In the last term, the probability of 0 successes, P^0 is, of course, assumed.

The Single-Term Formula

Each of the terms of this expansion can be represented by the individual formula previously derived:

$$P(d) = C_d^n p^d q^{n-d}$$

where

$P(d)$ = the probability of d successes

C_d^n = the coefficient = combination of n things taken d at a time

p = the probability of an event (the fraction defective)

q = the probability of a non-event $= 1 - p$

d = the number of desired events in n trials

n = the number of trials or sample size

This formula is extremely useful as it allows the calculation of an individual probability without having to first expand the binomial (a tedious process for large sample sizes).

Example 7.20 A random sample of 10 is selected from a steady stream of product from a punch press, which past experience has shown to produce 10% defective parts. Find the probability of: (1) one bad part, (2) two bad parts, (3) one or less bad parts, and (4) three or more bad parts in the sample.

1. One bad part:

$$P(d) = C_d^n p^d q^{n-d}$$

$$P(1) = C_1^{10}(0.10)^1(0.90)^{10-1}$$

$$= 10!/1!(10-1)! \times (0.10)^1(0.90)^9 = 0.3874$$

2. Two bad parts:

$$P(2) = 10!/2!(10-2)! \times (0.10)^2(0.90)^8 = 0.1937$$

3. One or less bad parts:

$$P(1 \text{ or less}) = P(0) + P(1)$$

$$P(0) = 10!/0!(10-0)! \times (0.10)^0(0.90)^{10} = 0.3487$$

$$P(1 \text{ or less}) = P(0) + P(1)$$
$$= 0.3487 + 0.3874 = 0.7361(73.61\%)$$

4. Three or more bad parts:

$$P(3 \text{ or more}) = 1 - P(2 \text{ or less})$$
$$= 1 - [P(0) + P(1) + P(2)]$$
$$= 1 - (0.3487 + 0.3874 + 0.1937) = 0.0702$$

Note how the additive and complementary rules of probability are especially useful in solving binomial problems. In determining the probability of more than one event, two or more terms must be added together (additive rule). In determining the probability of more than a certain number of events, the probability of that number or less can be subtracted from 1.00. For example, the probability of fewer than 2 defectives from a sample of 50 would be found by adding $P(0)$, $P(1)$, and $P(2)$. The probability of more than 2 could be found by subtracting this sum from 1.00. Of course, the probability of more than 2 could also be found by summing the probabilities of the 48 terms above 2, but this would be prohibitively time-consuming.

Example 7.20 can also be solved using the binomial expansion of $(p+q)^{10}$. In this case, the eighth, ninth, and tenth terms would have been used to solve the problem.

Calculations of Control Chart Pattern Probabilities

In Chapter 6 it was noted that various control chart patterns were indications of possible out-of-control conditions. These patterns were developed from applications of the 1% rule, which states: "any pattern that has less than a 1% probability of occurring by chance alone is considered a candidate for an out-of-control condition." In such cases, the process must be examined for an assignable cause. Because of their complexity, most of the calculations for these pattern probabilities were deferred until now, until the binomial could be used. These patterns, and their probabilities, are:

1. Seven in a row. By chance alone, it is equally likely that any one value (subsample mean) will be either part of the pattern or will not. Therefore, the probability that any one value is part of a pattern is 0.5 or 50%. This is equivalent to the fraction defective, or p, of the binomial. So:

$$P(7) = C_7^7 p^7 (1-p)^{7-7} = 7!/7!(7-7)!(0.5)^7(1-0.5)^0$$
$$= 0.0078$$

In contrast, six in a row does not meet the 1% rule.

$$P(6) = C_6^6 p^6 (1-p)^{6-6} = 6!/6!(6-6)!(0.5)^6(1-0.5)^0$$
$$= 0.0156$$

2. Ten of 11 in a row. The probability of an assignable cause for 10 of 11 in a row is the probability that exactly 10 will form a pattern (up or down, etc.) AND exactly one will not OR exactly 11 will. So:

$$P(10)=C_{10}^{11}p^{10}(1-p)^{11-10}$$
$$=11!/10!(11-10)!(0.5)^{10}(1-0.5)^{1}=0.00537$$
$$P(11)=C_{11}^{11}p^{11}(1-p)^{11-11}$$
$$=11!/11!(11-11)!(0.5)^{11}(1-0.5)^{0}=0.000488$$
$$P(10\text{ OR }11)=P(10)+P(11)$$
$$=0.00537+0.000488=0.0059$$

In contrast, $P(9\text{ of }10) = 0.107$, obviously greater than 1%.

3. Twelve of 14 in a row. This is $P(12)$ OR $P(13)$ OR $P(14)$:

$$P(12)=C_{12}^{14}p^{12}(1-p)^{14-12}$$
$$=14!/12!(14-12)!(0.5)^{12}(1-0.5)^{2}=0.00555$$
$$P(13)=C_{13}^{14}p^{13}(1-p)^{14-13}$$
$$=14!/13!(14-13)!(0.5)^{13}(1-0.5)^{1}=0.000854$$
$$P(14)=C_{14}^{14}p^{14}(1-p)^{14-14}$$
$$=14!/14!(14-14)!(0.5)^{14}(1-0.5)^{0}=0.000061$$
$$P(12\text{ OR }13\text{ OR }14)=0.00555+0.000854+0.000061=0.0065$$

In contrast, $P(11\text{ of }13) = 0.0112$.

4. Patterns between the mean and +1 standard deviation and between the mean and −1 standard deviation. Since the control chart is based on the normal curve, the probability that any one value will be in one of these areas is 34.13% (Chapter 3). The critical patterns are:
   a. Five in a row in one of these areas (either above or below the mean):

$$P(5)=C_{5}^{5}p^{5}(1-p)^{5-5}$$
$$=5!/5!(5-5)!(0.3413)^{5}(1-0.3413)^{0}$$
$$=0.00463$$

   b. Six of seven in a row in one of these areas (either above or below the mean):

$$P(6)=C_{6}^{7}p^{6}(1-p)^{7-6}$$
$$=7!/6!(7-6)!(0.3413)^{6}(1-0.3413)^{1}$$
$$=0.00729$$
$$P(7)=C_{7}^{7}p^{7}(1-p)^{7-7}$$

$$= 7!/7!(7-7)!(0.3413)^7(1-0.3413)^0$$

$$= 0.00054$$

$$P(6 \text{ of } 7) = 0.00729 + 0.00054 = 0.00783$$

5. Patterns between +1 and +2 standard deviations from the mean and −1 and −2 standard deviations from the mean. The probability that any one value will be in one of these areas is 0.136 (Chapter 3). The patterns are:
   a. Three in a row in one of these areas.

$$P(3) = C_3^3 p^3(1-p)^{3-3}$$

$$= 3!/3!(3-3)!(0.136)^3(1-0.136)^0$$

$$= 0.0025$$

   b. Four of five in a row.

$$P(4) = C_4^5 p^4(1-p)^{5-4}$$

$$= 5!/4!(5-4)!(0.136)^4(1-0.136)^1$$

$$= 0.0015$$

$$P(5) = C_5^5 p^5(1-p)^{5-5}$$

$$= 5!/5!(5-5)!(0.136)^5(1-0.136)^0$$

$$= 0.00005$$

$$P(4 \text{ of } 5) = 0.0015 + 0.00005 = 0.00155$$

6. Patterns between $+2\sigma$ and $+3\sigma$ (the UCL) and between -2σ and -3σ (the LCL) from the mean. The probability that any one value will be in one of these areas is 0.02135 (Chapter 3). There is only one pattern, two in a row in either one of the areas.

$$P(2) = C_2^2 p2(1-p)^{2-2}$$

$$= 2!/2!(2-2)!(0.02135)^2(1-0.02135)^0$$

$$= 0.00045558$$

7.4 The Poisson Formula

Although the Poisson is a single-term formula only, like the binomial, it can be expanded to a number of terms, each of which represents the probability of a particular number of occurrences. Also like the binomial, the sum of all the terms equals 1.00. This is true even though the Poisson can, theoretically, have an infinite number of terms, representing an infinite number of defects per unit. (The sum of the probabilities of all possible conditions must equal 1.00, even if there are an infinite number of these conditions.) Because of the possible infinite nature of the Poisson sample sizes (the Poisson can also be used when the sample size is known), Poisson expansions must begin with $d=0$. (Most Poisson tables use c number of defects rather than d.)

As the Poisson is expanded to more and more terms, the probabilities quickly become so small as to be infinitesimal and so can be ignored. Thus, the Poisson tables give the probabilities of only a limited number of the Poisson terms (to three places). When the probabilities get so small that the first three decimal places are zeros, the table ends. The equation for the Poisson is:

$$P(d) = e^{-np}\ (np)^d/d!$$

where

$P(d)$ = the probability of d defects or failures
d = the number of defects or failures that can be tolerated (usually determined by engineering or management and must be whole numbers only)
p = the fraction defective (as in the binomial)
n = the sample size
np = the average number of defects or failures (determined by actual sampling)
e = the base of the Naperian logorithms = 2.71828

It is important to understand the differences between d and np. Since these two terms have similar meanings, it is easy to confuse them. Remember that d is an individual value set by engineering (and must be in whole numbers), while np is the average of the distribution (and so can be a fraction) and is usually determined by actual sampling (occasionally, np is assumed).

Example 7.21 Ten speedboat shells were inspected and found to have 2, 1, 0, 3, 1, 2, 0, 0, 1, and 2 defects, respectively. Calculate the average number of defects per shell (np) and the probability of occurrence of 0, 1, 2, 3, 4, 5, or 6 defects in any one shell chosen at random.

Solution

The average number of defects per shell (np) is:

$$np = 12/10 = 1.2$$

Table 7.2 shows the calculations for determining the probabilities of 0, 1, 2, 3, 4, 5, and 6 defects per unit for an average (np) of 1.2.

Analysis of Table 7.2 reveals the following:

1. The total of the six probabilities do not quite equal 1.00 because the distribution never ends (theoretically, the number of defects can be infinite). It would serve no useful purpose, however, to continue the calcu-

Table 7.2 Probability Calculations for Defects per Unit

Number of Defects	Calculations	P
0	$(2.71828)^{-1.2}\ (1.2^0/0!)=$	0.301
1	$(2.71828)^{-1.2}\ (1.2^1/1!)=$	0.361
2	$(2.71828)^{-1.2}\ (1.2^2/2!)=$	0.217
3	$(2.71828)^{-1.2}\ (1.2^3/3!)=$	0.087
4	$(2.71828)^{-1.2}\ (1.2^4/4!)=$	0.026
5	$(2.71828)^{-1.2}\ (1.2^5/5!)=$	0.006
6	$(2.71828)^{-1.2}\ (1.2^6/6!)=$	0.001
	Total	0.999

lations because the remaining probabilities are effectively equal to zero (the probability of 7 defects, for example, is 0.0002).

2. The *additive* law of probability is quite useful. For example,

$$P(1 \text{ or less}) = P(0) + P(1) = 0.301 + 0.361 = 0.662$$

3. The *complementary* law of probability can also be useful. For example, suppose it were desirable to know the probability of two or more defects. One way to calculate this would be to use the additive law and add all the probabilities above one. For this problem, however, this is impossible (it would only be possible if defectives in a known sample size were being measured). So:

$$P(2 \text{ or more}) = 1 - P(1 \text{ or less}) = 1 - 0.662 = 0.338$$

The Poisson Tables

The calculation of the Poisson formula, though possible, is tedious and time-consuming when many terms are involved, such as P(5 or less). The Poisson tables (Table A2) have been prepared to overcome this problem. The tables are easy to use, which is one reason the Poisson has found such wide application in so many fields.

To use the tables, two values are needed: np and d. np is found in the left-hand column and d across the top. The body of the table is a probability value and is cumulative; it is an "or less than" value. The additive and complementary laws are especially useful in using these tables. The following rules have been developed to assist in using the tables (using $np = 1$):

1. $P(d$ or less$)$ = use the table directly. Find np in the left-hand column and move to the right to find the probability value under the proper d value. For example, if $np = 1.00$ and $d = 3$ or less, P(3 or less) = 0.981 or 98.1%.
2. $P(d) = P(d \text{ or less}) - P(d - 1 \text{ or less})$
   $P(3) = P(3 \text{ or less}) - P(2 \text{ or less})$
   $= 0.981 - 0.920 = 0.061$

3. $P(\text{more than } d) = 1 - P(d \text{ or less})$
   $P(\text{more than } 3) = 1 - P(3 \text{ or less})$
   $= 1 - 0.981 = 0.019$
4. $P(d \text{ or more}) = 1 - P(d - 1 \text{ or less})$
   $P(3 \text{ or more}) = 1 - P(2 \text{ or less})$
   $= 1 - 0.920 = 0.080$
5. $P(\text{less than } d) = P(d - 1 \text{ or less})$
   $P(\text{less than } 3) = P(2 \text{ or less}) = 0.920$

Example 7.22 The manager of an airport found that 20 airplanes per hour could be safely landed at the airport. Last year an average of 16 planes per hour had landed (during the peak hours of the day), and these arrival rates were found to be Poisson distributed. What is the probability that there will be more than 20 planes trying to land in any one hour?

Solution

$$P = \text{unknown and } n = \text{unknown}$$

$$np = 16 \text{ planes per hour (average)}$$

$$d = \text{more than } 20$$

$$P(\text{more than } 20) = 1 - P(20 \text{ or less}) = 1 - 0.868 = 0.132$$

A new computer will allow 25 planes to land safely each hour. What is the probability that more than 25 will try to land in any one hour?

$$P(\text{more than } 25) = 1 - P(25 \text{ or less}) = 1 - 0.987 = 0.013$$

(Note: Cost and safety factors would also be involved in the actual decision.)

The Inverse Use of the Poisson

There are times when management would like to know what the required sample size should be for a given probability (or what the process average must be). To get these answers the formulas and rules already given must be worked out backward. This is called the *inverse use of the Poisson,* and the steps are as follows:

1. Find the given probability in the body of the table under the appropriate d value.
   a. If $P(d$ or less) use the probability value and d value as given, go directly to the body of the table for P under d.
   b. If $P(d$ or more) go to the body of table for $1 - P$ under $d - 1$.
   c. If $P(\text{more than } d)$ go to the body of table for $1 - P$ under d.
2. Find np in the left-hand column (interpolate if necessary).
3. Calculate $n = np/p$ (if the sample size is desired and the process average, p, is known) or $p = np/n$ (if the sample size is known and the process average is desired).

Example 7.23 In order to reduce excessive testing costs, a sample of 10 is desired. What must the process average be if $P(3 \text{ or less}) = 0.891$?

Solution

1. Find 0.891 in the body of Table A2 under $d = 3$.
2. np for this value is 1.8
3. $p = np/n = 1.8/10 = 0.18$ or 18%.

Example 7.24 Find the sample size needed if the fraction defective is 0.03 and $P(\text{less than } 2) = 0.764$.

Solution

1. $P(\text{less than } 2) = P(1 \text{ or less}) = 0.764$.
2. Find 0.764 in the body of Table A2 under $d = 1$ and interpolate to find $np = 0.922$.
3. $n = np/p = 0.922/0.03 = 30.7$ or 31 units.

Note: The interpolation procedure (see the appendix) for finding 0.922 on the table is as follows:

1. $P = 0.764$ falls between 0.772 and 0.754 in the $d = 1$ column.
2. 0.772 is associated with an np of 0.90 while 0.754 has an np of 0.95.
3. $0.754 - 0.772 = 0.018$ and $0.764 - 0.772 = 0.008$.
4. $0.008/0.018 = 0.44$ (the fraction of the distance between 0.772 and 0.754, starting from 0.772). The np associated with 0.764 will be the same fraction of the distance between 0.90 and 0.95, starting from 0.90.
5. $0.44 \times (0.95 - 0.90) = 0.022$ (the distance between 0.90 and 0.95, starting at 0.90).
6. $0.022 + 0.90 = 0.922$ (np for a P of 0.764 at $d = 1$).

Example 7.25 Find the sample size necessary if the process average is 0.03 and $P(\text{more than } 2) = 0.236$.

Solution

1. $P(\text{more than } 2) = 1 - P(2 \text{ or less}) = 0.236$.
2. $1 - P(2 \text{ or less}) = 1 - 0.236 = 0.764$.
3. Find 0.764 in the body of Table A2 under $d = 2$ and interpolate to find $np = 1.6073$.
4. $n = np/p = 1.6073/0.03 = 55.77$ or 56 units.

7.5 The Student's *t* Distribution

In the normal curve (Gaussian distribution) examples from Chapter 3, the mean and standard deviation were assumed to be universe parameters that were derived from the entire population of product. For a long-term project or for ongoing production where a wealth of information is available about past performance (say the previous year's production), this assumption is usually valid. (The calculated statistics from this much data can be assumed to equal the real universe parameters.) Also, in SPC, the amount of data used for analysis purposes is usually large enough (normally over 100 measurements) that it does not matter if the Z or t is used (the answers will be essentially identical for large amounts of data). If small sample sizes are used, the universe parameters must be estimated from sample data ($\overline{X}$ and s instead of μ and σ), and the t distribution must be used instead of the normal.

The t distribution is actually the normal adjusted to overcome inherent errors due to small sample sizes (and to provide a bit of safety factor for the estimates). Thus, as the sample size increases, the t distribution approaches the normal (at about $n = 30$). The t distribution is used in the same way as the normal except that the P (probability) values (area under the curve or percent of items) depend on the size of the sample and the table must be entered at $n-1$ as well as at t. The t distribution is a continuous distribution, like the normal; in fact, it is just the normal with the tails spread out. The formula for the t score is:

$$t_{\alpha,n-1} = (X - \overline{X})/s$$

where

$t_{\alpha,n-1}$ = the number of standard deviations from the mean
α = the area under the curve below the desired value (X), or the probability that any one measurement is below a given value
n = the sample size
X = the desired value or measurement
$\overline{X}$ = the mean of the sample
s = the standard deviation of the sample

As with the normal curve, the t distribution can be used to find the percent of items below or above a certain value, between two values, and a desired mean or value from a given percent. To use the t table (Table A3), enter the table at $n-1$, move to the right to find the t value (it may be necessary to interpolate) and read the α from the top of the table if t is positive, or from the bottom of the table if t is negative.

To find a t value from a given sample size and probability value (inverse use of the table), enter the table at the desired probability value (α), move down (or up) the column until the desired degree of freedom line is reached ($n-1$), and read the t value from the body of the table (it may be necessary to interpolate). If the α value is less than 0.50, the table is entered from below and read up, and the t value is negative.

The t can be used to solve the same seven problems solved with the normal in Chapter 3, and in the same way (except that a different table and a different formula are used, of course). The same examples will be used here for comparison. The seven problems are as follows:

1. Find a percent of items below a given value.
2. Find a percent of items above a given value.
3. Find a percent of items between two values.
4. Find a value given a maximum percent of items desired to be below that value (what must the specification be, for example, if no more than a certain percentage is allowed to be below that specification).
5. Find a value given a maximum percent of items desired to be above that value.
6. Find the new mean given a maximum percent of items desired to be below a certain value (to what mean value must we produce our product, for instance, given that no more than a certain percent of our product is to measure below a given lower specification).
7. Find the new mean given a maximum percent of items desired to be above a certain value.

Problems 4 through 7 are examples of what is known as the inverse use of the t (solving for t from a given α). Note that pictures of the normal curve are used in every problem, just as in Chapter 3 (the t is simply the normal with the tails spread out). Pictures simplify the thought processes involved in these types of analyses and act as excellent guides in directing the solution to the problem.

Find the Percent of Items Below a Given Value

The steps are as follows:

1. Draw the curve.
2. Locate all given and calculated values on the drawing.
3. Calculate t.
4. Get the α value from Table A3 (this is the answer).

Example 7.26 The mean weight of a sample of 10 is 30 oz. with a standard deviation of 2 oz. Find the percent of product likely to weigh less than 27.5 oz.

Solution (see Figure 7.1)

$$t_{\alpha,n-1} = t_{\alpha,10\text{-}1} = (27.5 - 30)/2 = -2.5/2 = -1.25$$

$$\alpha = P(t \leq -1.25) = 0.1242 = 12.42\%$$

This can be interpreted as the probability that t less than or equal to -1.25 is 0.1242, or 12.42%. It also means any one of the following three equivalent statements (they mean the same thing):

1. 12.42% of the items are below 27.5 oz., OR
2. The chance of any one item being below 27.5 oz. is 12.42%, OR

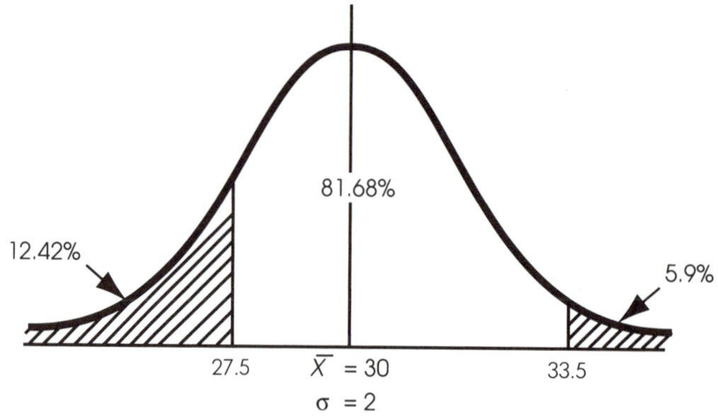

Figure 7.1. Curve illustrating Examples 7.26, 7.27, and 7.28.

3. Out of 10,000 items, 1,242 will weigh less than 27.5 oz. while 10,000 − 1,242 or 8,758 will weigh more.

Notice that the area of rejection (the percent of expected defectives) for the t is always larger than that for the Z. When the Z was used for the same problem (Example 3.11), the answer was smaller (0.1057). The t provides for more protection for small sample sizes.

Find the Percent of Items Above a Certain Value

The steps are as follows:

1. Draw the curve.
2. Locate all values on the curve.
3. Calculate t.
4. Get the α value from Table A3.
5. Subtract the α value from 1.00.

Example 7.27 The mean weight of a sample of 10 is 30 oz. with a standard deviation of 2 oz. Find the percent of product likely to weigh more than 33.5 oz.

Solution (see Figure 7.1)

$$t_{\alpha,n\text{-}1} = t_{\alpha,10\text{-}1} = (33.5 - 30)/2 = 3.5/2 = 1.75$$

$$\alpha = P(t > 1.75) = 1 - P(t \leq 1.75) = 1 - 0.941 = 5.9\%$$

Find the Percent of Items Between Two Values

The steps are as follows:

1. Draw the curve.
2. Locate all values on the curve.
3. Calculate t for each given value.

4. Find the α value for each t from Table A3.
5. Subtract the smaller table value from the larger.

Example 7.28 The mean weight of a sample of 10 is 30 oz. with a standard deviation of 2 oz. Find the percent of product likely to weigh between 27.5 oz. and 33.5 oz.

Solution (see Figure 7.1)

$$t_{27.5} \text{ (from Example 7.26)} = -1.25$$

$$t_{33.5} \text{ (from Example 7.27)} = 1.75$$

$$\alpha = P(-1.25 \leq t \leq 1.75) = 0.9410 - 0.1242 = 81.68\%$$

Another way to calculate this area (percent of items) is to subtract the sum of the areas in the tails from one $[1-(0.1242+0.059)=0.8168]$.

Find the Lower Limit Given a Maximum Desired Percent of Items Below that Limit

The steps are as follows:

1. Draw the curve.
2. Locate all values on the curve.
3. Find the t score from Table A3 using the given percentage.
4. Calculate the limit from the t formula.

Example 7.29 The mean weight of a sample of 10 is 30 oz. with a standard deviation of 2 oz. Find what the lower specification must be to ensure that no more than 5% of the items, on the average, will weigh less than that specification. (Remember to divide the 5% by 100 before beginning the calculations.)

Solution (see Figure 7.2)

$$t_{0.05,10-1} = -1.833 \text{ (from Table A3)}$$

$$t_{0.05,9} = -1.833 = (X - \overline{X})/s = (X - 30)/2$$

$$X = 30 - 1.833(2) = 26.33 \text{ oz.}$$

Find the Upper Limit Given a Maximum Desired Percent of Items Above that Limit

The steps are as follows:

1. Draw the curve.
2. Locate all values on the curve.
3. Find the t score from Table A3 using the given percentage.
4. Calculate the limit from the t formula.

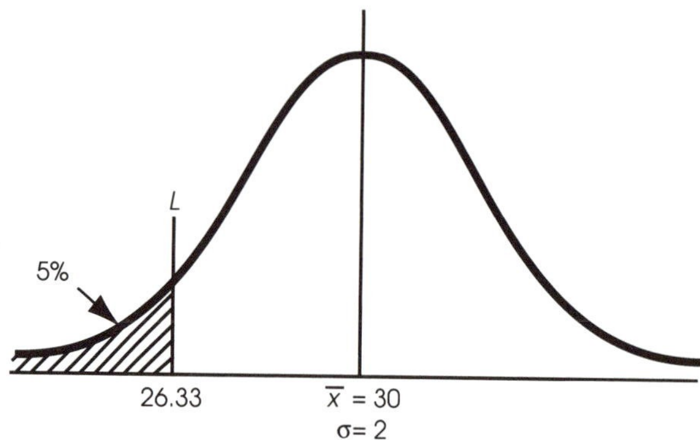

Figure 7.2. Curve illustrating Example 7.29.

Example 7.30 The mean weight of a sample of 10 is 30 oz. with a standard deviation of 2 oz. Find what the upper specification must be to ensure that no more than 1% of the items will weigh more than that specification.

Solution (see Figure 7.3)

$$t_{1-0.01,10-1} = t_{0.99,10-1} = 2.821 \text{ (Table A3)}$$

$$t_{0.99,9} = 2.821 = (X - \overline{X})/s = (X - 30)/2$$

$$X = 30 + 2.821(2) = 35.64 \text{ oz.}$$

Find the New Mean Given a Maximum Desired Percent of Items Below a Given Lower Specification Limit

The steps are as follows:

1. Draw the curve.
2. Locate all values on the curve.
3. Find the t score from Table A3 using the given percentage.
4. Calculate the mean from the t formula.

Example 7.31 The mean weight of a sample of 10 is 30 oz. with a standard deviation of 2 oz. Find what the new mean value must be (what the machine setting must be) to ensure that no more than 5% of the items will weigh less than the lower specification of 27.5 oz.

Solution (see Figure 7.4)

$$t_{0.05,10-1} = -1.833 \text{ (from Table A3)}$$

$$t_{0.05,9} = -1.833 = (X - \overline{X})/s = (27.5 - \overline{X})/2$$

$$\overline{X} = 27.5 + 1.833(2) = 31.17 \text{ oz.}$$

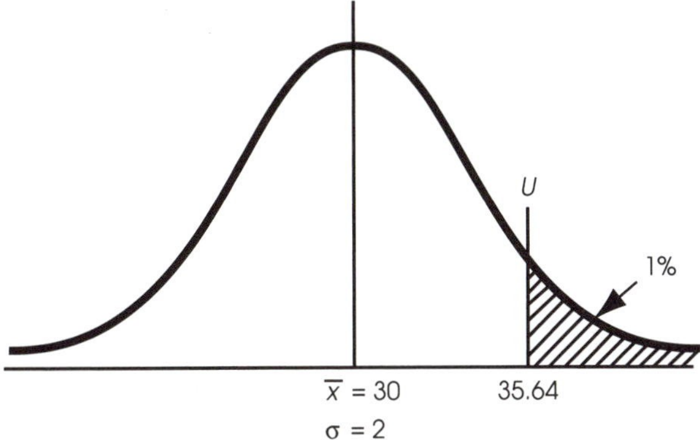

Figure 7.3. Curve illustrating Example 7.30.

Example 7.32 How does this new mean (31.17 oz.) affect the percent of items above the upper specification limit of 33.5 oz?

Solution (see Figure 7.4)

$$t_{\alpha,10-1} = (33.5 - 31.17)/2 = 1.165$$

$$\alpha = P(t > 1.165) = 1 - P(t \leq 1.165) = 1 - 0.9282 = 7.18\%$$

Find the New Mean Given a Maximum Desired Percent of Items Above a Given Upper Specification Limit

The steps are as follows:

1. Draw the curve.
2. Locate all values on the curve.
3. Find the *t* score from Table A3 using the given percentage.
4. Calculate the mean from the *t* score.

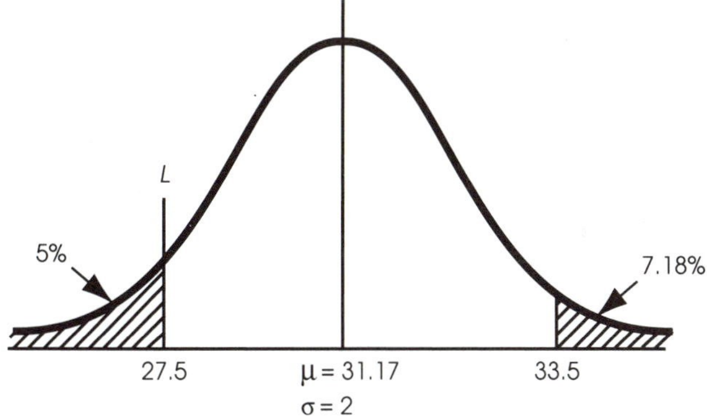

Figure 7.4. Curve illustrating Examples 7.31 and 7.32.

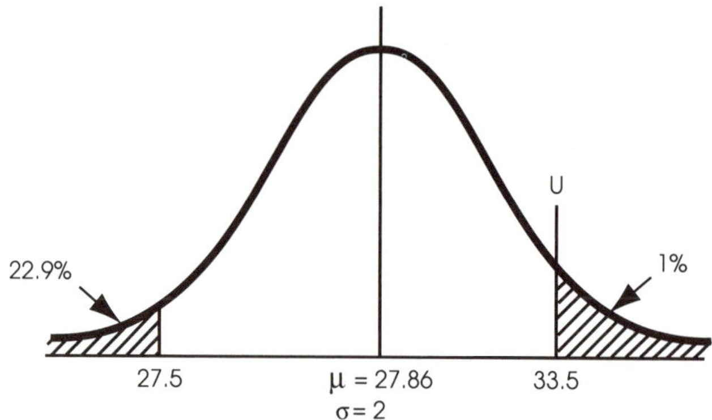

Figure 7.5. Curve illustrating Examples 7.33 and 7.34.

Example 7.33 The mean weight of a sample of 10 is 30 oz. with a standard deviation of 2 oz. Find what the new mean value must be (what the machine setting must be) to ensure that no more than 1% of the items will weigh more than 33.5 oz.

Solution (see Figure 7.5)

$$t_{1-0.01,10-1} = t_{0.99,10-1} = 2.821 \text{ (from Table A3)}$$

$$t_{0.99,9} = 2.821 = (X - \overline{X})/s = (33.5 - \overline{X})/2$$

$$\overline{X} = 33.5 - 2.821(2) = 27.858 \text{ oz.}$$

Example 7.34 How does this new mean of 27.858 affect the percent below the lower limit of 27.5 oz.?

Solution (see Figure 7.5)

$$t_{\alpha,10-1} = (X - \overline{X})/s = (27.5 - 27.858)/2 = -0.179$$

$$\alpha = P(t \leq -0.179) = 22.91\%$$

Practice Problems

7–1 A single ball is to be selected at random from a container containing a mixture of several different colored balls. The probability of selecting a red ball is 0.20, a green ball is 0.23, a yellow ball is 0.25, and a pink ball is 0.18. Although there are a few purple balls in the container, their probability is unknown. What is the probability that the ball selected is either green or yellow? Green or purple? Green or red or pink?

Answers
0.48; 0.37; 0.61

7–2 Four different types of shafts, all numbered for identification, are mixed in a tote box. There are eight straight shafts numbered 1 to 8, 12 tapered shafts numbered 1 to 12, six stepped shafts numbered 1 to 6, and four square shafts numbered 1 to 4. If one shaft is to be selected at random, what is the probability of selecting the following:

a. A square shaft or a shaft numbered 4?
b. A tapered shaft or a shaft numbered 7?
c. A stepped shaft or a shaft numbered 5?

Answers
0.23; 0.43; 0.267

7–3 A basket contains 110 parts of which 24 are known to be defective. If a sample of two is drawn at random and not replaced, what is the probability that both are defective? What is the probability that one is defective and one is not? What is the probability that the first one selected is good and the second is defective?

Answers
0.046; 0.344; 0.172

7–4 In Problem 7–3, suppose that three parts are drawn at random. What is the probability that one is defective? What is the probability that the first is defective and the next two are good? What is the probability that all three are defective?

Answers
0.399; 0.133; 0.0104

7–5 A delivery truck can travel three different routes on Monday, four on Tuesday, five on Wednesday, six on Thursday, and seven on Friday. If a route is chosen at random each day, how many different weekly routes are possible?

Answer
2520

7–6 A sample of four is selected from a lot of 40. How many permutations are possible? How many combinations are possible?

Answers
2,193,360; 91,390

7–7 A sample of 10 is selected from a lot of 20 parts. How many permutations are possible? How many combinations are possible?

Answers
6.70442×10^{11}; 184,756

7–8 Using the hypergeometric distribution, find:
  a. The probability of obtaining 1 defective in a sample of 5 from a lot of 50 known to be 10% defective.
  b. The probability of obtaining no defectives in the sample.
  c. The probability of obtaining more than 1 defective in the sample.

Answers
0.352; 0.577; 0.071

7–9 A lot of 40 parts has 10 defective. Using the hypergeometric, find:
  a. The probability of obtaining 1 defective in a sample of 5?
  b. The probability of obtaining 2 defectives in a sample of 5?
  c. The probability of obtaining 2 or more defectives in a sample of 5?

Answers
0.416; 0.278; 0.367

7–10 Answer Problem 7–8 using the binomial.

Answers
0.328; 0.590; 0.081

7–11 A certain process normally runs 4% defective parts. Find:
  a. The probability that a sample of 10 has exactly 2 defectives.
  b. The probability that a sample of 10 has exactly 1 defective.
  c. The probability that a sample of 10 has 2 or more defectives.

Answers
0.052; 0.277; 0.058

7–12 Answer Problem 7–8 using the Poisson.

Answers
0.303; 0.607; 0.090

7–13 Answer Problem 7–11 using the Poisson.

Answers
0.054; 0.268; 0.062

7–14 For the data of Problem 2–1 (where the mean is 1.567, the standard deviation is 0.261, and the sample size is 10) find:

a. The percentage of items expected to measure below 1.20.
b. The percentage of items expected to measure above 2.10.
c. The percentage of items expected to measure between 1.20 and 2.10.

Answers
9.7%; 3.8%; 86.5%

7–15 For the data of Problem 2–2 (where the mean is 12.7, the standard deviation is 2.6, and the sample size is 5) find:

a. The percentage of items expected to measure below 10.
b. The percentage of items expected to measure above 20.
c. The percentage of items expected to measure between 10 and 20.

Answers
19.3%; 2.4%; 78.3%

7–16 For the data of Problem 3–1 (where the mean is 1.567, the standard deviation is 0.261, and the sample size is 10), find:

a. The necessary lower specification limit if no more than 5% of the items can measure below that limit.
b. The necessary upper specification limit if no more than 2% of the items can measure above that limit.

Answers
1.089; 2.206

7–17 For the data of Problem 3–2 (where the mean is 12.7, the standard deviation is 2.6, and the sample size is 5), find:

a. The necessary lower specification limit if no more than 3% of the items can measure below that limit.
b. The necessary upper specification limit if no more than 1% of the items can measure above that limit.

Answers
5.82; 22.44

7–18 For the data of Problem 3–1 (where the mean is 1.567, the standard deviation is 0.261, and the sample size is 10), find:

a. The new mean needed for no more than 5% to measure below the lower specification limit of 1.2.
b. The percent above the upper specification of 2.1, for the new mean of part (a) above.

Answers
1.678; 7.4%

7–19 For the data of Problem 3–1 (where the mean is 1.567, the standard deviation is 0.261, and the sample size is 10), find:

a. The new mean needed for no more than 2% to measure above the upper specification limit of 2.1.
b. The percent below the lower specification of 1.2, for the new mean of part (a) above.

Answers
1.461; 18.4%

7–20 For the data of Problem 3–2 (where the mean is 12.7, the standard deviation is 2.6, and the sample size is 5), find:

a. The new mean needed for no more than 3% to measure below the lower specification limit of 10.
b. The percent above the upper specification of 20, for the new mean of part (a) above.

Answers
16.9; 14.3%

7–21 For the data of Problem 3–2 (where the mean is 12.7, the standard deviation is 2.6, and the sample size is 5) find:

a. The new mean needed for no more than 1% to measure above the upper specification limit of 20.
b. The percent below the lower specification of 10, for the new mean of part (a) above.

Answers
10.3; 45.0%

CHAPTER 8 ACCEPTANCE SAMPLING

Acceptance sampling plans provide procedures and standards for determining the most efficient sample to be used in lot acceptance/rejection decisions. This chapter will explore the theory underlying sampling plan determination. Chapter 9 will examine the most important and most used of the various standard sampling plans.

Objectives

1. Know the basic terms and symbols defining a sampling plan, and the logic of lot determination and control.
2. Understand the nature and derivation of the four values, or criteria, used in calculating the sampling plan.
3. Know how to calculate a sampling plan from basic theory, using the four fundamental criteria and the Poisson probability distribution.
4. Understand the nature, use, and derivation of the operating characteristic curve (OC curve).
5. Understand the nature, use, and derivation of the average outgoing quality curve (AOQ curve), and the average outgoing quality limit (AOQL).

8.1 Sampling Plan Definition

A sampling plan precisely defines the sample size (n), the acceptable number of defects (A), and the unacceptable number of defects (R). Frequently a lot size (N) is also shown. In quality control, there is some relationship between lot size and sample size. For example, a good sampling plan will provide for effective decisions with a sample of 10% or less of the lot size. The following shows a sampling plan as it is usually presented:

$$N = 1{,}200$$
$$n = 100$$
$$A = 2$$
$$R = 3$$

This plan means: Choose a random sample of 100 units from the lot of 1,200, inspect the applicable characteristic, and compare to a standard (specification). If there are 2 or less defective parts (that is, they do not meet the standards of the specification), accept the entire lot of 1,200. If there are 3 or more, reject the lot.

Some plans show a gap between A and R:

$$N = 1{,}200$$
$$n = 60$$
$$A = 2$$
$$R = 4$$

This plan is similar to the previous plan except that a separate decision is required when the number of defects equals 3. This type of plan occurs, for example, when a reduced sampling plan is used (such as when only 60 units are sampled rather than 100). If a sample from this type of plan were to have 3 defectives, the lot of 1,200 would be accepted, but the next lot, from the same vendor or machine, would be returned to regular inspection (where $n = 100$ rather than 60 and $R = 3$ rather than 4). (See MIL-STD-105E.)

Sampling plans can also require multiple samples:

$$N = 1{,}200$$
$$n_1 = 60$$
$$n_2 = 60$$
$$A_1 = 0$$
$$A_2 = 3$$
$$R_1 = 3$$
$$R_2 = 4$$

This type of plan means: Take a random sample of 60 from the lot and measure the applicable characteristic. If no defects are found, accept the lot. If 3 or more defects are found on the first try, reject the lot. If 1 or 2 defects are found, take a second sample of 60 and measure. If the total number of defects from both samples (from the full 120 units measured) is 3 or less, accept; if not, reject. Multiple sampling plans have been devised for as many as 7 successive samples. (See MIL-STD-105D.)

The advantage of this type of plan (multiple sampling) is that vendors with very good lots almost always have their lots accepted on the first sample, with smaller samples and fewer costs. (Very bad lots are also rejected on the first sample.) Unfortunately, medium quality lots would be more expensive to inspect (120 units instead of 100) and so this plan could be a disadvantage for some vendors. There is also a psychological advantage to multiple sampling plans as they appear to give a second chance for acceptance. Actually, the probability of acceptance is the same whether a single or a multiple plan is used.

Lot Sizes and Disposition

The size and organization of a lot depend on many factors including part size and configuration, material handling methods, consumer's plant dynamics, transportation methods, packaging, and economic quantities. Lots should be organized to facilitate sampling procedures. The best sampling procedure is one that ensures total randomality (an unbiased sample).

Randomality means that each unit in the lot has an equal chance of being chosen for the sample. The best way to ensure this is to assign a number to each unit and then use a random number to choose the units to be measured. Random numbers can be easily generated with most calculators. (Tables of random numbers are also available.) Random numbers from calculators occur in the form of decimal fractions of three or four decimals. For example, suppose the number 0.016 has been generated. The decimal point is ignored and the part assigned the number of 16 is chosen for measurement.

If lots are organized in regular patterns, stacked in orderly rows and columns, a stratified random sampling procedure can be used. In stratified sampling, the layers are chosen first, using the random numbers in exactly the same way; then the part within the layer is chosen, using the random numbers as before.

When a sample does not meet the sampling plan criteria (the percent defective is too high), the lot is considered unacceptable. One of three methods can be used for disposition of the lot. First, the lot can be accepted and sent to production regardless, with instructions to separate the defective parts as they are found. These rejected parts should then be returned to the vendor for credit. Proper credit should also include the extra production costs caused by these excessive defectives, but in actual practice it seldom does (due to the difficulty of identifying and proving those costs). This method is not considered acceptable in most firms today because of the problems to production. Even a 5%

defective lot can be enough to totally disrupt production and add enormously to its costs.

Another procedure is to rectify these lots at the consumer's plant prior to use. This requires 100% inspection to separate the defective parts from the good ones. The cost of this inspection should also be borne by the producer, but often is not.

The best procedure is to reject the entire lot and return it to the vendor for rectification. The vendor then inspects the rejected lots 100% and returns the rectified lot, with the good units only, to the consumer at the vendor's expense. The advantage to this procedure is that the extra cost and trouble to the vendors, as well as the vendor's direct involvement in the rectification process, is powerful motivation for vendors to improve their quality.

8.2 Sampling Plan Criteria

In order to design a sampling plan, four values must be known. These values are determined from past experience, engineering estimate, and/or management decisions. Sometimes they are specified by the buyer, as part of the contract.

1. Producer's risk, α (Greek letter alpha). This is defined as the probability that a good lot will be rejected, and is equivalent to the probability of d rejects in a sample (see Section 7.3). In calculating sampling plans, this value is always subtracted from 1 to get the probability of acceptance. This is done so that the same type of value, the probability of acceptance, can be used for both consumer's and producer's risk (to make proper comparisons).
2. Acceptable quality level (AQL). This is a numerical representation of "good" quality and is always associated with producer's risk. It is the maximum fraction defective considered acceptable off the producer's line. In other words, the AQL is a probability value, a p value (see Chapter 7). Therefore, the AQL is related to the p of the binomial and of the p chart. (Note that the AQL is a lower case p, a fraction defective, while the producer's risk, α, is an upper case P, as defined in Chapters 6 and 7.) Suppose the producer's risk (α) is 5% and the AQL is 1%. This means that there is a 5% chance that a lot with 1% or less defective parts will be rejected. Since 1% defective or less is considered to be "good" quality, and will be accepted by the vendor (if the vendor really knew that the lot was only 1% defective), rejection would be a mistake. In any sampling plan, there is always the possibility that an error can be made, that the percentage of defectives in the sample will be more, or less, than the percentage of defectives in the lot. The 5% (α) would be the chance that this type of mistake would be made. This is called a type I error in quality control and is defined as the rejection of an acceptable lot. In other words, 5 lots out of 100 "good" lots would

be unfairly rejected. This is an unnecessary cost (if only the facts were known) to the producer, hence, producer's risk.

3. Consumer's risk, β (Greek letter beta). This is the probability that a "bad" lot will be accepted. Since this is already a probability of acceptance, it does not have to be subtracted from 1. Bad lots, with high amounts of defective parts, can be quite expensive to the consumer. If a bad lot gets past the inspection process, it can cause a great deal of trouble in the consumer's plant (rework, shutdowns, etc.) This is another type of mistake a sampling plan can make and is called a type II error in quality control (accepting a bad lot). Since this type of mistake increases costs to the consumer, it is called consumer's risk.
4. Lot tolerance percent defective (LTPD). Some are now calling this term *limiting quality level* (LQL). This is the definition of bad quality associated with consumer's risk. It is the fraction defective that can be tolerated by a consumer, and is also a p value like the AQL. Note that the consumer's risk, β, is also an upper case P like the producer's risk, α.

Determining the Four Criteria

Suppose that a consumer describes that more than 9% defective parts will cause undue hardships during production. Nine percent or less defectives per lot, then, is acceptable. Past experience has shown that, in general, as much as 10% of these bad lots can be reasonably dealt with by the shop. The LTPD (0.09) and the β (0.10) have now been determined. If the producer were to produce at this 9% defective level, half the lots would be rejected. Remember that the 9% is an average figure and that, on the average (assuming normality), 50% of the lots would be greater than 9% defective. Therefore, the producer must produce at a much lower defective rate (AQL) to ensure that only a small percentage of the lots (α) will be rejected. This is the reason that the AQL is normally smaller than the LTPD. The AQL can be determined from this logic by using the techniques of the normal curve (or any other probability distribution that applies). α and β are management decisions usually based on experience. An α of 5% and a β of 10% usually work out well and are prevalent in sampling plans. (In some systems these values range from 1 to 10%, or higher.)

An example will be used to illustrate these concepts (Figure 8.1). Suppose that a sample size of 100 is normally used. Using the Poisson to approximate the normal distribution, the mean is 9 (0.09×100) and the standard deviation is 3 ($\sqrt{0.09 \times 100}$). The AQL, then, is:

$$Z_{0.05} = -1.645 = (X-9)/3$$

$$X = 9 - 1.645(3) = 4.065$$

$$\text{AQL} = X/100 = 4.065/100 = 0.041$$

Note: For small sample sizes, the t must be used.

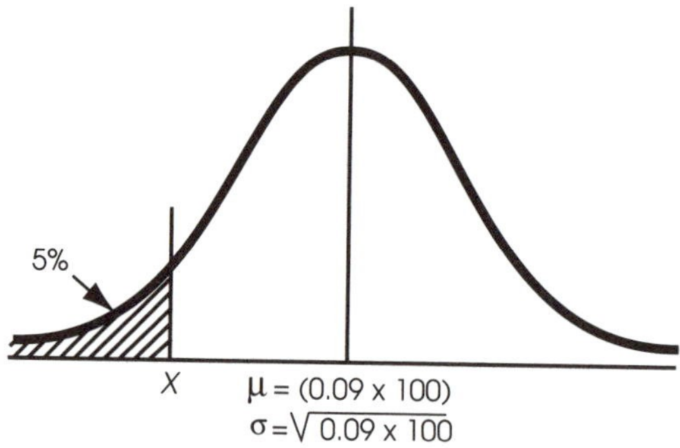

Figure 8.1. Illustration of an AQL determination.

This technique gives only an approximate figure (we don't know what the actual sample size will finally be), so it is usually adjusted by management, engineering, and/or the customer. This adjustment depends, to a large degree, on the projected sample size. In general, the larger the sample size, the higher the producer's defect rate (AQL) can be and still have an α of 0.05 (or the closer the producer's AQL can be to the consumer's LTPD). For a sample size of 1,000, for example, the AQL could be 0.077, while a sample size of 10 would require an AQL of -0.084 (a clear impossibility).

This illustrates a fundamental concept of acceptance sampling: The larger the sample, the greater the protection. Of course, the cost also increases with increased sample size. Therefore, the producer would like to see a large sample size required so that manufacturing controls can be relaxed (and thus costs reduced). The consumer, however, would like to see a small sample size to reduce inspection costs. This problem is further complicated by the fact that increased manufacturing costs eventually result in higher unit costs to the consumer. Because of this, the consumer is usually willing to tolerate some increase in the sample size, but only when the consumer's sampling costs are not excessive. A truly effective sampling plan, therefore, must efficiently balance these costs and still maintain proper sampling protection.

Please note that the description given in this section is not actually the way the four values have been determined. This explanation is just one way to think about these four values, and one way to understand how they interact and what they mean to each other.

8.3 Sampling Plan Calculations

Once the AQL, α, LTPD, and β are known, a sampling plan can be calculated using the inverse of the Poisson probability distribution. (Other distributions may be required for some plans, but the Poisson applies almost universally and is the easiest to use.) The needed sampling plan values are the sample number, n, and the acceptance number, A (called d in the Poisson). The rejection number, R, does not need to be calculated for most simple sampling plans as it is always one more than the acceptance number A (d in the Poisson).

The procedure is to assume an acceptance number at 0 ($A=d=0$) and calculate the sample size for the producer, n_p (using $1-\text{AQL}$ as the probability of acceptance), and for the consumer, n_c (using LTPD as the probability of acceptance). Two values (two sample sizes) are calculated and compared. The goal is for these two sample sizes to be equal (seldom achieved). If the two n's are not equal, the calculations must be repeated, successively (using $d=1$, $d=2$, etc.), until the two n's are either equal or as close to equal as possible. Only when the sample sizes are equal is the plan considered to be fair for both consumer and producer (the costs are balanced). The following values for AQL, α, LTPD, and β will now be used to illustrate the procedures:

$$\text{AQL}=1\%=0.01=p_p$$

$$\text{LTPD}=9\%=0.09=p_c$$

$$\alpha=5\%;\ 1-\alpha=0.95$$

$$\beta=10\%=0.10$$

First Trial ($A=d=0$)

(1) $n_p p_p=0.0516$ (using the Poisson tables at $P=0.95$ and $d=0$)

$$n_p=0.0516/0.01=5 \text{ units}$$

(2) $n_c p_c=2.3$ (using the Poisson tables at $P=0.10$ and $d=0$)

$$n_c=2.3/0.09=26 \text{ units}$$

The two n's (5 and 26) are not equal; try $d=1$

Second Trial ($A=d-1$)

(1) $n_p p_p=0.3458$

$$n_p=0.3458/0.01=35 \text{ units}$$

(2) $n_c p_c=3.89$

$$n_c=3.89/0.09=43 \text{ units}$$

The two n's (35 and 43) are not equal; try $d=2$.

Third Trial ($A=d=2$)

$$(1)\ n_p p_p = 0.8188$$

$$n_p = 0.8188/0.01 = 82 \text{ units}$$

$$(2)\ n_c p_c = 5.33$$

$$n_c = 5.33/0.09 = 59 \text{ units}$$

At this point no more calculations are needed. Notice that in trial 3, the n's switched and the consumer's sample size, n_c, became smaller than the producer's sample size, n_p. This trend will now continue forever, with greater and greater divergence for each higher d value. Calculations for multiple sampling plans are similar, except that the probability values are calculated from complex formulas rather than simply lifting a value from a table. Four possible sampling plans have been identified:

$$(1)\ n=35,\ A=1$$

$$(2)\ n=43,\ A=1$$

$$(3)\ n=82,\ A=2$$

$$(4)\ n=59,\ A=2$$

A decision must now be made as to which of these plans to use. One of four possible strategies can safely be followed:

1. Choose the plan with the lowest sample size. This plan is $n=35$, $A=1$ and is the one that provides the lowest cost.
2. Choose the plan with the largest sample size. This plan is $n=82$, $A=2$. Because of the large sample size, it provides the greatest protection against error.
3. Choose the plan that exactly meets the producer's stipulation and comes as close as possible to that of the consumer's. One of the two plans must be chosen: plan 1, $n=35$, $A=1$ or plan 3, $n=82$, $A=2$. If plan 1 is chosen, the consumer's risk (p_c or LTPD) is 3.89/35 or 0.111. If plan 3 is chosen, the consumer's risk (p_c or LTPD) is 5.33/82 or 0.065. Since 0.111 is closer to the consumer's stipulated risk of 0.09, choose plan 1.
4. Choose the plan that exactly meets the consumer's stipulation and comes as close as possible to the producer's risk. Either plan 2, $n=43$, $A=1$ or plan 4, $n=59$, $A=2$ must be chosen. For plan 2, the producer's risk (p_p or AQL) is 0.3538/43 or 0.0082. For plan 4, the producer's risk (p_p or AQL) is 0.8188/59 or 0.0139. Plan 2 is chosen because it is closer to the producer's stipulated risk of 0.01.

8.4 Operating Characteristic (OC) Curve

The operating characteristic (OC) curve is an excellent tool for evaluating quality sampling plans. The OC curve can be used for finding the probability that a lot of a certain fraction defective (p) will be ac-

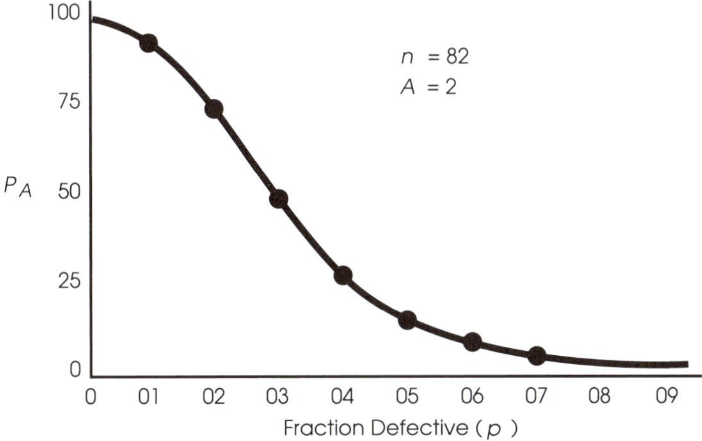

Figure 8.2. Operating characteristic (OC) curve.

cepted or rejected. Figure 8.2 shows the OC curve of sampling plan (1) of the previous section ($n=82$, $A=2$).

The ordinate (Y axis) gives the probability that a lot of a given fraction defective (p), found on the abscissa (X axis), will be accepted. The probability of rejecting the lot (P_f), then, is $1-P_A$ (or one minus the probability of accepting the lot). Thus, for an α of 0.05 (which is a P_f value), the corresponding P_A value is found by subtracting 0.05 from 1 (the chart only reads P_A, not P_f), locating the point on the ordinate, moving to the right to the curve, and then reading the p value from the abscissa below (on the X axis). A lot with a fraction defective of 0.01 would have a 95% chance of being accepted (a 5% chance of rejection), given the sampling plan of $n=82$, $A=2$ (or a 77.3% chance at a p of 0.02, etc.) (Figure 8.2).

The probability of acceptance, given a p value, can also be calculated from the basic probability distribution. For the sampling plan just mentioned, a fraction defective of 0.01 has a calculated probability of acceptance of 0.95, as follows: $p=0.01$, $np=82\times 0.01=0.82$; $P_A=0.95$ (from the Poisson tables at $np=0.82$ and $A=d=2$). The OC curve is constructed in just this way by assuming a series of p values and then computing their corresponding P_A. The position points given by each of these pairs of values is then charted and a line constructed through these points to get the OC curve for that sampling plan. Remember that A is actually d in the Poisson tables. The calculations shown in Table 8.1 would be used to generate the curve shown in Figure 8.2.

Note that as long as the shape of the curve does not change, the curve can be exactly defined by two points on the curve. These two points are normally chosen at α and β. For the curve in Table 8.1, these two points are: $\alpha=0.05$, $p=0.01$ and $\beta=0.10$, $p=0.065$.

Multiple Sampling Plans

OC curves for multiple sampling plans can also be constructed using the same logic and procedures already shown for single sampling plans. The only difference is that multiple sampling plans have multiple OC curves, one for each sample (a double sampling plan will have two curves, a triple three, etc.). Suppose a double sampling plan has the following values:

First Sample	Second Sample
$n_1=80$	$n_2=80$
$A_1=1$	$A_2=4$
$R_1=4$	$R_2=5$

Table 8.1. OC Curve Calculations ($n=82, A=d=2$)

1. $p=0.01$, $np=0.82$; $P_A=0.950$
2. $p=0.02$, $np=1.64$; $P_A=0.773$
3. $p=0.03$, $np=2.46$; $P_A=0.554$
4. $p=0.04$, $np=3.28$; $P_A=0.364$
5. $p=0.05$, $np=4.10$; $P_A=0.224$
6. $p=0.06$, $np=4.92$; $P_A=0.132$
7. $p=0.07$, $np=5.74$; $P_A=0.075$

Calculations for the first curve would use only the first sample information and would be similar to those of the single sampling plan already constructed; the OC curve would also be similar.

Calculations for the second curve, however, are more complex. Each point on the curve would have to be determined by assuming a value for p (as before) and then calculating its corresponding probability of acceptance, P_A, by the following formula:

$$P_A = P(d_1=1 \text{ or less}) + P(d_1=2)P(d_2=2 \text{ or less}) + P(d_1=3)P(d_2=1 \text{ or less})$$

Note that this formula is a combination of the additive and product rules of probability, that is, the probability that d_1 equals 1 or less OR the probability that d_1 equals 2 AND the probability that d_2 equals 2 or less OR the probability that d_1 equals 3 AND the probability that d_2 equals 1 or less.

Each of these probabilities must be interpolated from the Poisson tables and then plugged into the formula just given. This must be done for each of the chosen values of the fraction defective p (use the same formula to calculate P_A for each chosen value of p) to get the needed points for charting the curve. For example, if 7 points are needed, 7 P_A's will be calculated.

The probability of acceptance, P_A, for $p=0.01$ in the preceding formula is as follows:

1. $n_1p_1=80\times0.01=0.8$; $n_2p_2=80\times0.01=0.8$
2. $P(d_1=1$ or less$)=0.808$ (from the Poisson tables for $np=0.8$ and $d=1$ or less)
3. $P(d_1=2)P(d_2=2$ or less$)=0.144\times0.952$
4. $P(d_1=3)P(d_2=1$ or less$)=0.039\times0.808$
5. $P_A=0.808+(0.144\times0.952)+(0.039\times0.808)=0.977$

The same calculations must also be made for a fraction defective, p, of 0.02, 0.03, 0.04, etc., until enough points are determined so that the OC curve can be constructed (usually seven, at least). The calculations for determining this sampling plan, although following the same logic and procedures already described for single sampling plans, would be equally as complex. Multiple sampling plans of 3 or more samples, and their respective OC curves, would follow the same logic but would increase in complexity as the number of samples increased.

Properties of OC Curves

In general, the steeper the OC curve the better the protection for both consumer and producer. In fact, the ideal OC curve would be perpendicular from 0 to 100% at the maximum fraction defective (Figure 8.3). The only way to get this type of curve is to inspect 100% of the lot.

Many years ago, before statistical control procedures, sampling plans were determined as a fixed percentage of the lot size. However, this procedure does not provide the same protection (for different lot sizes). Figure 8.4 shows the OC curves from three different lots where the sampling sizes are 10% of their lot sizes. Obviously, the three curves are completely different.

The sample size and the acceptance number are the most important factors affecting the OC curve. If the sample sizes and the acceptance numbers are the same, the OC curves are very similar (almost identical for small sample sizes—see Figure 8.5). When sample sizes are increased, the curve becomes steeper (naturally, since a 100% sample produces a perpendicular curve), and provides better protection for both consumer and producer. The same thing also occurs when the acceptance number is decreased (the curve gets steeper and the plan provides better protection). Better protection, then, can be obtained by increasing the sample size, n, or by decreasing the acceptance number,

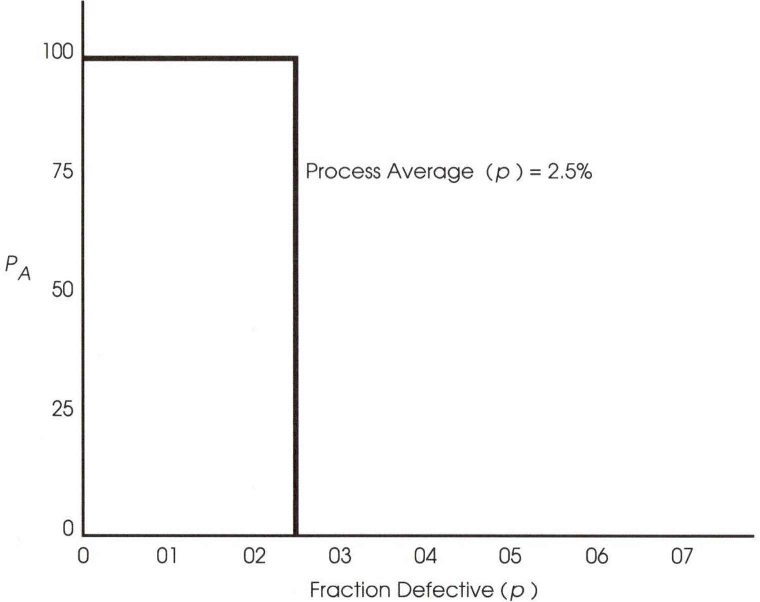

Figure 8.3. Ideal OC curve (100% inspection).

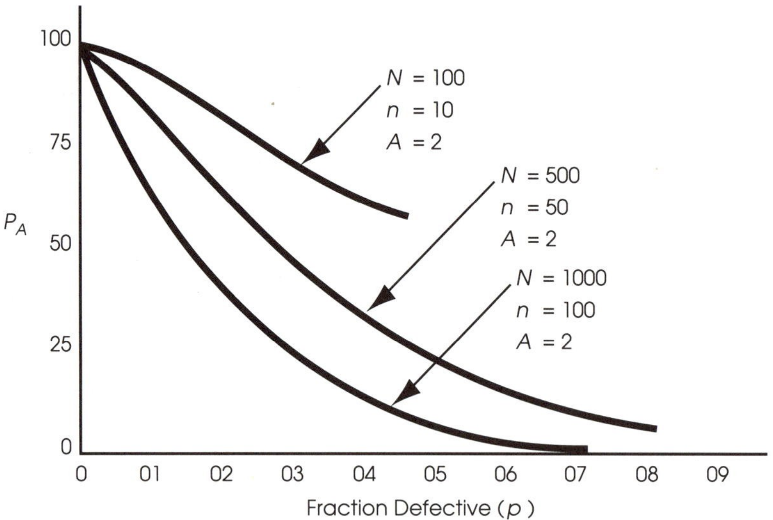

Figure 8.4. OC curves when sample sizes are 10% of lot sizes.

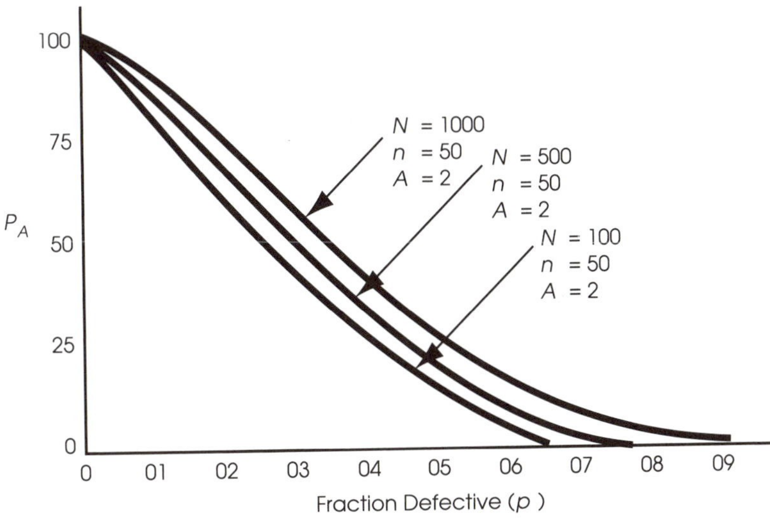

Figure 8.5. OC curves for constant sample size.

A, or both. Since an increase in the sample size also increases sampling costs, decreasing the acceptance number is usually preferred when better protection is needed.

8.5 Average Outgoing Quality

The average outgoing quality (AOQ) curve can be used to evaluate a sampling plan by showing the average quality accepted by the consumer (outgoing from the consumer's receiving inspection) for a given fraction defective. In Figure 8.6, the average quality going into the consumer's plant (accepted or outgoing from receiving inspection) for a fraction defective of 0.03 (3%) is 1.66%. This can also be determined mathematically by noting that 54.4% of these lots will be accepted with an average of 3% defectives ($P_A = 0.544$ at $np = 2.46$ and $A = d = 2$) while the remainder (45.6%) will be rectified. Rectified lots are rejected lots returned to the vendor for 100% inspection. Rectified lots, therefore, have 100% quality (no defectives, or $p = 0$) when returned to the customer. $(0.544 \times 0.03) + (0.456 \times 0)$, then, gives an AOQ of 1.66% (of course, 0.456×0, the outgoing quality of the rectified lots, can be dropped from the calculations). AOQ curves, in fact, are constructed in just this way (Table 8.2).

Table 8.2 AOQ Calculations ($n=82$, $A=d=2$)

p	np	P_A	AOQ($P_A \times 100p$)
0.01	0.82	0.950	0.95
0.02	1.64	0.773	1.55
0.03	2.46	0.554	1.66
0.04	3.28	0.364	1.46
0.05	4.10	0.224	1.12
0.06	4.92	0.132	0.79
0.07	5.74	0.075	0.53

The AOQ curve is constructed by determining a series of point pairs (p, AOQ) from a series of assumed fraction defective values p (just as in the OC curve). Table 8.2 shows how these point pairs are generated for the AOQ curve shown in Figure 8.6, using the sampling plan $n=82$, $A=2$. Note that Table 8.2 is identical to the table used for generating the OC curve, except that one additional column is added for the AOQ. Note that the AOQ is always presented as a percentage rather than as a decimal ratio.

AOQL

Another important value, the average outgoing quality limit (AOQL) is simply the maximum of the AOQ curve (Figure 8.6). It represents the maximum possible percent defective for the sampling plan (assuming rectification of rejected lots). AOQL values can be calculated by using successive approximations. (Use closer and closer p values until a value is reached on both sides that does not change for a satisfactory number of decimal places.)

Split-Risk Plans

In some plans, a point on the graph is specified through which a family of OC curves can be generated. At this point the producer's risk

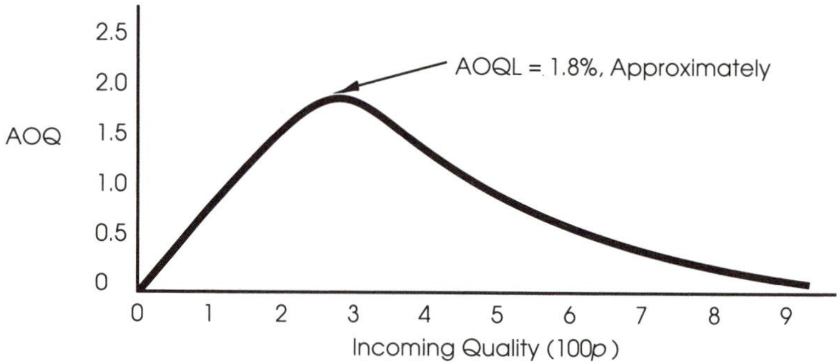

Figure 8.6. AOQ curve for $n=82$ and $A=2$.

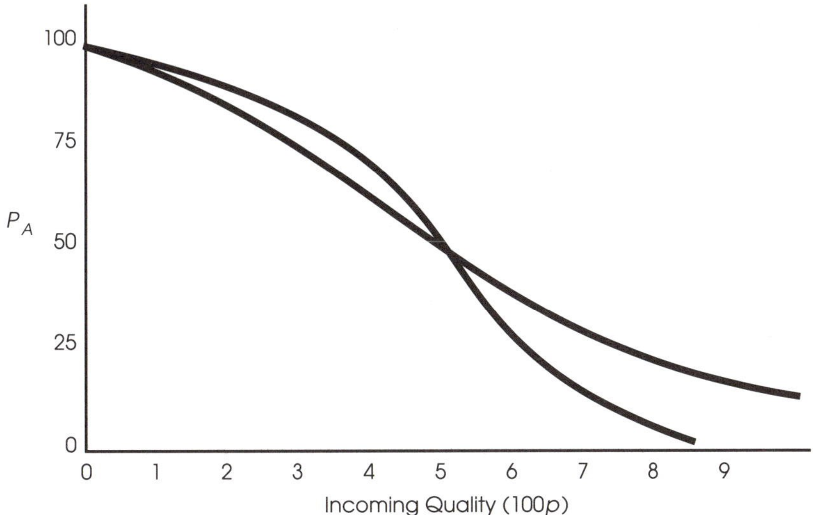

Figure 8.7. Split-risk sampling plans.

(α) and consumer's risk (β) are equal, but each curve requires a different sample size (n) and/or a different acceptance number (A). Theoretically, the number of these plans is infinite (even though limited to discrete values of n and A), but practical considerations limit them to manageable numbers. There are practical limits to a lot size (dictated by unit size, handling equipment, costs, etc.) and, of course, neither the sample size nor the acceptance number can be larger than the lot size (the sample size should be less than 10% of a large lot). Split-risk plans (Figure 8.7) set the producer's risk and consumer's risk equal at 50% ($\alpha = \beta = 0.5$) for a specified p value.

AQL plans (Figure 8.8), a special type of split-risk plan, have a stipulated AOQL for a specified p value. From this, a probability of acceptance (P_A) can be calculated inversely from the AOQL formula:

$$\text{AOQL} = p \times P_A$$

$$P_A = \text{AOQL}/p$$

The point identified by this P_A, at the specified p value, becomes the point through which a group of OC curves, and their associated sampling plans, can be generated.

Sampling Systems

It should be obvious, from this discussion, that the determination of the proper sampling plan is complex and tedious. Because of this, various sampling systems (standard sampling plans) have been devised to simplify this task. MIL-STD-105E is almost universally accepted, al-

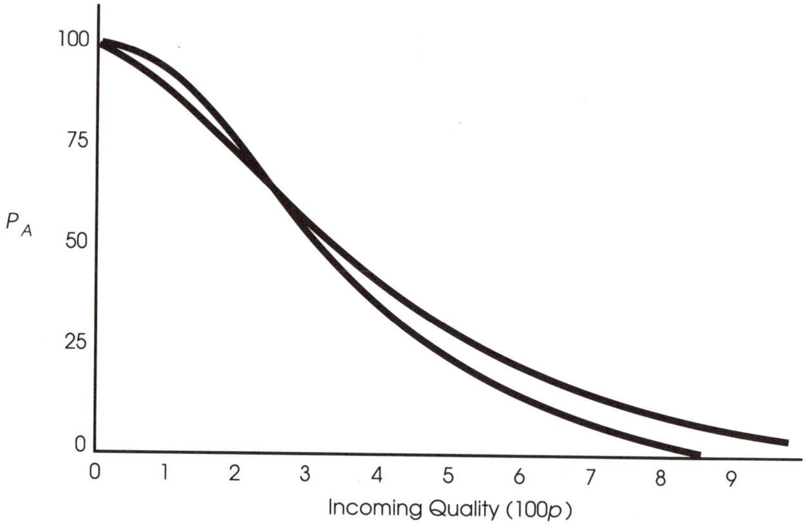

Figure 8.8. AQL sampling plans.

though some dissatisfaction with this system has been recently surfacing among quality professionals. It is an AQL system for attributes where the producer's stipulation is satisfied and the consumer's stipulation is approached as closely as possible. MIL-STD-414 is a lot-by-lot acceptance plan for variables that indexes on the AQL (like MIL-STD-105E). The Philips split-risk system is used somewhat in Europe, but hardly at all in the United States. Dodge-Romig tables meet the consumer's stipulation while coming as close as possible to the producer's stipulation by using the family of plans generated from the AOQL or LTPD. Many other systems have been derived from the sampling plan logic to fit specified situations. Chapter 9 will examine the most important of these plans.

Practice Problems

8–1 Find the AQL for a producer's risk of 5%, a consumer's risk of 10%, an LTPD of 6%, and a proposed sample size of 50.

Answer
0.38%

8–2 Find the AQL for a producer's risk of 1%, a consumer's risk of 5%, an LTPD of 8% and a proposed sample size of 100.

Answer
1.42%

8–3 Determine the following:

a. The four possible sampling plans for Problem 8–1.
b. Which plan provides the lowest sampling cost?
c. Which plan provides the greatest protection against sampling error?

Answers

(a) $n=131$, $A=4$; $n=174$, $A=5$
$n=132$, $A=4$; $n=155$, $A=5$
(b) $n=131$, $A=4$
(c) $n=174$, $A=5$

8–4 For Problem 8–3:

a. Which plan exactly meets the producer's stipulation and comes as close as possible to the consumer's?
b. What point on the curve precisely defines the producer's risk?
c. What point on the curve precisely defines the consumer's risk?

Answers

(a) $n=131$, $A=4$
(b) $P=0.015$, $P_A=0.95$
(c) $p=0.061$, $P_A=0.10$

8–5 For Problem 8–3:

a. Which plan exactly meets the consumer's stipulation and comes as close as possible to the producer's?
b. What point on the curve precisely defines the producer's risk?
c. What point on the curve precisely defines the consumer's risk?

Answers

(a) $n=132$, $A=4$
(b) $p=0.0149$, $P_A=0.95$
(c) $p=0.060$, $P_A=0.10$

8–6 Determine the following:

a. The four possible sampling plans for Problem 8–2.
b. Which plan provides the lowest sampling cost?
c. Which plan provides the greatest protection against sampling error?

Answers

(a) $n=127$, $A=5$; $n=163$, $A=6$
$n=131$, $A=5$; $n=148$, $A=6$
(b) $n=127$, $A=5$
(c) $n=163$, $A=6$

8–7 For Problem 8–6:

a. Which plan exactly meets the producer's stipulation and comes as close as possible to the consumer's?

b. What point on the curve precisely defines the producer's risk?

c. What point on the curve precisely defines the consumer's risk?

Answers

(a) $n=127$, $A=5$

(b) $p=0.0142$, $P_A=0.99$

(c) $p=0.083$, $P_A=0.05$

8–8 For Problem 8–6:

a. Which plan exactly meets the consumer's stipulation and comes as close as possible to the producer's?

b. What point on the curve precisely defines the producer's risk?

c. What point on the curve precisely defines the consumer's risk?

Answers

(a) $n=131$, $A=5$

(b) $p=0.0137$, $P_A=0.99$

(c) $p=0.080$, $P_A=0.05$

8–9 Construct the OC curve for Problem 8–3, part (b).

Answer

p	P_A
0.01	0.989
0.02	0.874
0.03	0.643
0.035	0.516
0.04	0.366
0.05	0.218
0.06	0.108

8–10 Construct the OC curve for Problem 8–6, part (c).

Answer

p	P_A
0.02	0.951
0.025	0.881
0.03	0.778
0.04	0.523
0.045	0.401
0.05	0.296
0.06	0.145

8–11 Construct the average outgoing quality curve (AOQ) for Problem 8–9.

Answer:

p	AOQ
0.01	0.989
0.02	1.748
0.03	1.929
0.035	1.806
0.04	1.646
0.05	1.090
0.06	0.648

8–12 Construct the average outgoing quality curve (AOQ) for Problem 8–10.

Answer

p	AOQ
0.02	1.902
0.025	2.203
0.03	2.334
0.04	2.092
0.045	1.805
0.05	1.480
0.06	0.870

8–13 What is the AOQL for Problem 8–11?

Answer
2.0% approximately

8–14 What is the AOQL for Problem 8–12?

Answer
2.3% approximately

CHAPTER 9 STANDARD SAMPLING PLANS

This chapter explores the important sampling plans that have been developed for various types of inspection systems.

Objectives

1. Know how to use MIL-STD-105E.
2. Know how to use the Dodge-Romig tables.
3. Know how to use the Philips split-risk system.
4. Know how to use sequential sampling.
5. Know how to use MIL-STD-1235B for continuous sampling.
6. Know how to use MIL-STD-414 for sampling variable (continuous) data.

9.1 MIL-STD-105E

MIL-STD-105E is an attribute acceptance sampling plan that indexes on the AQL. In other words, it basically matches the producer's stipulation (AQL) and comes as close as possible to the consumer's stipulated acceptable defect rate (LTPD). It should be noted that the alpha (α) and beta (β) risks are not fixed in the plan (they are not set at 0.05 and 0.10, respectively, as many believe). Instead they fluctuate between 0.001 and 0.15, although most are at or close to an AQL of 0.05 and an LTPD of 0.10. The plan is extensive and takes an entire volume of tables, graphs (OC curves, etc.), and explanations.

The plan indexes on the desired AQL and the lot size code letter. The lot size code letter depends on the following factors:

1. The lot size. There is some relationship between lot size and sample size in quality control. In general, the sample should be no larger than 10% of the lot size, except in small sizes where a 10% sample would be too small to provide adequate protection (and assurance of accuracy).
2. Inspection level. There are three general inspection levels provided by the plan: levels I, II, and III. (There are also three special inspection levels for use in special circumstances, but these require special training to apply and are rarely used.)
   a. Level I inspection. This level provides reduced sample sizes and a flatter OC curve for items that require destructive, dangerous, or expensive tests. Reduced sample sizes and flatter OC curves also lead to lowered inspection costs.
   b. Level II inspection. This is the general, or normal, inspection level that is used for items where no special circumstances exist. Most inspection is level II inspection.
   c. Level III inspection. This level provides for increased sample size and steeper OC curves (and higher inspection costs). Level III is used for expensive items where a higher level of protection is needed.

Three types of sampling are provided in the standard: single, double, and multiple (up to 7 samples). Each of these three types, in turn, is divided into normal, tightened, and reduced inspection categories. The standard is quite specific about how and when these different types of plans are to be used. Tightened inspection provides greater sampling protection and is used when the supplier's quality begins to deteriorate. Reduced inspection can be used when the supplier's quality has remained excellent for a period of time. Although reduced inspection does not provide quite the protection that the other two do, it is less costly. Tightened inspection is the most costly of all the plans. The procedures for using the standard will be illustrated by the following example:

$$\text{AQL} = 4\%$$

$$\text{Lot size} = 1{,}000$$

$$\text{Inspection level} = \text{II, normal inspection}$$

1. The first step is to determine the sampling size code letter. From Table 9.1, which is a partial reproduction of Table I from MIL-STD-105E, *J* is the code letter for a sample size of 1,000 (501 to 1,200) and an inspection level of II.
2. The next step is to read the sample plan from Table 9.2 (reproduced from Table II of MIL-STD-105E). Enter the table from the left at row *J*. Moving to the right, the first column gives the sample size, n, at 80. Now move to the right to the column headed 4.0. This is an AQL of 4%; the table uses percentages rather than fraction defective. This column has two values, the acceptance number A (called Ac in MIL-STD-105E) and the rejection number R (called Re in MIL-STD-105E). In

Table 9.1. Sample Size Code Letters (extracted from Table 1 of MIL-STD-105E)

Lot Size	General Inspection Levels I	II	III
to 8	A	A	B
15	A	B	C
25	B	C	D
50	C	D	E
90	C	E	F
150	D	F	G
280	E	G	H
500	F	H	J
1,200	G	J	K
3,200	H	K	L
10,000	J	L	M
35,000	K	M	N
150,000	L	N	P
500,000	M	P	Q
>500,000	N	Q	R

normal inspection, the rejection number is always one more than the acceptance number. The plan, then, is:

$$N = 1{,}000$$

$$n = 80$$

$$Ac = 7$$

$$Re = 8$$

If an arrow appears in the *Ac*/*Re* column, follow the arrow (either up or down) and use the plan that the arrow points to. For example, the sampling plan to be used for a code letter of *F* and an AQL of 0.40% is $n = 32$, $A = 0$, $R = 1$ (not $n = 20$, $A = 0$, $R = 1$). Double and multiple tables are read in the same way as single tables.

Note: The tables can also be used for defects per unit. Simply use the columns headed (AQL) 1.0 to 1,000 defects per unit.

Normal to Tightened

The plan just described for normal inspection would move to tightened inspection if any 2 out of any 5 consecutive lots are rejected (none of these can be rectified lots). For our example plan, the new requirements under tightened inspection would be (Table 9.3):

Table 9.2. Single Sampling Plans for Normal Inspection (Table II-A of MIL-STD-105E)

Sample size code letter	Sample size	Acceptable Quality Levels (normal inspection)																									
		0.010	0.015	0.025	0.040	0.065	0.10	0.15	0.25	0.40	0.65	1.0	1.5	2.5	4.0	6.5	10	15	25	40	65	100	150	250	400	650	1000
		Ac Re	Ac Re	Ac Re	Ac Re	Ac Re	Ac Re	Ac Re	Ac Re	Ac Re	Ac Re	Ac Re	Ac Re	Ac Re	Ac Re	Ac Re	Ac Re	Ac Re	Ac Re	Ac Re	Ac Re	Ac Re	Ac Re	Ac Re	Ac Re	Ac Re	Ac Re
A	2	↓	↓	↓	↓	↓	↓	↓	↓	↓	↓	↓	↓	↓	↓	0 1	↓	↓	1 2	2 3	3 4	5 6	7 8	10 11	14 15	21 22	30 31
B	3	↓	↓	↓	↓	↓	↓	↓	↓	↓	↓	↓	↓	↓	0 1	↑	↓	1 2	2 3	3 4	5 6	7 8	10 11	14 15	21 22	30 31	44 45
C	5	↓	↓	↓	↓	↓	↓	↓	↓	↓	↓	↓	↓	0 1	↑	↓	1 2	2 3	3 4	5 6	7 8	10 11	14 15	21 22	30 31	44 45	↑
D	8	↓	↓	↓	↓	↓	↓	↓	↓	↓	↓	↓	0 1	↑	↓	1 2	2 3	3 4	5 6	7 8	10 11	14 15	21 22	30 31	44 45	↑	↑
E	13	↓	↓	↓	↓	↓	↓	↓	↓	↓	↓	0 1	↑	↓	1 2	2 3	3 4	5 6	7 8	10 11	14 15	21 22	30 31	44 45	↑	↑	↑
F	20	↓	↓	↓	↓	↓	↓	↓	↓	↓	0 1	↑	↓	1 2	2 3	3 4	5 6	7 8	10 11	14 15	21 22	↑	↑	↑	↑	↑	↑
G	32	↓	↓	↓	↓	↓	↓	↓	↓	0 1	↑	↓	1 2	2 3	3 4	5 6	7 8	10 11	14 15	21 22	↑	↑	↑	↑	↑	↑	↑
H	50	↓	↓	↓	↓	↓	↓	↓	0 1	↑	↓	1 2	2 3	3 4	5 6	7 8	10 11	14 15	21 22	↑	↑	↑	↑	↑	↑	↑	↑
J	80	↓	↓	↓	↓	↓	↓	0 1	↑	↓	1 2	2 3	3 4	5 6	7 8	10 11	14 15	21 22	↑	↑	↑	↑	↑	↑	↑	↑	↑
K	125	↓	↓	↓	↓	↓	0 1	↑	↓	1 2	2 3	3 4	5 6	7 8	10 11	14 15	21 22	↑	↑	↑	↑	↑	↑	↑	↑	↑	↑
L	200	↓	↓	↓	↓	0 1	↑	↓	1 2	2 3	3 4	5 6	7 8	10 11	14 15	21 22	↑	↑	↑	↑	↑	↑	↑	↑	↑	↑	↑
M	315	↓	↓	↓	0 1	↑	↓	1 2	2 3	3 4	5 6	7 8	10 11	14 15	21 22	↑	↑	↑	↑	↑	↑	↑	↑	↑	↑	↑	↑
N	500	↓	↓	0 1	↑	↓	1 2	2 3	3 4	5 6	7 8	10 11	14 15	21 22	↑	↑	↑	↑	↑	↑	↑	↑	↑	↑	↑	↑	↑
P	800	↓	0 1	↑	↓	1 2	2 3	3 4	5 6	7 8	10 11	14 15	21 22	↑	↑	↑	↑	↑	↑	↑	↑	↑	↑	↑	↑	↑	↑
Q	1250	0 1	↑	↓	1 2	2 3	3 4	5 6	7 8	10 11	14 15	21 22	↑	↑	↑	↑	↑	↑	↑	↑	↑	↑	↑	↑	↑	↑	↑
R	2000	↑	↑	1 2	2 3	3 4	5 6	7 8	10 11	14 15	21 22	↑	↑	↑	↑	↑	↑	↑	↑	↑	↑	↑	↑	↑	↑	↑	↑

↓ Use first sampling plan below arrow. If sample size equals, or exceeds lot or batch size, do 100% inspection.

↑ Use first sampling plan above arrow.

Ac = Acceptance number

Re = Rejection number

Table 9.3. Single Sampling Plans for Tightened Inspection (Table II-B of MIL-STD-105E)

Acceptable Quality Levels (normal inspection); each cell gives Ac Re.

Sample size code letter	Sample size	0.010	0.015	0.025	0.040	0.065	0.10	0.15	0.25	0.40	0.65	1.0	1.5	2.5	4.0	6.5	10	15	25	40	65	100	150	250	400	650	1000
		Ac Re	Ac Re	Ac Re	Ac Re	Ac Re	Ac Re	Ac Re	Ac Re	Ac Re	Ac Re	Ac Re	Ac Re	Ac Re	Ac Re	Ac Re	Ac Re	Ac Re	Ac Re	Ac Re	Ac Re	Ac Re	Ac Re	Ac Re	Ac Re	Ac Re	Ac Re
A	2	↓	↓	↓	↓	↓	↓	↓	↓	↓	↓	↓	↓	↓	↓	↓	↓	↓	↓	1 2	2 3	3 4	5 6	8 9	12 13	18 19	27 28
B	3	↓	↓	↓	↓	↓	↓	↓	↓	↓	↓	↓	↓	↓	↓	0 1	↓	↓	1 2	2 3	3 4	5 6	8 9	12 13	18 19	27 28	41 42
C	5	↓	↓	↓	↓	↓	↓	↓	↓	↓	↓	↓	↓	↓	0 1	↓	↓	1 2	2 3	3 4	5 6	8 9	12 13	18 19	27 28	41 42	↑
D	8	↓	↓	↓	↓	↓	↓	↓	↓	↓	↓	↓	↓	0 1	↓	↓	1 2	2 3	3 4	5 6	8 9	12 13	18 19	27 28	41 42	↑	↑
E	13	↓	↓	↓	↓	↓	↓	↓	↓	↓	↓	↓	0 1	↓	↓	1 2	2 3	3 4	5 6	8 9	12 13	18 19	27 28	41 42	↑	↑	↑
F	20	↓	↓	↓	↓	↓	↓	↓	↓	↓	↓	0 1	↓	↓	1 2	2 3	3 4	5 6	8 9	12 13	18 19	↑	↑	↑	↑	↑	↑
G	32	↓	↓	↓	↓	↓	↓	↓	↓	↓	0 1	↓	↓	1 2	2 3	3 4	5 6	8 9	12 13	18 19	↑	↑	↑	↑	↑	↑	↑
H	50	↓	↓	↓	↓	↓	↓	↓	↓	0 1	↓	↓	1 2	2 3	3 4	5 6	8 9	12 13	18 19	↑	↑	↑	↑	↑	↑	↑	↑
J	80	↓	↓	↓	↓	↓	↓	↓	0 1	↓	↓	1 2	2 3	3 4	5 6	8 9	12 13	18 19	↑	↑	↑	↑	↑	↑	↑	↑	↑
K	125	↓	↓	↓	↓	↓	↓	0 1	↓	↓	1 2	2 3	3 4	5 6	8 9	12 13	18 19	↑	↑	↑	↑	↑	↑	↑	↑	↑	↑
L	200	↓	↓	↓	↓	↓	0 1	↓	↓	1 2	2 3	3 4	5 6	8 9	12 13	18 19	↑	↑	↑	↑	↑	↑	↑	↑	↑	↑	↑
M	315	↓	↓	↓	↓	0 1	↓	↓	1 2	2 3	3 4	5 6	8 9	12 13	18 19	↑	↑	↑	↑	↑	↑	↑	↑	↑	↑	↑	↑
N	500	↓	↓	↓	0 1	↓	↓	1 2	2 3	3 4	5 6	8 9	12 13	18 19	↑	↑	↑	↑	↑	↑	↑	↑	↑	↑	↑	↑	↑
P	800	↓	↓	0 1	↓	↓	1 2	2 3	3 4	5 6	8 9	12 13	18 19	↑	↑	↑	↑	↑	↑	↑	↑	↑	↑	↑	↑	↑	↑
Q	1250	↓	0 1	↓	↓	1 2	2 3	3 4	5 6	8 9	12 13	18 19	↑	↑	↑	↑	↑	↑	↑	↑	↑	↑	↑	↑	↑	↑	↑
R	2000	0 1	↑	↓	1 2	2 3	3 4	5 6	8 9	12 13	18 19	↑	↑	↑	↑	↑	↑	↑	↑	↑	↑	↑	↑	↑	↑	↑	↑
S	3150			1 2																							

↓ = Use first sampling plan below arrow. If sample size equals, or exceeds lot or batch size, do 100% inspection.
↑ = Use first sampling plan above arrow.
Ac = Acceptance number
Re = Rejection number

$$N = 1{,}000$$

$$n = 80$$

$$A = 5$$

$$R = 6$$

Normal inspection can be resumed only when 5 lots in a row are accepted.

Normal to Reduced

Some stringent rules govern the use of reduced inspection. Reduced inspection can only be used when all four of the following criteria are met:

1. Ten lots in a row in normal inspection have been accepted.
2. The total number of defectives from the 10 samples is equal to or less than the applicable number from Table 9.4 (reproduced from Table VIII of MIL-STD-105E). For example, if the sample size is 80, then the total number of units inspected from the 10 lots is 800. Suppose that all 10 lots had been accepted (none of the samples had more than 7 rejects) and that the total number of defective units had been 53. Reduced inspection cannot be instituted, then, because according to the table, only 24 defective units from all 10 samples are allowed in order to go to reduced inspection (row 800–1249 and column 4.0).
3. Production is in a steady state. Everything is running smoothly with no breakdowns, material problems, shortages, etc.
4. Reduced inspection has been authorized by the customer.

Suppose the previous plan has gone to reduced inspection. The new criteria are (Table 9.5):

$$N = 1{,}200$$

$$n = 32$$

$$A = 3$$

$$R = 6$$

With this plan, 32 are inspected. If 3 or less units are found defective, the lot is accepted. If 6 or more are defective, the lot is rejected (and the plan returns to normal inspection). If 4 or 5 are found defective, the lot is accepted, but the plan returns to normal inspection on the next lot. Reduced inspection should also be terminated whenever the production line begins to have problems, or when any other condition interferes. These rules apply equally to double and multiple sampling plans.

Table 9.4. Limit Numbers for Reduced Inspection (Table VIII of MIL-STD-105E)

Number of sample units from last 10 lots or batches	Acceptable Quality Level																									
	0.010	0.015	0.025	0.040	0.065	0.10	0.15	0.25	0.40	0.65	1.0	1.5	2.5	4.0	6.5	10	15	25	40	65	100	150	250	400	650	1000
20 - 29	*	*	*	*	*	*	*	*	*	*	*	*	*	*	*	0	0	2	4	8	14	22	40	68	115	181
30 - 49	*	*	*	*	*	*	*	*	*	*	*	*	*	*	0	0	1	3	7	13	22	36	63	105	178	277
50 - 79	*	*	*	*	*	*	*	*	*	*	*	*	*	0	0	2	3	7	14	25	40	63	110	181	301	
80 - 129	*	*	*	*	*	*	*	*	*	*	*	*	0	0	2	4	7	14	24	42	68	105	181	297		
130 - 199	*	*	*	*	*	*	*	*	*	*	*	0	0	2	4	7	13	25	42	72	115	177	301	490		
200 - 319	*	*	*	*	*	*	*	*	*	*	0	0	2	4	8	14	22	40	68	115	181	277	471			
320 - 499	*	*	*	*	*	*	*	*	*	0	0	1	4	8	14	24	39	68	113	189						
500 - 799	*	*	*	*	*	*	*	*	0	0	2	3	7	14	25	40	63	110	181							
800 - 1249	*	*	*	*	*	*	*	0	0	2	4	7	14	24	42	68	105	181								
1250 - 1999	*	*	*	*	*	*	0	0	2	4	7	13	24	40	69	110	169									
2000 - 3149	*	*	*	*	*	0	0	2	4	8	14	22	40	68	115	181										
3150 - 4999	*	*	*	*	0	0	1	4	8	14	24	38	67	111	186											
5000 - 7999	*	*	*	0	0	2	3	7	14	25	40	63	110	181												
8000 - 12499	*	*	0	0	2	4	7	14	24	42	68	105	181													
12500 - 19999	*	0	0	2	4	7	13	24	40	69	110	169														
20000 - 31499	0	0	2	4	8	14	22	40	68	115	181															
31500 - 49999	0	1	4	8	14	24	38	67	111	186																
50000 & Over	2	3	7	14	25	40	63	110	181	301																

*Denotes that the number of sample units from the last ten lots or batches is not sufficient for reduced inspection for this AQL. In this instance more than ten lots or batches may be used for the calculations, provided that the lots or batches used are the most recent ones in sequence, that they have all been on several inspections, and that none has been rejected while on original inspection.

Table 9.5. Single Sampling Plans for Reduced Inspection (Table II-C of MIL-STD-105E)

Sample size code letter	Sample size	Acceptable Quality Levels (reduced inspecton)†																									
		0.010	0.015	0.025	0.040	0.065	0.10	0.15	0.25	0.40	0.65	1.0	1.5	2.5	4.0	6.5	10	15	25	40	65	100	150	250	400	650	1000
		Ac Re	Ac Re	Ac Re	Ac Re	Ac Re	Ac Re	Ac Re	Ac Re	Ac Re	Ac Re	Ac Re	Ac Re	Ac Re	Ac Re	Ac Re	Ac Re	Ac Re	Ac Re	Ac Re	Ac Re	Ac Re	Ac Re	Ac Re	Ac Re	Ac Re	Ac Re
A	2	↓	↓	↓	↓	↓	↓	↓	↓	↓	↓	↓	↓	↓	↓	0 1	↓	↓	1 2	2 3	3 4	5 6	7 8	10 11	14 15	21 22	30 31
B	2	↓	↓	↓	↓	↓	↓	↓	↓	↓	↓	↓	↓	↓	0 1	↑	↓	0 2	1 3	2 4	3 5	5 6	7 8	10 11	14 15	21 22	30 31
C	2	↓	↓	↓	↓	↓	↓	↓	↓	↓	↓	↓	↓	0 1	↑	↓	0 2	1 3	1 4	2 5	3 6	5 8	7 10	10 13	14 17	21 24	↑
D	3	↓	↓	↓	↓	↓	↓	↓	↓	↓	↓	↓	0 1	↑	↓	0 2	1 3	1 4	2 5	3 6	5 8	7 10	10 13	14 17	21 24	↑	↑
E	5	↓	↓	↓	↓	↓	↓	↓	↓	↓	↓	0 1	↑	↓	0 2	1 3	1 4	2 5	3 6	5 8	7 10	10 13	14 17	21 24	↑	↑	↑
F	8	↓	↓	↓	↓	↓	↓	↓	↓	↓	0 1	↑	↓	0 2	1 3	1 4	2 5	3 6	5 8	7 10	10 13	↑	↑	↑	↑	↑	↑
G	13	↓	↓	↓	↓	↓	↓	↓	↓	0 1	↑	↓	0 2	1 3	1 4	2 5	3 6	5 8	7 10	10 13	↑	↑	↑	↑	↑	↑	↑
H	20	↓	↓	↓	↓	↓	↓	↓	0 1	↑	↓	0 2	1 3	1 4	2 5	3 6	5 8	7 10	10 13	↑	↑	↑	↑	↑	↑	↑	↑
J	32	↓	↓	↓	↓	↓	↓	0 1	↑	↓	0 2	1 3	1 4	2 5	3 6	5 8	7 10	10 13	↑	↑	↑	↑	↑	↑	↑	↑	↑
K	50	↓	↓	↓	↓	↓	0 1	↑	↓	0 2	1 3	1 4	2 5	3 6	5 8	7 10	10 13	↑	↑	↑	↑	↑	↑	↑	↑	↑	↑
L	80	↓	↓	↓	↓	0 1	↑	↓	0 2	1 3	1 4	2 5	3 6	5 8	7 10	10 13	↑	↑	↑	↑	↑	↑	↑	↑	↑	↑	↑
M	125	↓	↓	↓	0 1	↑	↓	0 2	1 3	1 4	2 5	3 6	5 8	7 10	10 13	↑	↑	↑	↑	↑	↑	↑	↑	↑	↑	↑	↑
N	200	↓	↓	0 1	↑	↓	0 2	1 3	1 4	2 5	3 6	5 8	7 10	10 13	↑	↑	↑	↑	↑	↑	↑	↑	↑	↑	↑	↑	↑
P	315	↓	0 1	↑	↓	0 2	1 3	1 4	2 5	3 6	5 8	7 10	10 13	↑	↑	↑	↑	↑	↑	↑	↑	↑	↑	↑	↑	↑	↑
Q	500	0 1	↑	↓	0 2	1 3	1 4	2 5	3 6	5 8	7 10	10 13	↑	↑	↑	↑	↑	↑	↑	↑	↑	↑	↑	↑	↑	↑	↑
R	800	↑	↑	0 2	1 3	1 4	2 5	3 6	5 8	7 10	10 13	↑	↑	↑	↑	↑	↑	↑	↑	↑	↑	↑	↑	↑	↑	↑	↑

↓ = Use first sampling plan below arrow. If sample size equals, or exceeds lot or batch size, do 100% inspection.
↑ = Use first sampling plan above arrow.
Ac = Acceptance number.
Re = Rejection number.
† = If the acceptance number has been exceeded, but the rejection number has not been reached, accept the lot, but reinstate normal inspection (see 10.1.4)

9.2 Dodge-Romig

Both Dodge and Romig were coworkers with Shewhart (developer of control charts) at Bell Laboratories in the 1920s. Working together, they extended the concepts of Shewhart into a set of tables for acceptance sampling by attributes (they also did some of the early work on chain sampling plans for ongoing production). Both single and double sampling are available (but not multiple). The tables differ from MIL-STD-105E in that they were designed to match the consumer's risk (β) rather than the producer's risk (α). They are also designed to minimize inspection effort and thus are more applicable to within plant inspection (MIL-STD-105E, for example, is especially well suited to vendor/customer inspection).

Tables 9.6 and 9.7 index the lot size and the LTPD, or the lot size and the AOQL (there are different tables for LTPD and for AOQL). For example, for a lot size of 1,200, an LTPD of 1% and a process average (p) of 4%, the inspection plan is:

$$N = 1{,}200$$

$$n = 220$$

$$A = 0$$

$$R = 1$$

The tables also show the AOQL for the plan, in this case 0.15% (the AOQL tables show the LTPD for each plan). Note that for these tables, some previous history must be available to the inspector. This may not be possible (or the accuracy uncertain) for a customer, which makes the Dodge-Romig tables inappropriate for vendor/customer situations. There are many more tables in the Dodge-Romig plan than the two shown here.

9.3 Philips Split-Risk

The Philips Standard Sampling System is a simple system that is used rather extensively in Europe but not much in the United States. It indexes the lot size and the process quality only, and one simple table is needed for both single and double sampling (Table 9.8). Small lots to 1,000 units use single sampling only, while lots larger than 1,000 use only double sampling. For a lot size of 1,000 and a process quality of 4% (the same example used for MIL-STD-105E), the plan is:

$$N = 1{,}000$$

$$n = 85$$

Table 9.6. Dodge-Romig Single Sampling Table Based on LTPD = 1%

	Process Average (%)																	
	0–0.010			*0.011–0.10*			*0.11–0.20*			*0.21–0.30*			*0.31–0.40*			*0.41–0.50*		
Lot Size	*n*	*c*	*AOQL (%)*	*n*	*c*	*AOQL (%)*	*n*	*c*	*AOQL (%)*	*n*	*c*	*AOQL (%)*	*n*	*c*	*AOQL (%)*	*n*	*c*	*AOQL (%)*
1–120	All	0	0	All	0	0	All	0	0	All	0	0	All	0	0	All	0	0
121–150	120	0	0.06	120	0	0.06	120	0	0.06	120	0	0.06	120	0	0.06	120	0	0.06
151–200	140	0	0.08	140	0	0.08	140	0	0.08	140	0	0.08	140	0	0.08	140	0	0.08
201–300	165	0	0.10	165	0	0.10	165	0	0.10	165	0	0.10	165	0	0.10	165	0	0.10
301–400	175	0	0.12	175	0	0.12	175	0	0.12	175	0	0.12	175	0	0.12	175	0	0.12
401–500	180	0	0.13	180	0	0.13	180	0	0.13	180	0	0.13	180	0	0.13	180	0	0.13
501–600	190	0	0.13	190	0	0.13	190	0	0.13	190	0	0.13	190	0	0.13	305	1	0.14
601–800	200	0	0.14	200	0	0.14	200	0	0.14	330	1	0.15	330	1	0.15	330	1	0.15
801–1,000	205	0	0.14	205	0	0.14	205	0	0.14	335	1	0.17	335	1	0.17	335	1	0.17
1,001–2,000	220	0	0.15	220	0	0.15	360	1	0.19	490	2	0.21	490	2	0.21	610	3	0.22
2,001–3,000	220	0	0.15	375	1	0.20	505	2	0.23	630	3	0.24	745	4	0.26	870	5	0.26
3,001–4,000	225	0	0.15	380	1	0.20	510	2	0.24	645	3	0.25	880	5	0.28	1,000	6	0.29
4,001–5,000	225	0	0.16	380	1	0.20	520	2	0.24	770	4	0.28	895	5	0.29	1,120	7	0.31
5,001–7,000	230	0	0.16	385	1	0.21	655	3	0.27	780	4	0.29	1,020	6	0.32	1,260	8	0.34
7,001–10,000	230	0	0.16	520	2	0.25	660	3	0.28	910	5	0.32	1,150	7	0.34	1,500	10	0.37
10,001–20,000	390	1	0.21	525	2	0.26	785	4	0.31	1,040	6	0.35	1,400	9	0.39	1,980	14	0.43
20,001–50,000	390	1	0.21	530	2	0.26	920	5	0.34	1,300	8	0.39	1,890	13	0.44	2,570	19	0.48
50,001–100,000	390	1	0.21	670	3	0.29	1,040	6	0.36	1,420	9	0.41	2,120	15	0.47	3,150	23	0.50

*n, size of sample; entry of "All" indicates that each piece in lot is to be inspected. c, allowable defect number for sample. AOQL, average outgoing quality limit.

Table 9.7. Dodge-Romig Single Sampling Table Based on AOQL = 3%

	Process Average (%)																	
	0–0.06			*0.07–0.60*			*0.61–1.20*			*1.21–1.80*			*1.81–2.40*			*2.41–3.00*		
Lot Size	*n*	*c*	*LQL (%)*	*n*	*c*	*LQL (%)*	*n*	*c*	*LQL (%)*	*n*	*c*	*LQL (%)*	*n*	*c*	*LQL (%)*	*n*	*c*	*LQL (%)*
1–10	All	0	—	All	0	—	All	0	—	All	0	—	All	0	—	All	0	—
11–50	10	0	19.0	10	0	19.0	10	0	19.0	10	0	19.0	10	0	19.0	10	0	19.0
51–100	11	0	18.0	11	0	18.0	11	0	18.0	11	0	18.0	11	0	18.0	22	1	16.4
101–200	12	0	17.0	12	0	17.0	12	0	17.0	25	1	15.1	25	1	15.1	25	1	15.1
201–300	12	0	17.0	12	0	17.0	26	1	14.6	26	1	14.6	26	1	14.6	40	2	12.8
301–400	12	0	17.1	12	0	17.1	26	1	14.7	26	1	14.7	41	2	12.7	41	2	12.7
401–500	12	0	17.2	27	1	14.1	27	1	14.1	42	2	12.4	42	2	12.4	42	2	12.4
501–600	12	0	17.3	27	1	14.2	27	1	14.2	42	2	12.4	42	2	12.4	60	3	10.8
601–800	12	0	17.3	27	1	14.2	27	1	14.2	43	2	12.1	60	3	10.9	60	3	10.9
801–1,000	12	0	17.4	27	1	14.2	44	2	11.8	44	2	11.8	60	3	11.0	80	4	9.8
1,001–2,000	12	0	17.5	28	1	13.8	45	2	11.7	65	3	10.2	80	4	9.8	100	5	9.1
2,001–3,000	12	0	17.5	28	1	13.8	45	2	11.7	65	3	10.2	100	5	9.1	140	7	8.2
3,001–4,000	12	0	17.5	28	1	13.8	65	3	10.3	85	4	9.5	125	6	8.4	165	8	7.8
4,001–5,000	28	1	13.8	28	1	13.8	65	3	10.3	85	4	9.5	125	6	8.4	210	10	7.4
5,001–7,000	28	1	13.8	45	2	11.8	65	3	10.3	105	5	8.8	145	7	8.1	235	11	7.1
7,001–10,000	28	1	13.9	46	2	11.6	65	3	10.3	105	5	8.8	170	8	7.6	280	13	6.8
10,001–20,000	28	1	13.9	46	2	11.7	85	4	9.5	125	6	8.4	215	10	7.2	380	17	6.2
20,001–50,000	28	1	13.9	65	3	10.3	105	5	8.8	170	8	7.6	310	14	6.5	560	24	5.7
50,001–100,000	28	1	13.9	65	3	10.3	125	6	8.4	215	10	7.2	385	17	6.2	690	29	5.4

[a] *n*, size of sample; entry of "All" indicates that each piece in lot is to be inspected. *c*, allowable defect number for sample. LQL, limiting quality level corresponding to a consumer's risk (β) = 0.10.

Table 9.8. Philips Standard Sampling Table

Lot Size	*Point of Control*																							
	0.25%			*0.5%*			*1%*			*2%*			*3%*			*5%*			*7%*			*10%*		
Single sampling	n		c	n		c	n		c	n		c	n		c	n		c	n		c	n		c
20–50	A			A			A			30		0	20		0	13		0	10		0	7		0
51–100	A			A			60		0	30		0	20		0	13		0	10		0	7		0
101–200	A			100		0	60		0	35		0	55		1	35		1	25		1	17		1
201–500	175		0	100		0	135		1	75		1	55		1	35		1	40		2	25		2
501–1,000	225		0	225		1	150		1	85		1	85		2	55		2	55		3	35		3
Double sampling	n_1	c_1	c_2	n_1	c_1	c_2	n_1	c_1	c_2	n_1	c_1	c_2	n_1	c_1	c_2	n_1	c_1	c_2	n_1	c_1	c_2	n_1	c_1	c_2
1,001–2,000	330	0	1	150	0	1	110	0	2	55	0	2	45	0	3	25	0	3	30	1	5	22	1	5
2,001–5,000	425	0	2	200	0	2	135	0	3	70	0	3	70	1	5	45	1	5	55	2	10	40	2	10
5,001–10,000	525	0	3	260	0	3	220	1	5	110	1	5	125	2	10	75	2	10	75	3	15	55	3	15
10,001–20,000	875	1	5	440	1	5	380	2	10	190	2	10	180	3	15	110	3	15	100	4	20	70	4	20
20,001–50,000	1,500	2	10	750	2	10	540	3	15	270	3	15	240	4	20	140	4	20	120	5	25	85	5	25
50,001–100,000	2,200	3	15	1,100	3	15	700	4	20	390	4	20	290	5	25	175	5	25	145	6	30	105	6	30

[a]Second sample $n_2 = 2n_1$. "A" means inspect entire lot.

$$A = 2$$

$$R = 3$$

In comparison to MIL-STD-105E, the lot size is slightly larger (85 instead of 80) but the acceptance number is smaller (7 in MIL-STD-105E). Obviously, the protection is not as good as it is in MIL-STD-105E.

9.4 Sequential Sampling

Sequential sampling is a piece-by-piece inspection plan where a decision is made after each piece is inspected. Two upward sloping limit lines are calculated and charted, the upper line being the rejection line and the lower the acceptance. As each piece is inspected, it is charted as either accepted on the abscissa or X axis, or rejected on the ordinate or Y axis. Only accumulated values are charted.

Lot acceptance is made whenever the accumulated number of defects is less than the number allowed, at that point, by the acceptance line. Lot rejection occurs when the accumulated rejects exceed the rejection line at that point. If neither of these alternatives occurs, inspection is continued until rejection or acceptance does occur, or until the number of items inspected exceeds three times the amount from a comparable single sampling plan. This plan is used for costly or destructive tests, and for acceptance sampling in reliability testing.

Figure 9.1 shows an example of a sequential chart for: $\alpha = 0.05$, $\beta = 0.10$, AQL $= 0.01$, and LTPD $= 0.06$. The formulas for the limit lines are:

$$\text{Rejection} = R = Y_R + Sn$$

$$\text{Acceptance} = A = -Y_A + Sn$$

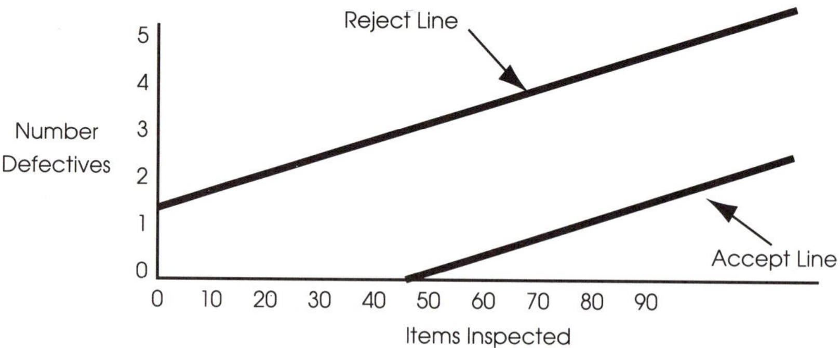

Figure 9.1. Sequential plan graph.

where

R = rejection

A = acceptance

Y_R = the intercept for the rejection line

Y_A = the intercept for the acceptance line

S = the slope of lines (both slopes must be equal)

n = the number inspected

The three unknowns, Y_R, Y_A, and S are developed as follows:

$$Y_R = Ln[(1-\beta)/\alpha]/\{Ln[(\text{LTPD}/\text{AQL})(1-\text{AQL})/(1-\text{LTPD})]\}$$

$$Y_A = Ln[1-\alpha)/\beta]/\{Ln[(\text{LTPD}/\text{AQL})(1-\text{AQL})/(1-\text{LTPD})]\}$$

$$S = Ln[(1-\text{AQL})/(1-\text{LTPD}])/\{Ln[(\text{LTPD}/\text{AQL})(1-\text{AQL})/(1-\text{LTPD})]\}$$

Calculating for our example ($\alpha = 0.05$, $\beta = 0.10$, AQL = 0.01, and LTPD = 0.06) gives the limit line formulas:

$$R = 1.57 + 0.028n$$

$$A = -1.22 + 0.028n$$

Rejection tables can also be constructed in place of the graph (see Table 9.9). Sequential values for n (starting at 1) can be substituted into each of the limit line equations to determine the number of defectives needed for rejection or acceptance at that sample size. For example, for the forty-fourth unit inspected, the lot would be rejected if 3 or more defectives (out of the 44 inspected) had been found, or accepted if all 44 were free of defectives.

$$R = 1.57 + 0.028(44) = 2.8 \text{ (use 3)}$$

$$A = -1.22 + 0.028(44) = 0.012 \text{ (use 0)}$$

In Table 9.9, if the acceptance number, A, falls below 0, acceptance cannot be accomplished on that sample; continue to inspect. If the rejection number, R, is greater than the number inspected, rejection cannot be accomplished on that sample (continue to inspect). An *a* means acceptance is not possible, continue to inspect; an *r* means rejection is not possible, continue to inspect.

9.5 MIL-STD-1235B

The previous four plans were lot-by-lot acceptance plans where the objective of the plan was the acceptance or rejection of an entire lot.

Table 9.9. Acceptance/ Rejection Table for Sequential Sampling

n	A	R
1	a	r
2	a	2
3	a	2
4	a	2
5	a	2
.	.	.
.	.	.
.	.	.
43	a	3
44	0	3

MIL-STD-1235B, on the other hand, provides for acceptance sampling of continuous production. The standard includes a group of these plans, called continuous sampling plans, each designed for a different objective.

CSP-1 is the basic continuous sampling plan. One-hundred percent inspection is initiated at the start of the process until a certain number in a row (called i in the standard) are found to be defect free. Then a sampling ratio or frequency (called f in the standard) is instituted until 1 defect is found, after which 100% inspection is reinstated and the plan starts over. The initial amount (for 100% inspection) is determined by indexing a table on the AOQL and the desired sampling fraction. There are a series of acceptable plans under each AOQL. The decision as to which plan to use depends on production run size, inspection labor, level of protection desired, etc., and is obviously a management decision. For example, if the AOQL is 1.22%, there are 11 possible plans from $i=23$, $f=1/2$, to $i=255$, $f=1/200$ (Table 9.10). If the plan $i=255$, $f=1/200$ is chosen, this means inspect 100% until 255 items in a row are found defect free, then inspect 1 out of each 200 until 1 defect is found, then return to 100% inspection and start the procedure over. The plan is usually chosen to balance the 100% inspection costs with the sampling costs and the protection level.

CSP-2 plans are identical to CSP-1 plans except that a second chance is provided when a defect is found while sampling. In this case, sampling is continued but a count is kept of the number inspected. If another defect is found before i number are inspected (the actual number inspected not the number produced), 100% inspection is reinstated and the plan restarted. (See Table 9.11 for an example of CSP-2 plans.) Other continuous sampling plans are available in the standard for spe-

Table 9.10. Values of "*i*" for CSP-1 Plans

	AOQL (%)															
f	0.018	0.033	0.046	0.074	0.113	0.143	0.198	0.33	0.53	0.79	1.22	1.90	2.90	4.94	7.12	11.46
1/2	1,540	840	600	375	245	194	140	84	53	36	23	15	10	6	5	3
1/3	2,550	1,390	1,000	620	405	321	232	140	87	59	38	25	16	10	7	5
1/4	3,340	1,820	1,310	810	530	420	303	182	113	76	49	32	21	13	9	6
1/5	3,960	2,160	1,550	965	630	498	360	217	135	91	58	38	25	15	11	7
1/7	4.950	2,700	1,940	1,205	790	623	450	270	168	113	73	47	31	18	13	8
1/10	6,050	3,300	2,370	1,470	965	762	550	335	207	138	89	57	38	22	16	10
1/15	7,390	4,030	2,890	1,800	1,180	930	672	410	255	170	108	70	46	27	19	12
1/25	9,110	4,970	3,570	2,215	1,450	1,147	828	500	315	210	134	86	57	33	23	14
1/50	11,730	6,400	4,590	2,855	1,870	1,477	1,067	640	400	270	175	110	72	42	29	18
1/100	14,320	7,810	5,600	3,485	2,305	1,820	1,302	790	500	330	215	135	89	52	36	22
1/200	17,420	9,500	6,810	4,235	2,760	2,178	1,583	950	590	400	255	165	106	62	43	26

Table 9.11 Values of "i" for CSP-2 Plans

	AOQL (%)							
f	0.53	0.79	1.22	1.90	2.90	4.94	7.12	11.46
1/2	80	54	35	23	15	9	7	4
1/3	128	86	55	36	24	14	10	7
1/4	162	109	70	45	30	18	12	8
1/5	190	127	81	52	35	20	14	9
1/7	230	155	99	64	42	25	17	11
1/10	275	185	118	76	50	29	20	13
1/15	330	220	140	90	59	35	24	15
1/25	395	265	170	109	71	42	29	18
1/50	490	330	210	134	88	52	36	22

cial cases, such as short production runs (CSP-F), short production runs and reduced sampling (CSP-T), reduced clearance or 100% sampling (CSP-V), and alternating clearance and sampling (CSP-F and CSP-T).

9.6 MIL-STD-414

MIL-STD-414 is similar to MIL-STD-105E in that it is a lot-by-lot acceptance sampling plan where normal, tightened, and reduced inspection are provided. MIL-STD-414, however, is a variable sampling plan (for measureable characteristics), whereas MIL-STD-105E is a sampling plan for attributes (good/bad characteristics). The standard assumes that the variables used are normally (Gaussian) distributed. Until recently this standard has received limited attention and application. However, a strong interest in the standard has been surfacing among quality professionals who have become disenchanted with MIL-STD-105E. It may be that MIL-STD-414 will be used more frequently in the future as a replacement for MIL-STD-105E, wherever possible.

MIL-STD-414 has four parts, with three different types of plans. Part A contains a general description of the system. Tables for sample size code letters and OC curves for all plans are also included in this section. Section B contains the standard deviation plan where the variability is unknown. In the Section C plans, the variability is still unknown, but the range is used instead of the standard deviation. Range-type plans are easier to construct, but do require larger sample sizes (thus increased sample costs). When the variability is known, the variability known plan, Section D, is the least costly. The first step, in any of the plans, is to determine the sample size code letter (from Table 9.12). This table is indexed by the lot size and the inspection level. Inspection level IV is the normal level and is used most often. The higher the inspection level, the steeper the OC curve and the greater

Table 9.12. Sample Size Code Letters (Extracted from Table A-2 of MIL-STD-414)

Lot Size	Inspection Level I	II	III	IV	V
to 8	B	B	B	B	C
15	B	B	B	B	D
25	B	B	B	C	E
40	B	B	B	D	F
65	B	B	C	E	G
110	B	B	D	F	H
180	B	C	E	G	I
300	B	D	F	H	J
500	C	E	G	I	K

the protection. The lower inspection levels are used when greater consumer risks can be tolerated.

The standard will be illustrated by using the unknown variability standard deviation method from Section B. Tables 9.13 and 9.14 are reproduced from Section B of the standard for use in developing the plan. Suppose a lot of 100 is submitted for inspection. Inspection level IV is desired, the AQL is 0.40%, tightened inspection is desired, and a lower specification limit of 3.0 is specified. The results of the 10 samples are 3.5, 3.6, 4.0, 4.0, 3.9, 3.6, 3.3, 3.5, 3.0, 3.8. Should the lot be accepted or rejected?

1. $\overline{X} = \Sigma X/n = 36.2/10 = 3.62$
2. $s = \sqrt{X^2 - (\Sigma X)^2/n/(n-1)}$
   $= \sqrt{(131.96 - 36.2^2/10)/(10-1)} = 0.319$

Table 9.13. Tables for Estimating P_L or P_U (Extracted from Table B-5 of MIL-STD-414)

Q_L or Q_U	Sample Size 5	10	20	30
1.0	16.36	15.97	15.89	15.88
1.1	13.48	13.50	13.52	13.53
1.2	10.76	11.24	11.38	11.42
1.3	8.21	9.22	9.48	9.55
1.4	5.88	7.44	7.80	7.90
1.5	3.80	5.87	6.34	6.46
1.6	2.03	4.54	5.09	5.23
1.7	0.66	3.41	4.02	4.18
1.8	0.00	2.49	3.13	3.30
1.9	0.00	1.75	2.40	2.57
2.0	0.00	1.17	1.81	1.98

Table 9.14. MIL-STD-414 Master Table for Plans Based on Variability Unknown, Standard Deviation Method

Sample size code letter	Sample size	Acceptable Quality Levels (normal inspection)													
		.04	.065	.10	.15	.25	.40	.65	1.00	1.50	2.50	4.00	6.50	10.00	15.00
		M	M	M	M	M	M	M	M	M	M	M	M	M	M
B	3	↓	↓	↓	↓	↓	↓	↓	▼	▼	7.59	18.86	26.94	33.69	40.47
C	4	↓	↓	↓	↓	↓	↓	↓	1.53	5.50	10.92	16.45	22.86	29.45	36.90
D	5	↓	↓	↓	↓	↓	↓	1.33	3.32	5.83	9.80	14.39	20.19	26.56	33.99
E	7	↓	↓	↓	↓	0.422	1.06	2.14	3.55	5.35	8.40	12.20	17.35	23.29	30.50
F	10	↓	↓	↓	0.349	0.716	1.30	2.17	3.26	4.77	7.29	10.54	15.17	20.74	27.57
G	15	0.099	0.186	0.312	0.503	0.818	1.31	2.11	3.05	4.31	6.56	9.46	13.71	18.94	25.61
H	20	0.135	0.228	0.365	0.544	0.846	1.29	2.05	2.95	4.09	6.17	8.92	12.99	18.03	24.53
I	25	0.155	0.250	0.380	0.551	0.877	1.29	2.00	2.86	3.97	5.97	8.63	12.57	17.51	23.97
J	30	0.179	0.280	0.413	0.581	0.879	1.29	1.98	2.83	3.91	5.86	8.47	12.36	17.24	23.58
K	35	0.170	0.264	0.388	0.535	0.847	1.23	1.87	2.68	3.70	5.57	8.10	11.87	16.65	22.91
L	40	0.179	0.275	0.401	0.566	0.873	1.26	1.88	2.71	3.72	5.58	8.09	11.85	16.61	22.86
M	50	0.163	0.250	0.363	0.503	0.789	1.17	1.71	2.49	3.45	5.20	7.61	11.23	15.87	22.00
N	75	0.147	0.228	0.330	0.467	0.720	1.07	1.60	2.29	3.20	4.87	7.15	10.63	15.13	21.11
O	100	0.145	0.220	0.317	0.447	0.689	1.02	1.53	2.20	3.07	4.69	6.91	10.32	14.75	20.66
P	150	0.134	0.203	0.293	0.413	0.638	0.949	1.43	2.05	2.89	4.43	6.57	9.88	14.20	20.02
Q	200	0.135	0.204	0.294	0.414	0.637	0.945	1.42	2.04	2.87	4.40	6.53	9.81	14.12	19.92
		.065	.10	.15	.25	.40	.65	1.00	1.50	2.50	4.00	6.50	10.00	15.00	
		Acceptability Quality Levels (tightened inspection)													

All AQL and table values are in percent defective.

↓ Use first sampling plan below arrow, that is, both sample size as well as M value. When sample size equals or exceeds lot size, every item in the lot must be inspected.

3. $Q_L = (\overline{X} - \text{LSL})/s = (3.62 - 3.0)/0.319 = 1.94$
4. $P_L = 1.75$ (from Table 9.13 at $QL = 1.94$ and $n = 10$)
5. $M = 0.716$ (from Table 9.14)
6. (P_L of 1.75) > (M of 0.716); reject the lot.

Note: For tightened inspection, read from the bottom of Table 9.14 up; for normal inspection, read from the top down (normal inspection has a P_L of 1.30).

In our example, the code letter is F for a lot size of 100 and an inspection level of IV. Table 9.14, then, is entered at code letter F and an AQL of 0.40%.

If an upper specification is given for control, the Q_U formula is:

$$Q_U = (\text{USL} - \overline{X})/s$$

The other formulas and procedures are identical.

Practice Problems

9–1 Using MIL-STD-105E, determine the single sampling plan for:

	Inspection Level	Lot Size	Inspection	AQL
a.	I	50	Normal	0.065%
b.	II	1,000	Tightened	1.0%
c.	III	50,000	Reduced	6.5%

Answers

a. 100% inspection
b. $n = 80$, $Ac = 1$, $Re = 2$
c. $n = 80$, $Ac = 10$, $Re = 13$

9–2 What action should be taken in Problem 9–1a if the number of defectives are 9, 14, and 11?

9–3 Using the Dodge-Romig tables, determine the single sampling plan and the AOQL for LTPD = 1.0% and:

a. $N = 1{,}000$ and $p = 0.40\%$
b. $N = 5{,}000$ and $p = 0.20\%$

Answers

a. $n = 335$, $A = 1$, AOQL = 0.17%
b. $n = 520$, $A = 2$, AOQL = 0.24%

9–4 Using the Dodge-Romig tables, determine the single sampling plan and the LTPD for AOQL = 3.0% and:

a. $N = 1{,}000$ and $p = 1.00\%$
b. $N = 5{,}000$ and $p = 2.00\%$

Answers

a. $n = 44$, $A = 2$, LTPD $= 11.8\%$
b. $n = 125$, $A = 6$, LTPD $= 8.4\%$

9–5 Using the Philips split-risk system, determine the plan for:

a. $N = 1{,}000$ and AQL $= 1.0\%$
b. $N = 5{,}000$ and AQL $= 2.0\%$

Answers

a. $n = 150$, $A = 1$
b. $n = 70$, $A_1 = 0$, $A_2 = 3$

9–6 In Problem 9–5b, what action should be taken if no defectives were found on the first sample? If 1 defective were found on the first sample? If 4 defectives were found on the first sample? If 1 defective were found on the first sample and 1 on the second? If 1 defective were found on the first sample and 3 on the second?

9–7 Determine the equations for a sequential sampling plan for $\alpha = 0.05$, $\beta = 0.10$, $p_\alpha = 0.09$ and $p_\beta = 0.01$.

Answers

$a = -0.99 + 0.037n$
$r = 1.27 + 0.037n$

9–8 For Problem 9–7, construct an acceptance-rejection table. At what point is rejection possible? At what point is acceptance possible?

Answers

$n = 1$; $n = 27$

9–9 Determine the equations for a sequential sampling plan for $\alpha = 0.05$, $\beta = 0.10$, $p_\alpha = 0.08$ and $p_\beta = 0.03$.

Answers

$a = -2.18 + 0.051n$
$r = 2.80 + 0.051n$

9–10 For Problem 9–9, at what point is rejection possible? At what point is acceptance possible?

Answers

$n = 3$; $n = 43$

9–11 Using CSP-1, determine the value of *i* for:
  a. AOQL of 1.2% and a frequency, *f*, of 1/7
  b. AOQL of 1.9% and a frequency, *f*, of 1/10

Answers
73; 57

9–12 Using CSP-2, determine the value of *i* for:
  a. AOQL of 1.2% and a frequency, *f*, of 1/7
  b. AOQL of 1.9% and a frequency, *f*, of 1/10

Answers
99; 64

9–13 Using MIL-STD-414, unknown variability standard deviation method, determine the sample size for:
  a. $N = 200$, inspection level = III
  b. $N = 40$, inspection level = IV

Answers
7; 5

9–14 Using MIL-STD-414, unknown variability standard deviation method, determine whether the lot is either accepted or rejected for a lot size, *N*, of 200, an inspection level of III, an AQL of 1.0%, an upper specification of 12.0, and sample measurements of: 10.2, 10.5, 10.7, 11.8, 9.9, 10.5, 10.6.

Answer
Accept

9–15 Using MIL-STD-414, unknown variability standard deviation method, determine whether the lot is either accepted or rejected for a lot size, *N*, of 40, an inspection level of IV, an AQL of 1.5%, a lower specification of 22, and sample measurements of: 25, 23, 34, 26, 28.

Answer
Reject

CHAPTER 10 DESIGN OF EXPERIMENTS

There are basically two methods for determining process capability, or effectiveness. The first uses control charts and capability analyses. These have already been explained in previous chapters. The second, the subject of this chapter, uses experiments in which test runs have been deliberately designed to vary critical characteristics to see what occurs. The results of these experiments are then used to determine the process's ability to make the product according to the specifications, and to assist design in determining process and product parameters.

Objectives

1. Understand the nature, concept, and philosophy of experimental design.
2. Design and conduct a two-level two-factor experiment using the one factor at a time (1FAAT) procedure. Also be able to design and conduct a two-level two-factor experiment using the factorial design procedure. Compare the two methods.
3. Design and conduct a two-level multi-factor experiment.
4. Understand the nature and use of some advanced factorial concepts and procedures: two-level fractional factorial designs, multi-level factorial designs, and the more important quantitative procedures that can be used to analyze the results of an experiment.
5. Perform an ANOVA analysis and design based on the Taguchi method.
6. Perform evolutionary operation (EVOP) procedure.

10.1 The Nature of Experimental Design

Experimental design, or design of experiments, refers to the deliberate organization of a series of tests in such a way that the desired information is obtained at the least expenditure of resources (money, materials, people, methods, etc.). Statistical procedures are essential to systematizing and controlling the experiment.

The objective of each of the individual tests in the experimental procedure is to determine what happens to the product or process when a particular input is used, or a particular amount of the input is used, or the input is varied in some way. The goal of the entire experiment is to obtain information about which combination of inputs does the best job, or to determine the effect of variation in the input variables on the performance of the process or product. In other words, the total of all the bits of information from each of the individual tests combines to provide the information needed to improve the process or product.

In order to maximize their efficiency (provide the most information at the least cost), experiments must be organized or designed (thus the term *design of experiments*). This means that the type of information needed must be carefully analyzed ahead of time. (If we don't know what we are looking for how can we know how to look for it?) The desired results (the objectives and goals) must be clearly stated. A thorough knowledge and understanding of the product and/or process is necessary. This knowledge comes from prior experience, engineering and process experts, study and training, etc. Decisions about how this information is to be used (what input factors will be used and at what levels, the objective of the experiment, etc.) should not be made lightly. Two procedures, brainstorming and cause and effect analysis, are used extensively in design of experiments to assist in these decisions. Other techniques are available.

The design of the experiments can be, and often is, more difficult than the actual running of the experiment, including calculating the results. As difficult as running the experiment and calculating the results can be, once it is learned, it is only a mechanical procedure. The design, however, can tax our ingenuity and creative energies to the fullest. Computers can be programmed to do the calculations no matter how intricate, but only a human can do the design. Improper design almost invariably leads to unusable conclusions.

Although the remaining sections of this chapter will concentrate on the operating and calculating aspects of experimental design, the critical aspect of this first step, design, cannot be emphasized enough. Also, a proper design must be made with the operational and calculational details in mind; the method of calculation and operation of the experiment will invariably affect the nature of the design. Thus, the designer must have a clear understanding of the different analysis procedures and calculations of experimental design, as well as the different types of designs and the methods for using them to initiate an experiment.

Definitions

The following terms are important in experimental design.

1. **Levels.** Usually only two or three levels are used (high, medium, or low). Actually, most experiments need only the simple two-level design. This is because most factor interactions in real life are linear in nature, that is, only two points are needed to completely define all other points on a straight line, or in a linear interaction. Three or more levels are used for effective interaction analysis when the interaction effects are suspected of being non-linear (curvilinear). When three or more levels are used, the resultant analysis can be extremely complex and difficult.
2. **Factors.** These are variables that are thought to affect the response, that is, the objective of the experiment. The identification of these variables requires prior knowledge or analysis; sometimes it requires one or more pre-tests.
3. **Response variables.** These define the way the process or product responds to the variation in the factors. They are the objectives of the experiment. In general, one of three types of responses can be generated from a design of experiments:
   a. Maximize. In this type of response, the larger the results, the better. Maximizing profits or maximizing production are examples of this type of response.
   b. Minimize. In this type of response, the smaller the results, the better. An excellent example of this type of response would be the minimization of costs.
   c. Normalize. In this type of response, the closer to a target or standard, the better. An example of this type of response would be the production of a part to an engineering specification.
4. **Treatment combination *(tc)*.** The term for a test using a particular combination of factors. There may be more than one trial run of each *tc*. This is often erroneously called an experiment. The entire group of *tc*'s is the experiment.
5. **Noise.** A term for the external factors of the product or process that affect, and obscure, the results. These are "outside" variables that either were not known at the time of the design of the experiment, were not considered important, or were considered as not part of the process or product. It is important in design of experiments that these noise factors be properly identified and their effects be minimized by the way the experiment is designed and/or run. Sometimes noise factors only interfere with the experiment and have no real effect on the product or process. At other times, the noise factors, when isolated, may provide valuable information about the problem, which can then lead

to changes in, and even a complete restructuring of, the entire experiment.

6. **Randomized tests.** The order in which the tests (*tc*'s) are conducted must be randomized to isolate and eliminate the noise effects. Some experimental design models use special procedures to accomplish this.
7. **Confounding.** This term means to mingle the factors so that the elements cannot be separated; the results of varying one factor may be mixed with another factor's results so that the answer is confounded, or erroneous. Design of experiments models frequently use this confounding principle to make the design more efficient. (Confounding is deliberately designed into the experiment to reduce the number of runs, and therefore, the costs.) Special analysis procedures are then instituted to separate the information from the errors associated with *confounding*.
8. **Orthogonal.** This term literally means *at right angles to*. If the factor equations are at right angles to each other, they are independent. An orthogonal array (Table 10.1) in experimental design is a set of tests (*tc*'s) that are independent of each other. (If the equations were to be graphed, they would appear at right angles to each other.) Independent means that the results of one combination of factors has no effect on the results of another combination.
9. **Observation.** Each individual measurement is called an observation in statistics. In experimental design, an observation is also the result of one test run.
10. **Trial or run.** The execution of a treatment combination is called a trial, or run. This is the test that was mentioned earlier. This refers to one test of one *tc*. A group of related tests, or trial runs, make up an experiment. Remember that an experiment is a set of tests and procedures designed to answer a specific question, or to solve a specific problem.
11. **Independent variables.** These are the factors that are chosen for test, that make up the variables in a *tc*. The variations in these variables are deliberately chosen for each test run; they do not vary as a result of variation in other variables (as do the dependent, or response, variables). These variables are also called controllable variables because their variations are deliberately chosen, or controlled.
12. **Dependent variables.** These are the response variables, the results of the tests, that vary as a result of variations in the independent variables. Response variables should be defined in the objectives. These are also called noncontrollable variables because they vary in accordance with the variation in the independent variable; their variations are not in the direct control of the experimenter.
13. **Factor interaction.** This refers to the effect on the response (dependent variable or problem objective) of varying two or more factors (independent variables) simultaneously. This effect is frequently more than a simple additive effect, it is often multiplicative or even exponential.

Procedures

The order of activities in an experimental design generally follows these steps:

1. **Recognize the problem.** This includes a clear definition of what the problem really is, and is not always as easy as it sounds. Careful analysis is needed at this point as the statement of the problem, along with the statement of objectives, provides a "road map" of the experimental procedures.
2. **Define the objectives.** As with all scientific endeavors, we must first define our objectives. These objectives must be:
   a. Precise, clear, and unambiguous, without extraneous words.
   b. Measurable. As a famous scientist said, if you can't measure it you don't really know what it is. It is extremely difficult, if not impossible, to compare the results to nonquantifiable data. Without this comparison, we really can't know if we have achieved our goal. There are ways to handle qualitative (nonmeasurable) data in design of experiments, but these are advanced concepts and beyond the scope of this text.
   c. Clearly related to the process or product in question. There can be a great number of quantifiable responses that may appear to be meaningful on superficial or cursory examination but which, upon careful analysis, will not relate to the problem.

   This type of objective will provide a clear standard against which to compare the result; it removes any uncertainties as to whether or not we have accomplished our goal.
3. **Choose the factors.** These are the independent, or input, variables (machines, processes, operators, materials, etc.). They must be carefully analyzed and defined. Combinations of these variables, at different levels or amounts, determine the character of the experimental results. Information about these inputs is extremely important, as improper variables and/or amounts (levels) can completely invalidate an expensive experiment.
4. **Choose the levels.** The factors previously chosen must be analyzed to determine the relevant degree of each. (How high is high, for example, and what constitutes a low measurement?) For example, a factor level can be chosen so high (or so low) that it will fall outside the area of action, that is, outside the area in which the factor can affect the response variable. The precise values are usually not too critical, as long as they are "reasonable," or not so close that important information will be missed, and not so widespread as to be impractical.
5. **Determine the response variables.** Response variables result from the actions of the independent variables, or factors. They should be defined in the statement of the problem and in the objectives.
6. **Choose a design.** A familiarity with the possible types of experimental design models is a necessity here. The actual design model chosen, along with the factors and other variables, may result from one or a combination of the following activities:

   a. Brainstorming.
   b. Cause and effect analysis.
   c. Informal group discussion and interaction.
   d. A pre-test involving a two-level two-factor experiment (Section 10.2). This is identical to a regular experiment except that the purpose is to identify the factors, levels, and design of the final problem experiment.
   e. A pre-test involving an EVOP analysis (evolutionary operation analysis).
   f. A statistical design catalog (Cochran and Cox 1957).
7. **Run the experiment** (run the various tests or treatment combinations). It is imperative that the various test runs be randomized, run in random order, so that any noise effect caused by the order in which the tests are made will be neutralized.
8. **Analyze the results.** This analysis can vary from a simple averaging procedure (as in Section 10.2) to a complex mathematical model.

Group involvement and input is almost a necessity in steps 1 through 5 just discussed. Everyone involved with the process and/or product from the design engineers, process engineers, production engineers, production supervisors, management, and quality control, to the production workers should be actively recruited and consulted for assistance and ideas.

Although these procedural steps should generally be followed in the order given, it should be noted that backtracking and changes are a frequent occurrence. Information from one step may provide insight for a previous step that may necessitate a return to the previous step for revision. The analyst must be flexible in the design and application of a design of experiments problem.

10.2 Two-Level Two-Factor Designs

If the input factors can be restricted to two levels (low and high), this is called a two-level design. The number of factors can be greater than two and the design can still be a two-level design, as long as none of the factors is evaluated at more than two levels. The levels must be specified at each end, the extremes (low and high, for example) of the area of action. They must be far enough apart to include the total area of variability (where changes in the factor will affect the response variable) but not so far that areas of non-effect are included. For example, suppose that it is known that a temperature of above 240° and below 100° will have no more effect on the part hardness (or that our furnaces cannot be effectively controlled beyond these temperatures). The area of action, then, would be between 100 and 240° and the levels would be specified at 240° for high and 100° for low.

In this section, the 1FAAT method will be presented using a two-factor two-level example only (the simplest of all experiments), and then the same example will be used for the factorial design method for comparison. The factorial, especially the fractional factorial, is perhaps the simplest means of overcoming the weaknesses of the 1FAAT method. The fractional factorial does not apply to 2^2 designs (two-level two-factor designs).

1FAAT

The simplest approach to design of experiments is to vary one factor at a time, while holding all others constant. This is called the one factor at a time design (1FAAT). This method, however, has two flaws. First, it takes a long time and many runs to obtain the results. Second, and much more important, it can seldom identify the factor interactions correctly (a combination of factors, such as time and temperature, that must occur together to maximize the effect of either). In the 1FAAT procedure, several trials of each *tc* must be run to obtain an average with which to use the statistical procedures (a minimum of four per *tc* is recommended). The factorial does not have this limitation; it can use one trial only for each *tc*, although replications are often done, especially when advanced analysis procedures are needed (such as ANOVA). Special procedures are used in factorials to obtain the averages needed.

Example 10.1 A certain part is to be tested for hardness. The steps in the problem solution are:

1. **Problem.** Variable hardness in the part.
2. **Objective.** Determine the controllable variables that affect the hardness and the extent of their effect.
3. **Factors.** Time (t) and temperature (T).
4. **Levels.**

Factor	Low	High
Time	20 sec.	40 sec.
Temperature	150°	200°

5. **Response variable.** Hardness.
6. **Choose a design.** Vary one factor at a time (1FAAT) and measure the resulting hardness. Three tests (*tc*'s) are required, one for the base combination where no variations are made and one each for varying the two factors. This type of design also needs at least four replications for each of the treatment combinations (*tc*'s) to average out chance variations. The possible treatment combinations (*tc*'s) are as follows:
   a. t_L and T_L—base combination
   b. t_L and T_H—increase the temperature
   c. t_H and T_L—increase the time
7. **Run.** The results of each trial run are shown in the following table.

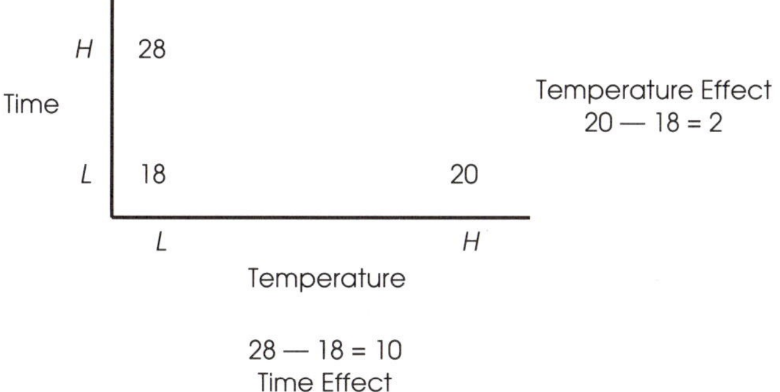

Figure 10.1. Graph of the results of Example 10.1.

Treatment	Trial 1	Trial 2	Trial 3	Trial 4	Average
t_L and T_L	17	19	16	20	18
t_L and T_H	19	21	22	18	20
t_H and T_L	27	28	28	29	28

8. **Analyze the results.** Low time (t_L) and low temperature (T_L) are used as a base from which the other three are compared.
   a. The increase in hardness as a result of increasing temperature is $20 - 18 = 2$.
   b. The increase in hardness as a result of increasing time is $28 - 18 = 10$.

Note that both factors have an effect on the hardness with time having the greatest effect. There appears to be some interaction effect from varying both time and temperature together, but the degree of interaction cannot be determined from this model.

Figure 10.1 shows a graph of the results of Example 10.1. A three factor experiment would be much more difficult to graph, as three dimensions would be required (a three-dimensional cube would be needed to illustrate such a graph). Obviously, four or more factors are impossible to graph. It is for this reason that these types of graphs are never actually used in real life experiments. They are used here only as an instructional tool.

Full Factorial Designs

It should be obvious from an examination of Example 10.1 and Figure 10.1 that an important treatment combination was missed. This is the combination where both factors are increased at the same time (t_H and T_H). In a full factorial design, all possible treatment combinations are examined. Therefore, a full factorial design for Example 10.1

would use four *tc*'s. The number of *tc*'s in a full factorial is determined by the following formula:

$$n_{tc} = L^F$$

where

n_{tc} = the number of treatment combinations

L = the number of levels

F = the number of factors

For Example 10.1, the calculations are:

$$n_{tc} = 2^2 = 4$$

If four repetitions (extra runs of the same *tc*) are desired, the total number of trial runs for a full factorial design for Example 10.1 would be $4 \times 4 = 16$. For the 1FAAT method of Example 10.1, the number of trials was 12 ($3 \times 4 = 12$). A full factorial then can be more expensive if it requires the same number of repetitions as the 1FAAT procedure does. Fortunately, the full factorial can utilize a special procedure not available to the 1FAAT method to reduce this need for repetitions. This procedure uses the results of other *tc*'s at the same level in place of some of the repetitions. In Figure 10.1, the averages at the high level for time (28 and 38) are averaged to get the average effect of time on the hardness. Since each of these figures is an average itself (of four repetitions) this means that the average of 33 for t_H is actually an average of eight trials rather than four. Therefore, four of the trials are unnecessary (for the full factorial). This means that only eight total trial runs are needed for the factorial to get the same degree of statistical certainty as was achieved for the 1FAAT with 12 trials. However, even if the factorial did require as many trials as the 1FAAT, it would still be worth it because of the extra and more correct response data achieved.

Advantages of the factorial over the 1FAAT method are:

1. Reduced costs due to a reduced number of trial runs needed.
2. More correct response information.
3. Interaction information.

Example 10.2 and Figure 10.2 illustrate these concepts.

Example 10.2 A certain part is to be tested for hardness. The steps in the problem solution are as follows (compare to Example 10.1):

1. **Problem.** Variable hardness in the part.
2. **Objective.** Determine the controllable variables that affect the hardness and the extent of their effect.

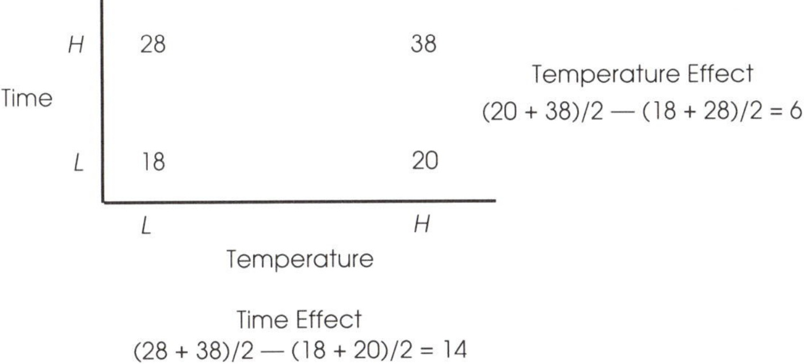

Figure 10.2. Graph of the results of Example 10.2.

3. **Factors.** Time (t) and temperature (T).
4. **Levels.**

Factor	Low	High
Time	20 sec.	40 sec.
Temperature	150°	200°

5. **Response variable.** Hardness.
6. **Choose a design.** Use a full factorial design and measure the resulting hardness. Four tests (*tc*'s) are required, one for the base combination where no variations are made, one each for varying the two factors, and a fourth for increasing both factors at once. When used with only two factors, this type of design also needs at least two replications for each of the treatment combinations (*tc*'s) to average out chance variations (the 1FAAT method needed four replications). The possible treatment combinations (*tc*'s) are as follows:
   a. t_L and T_L—base combination
   b. t_L and T_H—increase the temperature
   c. t_H and T_L—increase the time
   d. t_H and T_H—increase both time and temperature
7. **Run.** The results of each trial run are shown in the table below.

Treatment	Trial 1	Trial 2	Trial 3	Trial 4	Average
t_L and T_L	17	19	16	20	18
t_L and T_H	19	21	22	18	20
t_H and T_L	27	28	28	29	28
t_H and T_H	37	39	36	40	38

8. **Analyze the results.** Low time (t_L) and low temperature (T_L) are used as a base from which the other three are compared. The new base for temperature is the average of the two T_L's, $(18+28)/2=23$. The new base for time is the average of the two t_L's, $(18+20)/2=19$. The new

average hardness for the T_H's is $(20+38)/2=29$. Finally, the new average hardness for the t_H's is $(28+38)/2=33$.

a. The increase in hardness as a result of increasing temperature is:

$$(20+38)/2-(18+28)/2=6$$

b. The increase in hardness as a result of increasing time is:

$$(28+38)/2-(18+20)/2=14$$

c. The increase in hardness due to increasing both time and temperature, the interaction effect, is:

$$14+6=20$$

In comparing these results to the 1FAAT conclusions of Example 10.1, note that both factors still have an effect on the hardness, but the total effect on hardness is somewhat greater than the 1FAAT procedure had indicated. The interaction effect suspected from the 1FAAT experiment is now confirmed. The interaction effect of increasing both time and temperature is quite substantial. Obviously, the 1FAAT method had given some erroneous conclusions.

Although in retrospect this interaction may seem obvious (it takes time for temperature to affect the molecular structure changes that lead to increased hardness), many factors may have obscured this relationship. We should never assume that we or someone else "should have seen" the answer before the experiment was run just because it appears to be obvious afterward.

10.3 Two-Level Multi-Factor Factorial Designs

Although most processes and/or products can usually be analyzed using only two levels (due to the linear relationships usually present), such is certainly not the case with the factors. Most processes and/or products will usually be affected by many more than just two factors. It is not unusual for as many as 10 or more factors to be present in any one process, for instance. The problem is that as the number of factors is increased, the number of possible treatment combinations increases exponentially, which in turn can increase the cost of the experiment exponentially. The number of treatment combinations for two levels and 10 factors, for instance, is $2^{10}=1{,}024$. For five factors, the number of *tc*'s is $2^5=32$.

In addition to the definitions and procedures already presented, there are several other formalities used in the factorial, all concerned with the way the *tc*'s and factors are tabled for control and analysis purposes. These are as follows (see Table 10.1):

1. Label each factor with a capital letter, starting at *A*. For instance, time might be labeled *A*, temperature *B*, and pressure *C*.

Table 10.1 Orthogonal, Design, Table for Example 10.3

Treatment	tc Identifiers	A	B	C	Random Order	Hardness
t_L, T_L, P_L	1	−	−	−	2	18
t_H, T_L, P_L	*a*	+	−	−	3	28
t_L, T_H, P_L	*b*	−	+	−	6	22
t_H, T_H, P_L	*ab*	+	+	−	7	44
t_L, T_L, P_H	c	−	−	+	1	22
t_H, T_L, P_H	*ac*	+	−	+	5	26
t_L, T_H, P_H	*bc*	−	+	+	8	42
t_H, T_H, P_H	*abc*	+	+	+	4	38

Note 1: The random order assumes that the replications of each *tc* will be run successively. The replications can, of course, be randomized also.

Note 2: The hardness column is an average of the replications of each *tc*.

2. Label each treatment combination (*tc*) with lower case letters that correspond to the factor or factors being varied (that is, being varied from the base condition). For example, if pressure is being varied and pressure is labeled *C*, the *tc* would be labeled *c*. If both pressure and time were being varied together, the *tc* could be labeled *ac*. These labels serve as identifiers for each *tc* and uniquely describe each run so that the results will not get scrambled and confused by the randomization procedure. These labels are called *identifiers* in factorial design.
3. Use a special symbol for each level, such as a minus (−) for low level and a plus (+) for high level (other symbols can also be used here such as 1 and 2, 0 and 1, or −1 and +1). Now arrange these symbols and the factor and *tc* labels in a table according to the *Yates order*. In a Yates order, the pluses and minuses are alternated in the first column, alternated by twos in the second column, alternated by fours in the third column, by eights in the fourth, etc.

Randomization

In order to minimize the effects of any outside "noise" variables, the *tc*'s and replications must be run in random order. The best way to accomplish this is to number each *tc* and each replication of each *tc* in order and then randomize the numbers with a random order table (or use a calculator to generate the random numbers).

Interaction Effects

Possible interactions are identified by multiplying the signs. For example, an *AC* interaction is possible if both *A* and *C* are at their low levels $(- \times - = +)$, or if both are at their high levels $(+ \times + = +)$. If one is at its low level and the other is at its high level, the differences will result from the single effect of varying only one factor. Multiple effects above two interactions are much more complex, but are still calculated by using the simple multiplication of signs procedure. This in-

Table 10.2. Interaction Analysis Table for Example 10.3

tc Identifiers	A	B	C	AB	AC	BC	ABC	Hardness
1	−	−	−	+	+	+	−	18
a	+	−	−	−	−	+	+	28
b	−	+	−	−	+	−	+	22
ab	+	+	−	+	−	−	−	44
c	−	−	+	+	−	−	+	22
ac	+	−	+	−	+	−	−	26
bc	−	+	+	−	−	+	−	42
abc	+	+	+	+	+	+	+	38
Response	3	13	4	1	−8	3	−5	

teraction coding is not needed when setting up the experiment (Table 10.1), but only when analyzing the results (Table 10.2). A + sign in an interaction column does not mean that there *has* to be an interaction at that point, but only that there *may* be one. In two-level three-factor experiments, the interaction columns are not strictly necessary for analysis. In higher order experiments, they are.

Example 10.3 A certain part is to be tested for hardness. The steps in the problem solution are (compare to Examples 10.1 and 10.2):

1. **Problem.** Variable hardness in the part.
2. **Objective.** Determine the controllable variables that affect the hardness and the extent of their effect.
3. **Factors.** Time $(t) = A$, temperature $(T) = B$, and pressure $(P) = C$.
4. **Levels.** High and low, for all three factors.

Factor	Low	High
Time	20 sec.	40 sec.
Temperature	150°	200°
Pressure	200 PSI	300 PSI

5. **Response Variable.** Hardness.
6. **Choose a design.** Use a full factorial design and measure the resulting hardness. Eight tests (*tc*'s) are required, one for the base combination where no variations are made, one each for varying the three factors, and four for the four types of possible interactions. This type of design, strictly speaking, does not need replications (because four results can be used for calculating each combination). However, most practitioners do use some form of replication for most experiments. The possible treatment combinations (*tc*'s) are as follows:
   a. t_L, T_L, P_L—base combination
   b. t_L, T_L, P_H—increase the pressure only

c. t_L, T_H, P_L—increase the temperature only
d. t_H, T_L, P_L—increase the time only
e. t_H, T_H, P_L—increase both the time and temperature
f. t_H, T_L, P_H—increase both pressure and time
g. t_L, T_H, P_H—increase both temperature and pressure
h. t_H, T_H, P_H—increase all three

7. **Run.** The results of each trial run are shown in Table 10.1. This is the *design* table, that is, the table needed for designing the experiment and directing the application. Table 10.2 is the *analysis* table, that is, the table used for determining the results of the experiment. In essence, Table 10.2 consists of Table 10.1 with the interaction columns added to it. These new columns are constructed by multiplying the signs together algebraically. When unlike signs are multiplied together, the result is a negative (−). When like signs are multiplied together, the result is a plus (+). Relationships are then determined by averaging the results of similar signs.
8. **Analyze the results.**
   a. Factor analysis. Subtract the factor effect (the average of the hardness for each *tc* with that factor in the identifiers) from the base effect (average of those without that factor in the identifiers). For example, for the factor time (column *A*), subtract the average hardness for all minuses (−'s) in the column from the average hardness for all pluses (+'s) in the column.

$$(28+44+26+38)/4-(18+22+22+42)/4=3.0$$

   This is the increase in hardness as a result of varying time, the time response effect. The response effects of the other factors (columns *B* and *C*), and the factor interactions (columns *AB*, *AC*, etc.), are calculated in exactly the same way. These response effects are presented at the bottom of Table 10.2. Note that all three factors have a positive effect on hardness (increasing any one of these factors by itself will increase hardness), but that temperature affects it the most, and pressure hardly at all. Also note that the *AB* and *BC* interactions also have a positive effect on hardness, but that the *AC* and *ABC* interactions have negative effects. (Increasing these factors together will decrease hardness.)
   b. Graphical analysis. The interactions can also be graphed in a special way that provides better insight into their interacting effects on the response variable, hardness. The calculations are as follows (using the *A*/*C* interaction as an example). The results are shown in Figures 10.3 and 10.4. Since the interaction effects of Table 10.2 and Figure 10.3 are so difficult to analyze, the interaction graphs of Figure 10.4 are used to summarize and simplify these interactions. (1) Low *A* and low *C* (−, −). Find the two rows on Table 10.2 where both the *A* and the *C* columns are negative. The average of these two values is the hardness interaction for *A* and *C* when both are low. $(18+22)/2=20$. (2) Low *A* and high *C* (−, +). Find the two rows on Table 10.2 where the *A* column is − and the *C* column is +. The average

of these two values is the hardness interaction for A and C when A is low and C is high. $(22+42)/2=32$. (3) High A and low $C(+,-)$. Find the two rows on Table 10.2 where the A column is + and the C column is −. The average of these two values is the hardness interaction for A and C when A is low and C is high. $(28+44)/2=36$. (4) High A and high C $(+,+)$. Find the two rows on Table 10.2 where the A column is + and the C column is +. The average of these two values is the hardness interaction for A and C when A is low and C is high. $(26+38)/2=32$.

10.4 Advanced Factorial Concepts

As has already been stated, the number of treatment combinations (*tc*'s) increases as the number of factors increase. This is also true of the number of interactions. The number of *tc*'s can be calculated by the following formula:

$$n_{tc}=L^k$$

The number of interactions can be calculated by the following formula:

$$C^k_i$$

where

n_{tc} = the number of treatment combinations

L = the number of levels

k = the number of total factors in the problem

i = the number of factors in the interaction

C = the combination of k things taken i at a time

Fractional Factorials

It is rare for more than two factors to interact. The probability of them doing so is very low, and the probability of the interaction being significant if it does occur is very low. Therefore, combinations of more than two factors usually do not need to be run, saving a lot of time and cost in the experiment without materially affecting the results (without sacrificing much information).

In an eight-factor experiment, for example, there are only 36 one- and two-factor combinations (eight one-factor and 28 two-factor), with only 36 treatment combinations required to cover these 36 factor combinations. These 36 *tc*'s, and often less, will usually provide most or all of the essential information. The remainder of the *tc*'s (220 of them) can then be eliminated from the experiment without materially affecting the results. Therefore, only a fraction of the experiment needs to be run to obtain most of the information available (thus, *fractional* factorial). Ta-

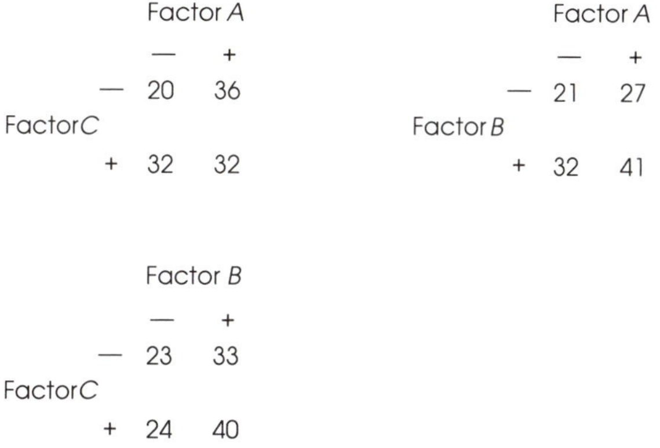

		Factor A —	Factor A +
Factor C	—	20	36
	+	32	32

		Factor A —	Factor A +
Factor B	—	21	27
	+	32	41

		Factor B —	Factor B +
Factor C	—	23	33
	+	24	40

Figure 10.3. Interaction values for Example 10.3.

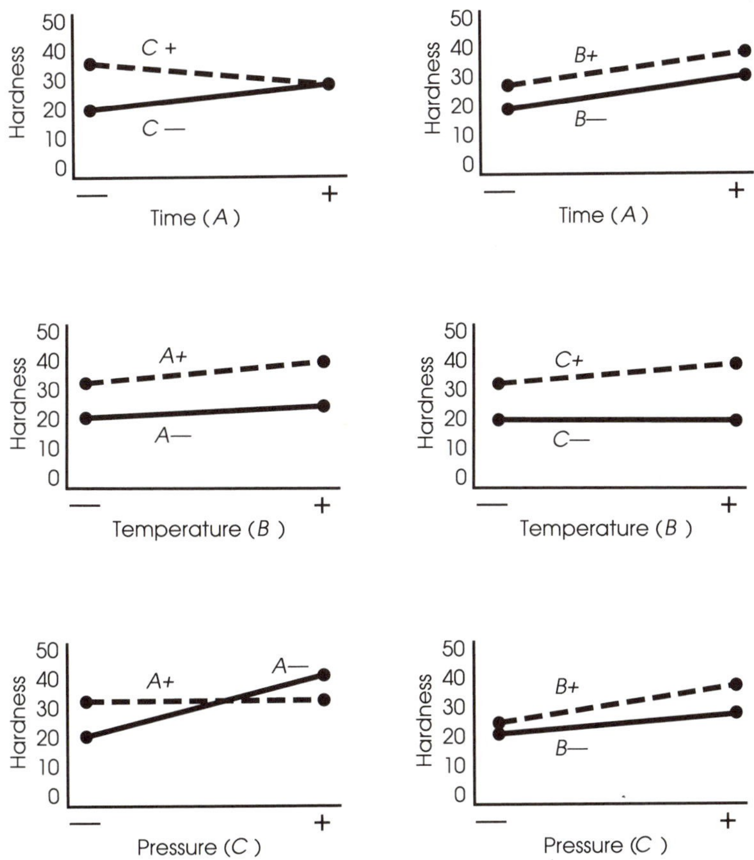

Figure 10.4. Interaction graphs for Example 10.3.

Table 10.3. Two-Level Factorial Combinations

Number of Factors k	Number of *tc*'s 2^k	Single-Factor Treatments	Two-Factor Combinations (C_i^n)
3	8	3	3
4	16	4	6
5	32	5	10
6	64	6	15
7	128	7	21
8	256	8	28
9	512	9	36
10	1,024	10	45

ble 10.3 presents the total number of *tc*'s, the number of single-factor treatments, and the number of two-factor combinations for 3 through 10 factors. In general, only the sum of the single-factor treatments and the two-factor combinations need to be run. In actual practice, however, there are ways to reduce even this relatively small amount of *tc*'s, especially when a large number of factors are present. The smallest number of *tc*'s that can be run in a fractional factorial is eight.

The final set of combinations run must equal a power of 2 (or 3 if three levels are used). If the 36 combinations mentioned for the eight-factor experiment were to be chosen, further adjustment must be made (36 is not a power of 2). The best way to do this is to eliminate four of the two-factor combinations (32 is a power of 2). It is at this point that the analyst's preknowledge of the process becomes very important. The process characteristics may suggest which combinations are unlikely; these combinations, then, will make excellent candidates for elimination.

The key to fractional factorial experimentation is in the choice of the proper combinations to eliminate. In actual practice, some of the complex combinations are run deliberately to facilitate the analysis. The results of one combination can be subtracted from another to get the single factor or double factor effect. A single complex combination can sometimes be used more than once in this way, and so take the place of several less complex combinations. This is the way that the *tc*'s are reduced to an absolute minimum in fractional factorial experiments. The choice of which to run is determined by a set of mathematical rules called *confounding rules*. When more than one factor is changed at a time, the effect caused by a single factor change is mixed or "confounded" in the results.

Procedures for confounding and fractionalizing experiments with more than five factors are complex and beyond the scope of this text.

The purpose of this section is to acquaint the reader with the concept and nature of fractional factorial experiments, not to develop an expertise in their use. This would require at least another full text (see Barker 1985 or Hicks 1973 or Montgomery 1976).

Multi-Level Multi-Factor Designs

Two-level designs (high and low) are restricted to linear relationships. Three levels (low, medium, and high), or more, can show curvilinear relationships (quadratic, cubic, etc.). An interaction, for instance, may peak in the middle and then go back down, or up, to its original level. A linear measurement would completely miss this relationship. Figure 10.5 shows a comparison of a two- and three-level factor. If the averaging technique is used, the two-level comparison would show an average of about 30, while the three levels show an actual hardness of closer to 45. In this case, the two-level analysis is completely inadequate. This is one reason why the relevant factors and levels must be clearly identified before the experiment is run.

Multi-level experiments are much more complex, but the theory is basically the same as in two-level experiments. A two-level experiment is frequently run to isolate the interacting factors; then a three-level (or more) experiment is run on just the isolated interacting factors for closer analysis. If handled properly, this two-step procedure can save a lot of money and still identify almost as much information. This two-step procedure illustrates what is known as the *25% rule* in experimental design. You should spend only 25% of your total available resources at the first part of your experiment, so that there will be enough time and money to complete the work to meet the problem objectives as originally defined.

Once again, the actual procedures for effecting a multi-level experimental design are beyond the scope of this book. This discussion is presented only as an introduction to the concepts. For a more exhaustive treatment of this subject see the texts by Barker (1985), Hicks (1973), Box et al. (1978), or Montgomery (1976).

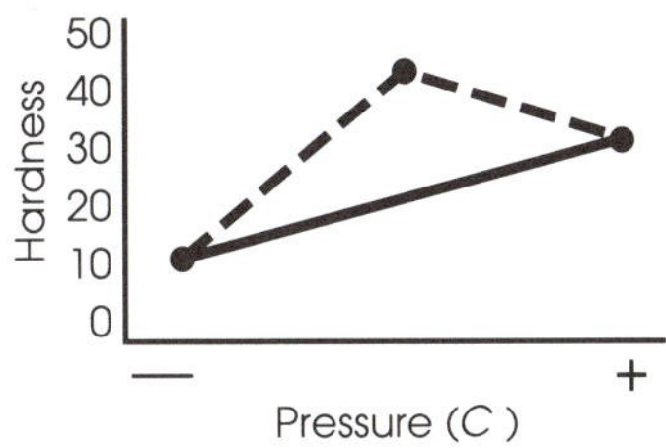

Figure 10.5. Interaction graphs for two and three levels.

Advanced Quantitative Analysis

Experimental results can be analyzed by many means, some of them so advanced and technical that a computer is required for the calculations. Fortunately, most experiments can be analyzed using one or two fairly simple techniques. The main analysis models for experimental design are:

1. **Simple average.** This technique has already been explained in Sections 10.2 and 10.3.
2. **Hypothesis testing.** In this model, an assumption is made about one or more inputs in relation to the response variable, after which calculations are made to determine the probability that this assumption is correct. If the calculated probability is less than a predetermined, desired probability, the hypothesis is rejected. For example, an hypothesis might be made that increases in time and temperature will cause the part hardness to increase. All experiments must use this procedure, either formally or assumed. In actual practice, most experimental analyses only assume the hypothesis; no actual formal statement of the hypothesis is presented. Such will be the case in this text.
3. ***t* tests.** This procedure uses the student's *t* distribution to analyze simple dichotomies (yes or no, good or bad, etc.) where only two populations or variables are compared at a time. For more than two, the ANOVA or least squares is needed (or some other, usually complex, procedure can be used).
4. **ANOVA** (ANalysis Of VAriance). This is a special technique to determine if the variation in the test results are large enough to be "statistically significant." If so, the factors being analyzed can be considered to be affecting the response variable (factors *A* and *B* do increase part hardness, for example). ANOVA techniques require at least two repetitions for each *tc* (four are better). The number of repetitions actually used in the experiment depends primarily on cost and is a management decision. If the experimental procedures are expensive (test costs are high), the number of repetitions is likely to be low. If test costs are low and the product is very important, the number of repetitions is likely to be higher. The more repetitions, the more confident we can be that the average information actually represents reality. The ANOVA is used extensively with the Taguchi method. (A modified Taguchi method is presented in Section 10.5.)
5. **Yates algorithm.** This is a special ANOVA technique that uses the Yates order (see Section 10.3) for its analysis. The actual Yates order is not often used in regular ANOVA—special experimental designs are used instead. The Yates algorithm can be used when no repetitions are used in the experiment (for four *tc*'s, for example, only four tests are made, one for each *tc*).
6. **Least squares.** In graphical analysis, least squares is used to fit a line to a series of points on the graph. This line, then, shows the relationship of two variables to each other. This is called linear regression. Least squares can be used to analyze more than two variables, of course, but

this cannot be charted on a graph. Actually, least squares is the base technique from which most other analysis procedures have been developed. Hypothesis, *t*, ANOVA, and Yates algorithm are special applications of least squares analysis.

10.5 The Taguchi Method

One of the most used experimental design models today is the Taguchi procedure, which is a modified fractional factorial model usually using ANOVA analysis procedures. The actual design of a Taguchi model is somewhat involved, but fortunately, generalized models from the method are available. It has been found that these catalogued models are able to cover most of the problems that arise in today's industry. The three smallest and most used of the two-level models are given in Figure 10.6. (Three-level arrays usually use 1, 2, and 3 or 0, 1, and 2 for low, medium, and high.)

The ANOVA concept is to compute the variance within each level (called the *noise*) and compare to the variance between each level (called the *signal*). The variance within each level (the noise) is then divided by the variance between each level (the signal) to get the *signal to noise* (*S/N*) ratio. If this *S/N* ratio exceeds that which is expected by

L_4

1	2	3
−	−	−
−	+	+
+	−	+
+	+	−

L_8

1	2	3	4	5	6	7
−	−	−	−	−	−	−
−	−	−	+	+	+	+
−	+	+	−	−	+	+
−	+	+	+	+	−	−
+	−	+	−	+	−	+
+	−	+	+	−	+	−
+	+	−	−	+	+	−
+	+	−	+	−	−	+

L_{12}

1	2	3	4	5	6	7	8	9	10	11
−	−	−	−	−	−	−	−	−	−	−
−	−	−	−	−	+	+	+	+	+	+
−	−	+	+	+	−	−	−	+	+	+
−	+	−	+	+	−	+	+	−	−	+
−	+	+	−	+	+	−	+	−	+	−
−	+	+	+	−	+	+	−	+	−	−
+	−	+	+	−	−	+	+	−	+	−
+	−	+	−	+	+	+	−	−	−	+
+	−	−	+	+	+	−	+	+	−	−
+	+	+	−	−	−	−	+	+	−	+
+	+	−	+	−	+	−	−	−	+	+
+	+	−	−	+	−	+	−	+	+	−

Figure 10.6. Generalized two-level orthogonal arrays.

chance alone (shown in the *F* table), then the levels are assumed to be different. (It is assumed that a change in the levels really does affect hardness, for example.) The maximum *S/N* ratio that can be expected by chance alone (for a particular α value) is shown in the appendix, Table A7 (the *F* table). This table is entered by dividing the degrees of freedom in the numerator of the *S/N* ratio calculation (df_1) by the degrees of freedom in the denominator (df_2). The procedure will be explained in conjunction with Example 10.4.

Examples 10.4 and 10.5 show *screening* type procedures. The main purpose of screening models is to more clearly identify the critical factors and factor levels. However, it has been found that Taguchi type screening models are adequate to analyze and solve most industrial problems. (Some think as much as 90% or more.) In the few cases where screening models are inadequate, the more advanced procedures can be used (see your friendly statistician). Example 10.4 will be analyzed using the more complex ANOVA model to illustrate the procedure. In Example 10.5, only the simpler averaging technique will be used, with suggestions on how to analyze the results with simple logic (the so-called "common" sense that at least one famous writer has called "uncommon" sense).

Example 10.4 Solve Example 10.3 (determine the effect of time, temperature, and pressure on part hardness) using an L8 array and ANOVA analysis, and assuming two repetitions per *tc* and an α of 0.05 (or a level of confidence of 95%). The L8 array is used because it provides room to analyze for factor interactions. Table 10.4 presents the data in array form. The measurements (observation or response variable or hardness) in the table are often coded (usually by subtracting an arbitrary constant and/or dividing by a constant) for ease of computation, especially if the numbers are large. In Table 10.4, for example, the measurements for hardness could have been coded by subtracting a

Table 10.4. Data Array for Example 10.4

tc Identifiers	A	B	AB	C	AC	BC	ABC	Hardness Trial 1	Trial 2
1	−	−	−	−	−	−	−	17	19
c	−	−	−	+	+	+	+	20	24
b	−	+	+	−	−	+	+	19	25
bc	−	+	+	+	+	−	−	37	47
a	+	−	+	−	+	−	+	27	29
ac	+	−	+	+	−	+	−	25	27
ab	+	+	−	−	+	+	−	42	46
abc	+	+	−	+	−	−	+	35	41

Table 10.5. ANOVA Analysis for Example 10.4 (Table 10.4)

Condition	SS	*df*	*MS*	*S/N*	F_{TABLE}
Time (*A*)	256	1	256	18.96	5.32
Temperature (*B*)	676	1	676	50.07	5.32
Pressure (*C*)	64	1	64	4.74	5.32
AB Interaction	4	1	4	0.30	5.32
AC Interaction	256	1	256	18.96	5.32
BC Interaction	36	1	36	2.67	5.32
ABC Interaction	100	1	100	7.41	5.32
Error	108	8	13.5	—	—
Total	1,500	15	—	—	—

rough mean (say 30) from each hardness measurement. Subsequent calculations would not be affected by this coding.

Solution

Table 10.5 gives the results of the ANOVA calculations. Note that the array of Table 10.4 does not match that of Table 10.2 for the full factorial analysis. This is due to the special nature of the Taguchi method. Each of the figures in this table will now be explained.

1. Sum of squares (*SS*) for time (factor *A*), temperature (factor *B*), pressure (factor *C*), and *AB*, *AC*, *BC*, and *ABC* interactions. These sums of squares are all calculated the same way. Simply add the responses for all the minuses in the column and subtract from the sum of all the plus responses, square, and divide by the sample size (the total number of trials). For factor *A*, this is:

$$SS_A = [(27+29+25+27+42+46+35+41)$$
$$-(17+19+20+24+19+25+37+47)]^2/16 = 256$$

2. Sum of squares (*SS*) for error. This is the difference between the total sum of squares and all the other sums of squares shown (and listed in #1):

$$SS_e = 1{,}500 - [256+676+64+4+256+36+100]$$
$$= 108$$

3. Total sum of squares. The total is (the *X*'s are the sixteen hardness results of the trials):

$$SS_T = \Sigma X^2 - (\Sigma X)^2/n$$
$$= 15{,}900 - 480^2/16 = 1{,}500$$

4. Degrees of freedom (*df*) for factors *A*, *B*, and *C*, and interactions *AB*, *AC*, *BC*, and *ABC* is the number of replications (trial runs) for the treat-

ment combination minus one. Since each of these combinations had two trial runs, the degrees of freedom *(df)* for each is $2-1=1$.

5. Degrees of freedom (*df*) for error is determined by the following formula:

$$2^n(r-1)=2^3(2-1)=8(1)=8$$

6. Total degrees of freedom *(df)* is computed by the following formula:

$$r(2^n)-1=2(2^3)-1=2(8)-1=15$$

The total for all combination *df*'s and the error *df* must equal the total *df*.

7. The mean square (*MS*) is another name for the variance. The variance is calculated by *SS*/*df*. For factor *A:*

$$MS_A=SS_A/df_A=256/1=256$$

8. The signal to noise ratio (*S*/*N*) is also called the calculated *F*. These values are calculated by dividing the *MS* of the factor by the *MS* of the error. For factor *A:*

$$S/N_A=MS_A/MS_e=256/13.5=18.96$$

9. The tabled *F* value is found in Table A7. The table is entered by using the two *df*'s of the *S*/*N* ratio. Find the column headed with the *df* of the numerator (the *S* or signal of the *S*/*N* ratio, the *df* of the factor being evaluated) and the row identified with the *df* of the denominator (the error or noise *df*, the *N* of the *S*/*N* ratio). For factor *A*, enter the table at column 1 (1 *df*) and move down the column to the eighth row to find the *F* value of 5.32. Note that this *F* value is the same for all factors of this problem.

Table 10.5 is interpreted as follows:

Whenever the *S*/*N* value is greater than the *F* value from the table, the factor is considered significant at the 0.05 level. In other words, there is a 95% probability that the factor actually does affect the response variable. In Table 10.5, note that factors *A* and *B*, and interactions *AC* and *ABC* all have *S*/*N* ratios greater than their *F* values; therefore, they are considered to affect part hardness. However, the effect can be negative or positive. This can be determined quite easily by graphing the factor interactions, as in Figure 10.4. In fact, the graphs in Figure 10.4 correctly represent the interaction effects from Example 10.4 (as well as Example 10.3), as the treatment combinations in each case have identical responses (the average hardnesses are the same in each case).

Example 10.5 A certain chemical process has seven input factors: A, B, C, D, E, F, and G. Run an L8 experiment to determine the proper treatment combination to maximize percent yield.

Table 10.6. Data Array for Example 10.5

tc Identifiers	A	B	C	D	E	F	G	% Yield
1	−	−	−	−	−	−	−	51
defg	−	−	−	+	+	+	+	53
bcfg	−	+	+	−	−	+	+	43
bcde	−	+	+	+	+	−	−	70
aceg	+	−	+	−	+	−	+	65
acdf	+	−	+	+	−	+	−	62
abef	+	+	−	−	+	+	−	71
abdg	+	+	−	+	−	−	+	46
Response	6.75	−0.25	4.75	0.25	14.25	−0.75	−6.25	

Solution

According to the response at the bottom of each column, factors *A*, *C*, and *E* all increase yield at the high level. Therefore, if the treatment combination includes these three factors at the high levels and the rest at the low, the resulting yield should be 76.75% ($51+6.75+4.75+14.75=76.75\%$). If this yield had been in the 90s, or if this is about the maximum that can be expected from this type of process (due to theoretical considerations), no more testing or analysis would be needed. Otherwise, further experimentation and/or higher level analysis (such as ANOVA) is indicated. Perhaps different input factors can be considered. Or a three-level experiment may indicate higher yields at interim (medium) levels. Of course, testing and product cost considerations would certainly limit the amount and type of experimentation that would be practical. This simple averaging type analysis may be all that is needed to make final product and process design decisions. In fact, this type of simple analysis is usually all that is needed in most experiments (perhaps 90% or more). However, it should be noted that this type of simple averaging analysis is always subject to measurement error. The only way that the error effect can be separated from the factor effect is by an ANOVA analysis (or some other advanced analysis technique). An ANOVA analysis, however, needs at least two replications of each treatment combination (*tc*) for a difference (variance) to be able to be computed. Also, for a seven-factor analysis, an L128 array would be needed to test for all possible interactions. Notice that this screening experiment has identified only three factors for probable effects on the response. A second, more complete, experiment (using an L8 array and ANOVA for interaction analysis) can now be run, with replications, using these three factors only.

10.6 Evolutionary Operation

Evolutionary operation (EVOP) is a simplified experimental design technique for simple systems where not too many (only 2 or 3) variables are present. The number of treatments (experiments) are minimized by running a series of individual experiments where the variable level for each successive trial is suggested by the results of the previous run. The succession of experiments ends when no more improvements can be made, when all possible experiments suggested by the previous trial result in a decrease in the objectives. The procedure will be explained in conjunction with an example.

Example 10.6 The variables affecting a certain plastic product are temperature, pressure, and time. The temperature can vary from 100 to 200° F while the time of operation can vary from 0 to 100 sec. Beyond these limits undesirable effects are known to occur. Although the pressure can theoretically vary from 150 to 300 lbs., previous experience and certain process characteristics suggest that the optimum pressure be 200 psi. An initial experiment has been run with a temperature of 130° F and at a time of 80 sec. The yield was found to be 13%. The objective is to find the combination of time and temperature that produces the best yield.

Solution

1. Draw a chart for graphing the succession of results (Figure 10.7). In this example, the chart increments have been chosen at 10 points (10° F and 10 sec.) because this type of process has suggested that a 10 point division allows significant changes without too much chance of moving too far beyond the optimum point at any one time.
2. The first trial is entered as a point at 80° F and 130 lbs., and with the trial results (13%) written alongside.
3. Draw an imaginary square at + and −10 points around this initial point. The corners of this square identify four possible experiments to be run. If none of these experiments results in a higher yield, the initial run is the best combination of variables that can produce the best yield. If one or more is higher, choose the highest and continue the procedure. In the example, the four new experiments identified by the procedure are: 90 sec. at 140°, 90 sec. at 120°, 70 sec. at 140°, and 70 sec. at 120°. The results of these experiments are shown on the graph. Notice that the two at the elevated temperatures have both increased the yield while those at the decreased time are split between an increased yield and a decreased yield. This already suggests that temperature is more important than time in our process.
4. Draw an arrow between the initial experiment and the one with the highest yield.
5. Draw another imaginary box around the point with the highest yield

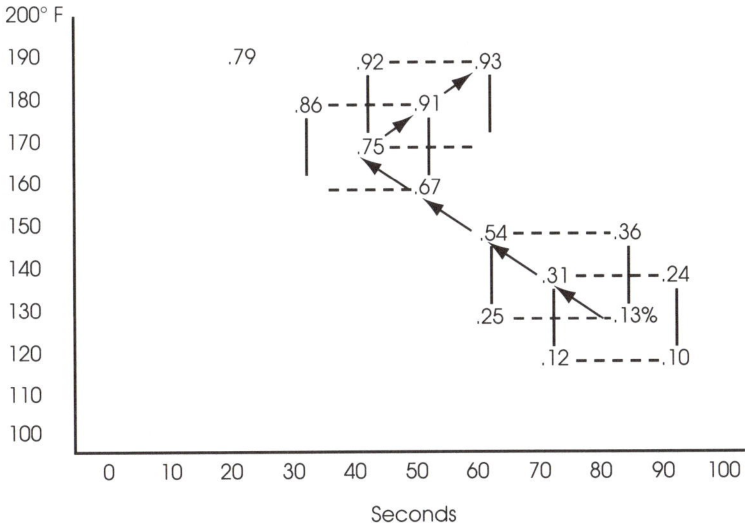

Figure 10.7. EVOP chart for Example 10.6.

(140° and 70 sec.) and repeat step 3. This time only three new experiments are identified because one of the corners of the new box is the initial experiment (which has, of course, already been run). Actually only two of these three need to be run (60 sec. at 150° and 80 sec. at 150°) as the results so far have clearly shown that decreasing the temperature decreases the yield. The results are shown on the graph.

6. Draw another arrow to the new high point. Note that a trend has now developed (the arrows all point in the same direction). From now on only one new experiment needs to be run at each new step (in the direction of the arrow) until the results show a decrease in yield. In our example, this finally occurs at 30 sec. and 180°.
7. When the trend finally results in a decrease in yield, retreat to the previous experiment and move in a different direction. Since increased temperature appears to be more important in our experiment, we will run the one higher temperature experiment remaining (50 sec. at 180°). This results in another increase in yield, from 86% to 91%.
8. Draw a new imaginary box around this new high point (50 sec. at 180°). Three new experiments are now identified. Once again, however, one of the three is at a lower temperature and is not likely to result in increased yields. The remaining two were run with both showing increases (to 92% and 93%). Note that the increase in the yields has now become quite small, only 2% at this point. It is highly unlikely that any further changes in the variables will have much of an effect on the yields.
9. Management must now make a decision as to whether or not to continue the tests. This decision should be based on a comparison between the costs of testing and the likely operating cost savings. If the decision is to continue, the procedure would be continued as before until no further

increase in yield results, or until the temperature and/or time limitations are reached. Even at this point it might be possible to further increase the yields by decreasing the chart increments (say from 10 points to five) and continue testing around this optimum point. This is called fine-tuning the variables. If the decision is made to stop at the 93% point, another management decision is indicated from the chart. Note that there is only a 1% difference in the yields between an experiment run at 60 sec. and 190° and one run at 40 sec. It could be possible that the 20 sec. time savings will more than offset the savings resulting from the increased yield.

In this example above, the pressure was kept constant at 200 psi. If the pressure is allowed to vary with the time and temperature, the procedure gets somewhat more complicated. One of the two following methods can be used:

1. Use a three-dimensional model for the graph. A physical three-dimensional model would be difficult to construct and use, although not impossible. A computer simulation would be much more feasible and much easier to use.
2. Assume an optimum point for one of the variables and then test the other two as was done in the example. When the optimum is reached with these two variables, choose one of them at this optimum point, hold it constant, and test the other two. Continue to do this until some acceptable result is reached. For example, in Example 10.6 a 93% yield was achieved without having to test the effects of varying the pressure. If the optimum results of testing the time and temperature had been only 60%, it would then pay to hold one of these variables constant (probably time at 40 sec.) and test the other two. If this still did not result in an acceptable yield, another series of experiments would have had to be run for time and pressure. At this point, of course, it might be more cost-effective to run a fractional factorial design.

APPENDIX

REVIEW OF ALGEBRA

A thorough knowledge of the following rules, definitions, and algebraic manipulations is necessary for a proper understanding of this text.

Rules

1. To add two numbers with like signs (both positive or both negative) add their absolute values and prefix their common sign:

$$-4 + (-6) = -10 \qquad \text{or} \qquad +4 + 6 = +10$$

2. To add two numbers with unlike signs, subtract the smaller absolute value from the larger one and prefix the sign of the numerically larger number. If the numbers are numerically equal, their sum is zero:

$$\begin{array}{r} -10 \\ +\ 5 \\ \hline -\ 5 \end{array} \qquad \begin{array}{r} +11 \\ -10 \\ \hline +\ 1 \end{array}$$

3. To subtract one number from another change the sign of the number subtracted and then add:

$$6 - (-5) = 6 + 5 = 11$$

$$6 - (+5) = 6 - 5 = 1$$

4. The product and the quotient of two numbers with like signs are positive; of two numbers with unlike signs, negative:

$$4 \times (-6) = -24 \qquad -24/+6 = -4$$
$$-4 \times (-6) = +24 \qquad -24/-6 = +4$$

5. The value of a number is unchanged when 0 is added to it or subtracted from it:

$$6 + 0 = 6$$
$$6 - 0 = 6$$

6. The product of any number and zero is always zero:

$$6 \times 0 = 0$$

7. The quotient obtained by dividing zero by any number is zero:

$$0/6 = 0$$

8. It is impossible to divide any number by zero:

$$6/0 = \text{undefined}$$

9. The sum of two or more algebraic terms is not changed by changing their order:

$$X + Y = Y + X$$

10. The sum of any group of algebraic terms is the same, however they are grouped:

$$x + y + z = (x + y) + z = x + (y + z)$$

11. The sum of the products of one term by each of several other terms is the product of this term by the sum of the others:

$$AB + AC + AD = A(B + C + D)$$

12. When parentheses preceded by a minus sign are removed, the signs of all terms which had been inside are changed:

$$4 - (x + y) = 4 - x - y$$
$$4 - (x - y) = 4 - x + y$$

13. The product of two or more factors is not changed by changing their order.

$$2 \times 3 = 3 \times 2 \qquad AB = BA$$

14. The product of three or more factors is not changed by grouping them in different ways:

$$(AB)C = A(BC) = B(AC)$$

15. Laws of exponents:

$$A^m A^n = A^{m+n} \qquad \frac{A^m}{A^n} = A^{m-n}$$

16. Identities:

$$A(B+C)=AB+AC$$
$$(A+B)^2=A^2+2AB+B^2$$
$$(A-B)^2=A^2-2AB+B^2$$
$$(A-B)(A+B)=A^2-B^2$$

17. The sign before a fraction is changed when the sign of either the numerator or the denominator is changed:

$$\frac{-6}{7} = -\frac{6}{7} = \frac{6}{-7} = -\frac{-6}{-7}$$

18. The sign before a fraction is changed when the sign of a factor of either the numerator or the denominator is changed:

$$+\frac{-6(7)}{8} = -\frac{-6(-7)}{8}$$

19. The product of two or more simple fractions is the product of the numerators divided by the product of the denominators.

$$\frac{A}{1} \times \frac{B}{C} \times \frac{D}{E} \times \frac{F}{G} = \frac{ABDF}{CEG}$$

20. To divide one fraction by another multiply the first one by the reciprocal of the second.

$$\frac{A}{B} \div \frac{C}{D} = \frac{A}{B} \times \frac{D}{C} = \frac{AD}{BC}$$

21. If $\log_a b = d$, then $b = a^d$:

$$\log_{10} 100 = 2 \quad or \quad \log_{10} 10^2 = 2 \quad or \quad 100 = 10^2$$

Definitions

1. $$A^0 = 1;\ A \neq 0$$

2. $$A^{-k} = 1/A^k$$

3. $$A^{1/n} = \sqrt[n]{A}$$

4. $$A^{p/q} = (\sqrt[q]{A})^p = \sqrt[q]{A^p}$$

5. $$\sqrt[n]{A^{kn}} = A^{kn/n} = A^k$$

6. $$\sqrt[n]{AB} = \sqrt[n]{A}\sqrt[n]{B}$$

7. $$\frac{\sqrt[n]{A}}{\sqrt[n]{B}} = \sqrt[n]{\frac{A}{B}}$$

8. $$\sqrt[3]{\sqrt[n]{A}} = \sqrt[n]{\sqrt[3]{A}} = \sqrt[3n]{A}$$

Problems

1. Simplify the symbols by grouping and combining like terms.

   a. $(x + 3y - z) - (2y - x + 3z) + (4z - 3x + 2y)$

   Answer: $-x + 3y$

   b. $3(x^2 - 2yz + y^2) - 4(x^2 - y^2 - 3yz) + x^2 + y^2$

   Answer: $6yz + 8y^2$

   c. $3x + 4y + 3[x - 2(y - x) - y]$

   Answer: $12x - 5y$

   d. $3 - 2x - [-(x + y)] + [x - 2y]$

   Answer: $3 - y$

2. *Find the products:*

   a. $2xy(3x^2y - 4y^3)$

   Answer: $6x^3y^2 - 8xy^4$

   b. $3x^2y^3(2xy - x - 2y)$

   Answer: $6x^3y^4 - 3x^3y^3 - 6x^2y^4$

   c. $(3a + 5b)(3a - 5b)$

   Answer: $9a^2 - 25b^2$

   d. $(5xy + 4)(5xy - 4)$

   Answer: $25x^2y^2 - 16$

   e. $(2 - 5y^2)(2 + 5y^2)$

   Answer: $4 - 25y^4$

   f. $(2x + 1)^3$

   Answer: $8x^3 + 12x^2 + 6x + 1$

3. *Factor:*

   a. $3x^2y^4 + 6x^3y^3$

   Answer: $3x^2y^3(y + 2x)$

   b. $12s^2t^2 - 6s^5t^4 + 4s^4t$

   Answer: $2s^2t(6t - 3s^3t^3 + 2s^2)$

   c. $64x - x^3$

   Answer: $x(8 + x)(8 - x)$

   d. $18x^3y - 8xy^3$

   Answer: $2xy(3x + 2y)(3x - 2y)$

   e. $2z^3 + 10z^2 - 28z$

   Answer: $2z(z + 7)(z - 2)$

   f. $2s^4t - 4s^3t^2 - 6s^2t^3$

   Answer: $2s^2t(s - 3t)(s + t)$

4. *Factor and reduce:*

a.
$$\frac{24x^3y^2}{18xy^3}$$

Answer: $\frac{4x^2}{3y}$

b.
$$\frac{36xy^4z^2}{-15x^4y^3z}$$

Answer: $\frac{-12zy}{5x^3}$

c.
$$\frac{5a^2 - 10ab}{a - 2b}$$

Answer: $5a$

d.
$$\frac{4x^2 - 16}{x^2 - 2x}$$

Answer: $\frac{4(x + 2)}{x}$

e.
$$\frac{3a^2}{4b^3}\left(\frac{2b^4}{9a^3}\right)$$

Answer: $\frac{b}{6a}$

f.
$$\frac{3x}{8y} \div \frac{9x}{16y}$$

Answer: $\frac{2}{3}$

g.
$$\frac{24x^3y^2}{5z^2} \div \frac{8x^2y^3}{15z^4}$$

Answer: $\frac{9xz^2}{y}$

h.
$$\frac{2x}{3} - \frac{x}{2}$$

Answer: $\frac{x}{6}$

i.
$$\frac{4}{3x} - \frac{5}{4x}$$

Answer: $\frac{1}{12x}$

5. *Evaluate:*

a. $(-2x)^3$

Answer: $-8x^3$

b. $\left(\frac{3y}{4}\right)^3$

Answer: $\frac{27y^3}{64}$

c. 4^{-3}

Answer: $\frac{1}{64}$

d. $(-4x)^{-2}$

Answer: $\frac{1}{16x^2}$

e. $(2y^{-1})^{-1}$

Answer: $\frac{y}{2}$

f. $\frac{3^{-1}x^2y^{-4}}{2^{-2}x^{-3}y^3}$

Answer: $\frac{4x^5}{3y^7}$

g. $(16)^{1/4}$

Answer: 2

h. $(-a^3b^3)^{-2/3}$

Answer: $\frac{1}{a^2b^2}$

i. $(10^3)^0$

Answer: 1

j. $3y^{2/3}(y^{4/3})$

Answer: $3y^2$

k. $\frac{1}{\sqrt[3]{8x}}(6)$

Answer: $\frac{3}{x^{1/3}}$

6. *Solve the following exponents:*

a. $a^p(a^q)$

Answer: a^{p+q}

b. $a^3(a^5)$

Answer: a^8

c. $3^4(3^5)$

Answer: 3^9

d. $a^{n+1}(a^{n-2})$

Answer: a^{2n-1}

e. $[4(10^{-6})]\,[2(10^4)]$

Answer: $8(10^{-2}) = 0.08$

f. $\dfrac{a^p}{a^q}$

Answer: a^{p-q}

g. $\dfrac{a^5}{a^3}$

Answer: a^2

h. $(ab)^p$

Answer: $a^p b^p$

i. $(2a)^4$

Answer: $2^4 a^4 = 16a^4$

j. $\left(\dfrac{a}{b}\right)^p$

Answer: $\dfrac{a^p}{b^p}$

k. $\left(\dfrac{2}{3}\right)^4$

Answer: $\dfrac{2^4}{3^4} = \dfrac{16}{81}$

l. $\sqrt[3]{\dfrac{8x^{3n}}{27y^6}}$

Answer: $\dfrac{2x^n}{3y^2}$

m.

$$\left(\frac{a^{1/3}}{x^{1/3}}\right)^{3/2}$$

Answer: $\frac{a^{1/2}}{x^{1/2}} = \frac{\sqrt{a}}{\sqrt{x}} = \sqrt{\frac{a}{x}}$

7. *Solve the following equations.*

a.

$$3x - 2 = 7$$

Answer: $x = 3$

b.

$$y + 3(y - 4) = 4$$

Answer: $y = 4$

c.

$$4x - 3 = 5 - 2x$$

Answer: $x = 4/3$

d.

$$\frac{2t - 9}{3} = \frac{3t + 4}{2}$$

Answer: $t = -6$

e.

$$x^2 - 40 = 9$$

Answer: $x = \pm 7$

f.

$$x^2 - 6 = x$$

Answer: $x = +3, -2$

g.

$$x^2 - 7x = -12$$

Answer: $x = 3, 4$

h.

$$x^2 + x = 6$$

Answer: $x = 2, -3$

i.

$$x^2 = 5x + 24$$

Answer: $x = 8, -3$

j.

$$9x^2 = 9x - 2$$

Answer: $x = 1/3, 2/3$

8. *Solve by quadratic formula:* $x = \frac{-b \pm \sqrt{b^2 - 4ac}}{2a}$

a.

$$x^2 - 5x = 6$$

Answer: $x = 6, -1$

b. $$x^2 - 6 = x$$

Answer: 3, −2

c. $$3x^2 - 2x = 8$$

Answer: $x = 2, -4/3$

9. *Express each as an algebraic sum of logarithms:*

a. $$\log_b UVW$$

Answer: $\log_b U + \log_b V + \log_b W$

b. $$\log_b \frac{UV}{W}$$

Answer: $\log_b U + \log_b V - \log_b W$

c. $$\log_b \frac{XYZ}{PQ}$$

Answer: $\log_b X + \log_b Y + \log_b Z - (\log_b P + \log_b Q)$

d. $$\log_b \frac{U^2}{V^3}$$

Answer: $2 \log_b U - 3 \log_b V$

e. $$\log_b \frac{U^2 V^3}{W^4}$$

Answer: $2 \log_b U + 3 \log_b V - 4 \log_b W$

f. $$\log_e \frac{\sqrt{x^3}}{\sqrt[4]{y^3}}$$

Answer: $\frac{3}{2} \log_e X - \frac{3}{4} \log_e Y$ *or* $\frac{3}{2} \ln X - \frac{3}{4} \ln Y$

10. *Graph*

a. $$y = x - 2$$

Answer:

x	y
0	−2
1	−1
2	0
−1	−3
−2	−4

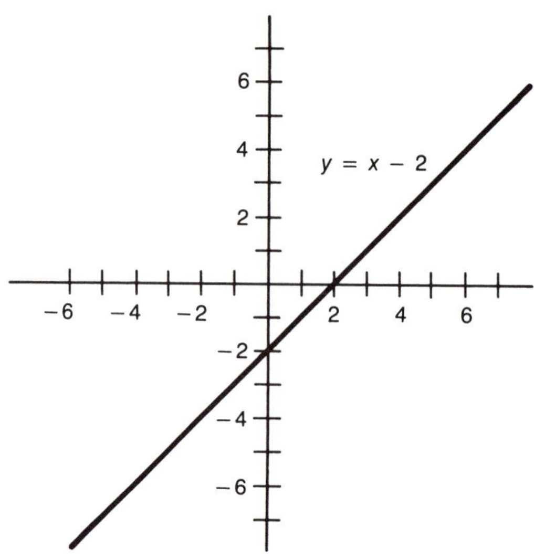

b. $y = 2x - 3$

Answer:

x	y
0	−3
1	−1
2	1
−1	−5

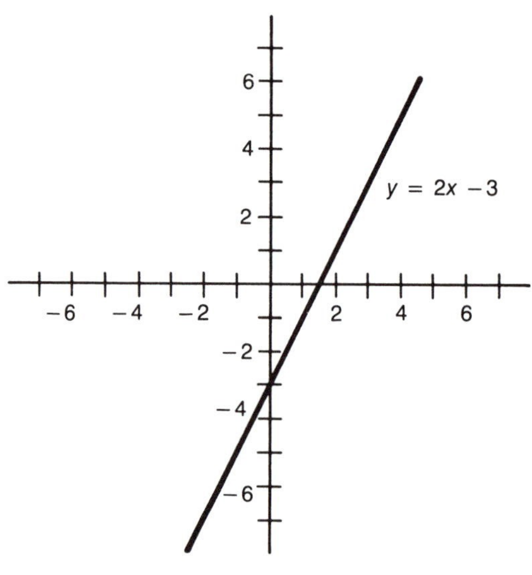

c. $y = 2x^2 - 2$

Answer:

x	y
0	−2
1	0
2	6
−1	0
−2	6

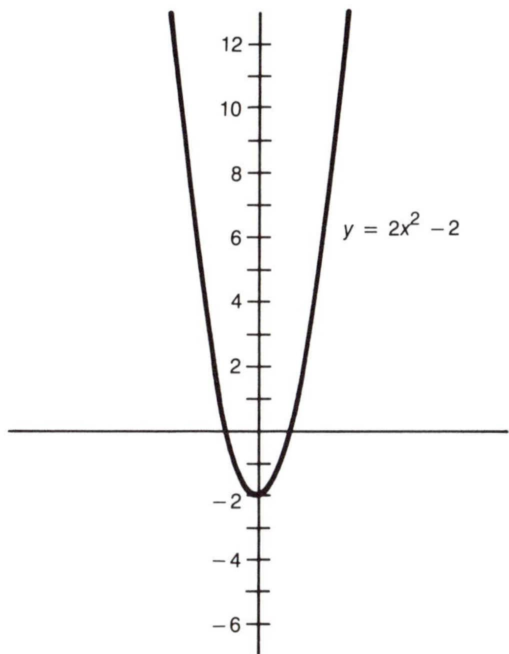

Linear Interpolation

The first step in linear interpolation is to determine the known and unknown values. A ratio equation is then set up and solved for the unknown value, say c, as follows:

$$a/b = c/d, \quad \text{so}$$

$$c = ad/b$$

a, b, c, and d represent the differences between the numbers shown in the tables. The Z tables will be used to illustrate.

Example 1 Find Z for a P of 0.20.

Solution

$$a = 0.1977 - 0.2000 = -0.0023$$

$$b = 0.1977 - 0.2005 = -0.0028$$

$$c = \text{Unknown}$$

$$d = -0.85 - (-0.84) = -0.01$$

$$c = ad/b = -0.0023(-0.01)/-0.0028 = -0.0082$$

$$Z = -0.85 - (-0.0082) = -0.8418$$

a, b →	0.1977	−0.85 ← c, d
a →	0.2000	? ← c
b →	0.2005	−0.84 ← d

Example 2 Find P for a Z of 1.264.

Solution

$$a = 1.26 - 1.264 = -0.004$$

$$b = 1.26 - 1.27 = -0.010$$

$$c = \text{Unknown}$$

$$d = 0.8962 - 0.8980 = -0.0018$$

$$c = ad/b = -0.004(-0.018)/-0.010 = -0.0072$$

$$P = 0.8962 - (-0.0072) = 0.889 \text{ or } 88.9\%$$

a, b →	1.260	0.8962 ← c, d
a →	1.264	? ← c
b →	1.270	0.8960 ← d

Table A1a Areas Under the Normal Curve

(Proportion of Total Area Under the Curve From $-\infty$ to Designated Z Value)

Z	0.09	0.08	0.07	0.06	0.05	0.04	0.03	0.02	0.01	0.00
−3.5	0.00017	0.00017	0.00018	0.00019	0.00019	0.00020	0.00021	0.00022	0.00022	0.00023
−3.4	0.00024	0.00025	0.00026	0.00027	0.00028	0.00029	0.00030	0.00031	0.00033	0.00034
−3.3	0.00035	0.00036	0.00038	0.00039	0.00040	0.00042	0.00043	0.00045	0.00047	0.00048
−3.2	0.00050	0.00052	0.00054	0.00056	0.00058	0.00060	0.00062	0.00064	0.00066	0.00069
−3.1	0.00071	0.00074	0.00076	0.00079	0.00082	0.00085	0.00087	0.00090	0.00094	0.00097
−3.0	0.00100	0.00104	0.00107	0.00111	0.00114	0.00118	0.00122	0.00126	0.00131	0.00135
−2.9	0.0014	0.0014	0.0015	0.0015	0.0016	0.0016	0.0017	0.0017	0.0018	0.0019
−2.8	0.0019	0.0020	0.0021	0.0021	0.0022	0.0023	0.0023	0.0024	0.0025	0.0026
−2.7	0.0026	0.0027	0.0028	0.0029	0.0030	0.0031	0.0032	0.0033	0.0034	0.0035
−2.6	0.0036	0.0037	0.0038	0.0039	0.0040	0.0041	0.0043	0.0044	0.0045	0.0047
−2.5	0.0048	0.0049	0.0051	0.0052	0.0054	0.0055	0.0057	0.0059	0.0060	0.0062
−2.4	0.0064	0.0066	0.0068	0.0069	0.0071	0.0073	0.0075	0.0078	0.0080	0.0082
−2.3	0.0084	0.0087	0.0089	0.0091	0.0094	0.0096	0.0099	0.0102	0.0104	0.0107
−2.2	0.0110	0.0113	0.0116	0.0119	0.0122	0.0125	0.0129	0.0132	0.0136	0.0139
−2.1	0.0143	0.0146	0.0150	0.0154	0.0158	0.0162	0.0166	0.0170	0.0174	0.0179
−2.0	0.0183	0.0188	0.0192	0.0197	0.0202	0.0207	0.0212	0.0217	0.0222	0.0228
−1.9	0.0233	0.0239	0.0244	0.0250	0.0256	0.0262	0.0268	0.0274	0.0281	0.0287
−1.8	0.0294	0.0301	0.0307	0.0314	0.0322	0.0329	0.0336	0.0344	0.0351	0.0359
−1.7	0.0367	0.0375	0.0384	0.0392	0.0401	0.0409	0.0418	0.0427	0.0436	0.0446
−1.6	0.0455	0.0465	0.0475	0.0485	0.0495	0.0505	0.0516	0.0526	0.0537	0.0548
−1.5	0.0559	0.0571	0.0582	0.0594	0.0606	0.0618	0.0630	0.0643	0.0655	0.0668
−1.4	0.0681	0.0694	0.0708	0.0721	0.0735	0.0749	0.0764	0.0778	0.0793	0.0808
−1.3	0.0823	0.0838	0.0853	0.0869	0.0885	0.0901	0.0918	0.0934	0.0951	0.0968
−1.2	0.0985	0.1003	0.1020	0.1038	0.1057	0.1075	0.1093	0.1112	0.1131	0.1151
−1.1	0.1170	0.1190	0.1210	0.1230	0.1251	0.1271	0.1292	0.1314	0.1335	0.1357
−1.0	0.1379	0.1401	0.1423	0.1446	0.1469	0.1492	0.1515	0.1539	0.1562	0.1587
−0.9	0.1611	0.1635	0.1660	0.1685	0.1711	0.1736	0.1762	0.1788	0.1814	0.1841
−0.8	0.1867	0.1894	0.1922	0.1949	0.1977	0.2005	0.2033	0.2061	0.2090	0.2119
−0.7	0.2148	0.2177	0.2207	0.2236	0.2266	0.2297	0.2327	0.2358	0.2389	0.2420
−0.6	0.2451	0.2483	0.2514	0.2546	0.2578	0.2611	0.2643	0.2676	0.2709	0.2743
−0.5	0.2776	0.2810	0.2843	0.2877	0.2912	0.2946	0.2981	0.3015	0.3050	0.3085
−0.4	0.3121	0.3156	0.3192	0.3228	0.3264	0.3300	0.3336	0.3372	0.3409	0.3446
−0.3	0.3483	0.3520	0.3557	0.3594	0.3632	0.3669	0.3707	0.3745	0.3783	0.3821
−0.2	0.3859	0.3897	0.3936	0.3974	0.4013	0.4052	0.4090	0.4129	0.4168	0.4207
−0.1	0.4247	0.4286	0.4325	0.4364	0.4404	0.4443	0.4483	0.4522	0.4562	0.4602
−0.0	0.4641	0.4681	0.4721	0.4761	0.4801	0.4840	0.4880	0.4920	0.4960	0.5000

(Continued)

Table A1a Areas Under the Normal Curve (*Continued*)

Z	0.00	0.01	0.02	0.03	0.04	0.05	0.06	0.07	0.08	0.09
+0.0	0.5000	0.5040	0.5080	0.5120	0.5160	0.5199	0.5239	0.5279	0.5319	0.5359
+0.1	0.5398	0.5438	0.5478	0.5517	0.5557	0.5596	0.5636	0.5675	0.5714	0.5753
+0.2	0.5793	0.5832	0.5871	0.5910	0.5948	0.5987	0.6026	0.6064	0.6103	0.6141
+0.3	0.6179	0.6217	0.6255	0.6293	0.6331	0.6368	0.6406	0.6443	0.6480	0.6517
+0.4	0.6554	0.6591	0.6628	0.6664	0.6700	0.6736	0.6772	0.6808	0.6844	0.6879
+0.5	0.6915	0.6950	0.6985	0.7019	0.7054	0.7088	0.7123	0.7157	0.7190	0.7224
+0.6	0.7257	0.7291	0.7324	0.7357	0.7389	0.7422	0.7454	0.7486	0.7517	0.7549
+0.7	0.7580	0.7611	0.7642	0.7673	0.7704	0.7734	0.7764	0.7794	0.7823	0.7852
+0.8	0.7881	0.7910	0.7939	0.7967	0.7995	0.8023	0.8051	0.8079	0.8106	0.8133
+0.9	0.8159	0.8186	0.8212	0.8238	0.8264	0.8289	0.8315	0.8340	0.8365	0.8389
+1.0	0.8413	0.8438	0.8461	0.8485	0.8508	0.8531	0.8554	0.8577	0.8599	0.8621
+1.1	0.8643	0.8665	0.8686	0.8708	0.8729	0.8749	0.8770	0.8790	0.8810	0.8830
+1.2	0.8849	0.8869	0.8888	0.8907	0.8925	0.8944	0.8962	0.8980	0.8997	0.9015
+1.3	0.9032	0.9049	0.9066	0.9082	0.9099	0.9115	0.9131	0.9147	0.9162	0.9177
+1.4	0.9192	0.9207	0.9222	0.9236	0.9251	0.9265	0.9279	0.9292	0.9306	0.9319
+1.5	0.9332	0.9345	0.9357	0.9370	0.9382	0.9394	0.9406	0.9418	0.9429	0.9441
+1.6	0.9452	0.9463	0.9474	0.9484	0.9495	0.9505	0.9515	0.9525	0.9535	0.9545
+1.7	0.9554	0.9564	0.9573	0.9582	0.9591	0.9599	0.9608	0.9616	0.9625	0.9633
+1.8	0.9641	0.9649	0.9656	0.9664	0.9671	0.9678	0.9686	0.9693	0.9699	0.9706
+1.9	0.9713	0.9719	0.9726	0.9732	0.9738	0.9744	0.9750	0.9756	0.9761	0.9767
+2.0	0.9773	0.9778	0.9783	0.9788	0.9793	0.9798	0.9803	0.9808	0.9812	0.9817
+2.1	0.9821	0.9826	0.9830	0.9834	0.9838	0.9842	0.9846	0.9850	0.9854	0.9857
+2.2	0.9861	0.9864	0.9868	0.9871	0.9875	0.9878	0.9881	0.9884	0.9887	0.9890
+2.3	0.9893	0.9896	0.9898	0.9901	0.9904	0.9906	0.9909	0.9911	0.9913	0.9916
+2.4	0.9918	0.9920	0.9922	0.9925	0.9927	0.9929	0.9931	0.9932	0.9934	0.9936
+2.5	0.9938	0.9940	0.9941	0.9943	0.9945	0.9946	0.9948	0.9949	0.9951	0.9952
+2.6	0.9953	0.9955	0.9956	0.9957	0.9959	0.9960	0.9961	0.9962	0.9963	0.9964
+2.7	0.9965	0.9966	0.9967	0.9968	0.9969	0.9970	0.9971	0.9972	0.9973	0.9974
+2.8	0.9974	0.9975	0.9976	0.9977	0.9977	0.9978	0.9979	0.9979	0.9980	0.9981
+2.9	0.9981	0.9982	0.9983	0.9983	0.9984	0.9984	0.9985	0.9985	0.9986	0.9986
+3.0	0.99865	0.99869	0.99874	0.99878	0.99882	0.99886	0.99889	0.99893	0.99896	0.99900
+3.1	0.99903	0.99906	0.99910	0.99913	0.99915	0.99918	0.99921	0.99924	0.99926	0.99929
+3.2	0.99931	0.99934	0.99936	0.99938	0.99940	0.99942	0.99944	0.99946	0.99948	0.99950
+3.3	0.99952	0.99953	0.99955	0.99957	0.99958	0.99960	0.99961	0.99962	0.99964	0.99965
+3.4	0.99966	0.99967	0.99969	0.99970	0.99971	0.99972	0.99973	0.99974	0.99975	0.99976
+3.5	0.99977	0.99978	0.99978	0.99979	0.99980	0.99981	0.99981	0.99982	0.99983	0.99983

$z = (x_i - \mu)/\sigma$

$P_s = P(z \leq z_i)$

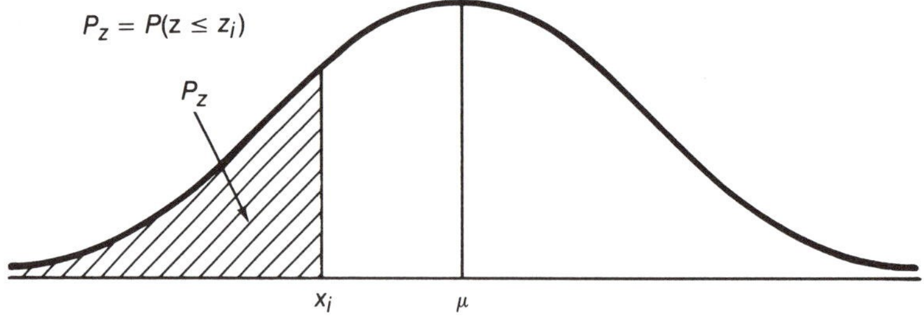

Table A1b Areas Under the Normal Curve, 3.50 to 5.99

Z		0.00	0.01	0.02	0.03	0.04	0.05	0.06	0.07	0.08	0.09
3.5	0.0^3	233	224	216	208	200	193	185	178	172	165
3.6		159	153	147	142	136	131	126	121	117	112
3.7		108	104	0996	0957	0920	0884	0850	0816	0784	0753
3.8	0.0^4	723	695	667	641	615	591	567	544	522	501
3.9		481	461	443	425	407	391	375	359	345	330
4.0		317	304	291	279	267	256	245	235	225	215
4.1		207	198	189	181	174	166	159	152	146	139
4.2		133	128	122	117	112	107	102	0977	0934	0893
4.3	0.0^5	854	816	780	746	712	681	650	621	593	566
4.4		541	517	494	471	450	429	410	391	373	356
4.5		340	324	309	295	281	268	256	244	232	222
4.6		211	201	192	183	174	166	158	151	143	137
4.7		130	124	118	112	107	102	0968	0921	0876	0834
4.8	0.0^6	793	755	718	683	649	617	587	558	530	504
4.9		479	455	433	411	391	371	352	335	318	302
5.0		287	272	258	245	233	221	210	199	189	179
5.1		170	161	153	145	137	130	123	117	111	105
5.2	0.0^7	996	944	895	848	803	751	720	682	646	612
5.3		579	548	519	491	465	440	416	394	372	352
5.4		353	315	298	282	266	252	238	225	213	201
5.5		190	179	170	160	151	143	135	127	120	114
5.6		107	101	0955	0901	0850	0802	0757	0714	0673	0635
5.7	0.0^8	599	565	533	502	473	446	421	396	374	352
5.8		332	312	294	277	261	246	231	218	205	193
5.9		182	171	161	151	143	134	126	119	112	105

0.0^3 means 0.000; 0.0^7 means 0.0000000; etc.

Examples:

$P_z = P_{4.45} = 0.00000450$ (Area under the *right* tail)

$P_z = P_{-4.45} = 0.00000450$ (Area under the *left* tail)

$P_z = P_{-3.62} = 0.000147$ (Area under the *left* tail)

$P_z = P_{3.62} = 0.000147$ (Area under the *right* tail)

$P_z = P_{5.21} = 0.0000000417$ (Area under the *right* tail)

Use A − (minus) *Z* for a left-handed area. Negative *Z*'s give area in the left tails. Positive *Z*'s give area in the right tail.

Table A2 Summation of Terms of Poisson's Exponential Binomial Limit[a]

(1,000 × Probability of c or Less Occurrences of Event That Has Average Number of Occurrences Equal to np or λT)

np / λT \ d (or) c	0	1	2	3	4	5	6	7	8	9
0.02	980	1,000								
0.04	961	999	1,000							
0.06	942	998	1,000							
0.08	923	997	1,000							
0.10	905	995	1,000							
0.15	861	990	999	1,000						
0.20	819	982	999	1,000						
0.25	779	974	998	1,000						
0.30	741	963	996	1,000						
0.35	705	951	994	1,000						
0.40	670	938	992	999	1,000					
0.45	638	925	989	999	1,000					
0.50	607	910	986	998	1,000					
0.55	577	894	982	998	1,000					
0.60	549	878	977	997	1,000					
0.65	522	861	972	996	999	1,000				
0.70	497	844	966	994	999	1,000				
0.75	472	827	959	993	999	1,000				
0.80	449	809	953	991	999	1,000				
0.85	427	791	945	989	998	1,000				
0.90	407	772	937	987	998	1,000				
0.95	387	754	929	984	997	1,000				
1.00	368	736	920	981	996	999	1,000			
1.1	333	699	900	974	995	999	1,000			
1.2	301	663	879	966	992	998	1,000			
1.3	273	627	857	957	989	998	1,000			
1.4	247	592	833	946	986	997	999	1,000		
1.5	223	558	809	934	981	996	999	1,000		
1.6	202	525	783	921	976	994	999	1,000		
1.7	183	493	757	907	970	992	998	1,000		
1.8	165	463	731	891	964	990	997	999	1,000	
1.9	150	434	704	875	956	987	997	999	1,000	
2.0	135	406	677	857	947	983	995	999	1,000	

(Continued)

Table A2 Summation of Terms of Poisson's Exponential Binomial Limit (*Continued*)

d (or) c / np / λT	0	1	2	3	4	5	6	7	8	9
2.2	111	355	623	819	928	975	993	998	1,000	
2.4	091	308	570	779	904	964	988	997	999	1,000
2.6	074	267	518	736	877	951	983	995	999	1,000
2.8	061	231	469	692	848	935	976	992	998	999
3.0	050	199	423	647	815	916	966	988	996	999
3.2	041	171	380	603	781	895	955	983	994	998
3.4	033	147	340	558	744	871	942	977	992	997
3.6	027	126	303	515	706	844	927	969	988	996
3.8	022	107	269	473	668	816	909	960	984	994
4.0	018	092	238	433	629	785	889	949	979	992
4.2	015	078	210	395	590	753	867	936	972	989
4.4	012	066	185	359	551	720	844	921	964	985
4.6	010	056	163	326	513	686	818	905	955	980
4.8	008	048	143	294	476	651	791	887	944	975
5.0	007	040	125	265	440	616	762	867	932	968
5.2	006	034	109	238	406	581	732	845	918	960
5.4	005	029	095	213	373	546	702	822	903	951
5.6	004	024	082	191	342	512	670	797	886	941
5.8	003	021	072	170	313	478	638	771	867	929
6.0	002	017	062	151	285	446	606	744	847	916

	10	11	12	13	14	15	16
2.8	1,000						
3.0	1,000						
3.2	1,000						
3.4	999	1,000					
3.6	999	1,000					
3.8	998	999	1,000				
4.0	997	999	1,000				
4.2	996	999	1,000				
4.4	994	998	999	1,000			
4.6	992	997	999	1,000			
4.8	990	996	999	1,000			
5.0	986	995	998	999	1,000		
5.2	982	993	997	999	1,000		
5.4	977	990	996	999	1,000		
5.6	972	988	995	998	999	1,000	
5.8	965	984	993	997	999	1,000	
6.0	957	980	991	996	999	999	1,000

(*Continued*)

Table A2 Summation of Terms of Poisson's Exponential Binomial Limit (*Continued*)

np / λT \ *d* (or) *c*	0	1	2	3	4	5	6	7	8	9
6.2	002	015	054	134	259	414	574	716	826	902
6.4	002	012	046	119	235	384	542	687	803	886
6.6	001	010	040	105	213	355	511	658	780	869
6.8	001	009	034	093	192	327	480	628	755	850
7.0	001	007	030	082	173	301	450	599	729	830
7.2	001	006	025	072	156	276	420	569	703	810
7.4	001	005	022	063	140	253	392	539	676	788
7.6	001	004	019	055	125	231	365	510	648	765
7.8	000	004	016	048	112	210	338	481	620	741
8.0	000	003	014	042	100	191	313	453	593	717
8.5	000	002	009	030	074	150	256	386	523	653
9.0	000	001	006	021	055	116	207	324	456	587
9.5	000	001	004	015	040	089	165	269	392	522
10.0	000	000	003	010	029	067	130	220	333	458
	10	**11**	**12**	**13**	**14**	**15**	**16**	**17**	**18**	**19**
6.2	949	975	989	995	998	999	1,000			
6.4	939	969	986	994	997	999	1,000			
6.6	927	963	982	992	997	999	999	1,000		
6.8	915	955	978	990	996	998	999	1,000		
7.0	901	947	973	987	994	998	999	1,000		
7.2	887	937	967	984	993	997	999	999	1,000	
7.4	871	926	961	980	991	996	998	999	1,000	
7.6	854	915	954	976	989	995	998	999	1,000	
7.8	835	902	945	971	986	993	997	999	1,000	
8.0	816	888	936	966	983	992	996	998	999	1,000
8.5	763	849	909	949	973	986	993	997	999	999
9.0	706	803	876	926	959	978	989	995	998	999
9.5	645	752	836	898	940	967	982	991	996	998
10.0	583	697	792	864	917	951	973	986	993	997
	20	**21**	**22**							
8.5	1,000									
9.0	1,000									
9.5	999	1,000								
10.0	998	999	1,000							

(*Continued*)

Table A2 Summation of Terms of Poisson's Exponential Binomial Limit (*Continued*)

d (or) c / np / λT	0	1	2	3	4	5	6	7	8	9
10.5	000	000	002	007	021	050	102	179	279	397
11.0	000	000	001	005	015	038	079	143	232	341
11.5	000	000	001	003	011	028	060	114	191	289
12.0	000	000	001	002	008	020	046	090	155	242
12.5	000	000	000	002	005	015	035	070	125	201
13.0	000	000	000	001	004	011	026	054	100	166
13.5	000	000	000	001	003	008	019	041	079	135
14.0	000	000	000	000	002	006	014	032	062	109
14.5	000	000	000	000	001	004	010	024	048	088
15.0	000	000	000	000	001	003	008	018	037	070
	10	11	12	13	14	15	16	17	18	19
10.5	521	639	742	825	888	932	960	978	988	994
11.0	460	579	689	781	854	907	944	968	982	991
11.5	402	520	633	733	815	878	924	954	974	986
12.0	347	462	576	682	772	844	899	937	963	979
12.5	297	406	519	628	725	806	869	916	948	969
13.0	252	353	463	573	675	764	835	890	930	957
13.5	211	304	409	518	623	718	798	861	908	942
14.0	176	260	358	464	570	669	756	827	883	923
14.5	145	220	311	413	518	619	711	790	853	901
15.0	118	185	268	363	466	568	664	749	819	875
	20	21	22	23	24	25	26	27	28	29
10.5	997	999	999	1,000						
11.0	995	998	999	1,000						
11.5	992	996	998	999	1,000					
12.0	988	994	997	999	999	1,000				
12.5	983	991	995	998	999	999	1,000			
13.0	975	986	992	996	998	999	1,000			
13.5	965	980	989	994	997	998	999	1,000		
14.0	952	971	983	991	995	997	999	999	1,000	
14.5	936	960	976	986	992	996	998	999	999	1,000
15.0	917	947	967	981	989	994	997	998	999	1,000

(*Continued*)

Table A2 Summation of Terms of Poisson's Exponential Binomial Limit[a] (*Continued*)

np / λT \ *d (or) c*	4	5	6	7	8	9	10	11	12	13
16	000	001	004	010	022	043	077	127	193	275
17	000	001	002	005	013	026	049	085	135	201
18	000	000	001	003	007	015	030	055	092	143
19	000	000	001	002	004	009	018	035	061	098
20	000	000	000	001	002	005	011	021	039	066
21	000	000	000	000	001	003	006	013	025	043
22	000	000	000	000	001	002	004	008	015	028
23	000	000	000	000	000	001	002	004	009	017
24	000	000	000	000	000	000	001	003	005	011
25	000	000	000	000	000	000	001	001	003	006
	14	15	16	17	18	19	20	21	22	23
16	368	467	566	659	742	812	868	911	942	963
17	281	371	468	564	655	736	805	861	905	937
18	208	287	375	469	562	651	731	799	855	899
19	150	215	292	378	469	561	647	725	793	849
20	105	157	221	297	381	470	559	644	721	787
21	072	111	163	227	302	384	471	558	640	716
22	048	077	117	169	232	306	387	472	556	637
23	031	052	082	123	175	238	310	389	472	555
24	020	034	056	087	128	180	243	314	392	473
25	012	022	038	060	092	134	185	247	318	394
	24	25	26	27	28	29	30	31	32	33
16	978	987	993	996	998	999	999	1,000		
17	959	975	985	991	995	997	999	999	1,000	
18	932	955	972	983	990	994	997	998	999	1,000
19	893	927	951	969	980	988	993	996	998	999
20	843	888	922	948	966	978	987	992	995	997
21	782	838	883	917	944	963	976	985	991	994
22	712	777	832	877	913	940	959	973	983	989
23	635	708	772	827	873	908	936	956	971	981
24	554	632	704	768	823	868	904	932	953	969
25	473	553	629	700	763	818	863	900	929	950
	34	35	36	37	38	39	40	41	42	43
19	999	1,000								
20	999	999	1,000							
21	997	998	999	999	1,000					
22	994	996	998	999	999	1,000				
23	988	993	996	997	999	999	1,000			
24	979	987	992	995	997	998	999	999	1,000	
25	966	978	985	991	994	997	998	999	999	1,000

Table A3 Percentiles of the *t* Distribution

df	$t_{0.60}$	$t_{0.70}$	$t_{0.80}$	$t_{0.90}$	$t_{0.95}$	$t_{0.975}$	$t_{0.99}$	$t_{0.995}$
1	0.325	0.727	1.376	3.078	6.314	12.706	31.821	63.657
2	0.280	0.617	1.061	1.886	2.920	4.303	6.965	9.925
3	0.277	0.584	0.978	1.638	2.353	3.182	4.541	5.841
4	0.271	0.569	0.941	1.533	2.132	2.776	3.747	4.604
5	0.267	0.559	0.920	1.476	2.015	2.571	3.365	4.032
6	0.265	0.553	0.906	1.440	1.943	2.447	3.143	3.707
7	0.263	0.549	0.896	1.415	1.895	2.365	2.998	3.499
8	0.262	0.546	0.889	1.397	1.860	2.306	2.896	3.355
9	0.261	0.543	0.883	1.383	1.833	2.262	2.821	3.250
10	0.260	0.542	0.879	1.372	1.812	2.228	2.764	3.169
11	0.260	0.540	0.876	1.363	1.796	2.201	2.718	3.106
12	0.259	0.539	0.873	1.356	1,782	2.179	2.681	3.055
13	0.259	0.538	0.870	1.350	1.771	2.160	2.650	3.012
14	0.258	0.537	0.868	1.345	1,761	2.145	2.624	2.977
15	0.258	0.536	0.866	1.341	1.753	2.131	2.602	2.947
16	0.258	0.535	0.865	1.337	1.746	2.120	2.583	2.921
17	0.257	0.534	0.863	1.333	1.740	2.110	2.567	2.898
18	0.257	0.534	0.862	1.330	1.734	2.101	2.552	2.878
19	0.257	0.533	0.861	1.328	1.729	2.093	2.539	2.861
20	0.257	0.533	0.860	1.325	1.725	2.086	2.528	2.845
21	0.257	0.532	0.859	1.323	1.721	2.080	2.518	2.831
22	0.256	0.532	0.858	1.321	1.717	2.074	2.508	2.819
23	0.256	0.532	0.858	1.319	1.714	2.069	2.500	2.807
24	0.256	0.531	0.857	1.318	1.711	2.064	2.492	2.797
25	0.256	0.531	0.856	1.316	1.708	2.060	2.485	2.787
26	0.256	0.531	0.856	1.315	1.706	2.056	2.479	2.779
27	0.256	0.531	0.855	1.314	1.703	2.052	2.473	2.771
28	0.256	0.530	0.855	1.313	1.701	2.048	2.467	2.763
29	0.256	0.530	0.854	1.311	1.699	2.045	2.462	2.756
30	0.256	0.530	0.854	1.310	1.697	2.042	2.457	2.750
40	0.255	0.529	0.851	1.303	1.684	2.021	2.423	2.704
60	0.254	0.527	0.848	1.296	1.671	2.000	2.390	2.660
120	0.254	0.526	0.845	1.289	1.658	1.980	2.358	2.617
∞	0.253	0.524	0.842	1.282	1.645	1.960	2.326	2.576
df	$-t_{0.40}$	$-t_{0.30}$	$-t_{0.20}$	$-t_{0.10}$	$-t_{0.05}$	$-t_{0.025}$	$-t_{0.01}$	$-t_{0.005}$

When the table is read from the foot, the tabled values are to be prefixed with a negative sign. Interpolation should be performed using the reciprocals of the degrees of freedom.

Table A4 Factors for Computing 3σ Control Chart Limits

Subsample Size	A_2	A_3	B_3	B_4	D_3	D_4
2	1.880	2.659	0	3.267	0	3.267
3	1.023	1.954	0	2.568	0	2.575
4	0.729	1.628	0	2.266	0	2.282
5	0.577	1.427	0	2.089	0	2.115
6	0.483	1.287	0.030	1.970	0	2.004
7	0.419	1.182	0.118	1.882	0.076	1.924
8	0.373	1.099	0.185	1.815	0.136	1.864
9	0.337	1.032	0.239	1.761	0.184	1.816
10	0.308	0.975	0.284	1.716	0.223	1.777
11	0.285	0.927	0.321	1.679	0.256	1.774
12	0.266	0.886	0.354	1.646	0.284	1.716
13	0.249	0.850	0.382	1.618	0.308	1.692
14	0.235	0.817	0.406	1.594	0.329	1.671
15	0.223	0.789	0.428	1.572	0.348	1.652

Subsample Size	d_2	D_1	D_2
2	1.128	0	3.686
3	1.693	0	4.358
4	2.059	0	4.698
5	2.326	0	4.918
6	2.534	0	5.078
7	2.704	0.205	5.203
8	2.847	0.387	5.307
9	2.970	0.546	5.394
10	3.078	0.687	5.469
11	3.173	0.812	5.534
12	3.258	0.924	5.592
13	3.336	1.026	5.646
14	3.407	1.121	5.693
15	3.472	1.207	5.737

Values for subsample sizes to 25 and above are available (see Montgomery 1985, Appendix VI).

BIBLIOGRAPHY

"An Education and Training Strategy for Total Quality Management in the Department of Defense," Office of the Assistant Secretary of Defense, (P&L) TQM/IPO, Washington, DC 20301, 1989.

"American National Standard—ANSI/ASQC Q91—1993," American Society for Quality Control, 611 East Wisconsin Avenue, Milwaukee, WI 53202. There are similar publications for ISO 9000 (Q90), ISO 9002 (Q92), ISO 9003 (Q93), and ISO 9004 (Q94).

ASQC Statistics Division, "Glossary and Tables for Statistical Quality Control," Milwaukee, 1983.

ASTM, "Manual on Presentation of Data and Control Chart Analysis," Committee E-11, 1916 Race Street, Philadelphia, PA 19103.

Atkinson, P. E. *Creating Culture Change*. San Diego, CA: Pfeiffer and Company, 1990.

Barker, T. B. *Quality by Experimental Design*. New York: Marcel Dekker, 1985.

Besterfield, D. H. *Quality Control,* 3rd ed. Englewood Cliffs, NJ: Prentice-Hall, 1991.

Bhote, K. R. *World Class Quality*. New York: AMA Publications, 1988.

Box, G. E. P., Hunter, W. G., and Hunter, J. S. *Statistics for Experimenters*. New York: Wiley, 1978.

Brassard, M. "The Memory Jogger Plus +," Goal/QPC, 13 Branch St., Methuen, MA 01844, (508) 685-3900, 1989.

Braverman, J. D. *Fundamentals of Statistical Quality Control*. Reston, VA: Reston Publishing, 1981.

Covey, S. R. *The Seven Habits of Highly Effective People*. New York: Simon and Schuster, 1989.

Crosby, P. B. *Quality is Free*. New York: McGraw-Hill, 1979.

Crosby, P. B. *Quality Without Tears*. New York: McGraw-Hill, 1984.

Dockstader, S. L. and Houston, A. "A Total Quality Management Process Improvement Model," Navy Personnel Research and Development Center, San Diego, CA 92152, 1988.

Deming, W. E. *Quality, Productivity and Competitive Position*. Cambridge, MA: MIT Press, 1982.

Deming, W. E. *Out of the Crisis*. Cambridge, MA: MIT Press, 1986.

Doty, L. A. *Reliability for the Technologies*, 2nd ed. New York: Industrial Press, 1989.

Doty, L. A. *Work Methods and Measurement for Management*. Albany, NY: Delmar, 1989.

Fawcett, M. *An ISO 9000 Implementation Plan*. Anaheim, CA: DK Institute Press, 1993.

Feigenbaum, A. V. *Total Quality Control*. New York: McGraw-Hill, 1961.

Glasser, W., M.D. *Control Theory*. New York: Harper and Row, 1984.

Glasser, W., M.D. *Control Theory in the Classroom*. New York: Harper and Row, 1985.

Glasser, W., M.D. *The Identity Society*. New York: Harper and Row, 1972.

Glasser, W., M.D. *Schools Without Failure*. New York: Harper and Row, 1969.

Hayes and Romig, *Modern Quality Control*. Encino, CA: Glencoe Publishing, 1982.

Herzberg, F. *The Motivation to Work*. New York: John Wiley and Sons, 1959.

Hicks, C. R. *Fundamental Concepts in the Design of Experiments*. New York: Holt, Rinehart and Winston, 1973.

Imai, M. *Kaizen*. New York: McGraw-Hill, 1986.

Ishikawa, K. *Guide to Quality Control*. White Plains, NY: Quality Resources, 1990.

Jaehn, A. "All Purpose Charts Can Make SPC Easy," Quality Progress, Feb. 1989, p. 112, American Society for Quality Control, Milwaukee, WI.

Johnson, P. L. *Keeping Score*. New York: Harper and Row, 1989.

Jones, L. and McBride, R. *An Introduction to Team Approach Problem Solving*. Milwaukee, WI: ASQC Press, 1990.

Juran, J. M. *Juran on Leadership for Quality*. New York: Free Press, 1989.

Juran, J. M. *Juran on Planning for Quality.* New York: Free Press, 1988.

Juran, J. M. *Quality Control Handbook,* 4th ed. New York: McGraw-Hill, 1988.

Juran, J. M. and Gryna, F. *Quality Planning and Analysis,* 2nd ed. New York: McGraw-Hill, 1980.

Kanholm, J. *ISO 9000 Documentation.* Los Angeles, CA: AQA Press, 1993.

Kanholm, J. *ISO 9000 Explained.* Los Angeles, CA: AQA Press, 1993.

Kanholm, J. *ISO 9000 in Your Company.* Los Angeles, CA: AQA Press, 1993.

Likert, T. *New Patterns of Management.* New York: McGraw-Hill, 1961.

Livingston, J. S. "Pygmalion in Management," *Harvard Business Review,* July–Aug. 1969.

Maslow, A. H. *Motivation and Personality.* New York: Harper and Row, 1970.

McGregor, D. *The Human Side of Enterprise.* New York: McGraw-Hill, 1960.

Montgomery, D. C. *Design and Analysis of Experiments,* 3rd ed. New York: John Wiley, 1991.

Montgomery, D. C. *Introduction to Statistical Quality Control.* New York: John Wiley, 1985.

Ott, E. R. *Process Quality Control.* New York: McGraw-Hill, 1975.

Perez-Wilson, M. "Machine/Process Capability Study," Advanced Systems Consultants, P.O. Box 1176, Scottsdale, AZ 85252, 1989.

Peters, T. and Waterman, R. *In Search of Excellence.* New York: Harper and Row, 1982.

Peters, T. *Thriving on Chaos.* New York: Harper and Row, 1987.

Pyzdek, T. *Pyzdek's Guide to SPC, Volume One: Fundamentals.* Tucson, AZ: Quality Publishing, 1989 (a Quality Press, ASQC, Publication).

Pyzdek, T. *An SPC Primer.* Tucson, AZ: Quality Publishing, 1986 (a Quality Press, ASQC, Publication).

ReVelle, J. B. *The New Quality Technology.* Los Angeles, CA: Hughes Aircraft, 1988.

Schatz and Schatz, *Managing by Influence.* Englewood Cliffs, NJ: Prentice-Hall, 1986.

Scholtes, P. R. *The Team Handbook.* Madison, WI: Joiner Associates, 1988.

Scott and Jaffe, *Empowerment.* Los Altos, CA: Crisp Publications, 1991.

Senge, P. M. *The Fifth Discipline.* New York: Doubleday, 1990.

Sepehri, M. *Quest for Quality.* Norcross, GA: Industrial Engineering and Management Press, IIT, 1987.

"Total Quality Management Guide," Office of the Deputy Assistant Secretary of Defense, OASD (P&L) TQM, Pentagon, Washington, DC 20301, 1989.

"Total Quality Management Implementation: Selected Readings," Office of the Assistant Secretary of Defense, (P&L) TQM/IPO, Washington, DC 20301, 1989.

Traver, R. W. *Industrial Problem Solving*. Carol Stream, IL: Hitchcock, 1989.

Watson, G. *Strategic Benchmarking*. Milwaukee, WI: ASQC Press, 1994.

Whitehouse, G. E. *Systems Analysis and Design Using Network Techniques*. Englewood Cliffs, NJ: Prentice-Hall, 1973.

INDEX